BOLLINGEN SERIES XLII

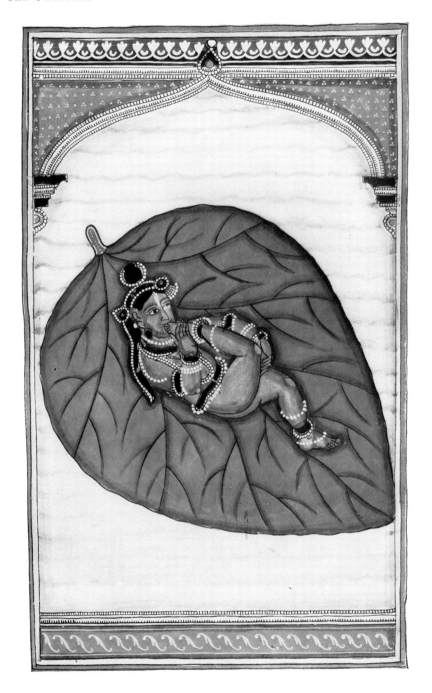

1. The Birth of Vishnu

India, illustration from an 18th-century manuscript

ERICH NEUMANN

THE
ORIGINS AND HISTORY
OF
CONSCIOUSNESS

WITH A FOREWORD BY C. G. JUNG
TRANSLATED FROM THE GERMAN
BY R. F. C. HULL

BOLLINGEN SERIES XLII

PRINCETON UNIVERSITY PRESS

Copyright 1954 by Bollingen Foundation Inc., New York, N.Y.
Published by Princeton University Press, Princeton, N.J.

First Princeton/Bollingen Paperback Printing, 1970
Second printing, 1971

THIS VOLUME IS THE FORTY-SECOND IN A SERIES OF BOOKS
SPONSORED BY BOLLINGEN FOUNDATION.

Originally published in German as
Ursprungsgeschichte des Bewusstseins
by Rascher Verlag, Zurich, 1949

Library of Congress Catalogue Card No.: 53-12527
ISBN 0-691-01761-1

MANUFACTURED IN THE UNITED STATES OF AMERICA
BY PRINCETON UNIVERSITY PRESS AT PRINCETON, N.J.

He whose vision cannot cover
History's three thousand years,
Must in outer darkness hover,
Live within the day's frontiers.

GOETHE, *Westöstlicher Diwan*

TRANSLATOR'S NOTE

THE PRESENT EDITION of this book contains the author's corrections and revisions of his original text. Certain minor omissions, mostly of repetitive material, have been made with his permission, and a few small passages added in connection with the illustrations, which the author has assembled for this edition.

Quotations are in most cases taken from or based upon the standard English or American translations indicated in the footnotes; but where it was necessary to translate directly from the German texts cited by the author, reference is made to the German sources only.

I would like to express my most cordial thanks to Dr. Gerhard Adler for his help in elucidating many difficult passages in the text, and for his careful revision of the translation in typescript.

R. F. C. HULL

NOTE OF ACKNOWLEDGMENT

GRATEFUL ACKNOWLEDGMENT for permission to quote is made to the following: the Cambridge University Press for illustrations and text passages from J. M. Woodward, PERSEUS; The Dial Press, New York, for the prefatory motto, from THE PERMANENT GOETHE, edited by Thomas Mann, copyright 1948 by The Dial Press; Harrap and Co., London, for a passage from J. C. Andersen, MYTHS AND LEGENDS OF THE POLYNESIANS; the Princeton University Press for a part of E. A. Speiser's translation of the Gilgamesh Epic, from ANCIENT NEAR EASTERN TEXTS, edited by J. B. Pritchard; to Routledge and Kegan Paul, London, for a passage from E. A. Wallis Budge's translation of the Egyptian Book of the Dead; and to the Viking Press, New York, for D. H. Lawrence's poem "The Ship of Death," from his LAST POEMS, copyright 1933 by Frieda Lawrence.

CONTENTS

LIST OF ILLUSTRATIONS

Frontispiece:

THE UROBOROS

1. The Birth of Vishnu. India, illustration from an 18th-century manuscript. (Paris, Bibliothèque nationale. Photo: Bibliothèque.)

Following page 32:

2. Serpent biting its tail, encircling an inscription. Bowl from the Mandaeans, Mesopotamia, *c.* 500 A.D. (Present location unknown.)

3. The ocean ringing the world. *Mappa mundi,* with Babylon in the center, from a cuneiform tablet. (Drawing from *Cuneiform Texts from Babylonian Tablets &c. in the British Museum,* Part XXII, London, 1906, plate 48.)

4. The four corners of the world, with encircling serpent. Coptic. (Woodcut from Athanasius Kircher, *Oedipus Aegyptiacus,* Rome, 1652–54.)

5. "Snake going round the world and a boat." Drawing by a five-year-old English girl of working-class origin. (From Herbert Read, *Education through Art,* New York, 1948.)

6. Serpent design on a brass shield. Benin, Nigeria, west Africa. (Drawing from Leo Frobenius, *Kulturgeschichte Afrikas,* Zurich, 1933, after A. H. L. Fox-Pitt-Rivers, *Antique Works of Art from Benin,* London, 1900, fig. 102.)

7. Mexican calendar stone, with encircling serpent. (Etching after G. F. Gemelli Careri, *Giro del Mondo,* Naples, 1721, reproducing an Aztec drawing.)

FOREWORD

THE AUTHOR has requested me to preface his book with a few words of introduction, and to this I accede all the more readily because I found his work more than usually welcome. It begins just where I, too, if I were granted a second lease of life, would start to gather up the *disjecta membra* of my own writings, to sift out all those "beginnings without continuations" and knead them into a whole. As I read through the manuscript of this book it became clear to me how great are the disadvantages of pioneer work: one stumbles through unknown regions; one is led astray by analogies, forever losing the Ariadne thread; one is overwhelmed by new impressions and new possibilities, and the worst disadvantage of all is that the pioneer only knows afterwards what he should have known before. The second generation has the advantage of a clearer, if still incomplete, picture; certain landmarks that at least lie on the frontiers of the essential have grown familiar, and one now knows what must be known if one is to explore the newly discovered territory. Thus forewarned and forearmed, a representative of the second generation can spot the most distant connections; he can unravel problems and give a coherent account of the whole field of study, whose full extent the pioneer can only survey at the end of his life's work.

This difficult and meritorious task the author has performed with outstanding success. He has woven his facts into a pattern and created a unified whole, which no pioneer could have done nor could ever have attempted to do. As though in confirmation of this, the present work opens at the very place where I unwittingly made landfall on the new continent long ago, namely the realm of *matriarchal symbolism;* and, as a conceptual framework for his discoveries, the author uses a symbol whose significance first dawned on me in my recent writings on the psychology of alchemy: the *uroboros*. Upon this foundation he has succeeded in constructing a unique history of the evolution of consciousness, and at the same time in representing the body of myths as the phenomenology of this same evolution. In this way he arrives at conclusions and insights which are among the most important ever to be reached in this field.

Naturally to me, as a psychologist, the most valuable aspect of the work is the fundamental contribution it makes to a psychology of the unconscious. The author has placed the concepts of analytical psychology—which for many people are so bewildering—on a firm evolutionary basis, and erected upon this a comprehensive structure in which the empirical forms of thought find their rightful place. No system can ever dispense with an over-all hypothesis which in its turn depends upon the temperament and subjective assumptions of the author as well as upon objective data. This factor is of the greatest importance in psychology, for the "personal equation" colors the mode of seeing. Ultimate truth, if there be such a thing, demands the concert of many voices.

I can only congratulate the author on his achievement. May this brief foreword convey to him my heartfelt thanks.

C. G. JUNG

March 1, 1949

INTRODUCTION

THE FOLLOWING ATTEMPT to outline the archetypal stages in the development of consciousness is based on modern depth psychology. It is an application of the analytical psychology of C. G. Jung, even where we endeavor to amplify this psychology, and even though we may speculatively overstep its boundaries.

Unlike other possible and necessary methods of inquiry which consider the development of consciousness in relation to external environmental factors, our inquiry is more concerned with the internal, psychic, and archetypal factors which determine the course of that development.

The structural elements of the collective unconscious are named by Jung "archetypes" or "primordial images." They are the pictorial forms of the instincts, for the unconscious reveals itself to the conscious mind in images which, as in dreams and fantasies, initiate the process of conscious reaction and assimilation.

These fantasy-images undoubtedly have their closest analogues in mythological types. We must therefore assume that they correspond to certain *collective* (and not personal) structural elements of the human psyche in general, and, like the morphological elements of the human body, are *inherited*.[1]

The archetypal structural elements of the psyche are psychic organs upon whose functioning the well-being of the individual depends, and whose injury has disastrous consequences:

Moreover, they are the unfailing causes of neurotic and even psychotic dis-

[1] Jung, "The Psychology of the Child Archetype," p. 155.

orders, behaving exactly like neglected or maltreated physical organs or organic functional systems.[2]

It is the task of this book to show that a series of archetypes is a main constituent of mythology, that they stand in an organic relation to one another, and that their stadial [3] succession determines the growth of consciousness. In the course of its ontogenetic development, the individual ego consciousness has to pass through the same archetypal stages which determined the evolution of consciousness in the life of humanity. The individual has in his own life to follow the road that humanity has trod before him, leaving traces of its journey in the archetypal sequence of the mythological images we are now about to examine. Normally the archetypal stages are lived through without disturbance, and the development of consciousness proceeds in them just as naturally as physical development proceeds in the stages of bodily maturation. As organs of the psyche's structure the archetypes articulate with one another autonomously, like the physical organs, and determine the maturation of the personality in a manner analogous to the biological hormone-components of the physical constitution.

Besides possessing an "eternal" significance, the archetype also has an equally legitimate historical aspect. Ego consciousness evolves by passing through a series of "eternal images," and the ego, transformed in the passage, is constantly experiencing a new relation to the archetypes. Its relation to the eternality of the archetypal images is a process of succession in time— that is to say, it takes place in stages. The ability to perceive, to understand, and to interpret these images changes as ego consciousness changes in the course of man's phylogenetic and ontogenetic history; consequently the relativity of the eternal image to the evolving ego consciousness becomes more and more pronounced.

The archetypes that determine the stages of conscious devel-

2 Ibid., p. 157.
3 [An adjective derived from Lat. *stadium* in the biological sense of "stage of development."–TRANS.]

opment form only a segment of archetypal reality as a whole. But by availing ourselves of the evolutionary or synoptic view we can make out a kind of guiding line running through limitless symbolism of the collective unconscious which helps us to orient ourselves in the theory and practice of depth psychology.

An investigation of the archetypal stages also affords a better psychological orientation in a number of ancillary subjects, e.g., the history of religion, anthropology, folk psychology, and the like. All these can then be brought together on a psycho-evolutionary basis which would promote a deeper understanding.

Surprisingly enough, these specialized sciences have not so far allowed themselves to be sufficiently enriched by depth psychology, and least of all by Jungian psychology. In spite of that, the psychological starting point of these disciplines emerges more and more plainly, and it is beginning to become obvious that the human psyche is the source of all cultural and religious phenomena. Hence a final reckoning with depth psychology cannot be evaded much longer.

We must emphasize that our exposition of myth is not based on any specialized branch of science, whether archaeology, comparative religion, or theology, but simply and solely on the practical work of the psychotherapist, whose concern is the psychic background of modern man. The connection between his psychology and the deeper layers of humanity still alive in him is therefore the real starting point and subject of this work. The deductive and systematic method of exposition here adopted may at first obscure the topical and therapeutic significance of our findings, but anyone familiar with psychic events at the deepest level will recognize the importance and relevance of these connections, whose detailed illustration by modern empirical material is reserved for later examination.

As is well known, the "comparative" method of analytical psychology collates the symbolic and collective material found in individuals with the corresponding products from the history of religion, primitive psychology, and so on, and in this way arrives at an interpretation by establishing the "context." This method we now supplement by the evolutionary approach, which considers the material from the standpoint of the stage reached by the developing consciousness, and hence by the ego in its relations with the unconscious. Our work therefore links up with that fundamental early work of Jung's, *The Psychology of the Unconscious,* even though we may be obliged to make certain emendations. Whereas in Freudian psychoanalysis the evolutionary approach led only to a concretistic and narrowly personalistic theory of libido, analytical psychology has so far failed to pursue this line of inquiry any further.

The emergence of the collective human background as a transpersonal reality has forced us to recognize the relativity of our own position. The multiplicity of forms and phenomena in which the infinite diversity of the human psyche is expressed, the wealth of cultures, values, patterns of behavior, and world views produced by the vitality of man's psychic structure, must make any attempt at a general orientation seem, at the outset, a perilous venture. Yet such an attempt has to be made, even with the knowledge that our specifically Western orientation is only one among many. The evolution of consciousness as a form of creative evolution is the peculiar achievement of Western man. Creative evolution of ego consciousness means that, through a continuous process stretching over thousands of years, the conscious system has absorbed more and more unconscious contents and progressively extended its frontiers. Although from antiquity right down to recent times we see a new and differently patterned canon of culture continually superseding the previous one, the West has nevertheless succeeded in achieving an historical and cultural continuity in which each canon gradually came to be integrated. The structure of modern consciousness rests on this integration, and at each period of its development the ego has to absorb essential portions of the cultural past transmitted to it by the canon of values embodied in its own culture and system of education.

The creative character of consciousness is a central feature of the cultural canon of the West. In Western culture, and partly

xviii

also in the Far East, we can follow the continuous, though often fitful, development of consciousness over the last ten thousand years. Here alone has the canon of stadial development, collectively embodied in mythological projections, become a model for the development of the individual human being; here alone have the creative beginnings of individuality been taken over by the collective and held up as the ideal of all individual development. Wherever this type of creative ego consciousness has developed, or is still developing, the archetypal stages of conscious evolution are in force. In stationary cultures, or in primitive societies where the original features of human culture are still preserved, the earliest stages of man's psychology predominate to such a degree that individual and creative traits are not assimilated by the collective. Indeed, creative individuals possessed of a stronger consciousness are even branded by the collective as antisocial.[4]

The creativity of consciousness may be jeopardized by religious or political totalitarianism, for any authoritarian fixation of the canon leads to sterility of consciousness. Such fixations, however, can only be provisional. So far as Western man is concerned, the assimilative vitality of his ego consciousness is more or less assured. The progress of science and the increasingly obvious threat to humanity from unconscious forces impel his consciousness, from within and without, to continual self-analysis and expansion. The individual is the bearer of this creative activity of the mind and therefore remains the decisive factor in all future Western developments. This holds true regardless of the fact that individuals co-operate and mutually determine the spiritual democracy in which they live.

Any attempt to outline the archetypal stages from the standpoint of analytical psychology must begin by drawing a fundamental distinction between personal and transpersonal psychic factors. Personal factors are those which belong to one individual personality and are not shared by any other individual, regardless of whether they are conscious or unconscious. Transper-

[4] Mead, *Sex and Temperament in Three Primitive Societies*, pp. 228 f.

xix

sonal factors, on the other hand, are collective, supra- or extra-personal, and are to be regarded not as *external* conditions of society, but as *internal* structural elements. The transpersonal represents a factor that is largely independent of the personal, for the personal, both collectively and individually, is a late product of evolution.

Every historical inquiry—and every evolutionary approach is in this sense historical—must therefore begin with the transpersonal. In the history of mankind as in the development of the individual there is an initial preponderance of transpersonal factors, and only in the course of development does the personal realm come into view and achieve independence. The individualized conscious man of our era is a late man, whose structure is built on early, pre-individual human stages from which individual consciousness has only detached itself step by step.

The evolution of consciousness by stages is as much a collective human phenomenon as a particular individual phenomenon. Ontogenetic development may therefore be regarded as a modified recapitulation of phylogenetic development.

This interdependence of collective and individual has two psychic concomitants. On the one hand, the early history of the collective is determined by inner primordial images whose projections appear outside as powerful factors—gods, spirits, or demons—which become objects of worship. On the other hand, man's collective symbolisms also appear in the individual, and the psychic development, or misdevelopment, of each individual is governed by the same primordial images which determine man's collective history.

Since we have undertaken to expound the whole canon of mythological stages, their sequence, their interconnections, and their symbolism, it is not only permissible but imperative to draw the relevant material from different spheres of culture and different mythologies, irrespective of whether or not all stages are present in any one culture.[5]

[5] A thorough investigation of the archetypal stages in individual spheres of culture and mythology would be exceedingly interesting, because the absence or

We do not therefore maintain that all the stages of conscious development are to be found always, everywhere, and in every mythology, any more than the theory of evolution maintains that the evolutionary stages of every animal species are repeated in man's evolution. What we do maintain is that these developmental stages arrange themselves in an orderly sequence and thus determine all psychic development. Equally we maintain that these archetypal stages are unconscious determinants and can be found in mythology, and that only by viewing the collective stratification of human development together with the individual stratification of conscious development can we arrive at an understanding of psychic development in general, and individual development in particular.

Again, the relation between the transpersonal and the personal—which plays a decisive role in every human life—is prefigured in human history. But the collective aspect of this relationship does not mean that unique or recurrent historical events are inherited, for up to the present there has been no scientific proof of the inheritance of acquired characteristics. For this reason analytical psychology considers the structure of the psyche to be determined by a priori transpersonal dominants —archetypes—which, being essential components and organs of the psyche from the beginning, mold the course of human history.

The castration motif, for instance, is not the result of the inheritance of an endlessly repeated threat of castration by a primordial father, or rather by an infinity of primordial fathers. Science has discovered nothing that could possibly support such a theory, which moreover presupposes the inheritance of acquired characteristics. Any reduction of the castration threat, parricide, the "primal scene" of parental intercourse, and so on, to historical and personalistic data, which presumes to paint the early

overemphasis of individual stages would enable us to draw important conclusions about the cultures concerned. Such an inquiry will doubtless be undertaken at a later date.

history of humanity in the likeness of a patriarchal bourgeois family of the nineteenth century, is scientifically impossible.[6]

It is one of the tasks of this book to show that, in regard to these and similar "complexes," we are really dealing with symbols, ideal forms, psychic categories, and basic structural patterns whose infinitely varied modes of operation govern the history of mankind and the individual.[7]

The development of consciousness in archetypal stages is a transpersonal fact, a dynamic self-revelation of the psychic structure, which dominates the history of mankind and the individual. Even deviations from the path of evolution, their symbology and symptomatology, must be understood in relation to the prior archetypal pattern.

In the first part of our exposition—The Mythological Stages in the Evolution of Consciousness—the accent lies on the wide distribution of the mythological material, and on demonstrating the connections between the symbols and the various strata of conscious development. Only against this background can we understand the normal developments of the psyche, as well as the pathological phenomena in which collective problems constantly appear as the basic problems of human existence and so must be understood in that light.

Besides uncovering the evolutionary stages and their archetypal connections, our inquiry also has a therapeutic aim, which is both individual and collective. The integration of personal psychic phenomena with the corresponding transpersonal sym-

[6] See infra, p. 53, note 16.

[7] It is in this sense that we use the terms "masculine" and "feminine" throughout the book, not as personal sex-linked characteristics, but as symbolic expressions. When we say masculine or feminine dominants obtrude themselves at certain stages, or in certain cultures or types of person, this is a psychological statement which must not be reduced to biological or sociological terms. The symbolism of "masculine" and "feminine" is archetypal and therefore transpersonal; in the various cultures concerned, it is erroneously projected upon persons as though they carried its qualities. In reality every individual is a psychological hybrid. Even sexual symbolism cannot be derived from the person, because it is prior to the person. Conversely, it is one of the complications of individual psychology that in all cultures the integrity of the personality is violated when it is identified with either the masculine or the feminine side of the symbolic principle of opposites.

bols is of paramount importance for the further development of consciousness and for the synthesis of the personality.[8]

The rediscovery of the human and cultural strata from which these symbols derive is in the original sense of the word "*bildend*"—"informing." Consciousness thus acquires images (*Bilder*) and education (*Bildung*), widens its horizon, and charges itself with contents which constellate a new psychic potential. New problems appear, but also new solutions. As the purely personal data enter into association with the transpersonal, and the collective human aspect is rediscovered and begins to come alive, new insights, new possibilities of life, add themselves to the narrowly personalistic and rigid personality of the sick-souled modern man.

Our aim is not confined to pointing out the correct relation of the ego to the unconscious, and of the personal to the transpersonal. We have also to realize that the false, personalistic interpretation of everything psychic is the expression of an unconscious law which has everywhere constrained modern man to misinterpret his true role and significance. Only when we have made it clear to what degree the reduction of the transpersonal to the personal springs from a tendency which once had a very deep meaning, but which the crisis of modern consciousness has rendered wholly meaningless and nonsensical, will our task be fulfilled. Only when we have recognized how the personal develops out of the transpersonal, detaches itself from it but, despite the crucial role of ego consciousness, always remains rooted in it, can we restore to the transpersonal factors their original weight and meaning, lacking which a healthy collective and individual life is impossible.

This brings us to a psychological phenomenon which will be fully discussed in Part II, under the "law of secondary personalization." This maintains that contents which are primarily transpersonal and originally appeared as such are, in the course of de-

---

[8] Here we would only emphasize the material content of the symbols. The healing and "whole-making" effect of the emotional components of the collective unconscious is discussed in Part II.

velopment, taken to be personal. The secondary personalization of primary transpersonal contents is in a certain sense an evolutionary necessity, but it constellates dangers which for modern man are altogether excessive. It is necessary for the structure of personality that contents originally taking the form of transpersonal deities should finally come to be experienced as contents of the human psyche. But this process ceases to be a danger to psychic health only when the psyche is itself regarded suprapersonally, as a numinous world of transpersonal happenings. If, on the other hand, transpersonal contents are reduced to the data of a purely personalistic psychology, the result is not only an appalling impoverishment of individual life—that might remain merely a private concern—but also a congestion of the collective unconscious which has disastrous consequences for humanity at large.

Psychology, having penetrated to the collective layer in its investigation of the lower levels of the individual psyche, is faced with the task of evolving a collective and cultural therapy adequate to cope with the mass phenomena that are now devastating mankind. One of the most important objectives of any depth psychology in the future is its application to the collective. It has to correct and prevent the dislocation of collective life, of the group, by applying its specific points of view.[9]

The relation of the ego to the unconscious and of the personal to the transpersonal decides the fate not only of the individual, but of humanity. The theater of this encounter is the human mind. In the present work, a substantial part of mythology is seen as the unconscious self-delineation of the growth of consciousness in man. The dialectic between consciousness and the unconscious, its transformation, its self-liberation, and the birth of human personality from this dialectic form the theme of Part I.

[9] Cf. my *Depth Psychology and a New Ethic.*

PART I

The Mythological Stages
in the
Evolution of Consciousness

Nature rejoices in nature.
Nature subdues nature.
Nature rules over nature.

OSTANES

A. The Creation Myth

I. THE UROBOROS

II. THE GREAT MOTHER

III. THE SEPARATION OF THE WORLD PARENTS

Nature rejoices in nature.

I

THE UROBOROS

For what the center brings
Must obviously be
That which remains to the end
And was there from eternity.
GOETHE, *Westöstlicher Diwan*

THE MYTHOLOGICAL STAGES in the evolution of consciousness begin with the stage when the ego is contained in the unconscious, and lead up to a situation in which the ego not only becomes aware of its own position and defends it heroically, but also becomes capable of broadening and relativizing its experiences through the changes effected by its own activity.

The first cycle of myth is the creation myth. Here the mythological projection of psychic material appears in cosmogonic form, as the mythology of creation. The world and the unconscious predominate and form the object of myth. Ego and man are only nascent as yet, and their birth, suffering, and emancipation constitute the phases of the creation myth.

At the stage of the separation of the World Parents, the germ of ego consciousness finally asserts itself. While yet in the fold of the creation myth it enters upon the second cycle, namely, the hero myth, in which the ego, consciousness, and the human world become conscious of themselves and of their dignity.

In the beginning is perfection, wholeness. This original perfection can only be "circumscribed," or described symbolically; its nature defies any description other than a mythical one, because that which describes, the ego, and that which is described, the beginning, which is prior to any ego, prove to be

5

incommensurable quantities as soon as the ego tries to grasp its object conceptually, as a content of consciousness.

For this reason a symbol always stands at the beginning, the most striking feature of which is its multiplicity of meanings, its indeterminate and indeterminable character.

The beginning can be laid hold of in two "places": it can be conceived in the life of mankind as the earliest dawn of human history, and in the life of the individual as the earliest dawn of childhood. The self-representation of the dawn of human history can be seen from its symbolic description in ritual and myth. The earliest dawn of childhood, like that of mankind, is depicted in the images which rise up from the depths of the unconscious and reveal themselves to the already individualized ego.

The dawn state of the beginning projects itself mythologically in cosmic form, appearing as the beginning of the world, as the mythology of creation. Mythological accounts of the beginning must invariably begin with the outside world, for world and psyche are still one. There is as yet no reflecting, self-conscious ego that could refer anything to itself, that is, reflect. Not only is the psyche open to the world, it is still identical with and undifferentiated from the world; it knows itself as world and in the world and experiences its own becoming as a world-becoming, its own images as the starry heavens, and its own contents as the world-creating gods.

Ernst Cassirer [1] has shown how, in all peoples and in all religions, creation appears as the creation of light. Thus the coming of consciousness, manifesting itself as light in contrast to the darkness of the unconscious, is the real "object" of creation mythology. Cassirer has likewise shown that in the different stages of mythological consciousness the first thing to be discovered is subjective reality, the formation of the ego and individuality. The beginning of this development, mythologically regarded as the beginning of the world, is the coming of light, without which no world process could be seen at all.

[1] *The Philosophy of Symbolic Forms*, trans. Manheim, Vol. II, pp. 94 ff.

But the earliest dawn is still prior to this birth of light out of darkness, and a wealth of symbols surrounds it.

The form of representation peculiar to the unconscious is not that of the conscious mind. It neither attempts nor is able to seize hold of and define its objects in a series of discursive explanations, and reduce them to clarity by logical analysis. The way of the unconscious is different. Symbols gather round the thing to be explained, understood, interpreted. The act of becoming conscious consists in the concentric grouping of symbols around the object, all circumscribing and describing the unknown from many sides. Each symbol lays bare another essential side of the object to be grasped, points to another facet of meaning. Only the canon of these symbols congregating about the center in question, the coherent symbol group, can lead to an understanding of what the symbols point to and of what they are trying to express. The symbolic story of the beginning, which speaks to us from the mythology of all ages, is the attempt made by man's childlike, prescientific consciousness to master problems and enigmas which are mostly beyond the grasp of even our developed modern consciousness. If our consciousness, with epistemological resignation, is constrained to regard the question of the beginning as unanswerable and therefore unscientific, it may be right; but the psyche, which can neither be taught nor led astray by the self-criticism of the conscious mind, always poses this question afresh as one that is essential to it.

The question of the beginning is also the question "Whence?" It is the original and fateful question to which cosmology and the creation myths have ever tried to give new and different answers. This original question about the origin of the world is at the same time the question about the origin of man, the origin of consciousness and of the ego; it is the fateful question "Where did I come from?" that faces every human being as soon as he arrives upon the threshold of self-consciousness.

The mythological answers to these questions are symbolical, like all answers that come from the depths of the psyche, the unconscious. The metaphorical nature of the symbol says: this

7

is this, that is that. The statement of identity and the logic of consciousness erected upon it have no value for the psyche and the unconscious. The psyche blends, as does the dream; it spins and weaves together, combining each with each. The symbol is therefore an analogy, more an equivalence than an equation, and therein lies its wealth of meanings, but also its elusiveness. Only the symbol group, compact of partly contradictory analogies, can make something unknown, and beyond the grasp of consciousness, more intelligible and more capable of becoming conscious.

One symbol of original perfection is the circle. Allied to it are the sphere, the egg, and the *rotundum*—the "round" [2] of alchemy. It is Plato's round that was there in the beginning:

Therefore the demiurge made the world in the shape of a sphere, giving it that figure which of all is the most perfect and the most equal to itself.[3]

Circle, sphere, and round are all aspects of the Self-contained, which is without beginning and end; in its preworldly perfection it is prior to any process, eternal, for in its roundness there is no before and no after, no time; and there is no above and no below, no space. All this can only come with the coming of light, of consciousness, which is not yet present; now all is under sway of the unmanifest godhead, whose symbol is therefore the circle.

The round is the egg, the philosophical World Egg, the nucleus of the beginning, and the germ from which, as humanity teaches everywhere, the world arises.[4] It is also the perfect state in which the opposites are united—the perfect beginning because the opposites have not yet flown apart and the world has not yet begun, the perfect end because in it the opposites have come together again in a synthesis and the world is once more at rest.

The container of opposites is the Chinese *t'ai chi*, a round con-

[2] Jung, *Psychology and Alchemy*, index, s.v. "rotundum."
[3] Plato, *Timaeus* (based on the Cornford trans.).
[4] Frobenius, *Vom Kulturreich des Festlandes*, p. 69; Shatapatha Brahmana 6. 1. 1. 8; Geldner, *Vedismus und Brahmanismus*, pp. 92 f.

taining black and white, day and night, heaven and earth, male and female. Lao-tzu says of it:

> There was something formless yet complete,
> That existed before heaven and earth;
> Without sound, without substance,
> Dependent on nothing, unchanging,
> All pervading, unfailing.
> One may think of it as the mother of all things under heaven.[5]

Each of these pairs of opposites forms the nucleus of a group of symbols which cannot be described here in any great detail; a few examples must suffice.

The round is the calabash containing the World Parents.[6] In Egypt as in New Zealand, in Greece as in Africa and India, the World Parents, heaven and earth, lie one on top of the other in the round, spacelessly and timelessly united, for as yet nothing has come between them to create duality out of the original unity. The container of the masculine and feminine opposites is the great hermaphrodite, the primal creative element, the Hindu *purusha* who combines the poles in himself:

In the beginning this world was Soul (Atman) alone in the form of a person. Looking around, he saw nothing else than himself. He said first: "I am." . . . He was, indeed, as large as a woman and a man closely embraced. He caused that self to fall (*pat*) into two pieces. Therefrom arose a husband (*pati*) and a wife (*patni*).[7]

What is said here of the deity recalls Plato's Original Man; there too the hermaphroditic round stands at the beginning.

This perfect state of being, in which the opposites are contained, is perfect because it is autarchic. Its self-sufficiency, self-contentment, and independence of any "you" and any "other" are signs of its self-contained eternality. We read in Plato:

[5] Tao Teh Ching, No. XXV; trans. by Arthur Waley in *The Way and Its Power*.
[6] Frobenius, op. cit., p. 112.
[7] Brihadaranyaka Upanishad 1. 4. 1–3, trans. by Hume, *The Thirteen Principal Upanishads*.

And he established the universe a sphere revolving in a circle, one and solitary, yet by reason of its excellence able to bear itself company, and needing no other friendship or acquaintance.[8]

The perfection of that which rests in itself in no way contradicts the perfection of that which circles in itself. Although absolute rest is something static and eternal, unchanging and therefore without history, it is at the same time the place of origin and the germ cell of creativity. Living the cycle of its own life, it is the circular snake, the primal dragon of the beginning that bites its own tail, the self-begetting Ὀυϱόβοϱος.[8a]

This is the ancient Egyptian symbol [9] of which it is said: *"Draco interfecit se ipsum, maritat se ipsum, impraegnat se ipsum."* [10] It slays, weds, and impregnates itself. It is man and woman, begetting and conceiving, devouring and giving birth, active and passive, above and below, at once.

As the Heavenly Serpent, the uroboros was known in ancient Babylon; [11] in later times, in the same area, it was often depicted by the Mandaeans (*illus. 2*); its origin is ascribed by Macrobius to the Phoenicians.[12] It is the archetype of the ἕν τὸ πᾶν, the All One, appearing as Leviathan and as Aion, as Oceanus (*illus. 3 and 5*) and also as the Primal Being that says: "I am Alpha and Omega." As the Kneph of antiquity it is the Primal Snake, the "most ancient deity of the prehistoric world." [13] The uroboros can be traced in the Revelation of St. John and among the Gnostics [14] as well as among the Roman syncretists; [15] there are pictures of it in the sand paintings of the Navajo Indians [16] and in

8 Plato, *Timaeus,* 34 (based on the Cornford trans.).

8a Hereinafter transcribed as "uroboros."

9 Goldschmidt, "Alchemie der Aegypter."

10 Cf. Jung, "The Visions of Zosimos." Cited from the *Artis auriferae* (Basel, 1593), Vol. I, "Tractatulus Avicennae," p. 406.

11 Leisegang, "The Mystery of the Serpent."

12 Numerous examples of representations were collected in the Eranos Archives, Ascona, Switzerland; a duplicate of the Archives is in the possession of the Bollingen Foundation, New York, and the Warburg Institute, London.

13 Kees, *Der Götterglaube im alten Aegypten,* p. 347.

14 *Pistis Sophia,* trans. by Horner, pp. 160–64 and 166–68.

15 Kerényi, "Die Göttin Natur."

16 Cf. Newcomb and Reichard, *Sandpaintings of the Navajo Shooting Chant,* especially Pl. XIII.

Giotto; [17] it is found in Egypt (*illus. 4*), Africa (*illus. 6*), Mexico (*illus. 7*), and India (*illus. 8*), among the gypsies as an amulet,[18] and in the alchemical texts (*illus. 9*).[19]

The symbolic thinking portrayed in these images of the round endeavors to grasp contents which even our present-day consciousness can only understand as paradoxes, precisely because it cannot grasp them. If we give the name of "all" or "nothing" to the beginning, and speak in this connection of wholeness, unity, nondifferentiation, and the absence of opposites, all these "concepts," if we look at them more closely and try to "conceive" them instead of just going on thinking them, are found to be images derived and abstracted from these basic symbols. Images and symbols have this advantage over the paradoxical philosophical formulations of infinite unity and unimaged wholeness, that their unity can be seen and grasped as a unity at one glance.

More: all these symbols with which men have sought to grasp the beginning in mythological terms are as alive today as they ever were; they have their place not only in art and religion, but in the living processes of the individual psyche, in dreams and in fantasies. And so long as man shall exist, perfection will continue to appear as the circle, the sphere, and the round; and the Primal Deity who is sufficient unto himself, and the self who has gone beyond the opposites, will reappear in the image of the round, the mandala.[20]

This round and this existence in the round, existence in the uroboros, is the symbolic self-representation of the dawn state, showing the infancy both of mankind and of the child. The validity and reality of the uroboros symbol rest on a collective basis. It corresponds to an evolutionary stage which can be "recollected" in the psychic structure of every human being.

[17] See his "Envy," one of the Vices in the frescoes (c. 1305) of the Arena Chapel, Padua: the figure is of a horned, bat-eared witch, from whose mouth a serpent issues, circling back to bite her face.

[18] *Ciba-Zeitschrift*, No. 31, illustration, "Heil-Aberglaube der Zigeuner."

[19] See also illustrations in Jung, *Psychology and Alchemy* and "Paracelsus as a Spiritual Phenomenon."

[20] Cf. the work of Jung and his school on the mandala in normal and pathological people, children (*illus. 5*), etc.

It functions as a transpersonal factor that was there as a psychic stage of being before the formation of an ego. Moreover, its reality is re-experienced in every early childhood, and the child's personal experience of this pre-ego stage retraces the old track trodden by humanity.

An embryonic and still undeveloped germ of ego consciousness slumbers in the perfect round and awakens. It is immaterial whether we are dealing with a self-representation of this psychic stage, manifesting itself in a symbol, or whether a later ego describes this preliminary stage as its own past. Since the ego has and can have no experiences of its own in the embryonic state, not even psychic experiences—for its experiencing consciousness still slumbers in the germ—the later ego will describe this earlier state, of which it has indefinite but symbolically graspable knowledge, as a "prenatal" time. It is the time of existence in paradise where the psyche has her preworldly abode, the time before the birth of the ego, the time of unconscious envelopment, of swimming in the ocean of the unborn.

The time of the beginning, before the coming of the opposites, must be understood as the self-description of that great epoch when there was still no consciousness. It is the *wu chi* of Chinese philosophy, whose symbol is the empty circle.[21] Everything is still in the "now and for ever" of eternal being; sun, moon, and stars, these symbols of time and therefore of mortality, have not yet been created; and day and night, yesterday and tomorrow, genesis and decay, the flux of life and birth and death, have not yet entered into the world. This prehistoric state of being is not time, but eternity, just as the time before the coming of man and before birth and begetting is eternity. And just as there is no time before the birth of man and ego, only eternity, so there is no space, only infinity.

The question "Whence?"—which is both the original question and the question about the origin—has but one answer, and of

---

[21] Richard Wilhelm, in *Das Buch des Alten vom Sinn und Leben* (his German edn. of the Tao Teh Ching), p. 90.

this there are two interpretations. The answer is: the round, and the two interpretations: the womb and the parents.

It is crucial for every psychology, and especially for every psychology of childhood, to understand this problem and its symbolism.

The uroboros appears as the round "container," i.e., the maternal womb, but also as the union of masculine and feminine opposites, the World Parents joined in perpetual cohabitation. Although it seems quite natural that the original question should be connected with the problem of the World Parents, we must realize at once that we are dealing with symbols of origination and not with sexuality or a "genital theory." The problem around which mythological statements revolve and which was from the very beginning the crucial question for man is really concerned with the origins of life, of the spirit and the soul.

This is not to say that early man was something of a philosopher; abstract questions of this kind were wholly alien to his consciousness. Mythology, however, is the product of the collective unconscious, and anyone acquainted with primitive psychology must stand amazed at the unconscious wisdom which rises up from the depths of the human psyche in answer to these unconscious questions. The unconscious knowledge of the background of life and of man's dealings with it is laid down in ritual and myth; these are the answers of what he calls the human soul and the human mind to questions which were very much alive for him, even though no ego consciousness had consciously asked them.

Many primitive peoples do not recognize the connection between sexual intercourse and birth. Where, as among primitives, sexual intercourse often begins in childhood but does not lead to the begetting of children, it is natural to conclude that the birth of the child has nothing to do with impregnation by a man in the sexual act.

The question about the origin, however, must always be answered by "womb," for it is the immemorial experience of mankind that every newborn creature comes from a womb. Hence

13

the "round" of mythology is also called the womb and uterus, though this place of origin should not be taken concretely. In fact, all mythology says over and over again that this womb is an image, the woman's womb being only a partial aspect of the primordial symbol of the place of origin from whence we come. This primordial symbol means many things at once: it is not just *one* content or part of the body, but a plurality, a world or cosmic region where many contents hide and have their essential abode. "The Mothers" are not *a* mother.

Anything deep—abyss, valley, ground, also the sea and the bottom of the sea, fountains, lakes and pools, the earth (*illus. 10*), the underworld, the cave, the house, and the city—all are parts of this archetype. Anything big and embracing which contains, surrounds, enwraps, shelters, preserves, and nourishes anything small belongs to the primordial matriarchal realm.[22] When Freud saw that everything hollow was feminine, he would have been right if only he had grasped it as a symbol. By interpreting it as the "female genitalia" he profoundly misunderstood it, because female genitalia are only a tiny part of the archetype of the Primordial Mother.

Compared with this maternal uroboros, human consciousness feels itself embryonic, for the ego feels fully contained in this primordial symbol. It is only a tiny helpless newcomer. In the pleromatic phase of life, when the ego swims about in the round like a tadpole, there is nothing but the uroboros in existence. Humanity does not yet exist, there is only divinity; only the world has being. Naturally, then, the first phases of man's evolving ego consciousness are under the dominance of the uroboros. They are the phases of an infantile ego consciousness which, although no longer entirely embryonic and already possessing an existence of its own, still lives in the round, not yet detached from it and only just beginning to differentiate itself from it. This initial stage when ego consciousness is still on the infantile level is marked by the predominance of the maternal side of the uroboros.

[22] Jung, "Psychological Aspects of the Mother Archetype."

The world is experienced as all-embracing, and in it man experiences himself, as a self, sporadically and momentarily only. Just as the infantile ego, living this phase over again, feebly developed, easily tired, emerges like an island out of the ocean of the unconscious for occasional moments only, and then sinks back again, so early man experiences the world. Small, feeble, and much given to sleep, i.e., for the most part unconscious, he swims about in his instincts like an animal. Enfolded and upborne by great Mother Nature, rocked in her arms, he is delivered over to her for good or ill. Nothing is himself; everything is world. The world shelters and nourishes him, while he scarcely wills and acts at all. Doing nothing, lying inert in the unconscious, merely being there in the inexhaustible twilit world, all needs effortlessly supplied by the great nourisher—such is that early, beatific state. All the positive maternal traits are in evidence at this stage, when the ego is still embryonic and has no activity of its own. The uroboros of the maternal world is life and psyche in one; it gives nourishment and pleasure, protects and warms, comforts and forgives. It is the refuge for all suffering, the goal of all desire. For always this mother is she who fulfills, the bestower and helper. This living image of the Great and Good Mother has at all times of distress been the refuge of humanity and ever shall be; for the state of being contained in the whole, without responsibility or effort, with no doubts and no division of the world into two, is paradisal, and can never again be realized in its pristine happy-go-luckiness in adult life.

The positive side of the Great Mother seems to be embodied in this stage of the uroboros. Only at a very much higher level will the "good" Mother appear again. Then, when she no longer has to do with an embryonic ego, but with an adult personality matured by rich experience of the world, she reveals herself anew as Sophia, the "gracious" Mother, or, pouring forth her riches in the creative fullness of true productivity, as the "Mother of All Living."

The dawn state of perfect containment and contentment was never an historical state (Rousseau was still projecting this

15

psychic phase into the historical past, as the "natural state" of the savage.) It is rather the image of a psychic stage of humanity, just discernible as borderline image. However much the world forced early man to face reality, it was with the greatest reluctance that he consciously entered into this reality. Even today we can see from primitives that the law of gravity, the inertia of the psyche, the desire to remain unconscious, is a fundamental human trait. Yet even this is a false formulation, since it starts from consciousness as though that were the natural and self-evident thing. But fixation in unconsciousness, the downward drag of its specific gravity, cannot be called a desire to remain unconscious; on the contrary, *that* is the natural thing. There is, as a counteracting force, the desire to become conscious, a veritable instinct impelling man in this direction. One has no need to desire to remain unconscious; one is primarily unconscious and can at most conquer the original situation in which man drowses in the world, drowses in the unconscious, contained in the infinite like a fish in the environing sea. The ascent toward consciousness is the "unnatural" thing in nature; it is specific of the species Man, who on that account has justly styled himself Homo sapiens. The struggle between the specifically human and the universally natural constitutes the history of man's conscious development.

So long as the infantile ego consciousness is weak and feels the strain of its own existence as heavy and oppressive, while drowsiness and sleep are felt as delicious pleasure, it has not yet discovered its own reality and differentness. So long as this continues, the uroboros reigns on as the great whirling wheel of life, where everything not yet individual is submerged in the union of opposites, passing away and willing to pass away.

Man is not yet thrown back upon himself, against nature, nor the ego against the unconscious; being oneself is still a wearisome and painful experience, still the exception that has to be overcome. It is in this sense that we speak of "uroboric incest." It goes without saying that the term "incest" is to be understood symbolically, not concretistically and sexually.

16

Wherever the incest motif appears, it is always a prefiguration of the *hieros gamos,* of the sacred marriage consummation which attains its true form only with the hero.

Uroboric incest is a form of entry into the mother, of union with her, and it stands in sharp contrast to other and later forms of incest. In uroboric incest, the emphasis upon pleasure and love is in no sense active, it is more a desire to be dissolved and absorbed; passively one lets oneself be taken, sinks into the pleroma, melts away in the ocean of pleasure—a *Liebestod.* The Great Mother takes the little child back into herself, and always over uroboric incest there stand the insignia of death, signifying final dissolution in union with the Mother. Cave, earth, tomb, sarcophagus, and coffin are symbols of this ritual recombination, which begins with burial in the posture of the embryo in the barrows of the Stone Age and ends with the cinerary urns of the moderns.

Many forms of nostalgia and longing signify no more than a return to uroboric incest and self-dissolution, from the *unio mystica* of the saint to the drunkard's craving for unconsciousness and the "death-romanticism" of the Germanic races. The incest we term "uroboric" is self-surrender and regression. It is the form of incest taken by the infantile ego, which is still close to the mother and has not yet come to itself; but the sick ego of the neurotic can also take this form and so can a later, exhausted ego that creeps back to the mother after having found fulfillment.

Notwithstanding its own dissolution and the deadly aspect of the uroboros, the embryonic ego does not experience uroboric incest as anything hostile, even though it be annihilated. The return to the great round is a happening full of passive, childlike confidence; for the infantile ego consciousness always feels its reawakening, after having been immersed in death, as a rebirth. It feels protected by the maternal depths even when the ego has disappeared and there is no consciousness of itself. Man's consciousness rightly feels itself to be the child of these primordial depths; for not only in the history of mankind is

17

consciousness a late product of the womb of the unconscious, but in every individual life, consciousness re-experiences its emergence from the unconscious in the growth of childhood, and every night in sleep, dying with the sun, it sinks back into the depths of the unconscious, to be reborn in the morning and to begin the day anew.

The uroboros, the great round, is not only the womb, but the World Parents. The World Father is joined to the World Mother in uroboric union, and they are not to be divided. They are still under the rule of the primordial law: above and below, father and mother, heaven and earth, God and world, reflect one another and cannot be put apart. How could the conjunction of opposites, as the initial state of existence, ever be represented mythologically except by the symbol of the conjoined World Parents!

Thus the World Parents, who are the answer to the question about the origin, are themselves the universe and the prime symbol of everlasting life. They are the perfection from whence everything springs; the eternal being that begets, conceives, and brings itself to birth, that kills and revivifies. Their unity is a state of existence transcendent and divine, independent of the opposites—the inchoate "En-Soph" of the cabala, which means "unending plenitude" and "nothingness." The tremendous force of this primordial symbol of the psyche does not lie only in the fact that it contains in itself the non-differentiated state of union beyond the opposites. The uroboros also symbolizes the creative impulse of the new beginning; it is the "wheel that rolls of itself," the initial, rotatory movement in the upward spiral of evolution.[23]

This initial movement, the procreative thrust, naturally has an affinity with the paternal side of the uroboros and with the beginning of evolution in time, and is far harder to visualize than the maternal side.

[23] Schoch-Bodmer, "Die Spirale als Symbol und als Strukturelement des Lebendigen"; Leisegang, "Das Mysterium der Schlange."

18

For instance, when we read in Egyptian theology such passages as:

Atum, who indulged himself in Heliopolis, took his phallus in his hand in order to arouse pleasure. A brother and sister were produced, Shu and Tefnut.[24]

or:

I copulated in my hand, I joined myself to my shadow and spurted out of my own mouth. I spewed forth as Shu and spat forth as Tefnut.[25]

this clearly expresses the difficulty of grasping the creative beginning in a symbol. What is meant would nowadays be called spontaneous generation or the self-manifestation of a god. The original force of the images still shines through our rather more abstract terms. The uroboric mode of propagation, where begetter and conceiver are one, results in the image of immediate genesis from the semen, without partner and without duality.

To call such images "obscene" is to be guilty of a profound misunderstanding. Actually, life in those times was far more disciplined sexually, far purer, than in most of the later cultures; the sexual symbolism that appears in primitive cult and ritual has a sacral and transpersonal import, as everywhere in mythology. It symbolizes the creative element, not personal genitality. It is only personalistic misunderstanding that makes these sacral contents "obscene." Judaism and Christianity between them—and this includes Freud—have had a heavy and disastrous hand in this misunderstanding. The desecration of pagan values in the struggle for monotheism and for a conscious ethic was necessary, and historically an advance; but it resulted in a complete distortion of the primordial world of those times. The effect of secondary personalization in the struggle against paganism was to reduce the transpersonal to the personal. Sanctity became sodomy, worship became fornication,

[24] Pyramid Texts, spell 1248, in Sethe, *Pyramidentexte.*
[25] Book of Apopis, in Roeder, *Urkunden zur Religion des alten Aegypten,* p. 108.

19

and so on. An age whose eyes are once more open to the transpersonal must reverse this process.

Later creation symbols show how these matters came to be better formulated. Not that any repression had crept in. What was to be expressed had from the very outset no sexual connotations, it was meant symbolically; but the efforts with which early man wrestled for words give us some indication of what it was all about.

The image of the self-fecundating primal god undergoes new variations in Egypt and India, and in both cases there is a move in the direction of spiritualization. But this spiritualization is the same as the endeavor to apprehend the nature of the creative force that was there in the beginning:

> It is the heart which makes all that results, to come out, and it is the tongue which repeats (expresses) the thought of the heart. . . . That is what causes all the gods to be born. Atum with his Ennead, and every divine utterance manifests itself in the thought of the heart and speech of the tongue.[26]

Or:

> The Demiurge who created all the gods and their Kas is in his heart and in his tongue.[27]

And finally we come to the most abstract and spiritual symbolism of all, where God is the "breath of life":

> He did not bring me forth from his mouth, nor conceive me in his hand, but he breathed me forth from his nostrils.[28]

The transition from image to idea in this formulation of the creative principle becomes doubly clear when one knows that in the hieroglyphs "thought" is written with the image for "heart" and "speech" with that for "tongue."

At this point in Egyptian mythology and its wrestlings with the problem of creation, we have the first beginnings of what was to be expressed several thousand years later as the "Word of God" in the Bible story of the creation and in the doctrine of

[26] Moret, *The Nile and Egyptian Civilization*, p. 376.
[27] Kees, *Aegypten*, p. ii.
[28] Kees, *Götterglaube*, p. 312 n.

20

the Logos—an expression that was never able to break away altogether from the primordial image of the "self-manifesting" and "self-expressing" god.

Understandably enough, the creative principle that brings the world into being is derived from the creative nature of man himself. Just as a man—our figures of speech say the same thing today—brings forth his creations from his own depths and "expresses" himself, so do the gods. In like manner Vishnu the Boar scoops the earth out of the sea, and the god ponders the world in his heart and expresses it in the creative word. The word, speech, is a higher product, the utterance of one sunk in himself, in his own depths. When we talk of "introversion" we say the same thing. In India, *tapas*, "inward heat" and "brooding," is the creative force with whose help everything is made. The self-incubating effect of introversion, a fundamental experience of the self-generating spirit, is clearly expressed in the following text:

He, Prajapati, took to praying and fasting, because he desired offspring, and he made himself fruitful.[29]

An Egyptian text says:

My name was "he who created himself, first god of first gods." [30]

The same principle of "heating" is described in another Brahmana as the way of creation:

In the beginning this world was nothing at all. Heaven was not, nor earth, nor space. Because it was not, it bethought itself: I will be. It emitted heat.

After describing a long series of cosmogonic heatings and the production of elements, the text goes on:

He found foothold on the earth. When he had found a firm foothold there, he thought: I will propagate myself. He emitted heat and became pregnant.[31]

[29] Shatapatha Brahmana 11. 1. 6. 7, trans. from Geldner, *Vedismus und Brahmanismus.*
[30] Book of Apopis, in Roeder, op. cit.
[31] Taittiriya Brahmana 2. 2. 9. 5, trans. from Geldner, op. cit., p. 90.

Just as the maternal side of the uroboros gives birth without procreation, so the paternal side procreates without the maternal womb. The two sides are complementary and belong together. The original question asks about the origin of that which moves all life. To this question the creation myths give one answer: they say that creation is something not altogether expressible in the symbols of sexuality, and they proceed to formulate the unformulable in an image.

The creative word, creative breath—that is creative spirit. But this breath concept is only an abstraction from the image of the procreative wind-ruach-pneuma-animus, which animates through "inspiration." The solar phallus symbolizing the creative element is the source of the wind, both in an Egyptian magic papyrus and in the vision of a modern psychotic.[32] This wind, in the form of the ruach-dove of the Holy Ghost, is wafted under the robe of the immaculately conceiving Virgin Mary, through a tube held out to her by God the Father in the sun. The wind is the fructifying bird known to the primitives, the ancestral spirit that blows upon the women, and also upon tortoises and female vultures, and makes them fruitful.[33]

Animals as fructifiers, gods as fructifiers, gods as animals, animals as gods—everywhere the enigma of fructification is ranged alongside that of creative "inspiration." Mankind asks about the origin of life, and immediately life and soul fuse into one, as living psyche, power, spirit, motion, breath, and the life-giving mana. This One who stands at the beginning is the creative force contained in the uroboric unity of the World Parents, from whom it blows, begets, gives birth, moves, breathes, and speaks. "As the wind blows, everything grows," says the Upanishad.[34]

Although the ego experiences—and must experience—the uroboros as the terrible dark power of the unconscious, mankind does not by any means associate this stage of its preconscious

[32] Jung, "The Structure of the Psyche," p. 150.
[33] Briffault, The Mothers, Vol. II, p. 452.
[34] Brihadaranyaka 3. 9. 9, in The Ten Principal Upanishads, trans. by W. B. Yeats and Shree Purohit Swami.

existence only with feelings of dread and drowsiness. Even if, for the conscious ego, light and consciousness cleave together, like darkness and unconsciousness, man still has inklings of another and, so he thinks, a deeper "extraworldly" knowledge. In mythology this illumination is usually projected into a knowledge acquired before birth or after death.

In the Bardo Thödol, the Tibetan Book of the Dead, the dead man receives instruction, and the instruction culminates in the doctrine that he shall know himself identical with the great white light that shines beyond life and death:

Thine own consciousness, shining, void, and inseparable from the Great Body of Radiance, hath no birth, nor death, and is the Immutable Light— Buddha Amitabha.[35]

This knowledge is postconscious, outside and not of this world, a knowing and being in the perfection that comes after death, but it is also preconscious, preworldly, and prenatal. This is what the Jewish midrash means when it ascribes knowledge to the unborn babe in the womb, saying that over its head there burns a light in which it sees all the ends of the world.[36] Also, existence in the time before the beginning is supposedly connected with foreknowledge. The creature that still exists in the round participates in the knowledge of the unformed, is merged in the ocean of wisdom. The primal ocean, likewise an origination symbol—for as a ring-snake the uroboros is also the ocean—is the source not only of creation but of wisdom too. Hence the early culture heroes often come up from the sea in the shape of a half fish, like the Babylonian Oannes, and bring their wisdom as a revelation to mankind.

Since the original wisdom is preworldly, i.e., prior to the ego and the coming of consciousness, the myths say it is prenatal. But existence after death and prenatal existence in the uroboros are the same thing. The ring of life and death is a closed circuit; it is the wheel of rebirth, and the dead man instructed in the

[35] Evans-Wentz, *The Tibetan Book of the Dead*, p. 96.
[36] Wünsche, *Kleine Midraschim*, Vol. III, pp. 213 f.

Bardo Thödol will infallibly be born again if he fails to attain to the highest knowledge in his afterlife. So for him the instruction after death is equally a prenatal one.

The mythological theory of foreknowledge also explains the view that all knowing is "memory." Man's task in the world is to remember with his conscious mind what was knowledge before the advent of consciousness. In this sense it is said of the *saddik*, the "perfect righteous man" of Hasidism, the mystical Jewish movement dating from the end of the eighteenth century:

The Saddik finds that which has been lost since birth and restores it to men.[37]

It is the same conception as Plato's philosophical doctrine of the prenatal vision of ideas and their remembrance. The original knowledge of one who is still enfolded in the perfect state is very evident in the psychology of the child. For this reason many primitive peoples treat children with particular marks of respect. In the child the great images and archetypes of the collective unconscious are living reality, and very close to him; indeed, many of his sayings and reactions, questions and answers, dreams and images, express this knowledge which still derives from his prenatal existence. It is transpersonal experience not personally acquired, a possession acquired from "over there." Such knowledge is rightly regarded as ancestral knowledge, and the child as a reborn forebear.

The theory of heredity, proving that the child has the ancestral heritage biologically in himself, and to a large extent actually "is" this heritage, also has a psychological justification. Jung therefore defines the transpersonal—or the archetypes and instincts of the collective unconscious—as "the deposit of ancestral experience."[38] Hence the child, whose life as a prepersonal entity is largely determined by the collective unconscious, actually is the living carrier of this ancestral experience.

In the dawn world of consciousness, where the feebly devel-

---

[37] Horodezky, *Rabbi Nachman von Brazlaw*, p. 188.
[38] "Analytical Psychology and *Weltanschauung*," p. 376.

oped ego is still under the dominance of the unconscious, there rules, besides the symbolism whose mythological stages we are trying to describe, another set of symbols which correspond to the magic body image in the psyche. Certain groups of symbols are co-ordinated with certain regions of the body. Even today, the primitive body scheme of belly, breast, and head is used in ordinary psychology, where "belly" is an abbreviation for the instinctual world, "breast" and "heart" for the zone of feeling, and "head" and "brain" for the zone of spirit. Modern psychology and language have been influenced to this day by this original body scheme. The scheme is most developed in Indian psychology; in Kundalini yoga the ascending consciousness rouses and activates the different body-soul centers. The diaphragm is supposed to correspond to the earth's surface, and development beyond this zone is co-ordinated with the "rising sun," the state of consciousness that has begun to leave behind the unconscious and all ties with it.

The body scheme, as the archetype of the original man in whose image the world was created, is the basic symbol in all systems where parts of the world are co-ordinated with regions of the body. This co-ordination is to be found everywhere, in Egypt as in Mexico, in Indian literature as in the cabala. Not God alone, but the whole world is created in man's image. The relation of the world and the gods to the body scheme is the earliest concretistic form of the "anthropocentric world picture," with man standing in the middle or "at the heart" of the world. It derives from one's own body sensations, which are charged with mana and are commonly misunderstood as narcissistic.

The mana-charge originally associated with everything that belongs to the body is expressed in primitive man's fear of magical influences, due to the fact that every part of the body, from hair to excrement, can stand for the body as a whole and bewitch it. Also, the symbolism of the creation myths, where everything that comes out of the body is creative, derives from the latter's mana potency. Not only the semen, but urine and spittle,

25

sweat, dung, and breath, words and flatus, are heavy with creation. Out of it all comes the world, and the whole "turn-out" is "birth."

For primitive man and the child, with his overemphasized unconscious, the main accent falls on the visceral region and its dead weight of vegetative life. The "heart" is for him the highest center, representing what the thinking head means for us. For the Greeks, the midriff was the seat of consciousness, for the Indians and Hebrews, the heart. In both cases thinking is emotional, bound up with affects and passions. The dissolution of emotional components is not yet complete (see Part II). Only if a thought is a passion that grips the heart can it reach ego consciousness and be perceived; consciousness is only affected by the proximity of the idea to the archetype. But the heart is also the seat of ethical decision; it symbolizes the center of the personality, and, in the Egyptian Judgment of the Dead, it was weighed. The heart plays the same role in Jewish mysticism,[39] and even today we still speak of a man having a "good heart" as though it were an ethical organ. Anything situated lower down than the heart belongs to the realm of instinct. The liver and the kidneys are visceral centers of great importance for psychic life. "God trieth the heart and reins" of the man whose conscious and unconscious are to be searched, and the examination of the liver as the divinatory center in haruspicy is as well known as the fate of Prometheus, who, for the theft of fire and the hybristic overextension of his consciousness, was punished with the "agenbite of inwit" by Zeus, who sent an eagle to feed upon his liver. But all visceral centers, which also function as affective centers controlling sexuality, are already centers of a higher order. Deeper down lies the psychic plane of intestinal processes of the alimentary tract. The instinct to eat—hunger—is one of the most elementary of man's psychic instincts, and the psychology of the belly plays a correspondingly large part with primitives and children. One's state of mind is the more dependent upon whether one is satis-

[39] Bischoff, *Die Elemente der Kabbalah,* Vol. I, p. 234.

fied or not, or thirsty or not, the less one's consciousness and one's ego are developed. For the embryonic ego the nutritional side is the only important factor, and this sphere is still very strongly accentuated for the infantile ego, which regards the maternal uroboros as the source of food and satisfaction.

The uroboros is properly called the "tail-eater," and the symbol of the alimentary canal dominates this whole stage. The "swamp" stage of the uroboros and early matriarchate, as described by Bachofen, is a world in which every creature devours every other. Cannibalism is symptomatic of this state of affairs. On this level, which is pregenital because sex is not yet operative and the polar tension of the sexes still in abeyance, there is only a stronger that eats and a weaker that is eaten. In this animal world—since rutting is relatively rare—the visceral psychology of hunger occupies the foreground. Hunger and food are the prime movers of mankind.

Everywhere we find in the initial creation myths a pregenital food symbolism, transpersonal because sprung from the original collective layer of symbols. The systole and diastole of human existence center on the functions of the digestive tract. Eating = intake, birth = output, food the only content, being nourished the fundamental form of vegetative-animal existence—that is the motto. Life = power = food, the earliest formula for obtaining power over anything, appears in the oldest of the Pyramid Texts. They say of the risen dead:

The sky clouds over, the stars rain down (?); the mountains stir themselves, the cattle of the Earth-god tremble . . . at the sight of him, as he appears before them with the living soul of a god, who lives upon his fathers and devours his mothers.

It is he who devours men and lives upon the gods. . . . The catcher of skulls . . . he catches them for him. He of the resplendent head watches them for him and drives them to him (?). . . .

Their great ones are for his breakfast, their lesser ones for his dinner, and their little ones for his supper.

Whomsoever he meets on his ways, he eats raw.

He has taken away the hearts of the gods. He has eaten the Red Crown and swallowed the Green Crown. He eats the lungs of wise men; he is content to live upon hearts and their magic; he rejoices (?) ... if he can devour those who are in the Red Crown. He flourishes and their magic is in his body, and his glory is not taken from him. He has devoured the understanding of all the gods. . . .[40]

We find a corresponding symbolism in India. In one account of the creation, the first divinities fall headlong into the sea, and "Hunger" and "Thirst" are delivered up to the negative powers of the primeval waters. The account continues:

Hunger and Thirst said to him (the Self): "For us two also find an abode."

To them he said: "I assign you two a part among these divinities. I make you two partakers among them." Therefore to whatever divinity an oblation is made, hunger and thirst become partakers in it.

He bethought himself: "Here now are worlds and world-guardians. Let me create food for them."

He brooded upon the waters. And out of them that were brooded upon there arose a form. The form that arose is food.[41]

Food becomes a "cosmic content" to be seized hold of, and when the Self finally managed to seize it with *apana* (the digestive breath), "he consumed it." In another passage hunger is symbolized as death; he is the eater and devourer, as we know from the deadly and devouring aspect of the uroboros.

Even today language cannot get away from these elementary images. Eating, devouring, hunger, death, and maw go together; and we still speak, just like the primitive, of "death's maw," a "devouring war," a "consuming disease." "Being swallowed and eaten" is an archetype that occurs not only in all the medieval paintings of hell and the devil; we ourselves express the swallowing of something small by something big in the same imagery, when we say that a man is "consumed" by his work, by a movement or an idea, or "eaten up" with jealousy.

On this level, where the uroboros is co-ordinated with cosmogony, the world or cosmic content to be "assimilated" is food. Food is a phase of Brahma:

[40] Spells 273–74, in Erman, *Literature of the Ancient Egyptians*.
[41] Aitareya Upanishad 2. 5.–3. 2 (based on Hume and Deussen translations).

28

From food all creatures are produced,
All creatures that dwell on earth.
By food they live
And into food they finally pass.
Food is the chief among beings,
Therefore they call it the panacea.
Verily he obtains all food
Who worships Brahma as food.
For food is the chief among beings,
Therefore they call it the panacea.
All creatures are born of food,
By food they continue to grow.
Creatures feed on it, it upon creatures,
Therefore is it called food.[42]

Brahma arises through tapas.
From Brahma comes food,
From food—breath, spirit, truth,
Worlds, and in works, immortality.[43]

The same symbolism is used in the Maitrayana Upanishad,[44] where the relation between the world and God is equivalent to that between food and the eater of food. God, once glorified as the world nourisher, is now seen as the world devourer, for the world is God's sacrificial food.

Just as in primitive psychology and mythology the "alimentary uroboros" is a cosmic quantity, so its symbolism also appears in the relatively late philosophical speculations of India for the purpose of clarifying the relations between God as "subject" and world as "object," and vice versa.

In this connection we must mention the "sacrifice" that is offered to the god in the form of food and "eaten" by him. It is at once an act of incorporation or "inward digestion," and of seizure for increase of power.

So the world in India is the "food of the gods." As Deussen has explained, the world, according to an early Vedic idea, was

[42] Taittiriya Upanishad 2. 2.
[43] Mundaka Upanishad 1. 1. 8 (both based on Hume and Deussen translations).
[44] 6. 9. 1 ff.

created by Prajapati, who is at once life and death—or hunger. It was created in order to be eaten as the sacrifice which he himself offers to himself. This is how the horse sacrifice is interpreted,[45] the horse standing for the universe, like the bull in other cultures:

Whatever he brought forth, he resolved to eat. Because he eats (*ad*) everything, he is called infinite (*aditi*). Therefore he who knows the essence of *aditi*, becomes the eater of the world; everything becomes food for him.[46]

From this it is clear that a later age, correctly interpreting the old symbolism, has spiritualized it, or "inwardly digested" it; for the act of eating, digesting, and assimilating the world now appears as a means to possess and obtain power over it. To "know the essence of *aditi*" is to experience the infinite being of the creator who "eats" the world he has created. Thus, on the primitive level, conscious realization is called eating. When we talk of the conscious mind "assimilating" an unconscious content, we are not saying much more than is implied in the symbol of eating and digesting.

The examples from Indian and Egyptian mythology could be multiplied at will, for this sort of elementary food symbolism is archetypal. Wherever liquor, fruit, herbs, etc., appear as the vehicles of life and immortality, including the "water" and "bread" of life, the sacrament of the Host, and every form of food cult down to the present day, we have this ancient mode of human expression before us. The materialization of psychic contents, by which contents that we would call "psychic"—like life, immortality, and death—take on material form in myth and ritual and appear as water, bread, fruit, etc., is a characteristic of the primitive mind. Inside is projected outside, as we say. In reality there is a "psychization" of the object: everything outside us is experienced symbolically, as though saturated with a content which we co-ordinate with the psyche as something psychic or spiritual. This material object outside is then "assimilated," i.e., eaten. Conscious realization is "acted out" in the

---

[45] Brihadaranyaka Upanishad 1. 1. 1.
[46] Ibid., 1. 2. 5 (based on Hume and Deussen translations).

elementary scheme of nutritive assimilation, and the ritual act of concrete eating is the first form of assimilation known to man.[47] Over this whole sphere of symbolism looms the maternal uroboros in its mother-child aspect, where need is hunger and satisfaction means satiety.

The body and its "autoerotic-narcissistic" sense of itself—we shall be reviewing this idea later on—is an uroboric closed circuit. In this pregenital stage self-gratification is not masturbation, but the satisfaction of being nourished, with the infant's finger-sucking as a substitute.[47a] To "obtain" is to "eat," it does not mean to "be fertilized"; to "produce," to "express," means to "excrete," "spit," "urinate"—later to "speak"—but not to "give birth" or "beget." The masturbatory stage of uroboric creation is, on the other hand, genital in character, and precedes the sexual stage of the World Parents, which is the stage of propagation in duality, and both are preceded by the stage of the alimentary uroboros.

All the above bodily functions symbolize something that is at the same time a psychic process. The rites of cannibalism and the funeral feast, the eating of gods in the Pyramid Texts, and the communion mysteries, represent a spiritual act.

The assimilation and ingestion of the "content," the eaten food, produces an inner change. Transformation of the body cells through food intake is the most elementary of animal changes experienced by man. How a weary, enfeebled, and famished man can turn into an alert, strong, and satisfied being, or a man perishing of thirst can be refreshed or even transformed by an intoxicating drink: this is, and must remain, a fundamental experience so long as man shall exist.

[47] [Cf. Guénon, *Man and His Becoming According to the Vedanta.* It is here pointed out (p. 79, n. 2) that from the Latin word *sapere,* "to taste, perceive, know," are ultimately derived two groups of words, namely, "sap," *Saft, sève,* "savor," "sapid," etc., on the one hand, and *savoir,* "sapient," "sage," etc., on the other, "by reason of the analogy which exists between nutritive assimilation in the bodily order and cognitive assimilation in the mental and intellectual orders."—TRANS.]

[47a] See illus. 1 (frontispiece). The creator god Vishnu as a child sucking his big toe combines in himself the living circuit of the uroboros and its autonomy.

31

The emergence of corresponding symbolisms does not mean "regression to the oral zone" in the sense that this is an "infantile-perverse" zone of sexual pleasure which we ought to overcome, but simply a return to uroboric symbolism (*illus. 1*), positively accented by the unconscious. Being fertilized by eating does not imply ignorance of the sexual act, nor is it in any sense an "unenlightened substitute"; it means "total assimilation" rather than "union with." It is something different from the above-mentioned fertilization by the wind; in eating, the accent falls on the bodily intake, but in the latter case, on the invisibility of the animating and fertilizing agent.[48]

Accordingly, at the stage of the maternal alimentary uroboros, the breasts are always emphasized, as for instance in the mythological pictures of the many-breasted Great Mother (*illus. 12*) or in the innumerable statues of the goddess who presses her breasts. Here the nourishing Great Mother is more generative than parturient. Breast and lactic flow are generative elements which can also appear in phallic form, because the milk is then understood symbolically as a fertilizing agent. The milk-giving mother, whose commonest symbol is the cow, is procreative and on that account may even have a paternal character. Her child, as something she "fertilizes," is then receptive and feminine, regardless of its sex. The maternal uroboros is still hermaphroditic and presexual, like the child. So the mother propagates by nourishing, just as the child is fertilized by eating and gives birth by evacuating. For both of them the nutrient flow is a symbol of life without polar tension, and entirely unsexual.

The accentuation of the Mother's breast and its phallic character, however, already forms the transition stage. The original situation is one of complete containment in the uroboros. When the phallic character of the breast emerges, or the Mother is seen as the phallus bearer, it is a sign that the infantile subject

---

[48] A psychoanalytical interpretation (Abraham, "A Short Study of the Development of the Libido"; Jones, "Psychoanalysis of Christianity") which would reduce the one to the cannibalistic oral stage of libido organization, and the other to flatus at the anal level, is profoundly hurtful to the man whose symbolic products are misunderstood and depreciated in this way.

2. Serpent biting its tail, encircling an
inscription

Bowl from the Mandaeans, Mesopotamia,
c. 500 A.D.

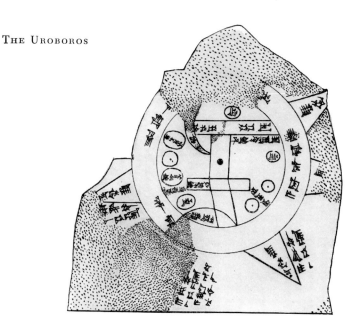

3. The ocean ringing the world

Mappa mundi, *with Babylon in center,*
from a cuneiform tablet

4. The four corners of the world, with
encircling serpent

Coptic, 17th-century Italian woodcut

5. "Snake going round the world and a boat"

Drawing by a five-year-old English girl of working-class origin

6. Serpent design on a brass shield

Benin, Nigeria

7. Mexican calendar stone, with encircling serpent

Etching from an 18th-century Swiss book

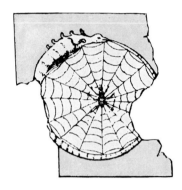

8. Maya, the eternal spinner,
encircled by serpent

*Damaged vignette from a
Brahmanic book of maxims*

9. Alchemical uroboros

*One of the allegorical figures of Lambspringk,
from a 17th-century German work*

10. Hieronymus Bosch: *Creation*

From the Garden of Earthly Delights, c. *1500*

11. The nine choirs of angels

Miniature from St. Hildegarde of Bingen, Scivias,
12th-century manuscript

is beginning to differentiate himself. Active and passive striv-
ings gradually become distinct; the opposites make their appearance. Conceiving by eating and giving birth by excreting
are differentiated as separate acts within the nutrient flow, and
the ego begins to distinguish itself from the uroboros. This
means the end of that beatific uroboric state of autarchy, perfection, and absolute self-sufficiency. So long as the ego was
swimming in the belly of the uroboros, a mere ego germ, it
shared in that paradisal perfection. This autarchy holds absolute
sway in the womb, where unconscious existence is combined
with absence of suffering. Everything is supplied of its own
accord; there is no need of the slightest exertion, not even an
instinctive reaction, let alone a regulating ego consciousness.
One's own being and the surrounding world—in this case, the
mother's body—exist in a *participation mystique,* never more to
be attained in any environmental relationship. This state of ego-
lessness, interrupted by no pleasure-pain reactions, is naturally
experienced by the later ego consciousness as one of the most
perfect forms of autarchy, bringing utter contentment. Plato
describes the formation of the world in words that recall this
containment within the uroboros:

It had no need of eyes, for there was nothing outside it to be seen; nor of
ears, for there was nothing outside it to be heard. There was no surrounding
air to be breathed, nor was it in need of any organ by which to supply itself
with food or to get rid of it when digested. Nothing went out from or came
into it anywhere, for there was nothing. Of design it was made thus, its own
waste providing its own food, acting and being acted upon entirely within
and by itself, because its designer considered that a being which was sufficient unto itself would be far more excellent than one which depended
upon anything.[49]

Once more we meet the uroboric cycle of self-propagation
on the alimentary level. Just as the uroboros fertilizes itself in
the mouth by eating its own tail, so "its own waste provides its
own food," an ever-recurrent symbol of autonomy and self-
sufficiency. This primordial image of the autarchic uroboros un-

[49] *Timaeus,* 33 (based on the Cornford trans.).

derlies the homunculus of alchemy, who is begotten in the round
—the retort—by rotation of the elements, and it even underlies
the *perpetuum mobile* of physics.

We shall have to concern ourselves with the problem of autarchy at all stages of our inquiry, because it is bound up with an
important trend in man's development, namely, with the problem of his self-formation. So far we have distinguished three
stages of uroboric autarchy: the first is the pleromatic stage of
paradisal perfection in the unborn, the embryonic stage of the
ego, which a later consciousness will contrast with the sufferings of the nonautarchic ego in the world. The second stage is
that of the alimentary uroboros, a closed circuit whose "own
waste provides its own food." The third, genital-masturbatory
phase is that of Atum "copulating in his own hand." All these
images, like the self-incubation of one made pregnant through
tapas—a later spiritual form of autarchy—are images of the self-
contained creative principle.

Uroboric autarchy, even when it appears as a dominant archetype, must not be reduced to the level of autoeroticism and narcissism. Both these conceptions are only valid in cases of mis-
development, when the evolutionary stage ruled by the uroboros
persists for an unnaturally long time. But even then the positive
aspect must be borne in mind. Autarchy is just as necessary a
goal of life and development as is adaptation. Self-development, self-differentiation, and self-formation are trends of the
libido no less legitimate than the extraverted relation to the
object and the introverted relation to the subject. The negative
evaluation implied by the terms "autoeroticism," "autism," and
"narcissism" is only justified in pathological cases where there
are deviations from this natural basic attitude; for the development of the ego, of consciousness, of personality, and, lastly, of
individuality itself is actually fostered by the autarchy whose
symbol is the uroboros. In many cases, therefore, the appearance of uroboric symbolism, especially if its formative and sta-
bilizing character is strongly marked, as, for instance, in the

mandala, indicates that the ego is moving toward the self, rather than in the direction of objective adaptation.

Detachment from the uroboros, entry into the world, and the encounter with the universal principle of opposites are the essential tasks of human and individual development. The process of coming to terms with the objects of the outer and inner worlds, of adapting to the collective life of mankind both within and without, governs with varying degrees of intensity the life of every individual. For the extravert, the accent lies on the objects outside, people, things, and circumstances; for the introvert, it lies on the objects inside, the complexes and archetypes. Even the introvert's development, which relates mainly to the psychic background, is in this sense "bound to the object," despite the fact that the objects lie inside him and not outside, being psychic forces rather than social, economic, or physical ones.

But besides this trend of development there is another, equally legitimate, which is self-related or "centroverted," and which makes for the development of personality and for individual realization. This development may derive its contents from outside and inside equally, and is fed by introversion as much as by extraversion. Its center of gravity, however, lies not in objects and objective dealings, irrespective of whether the objects be external or internal, but in self-formation; that is to say, in the building up and filling out of a personality which, as the nucleus of all life's activities, uses the objects of the inner and outer worlds as building material for its own wholeness. This wholeness is an end in itself, autarchic; it is quite independent of any utility value it may have either for the collective outside or for the psychic powers inside.

That we are nevertheless concerned here with a creative principle of decisive importance for civilization will be shown in its proper place.

Self-formation, whose effects in the second half of life Jung has termed "individuation," [50] has its critical developmental

[50] *Psychology and Alchemy*, index, s.v.

35

pattern not only in the first half of life, but also back in childhood. The growth of consciousness and of the ego is largely governed by this pattern. The stability of the ego, i.e., its ability to stand firm against the disintegrative tendencies of the unconscious and the world, is developed very early, as is also the trend toward extension of consciousness, which is likewise an important prerequisite for self-formation. Although in the first half of life, ego and consciousness are mainly preoccupied with adaptation, and the self-formative trend seems to be in abeyance, yet the beginnings of this self-realization process, while it only becomes noticeable with increasing maturity, lie far back in childhood; and it is here that the first struggles for self-formation are decided. The allegedly narcissistic, autistic, autoerotic, egocentric, and, as we saw, anthropocentric stage of the uroboros, so obvious in the child's autarchic and naïve self-relatedness, is the precondition of all subsequent self-development.

The same uroboric symbolism that stands at the beginning, before ego development starts, reappears at the end, when ego development is replaced by the development of the self, or individuation. When the universal principle of opposites no longer predominates, and devouring or being devoured by the world has ceased to be of prime importance, the uroboros symbol will reappear as the mandala in the psychology of the adult.

The goal of life now is to make oneself independent of the world, to detach oneself from it and stand by oneself. The autarchic character of the uroboros appears as a positive symbol pointing in a new direction. Whereas the uroboric incest of the neurotic and his pleromatic fixation denote an inability to break away from his origins and a refusal to be born into the world, the appearance of mandala and uroboros symbolism in the mature man is an indication that he must once more free himself from this world—for now he is "fed up" with it—and come to himself. He has, by a new process, to bear himself out of this world, just as he had to bear himself into it with his nascent ego.

Hence the "perfect" figure of the uroboros, standing as it does at the center of the unconscious world of the primitive and the child,[51] is simultaneously the central symbol of the second half of life and the nucleus of the developmental trend we have called self-formation or centroversion. The symbol of the circular mandala stands at the beginning as at the end. In the beginning it takes the mythological form of paradise; in the end, of the Heavenly Jerusalem. The perfect figure of the circle from whose center radiate the four arms of a cross, in which the opposites are at rest, is a very early and a very late symbol historically. It is found in the sanctuaries of the Stone Age; it is the paradise where the four streams have their source, and in Canaanite mythology it is the central point where the great god El sits, "at the source of the streams, in the midst of the sources of the two seas." [52]

The uroboros, traceable in all epochs and cultures, then appears as the latest symbol of individual psychic development, signifying the roundedness of the psyche, life's wholeness, and perfection regained. It is the place of transfiguration and illumination (*illus. 11*), of finality, as well as the place of mythological origination.

Thus the Great Round of the uroboros arches over man's life, encompassing his earliest childhood and receiving him again, in altered form, at the end. But in his own individual life, too, the pleroma of universal unity can be sought and found in religious experience. In mysticism, where the self-re-entrant figure of the uroboros appears as the "ocean of Godhead," there is often a dissolution of the ego, an ecstatic surrender which is equivalent to uroboric incest. But when, instead of the death ecstasy of the ego, the *"Stirb und Werde"* principle of rebirth predominates, and the theme of rebirth prevails over that of death, this is not a regression but a creative process.[53] Its relation to the uroboric stage will be fully discussed elsewhere, for the distinction between creative and pathological processes is of the utmost importance in all depth psychology.

[51] Cf. the role played by the circle in the earliest drawings of children (*illus. 5*).

[52] Albright, *Archaeology and the Religion of Israel*, p. 72.

[53] See my "Der mystische Mensch."

For both processes the uroboros is appropriate as a symbol of origination. In creative phenomena, too, and not only in religious phenomena, the life-spanning figure of the round signifies the regenerative sea and the source of higher life. It is, however, this same figure whose clinging embrace prevents the neurotic from being born into life. Then it is no longer the primordial figure of the uroboros, but, in the case of a more developed ego, the indication that a further stage has been reached, namely, the dominance of the uroboros over the ego, or the stage of the Great Mother.

II

THE GREAT MOTHER

The Ego under the Dominance of the Uroboros

WHEN THE EGO BEGINS to emerge from its identity with the uroboros, and the embryonic connection with the womb ceases, the ego takes up a new attitude to the world. The individual's view of the world changes with every stage of his development, and the variation of archetypes and symbols, gods and myths, is the expression, but also the instrument, of this change. Detachment from the uroboros means being born and descending into the lower world of reality, full of dangers and discomforts. The nascent ego becomes aware of pleasure-pain qualities, and from them it experiences its own pleasure and pain. Consequently the world becomes ambivalent. The unconscious life of nature, which is also the life of the uroboros, combines the most meaningless destruction with the supreme meaningfulness of instinctive creation; for the meaningful unity of the organism is as "natural" as the cancer which devours it. The same applies to the unity of life within the uroboros, which, like the swamp, begets, gives birth, and slays again in an endless cycle. The world experienced by the waking ego of humanity is the world of J. J. Bachofen's matriarchate with its goddesses of motherhood and destiny. The wicked, devouring mother and the good mother lavishing affection are two sides of the great uroboric Mother Goddess who reigns over this psychic stage.

This growing ambivalence gives rise to an equally ambivalent attitude on the part of the ego towards the archetype in whose power it lies.

The overwhelming might of the unconscious, i.e., the devouring, destructive aspect under which it may also manifest itself, is seen figuratively as the evil mother, whether as the bloodstained goddess of death, plague, famine, flood, and the force of instinct, or as the sweetness that lures to destruction. But, as the good mother, she is fullness and abundance; the dispenser of life and happiness, the nutrient earth, the cornucopia of the fruitful womb. She is mankind's instinctive experience of the world's depth and beauty, of the goodness and graciousness of Mother Nature who daily fulfills the promise of redemption and resurrection, of new life and new birth (*illus. 12, 13, and 18*).

Over against all this the ego—consciousness, the individual—remains small and impotent. It feels itself a tiny, defenseless speck, enveloped and helplessly dependent, a little island floating on the vast expanse of the primal ocean. At this stage, consciousness has not yet wrested any firm foothold from the flood of unconscious being. For the primitive ego, everything is still wrapped in the watery abyss, in whose eddyings it washes to and fro without orientation, with no sense of separateness, defenseless against this maelstrom of mysterious being which swamps it again and again from within and without.

Exposed to the dark forces of the world and the unconscious, early man's life feeling is necessarily one of constant endangerment. Life in the psychic cosmos of the primitive is a life full of danger and uncertainty; and the daemonism of the external world, with its sickness and death, famines and floods, droughts and earthquakes, is heightened beyond measure when contaminated with what we call the inner world. The terrors of a world ruled by the irrationality of chance and mitigated by no knowledge of the laws of causality are made even more sinister by the spirits of the dead, by demons and gods, witches and magicians; invisible workings emanate from all these beings, and the reality of these all-pervading effluences shows itself in fears, emotional outbursts, orgiastic frenzies, and psychic epidemics; seasonal bouts of lust, murderous impulses, visions, dreams, and hallucinations. One has only to know how great, even today, is Western man's primordial fear of the world despite his relatively highly developed consciousness, to understand the world fear of the primitive, and his feeling of endangerment.

This same horror of nameless, lurking forces is known also to the child, who is still incapable of conscious orientation and discrimination, confronting every event as though it were a devastating innovation, and exposed to every whim of the world and man. In him, too, there dwells this primitive dread which comes from an outside world contaminated with the inside and made mysterious by projection, as we see it in the dynamistic and animistic world picture. This dread is an expression of the dawn situation when a small and feeble ego consciousness pits itself against the cosmos. The supremacy of the world of objects and the world of the unconscious is an experience that has to be accepted. For this reason, fear is a normal phenomenon in the psychology of the child. Although it is outgrown as consciousness increases in strength, it provides at the same time a transpersonal incentive to such development. Vital components in the growth of the ego and in the evolution of consciousness, culture, religion, art, and science spring from the urge to overcome this fear by giving it concrete expression. It is therefore quite wrong to reduce it to personal or environmental factors and to seek to get rid of it in that way.

Owing to the disorientation of the infantile ego, the pleasure-pain components are experienced inseparately from one another, or at any rate the object of experience is colored by a mixture of both. The nonseparation of opposites and the resultant ambivalence of the ego towards all objects evoke a feeling of fear and impotence. The world is uroboric and supreme, whether this uroboric supremacy be experienced as the world or the unconscious, one's environment, or one's own body.

The dominance of the uroboros during the infantile phase of ego consciousness is what Bachofen describes as the time of the matriarchate, and all the symbols he associates with it still appear in this psychic stage. We must again emphasize that "stage" refers to a structural layer and not to any historical epoch. In individual development and perhaps also in that of the collective, these layers do not lie on top of one another in an orderly arrangement, but, as in the geological stratification of the earth, early layers may be pushed to the top and late layers to the bottom.

We shall have to consider, later on, the contrast between masculine and feminine development. But one thing, paradoxical though it may seem, can be established at once as a basic law: even in woman, consciousness has a masculine character. The correlation "consciousness-light-day" and "unconsciousness-darkness-night" holds true regardless of sex, and is not altered by the fact that the spirit-instinct polarity is organized on a different basis in men and women. Consciousness, as such, is masculine even in women, just as the unconscious is feminine in men.[1]

Bachofen's matriarchate stands for the stage when ego consciousness is undeveloped and still embedded in nature and the world. Consequently the uroboric principle is also associated with the predominance of earth and vegetation symbolism.

It is not the earth that imitates woman, but woman who imitates the earth. Marriage was regarded by the ancients as an agrarian matter; the whole terminology of matrimonial law is borrowed from agriculture,[2]

says Bachofen, recalling Plato's remark:

In fertility and generation, woman does not set an example to the earth, but the earth sets an example to woman.[3]

These sayings recognize the priority of the transpersonal and the derivative nature of the personal. Even marriage, the regulation of the sexual principle of opposites, derives from the earth principle of the matriarchate.

[1] This does not contradict Jung's statement that the ego of a woman has a feminine character, and her unconscious a masculine one. Woman fights part of the heroic struggle with the help of her masculine consciousness, or, in the language of analytical psychology, her "animus," but for her this struggle is not the only one and not the final one. However, the problem of "matriarchal consciousness" here at issue can only be dealt with in my work on the psychology of the feminine.

[2] Bachofen, *Urreligion und antike Symbole*, Vol. II, p. 309.

[3] Plato, *Menexenus*, 238.

At this stage, food symbolism and the organs co-ordinated with it are of prime importance. This explains why Mother Goddess cultures and their mythologies are closely connected with fertility and growth, and particularly with agriculture, hence with the sphere of food, which is the material and bodily sphere.

The stage of the maternal uroboros is characterized by the child's relation to its mother, who yields nourishment (*illus. 12*), but at the same time it is an historical period in which man's dependence on the earth and nature is at its greatest. Connected with both aspects is the dependence of the ego and consciousness on the unconscious. The dependence of the sequence "child-man-ego-consciousness" on the sequence "mother-earth-nature-unconscious" illustrates the relation of the personal to the transpersonal and the reliance of the one upon the other.

This stage of development is ruled by the image of the Mother Goddess with the Divine Child (*illus. 13*). It emphasizes the necessitous and helpless nature of the child and the protective side of the mother. In the form of a goat she suckles the Cretan boy Zeus and protects him from the devouring father; Isis brings the boy Horus back to life when he is stung by a scorpion; and Mary protects the Jesus child fleeing from Herod, just as Leto hides her divinely begotten children from the wrath of the hostile goddess. The child is the companion god of the Great Mother. As child and Cabir, it stands beside and beneath her, her dependent creature. Even for the youthful god, the Great Mother is fate. How much more, then, for the child, whose nature it is to be an appendage of her body.

This relationship is most vividly expressed in the "prehuman" symbols where the Mother is the sea, a lake, or a river, and the child a fish swimming in the enveloping waters.[4]

Little Horus the son of Isis, Hyacinthus, Erichthonius, and Dionysus, Melicertes the son of Ino, and countless other beloved children are all under the dominion of the all-powerful Mother Goddess. For them she is still the beneficent birth-giver

[4] *The Cambridge Ancient History,* Vol. of Plates I, p. 197.

and protectress, the young Mother, the Madonna. There is as yet no conflict, for the original containment of the child in the maternal uroboros is a state of uninterrupted reciprocal bliss. The adult ego connects the Madonna with this infantile stage, but the infantile ego, having as yet no central consciousness, still feels the amorphous pleromatic character of the maternal uroboros.

Nevertheless, this child suffers the same fate as the adolescent lover who succeeds him: he is killed. His sacrifice, death, and resurrection are the ritual center of all child-sacrifice cults. Born to die, dying to be reborn, the child is co-ordinated with the seasonal life of vegetation. The Cretan Zeus-child, nurtured by the Great Mother in the shape of a goat, cow, bitch, sow, dove, or bee,[5] is born every year, only to die every year. But the boy is also light and therefore more than mere vegetation:

One myth, very original in its primitivity although only recorded in later times, tells us that the child was born every year, for it speaks of a light which every year shone forth from a grotto "when the blood flowed at the birth of Zeus." [6]

The fate of the dying and sacrificed child, however, is not tragic like that of the adolescent lover. In the return to the deadly Mother, the *mater larum* of the Romans, he finds shelter and comfort, for containment in the Great Mother enfolds the child, whether in life or in death.[7]

[5] Nilsson, "Die Griechen," in Chantepie de la Saussaye, *Lehrbuch der Religionsgeschichte*, Vol. II, p. 319.

[6] Ibid.

[7] The book by Jung and Kerényi, *Essays on a Science of Mythology*, supplements our study at important points. Nevertheless a few critical observations are necessary here. The section in which Kerényi deals with the Kore-Demeter myth is of great importance for our projected study of feminine psychology and its deviations from the line of stadial development, and will be fully discussed there. The procedure we adopt, of examining a given group of archetypes from the evolutionary point of view, is "biographical" in the very sense which Kerényi rejects (pp. 35–38). Undoubtedly every archetype is timeless and therefore eternal, like God, so that the Divine Child never "becomes" the divine youth, it being rather the case that both exist side by side without any connection, as eternal ideas. And yet the gods do "become"; they have their fate and consequently their "biography." This evolutionary aspect of the eternal is viewed

During the phase when consciousness begins to turn into self-consciousness, that is, to recognize and discriminate itself as a separate individual ego, the maternal uroboros overshadows it like a dark and tragic fate. Feelings of transitoriness and mortality, impotence and isolation, now color the ego's picture of the uroboros, in absolute contrast to the original situation of contentment. Whereas, in the beginning, the waking state was sheer exhaustion for the feeble ego consciousness, and sleep was bliss, so that it could later surrender itself rapturously to uroboric incest and return to the Great Round, now this return becomes more and more difficult and is accomplished with increasing repugnance as the demands of its own independent existence grow more insistent. For the dawning light of consciousness, the maternal uroboros turns to darkness and night. The passage of time and the problem of death become a dominant life-feeling; Bachofen describes the mother-born, who know that they are born only of earth and mother, as being "sad by nature," for decay and the necessity of death are one side of the uroboros just because its other side signifies birth and life. The world wheel, the humming loom of time, the Weird Sisters, and the wheel of birth and death, all these symbols express the sadness that rules over the life of the adolescent ego.

In this third phase, the ego germ has already attained a cer-

---

as one aspect among many other true and possible ones, and we refer to the child stage only as the stage of transition from uroboros to adolescence, without elaborating its independent existence. In this sense the work of Jung and Kerényi greatly enriches our theme.

In the child archetype the conscious ego is still incompletely separated from the unconscious self, and everywhere there are traces of its containment in the uroboros, the primordial deity. Jung therefore speaks of the "hermaphroditism of the child," and of the "child as beginning and end." The "invincibility of the child" expresses not only the place where invincible deity has his seat, i.e., the uroboros, but the invincible nature of the new development which the child, as light and consciousness, represents. Both these elements belong to the eternality of the Divine Child.

With the phenomenon of its "abandonment," however, we enter upon the child's historical fate. Here his detachment, differentiation, and uniqueness are stressed, also the onset of that fateful opposition to the First Parents which determines the child's biographical career and at the same time the spiritual progress of mankind.

tain degree of autonomy. The embryonic and infantile stages are over, but although the adolescent no longer confronts the uroboros as a mere child, he has still not thrown off its suzerainty.

The development of the ego goes hand in hand with a heightened plastic representation of the objects to which the ego is related. The maternal uroboros, unformed in the sense that the human figure has a form, is now succeeded by the figure of the Great Mother.

The uroboric character of the Great Mother is apparent wherever she is worshiped in androgynous form, for instance as the bearded goddess in Cyprus and Carthage.[8] The woman with the beard, or with the phallus, betrays her uroboric character in the nondifferentiation between male and female. Only later will this hybrid be replaced by sexually unequivocal figures, for its mixed and ambivalent character represents the earliest stage from which the opposites will subsequently be differentiated.

Thus the infantile consciousness, constantly aware of its ties with, and dependence upon, the matrix from which it sprang, gradually becomes an independent system; consciousness becomes self-consciousness, and a reflecting ego having cognizance of itself emerges as the center of consciousness. Even before the centering of the ego there is consciousness of a sort, just as we can observe conscious acts in the infant before the appearance of ego consciousness. But only when the ego experiences itself as something distinct and different from the unconscious is the embryonic stage overcome, and only then can a conscious system be formed that stands entirely on its own. This early stage of conscious-unconscious relations is reflected in the mythology of the Mother Goddess and her connection with the son-lover. The Attis, Adonis, Tammuz, and Osiris figures [9] in the Near Eastern cultures are not merely born of a mother; on the contrary, this aspect is altogether eclipsed by the fact that they are their mother's lovers: they are loved, slain, buried, and bewailed by

[8] Przyluski, "Ursprünge und Entwicklung des Kultes der Mutter-Göttin."
[9] Frazer, *The Golden Bough* (abridged edition, 1951), p. 378.

her, and are then reborn through her. The figure of the son-lover follows on the stage of embryo and child. By differentiating himself from the unconscious and reaffirming his masculine otherness, he very nearly becomes the partner of the maternal unconscious; he is her lover as well as her son. But he is not yet strong enough to cope with her, he succumbs to her in death and is devoured. The mother-beloved turns into the terrible Death Goddess. She is still playing cat-and-mouse with him, and she overshadows even his rebirth. Where, as the god who dies to rise again, he is connected with the fertility of the earth and vegetation, the sovereignty of the Earth Mother is as obvious as his own independence is questionable. The masculine principle is not yet a paternal tendency balancing the maternal-female principle; it is still youthful and vernal, the merest beginning of an independent movement away from the place of origin and the infantile relation.

These relations are summarized in Bachofen:

The mother is earlier than the son. The feminine has priority, while masculine creativity only appears afterwards as a secondary phenomenon. Woman comes first, but man "becomes." The prime datum is the earth, the basic maternal substance. Visible creation proceeds from her womb, and it is only then that the sexes are divided into two, only then does the masculine form come into being. Thus, male and female do not appear simultaneously; they are not of the same order. . . . The female is primary, the male is only what comes out of her. He is part of the visible but ever-changing created world; he exists only in perishable form. Woman exists from everlasting, self-subsistent, immutable; man, evolving, is subject to continual decay. In the realm of the physical, therefore, the masculine principle is of second rank, subordinate to the feminine. Herein lies the prototype and justification of gynocracy; herein is rooted that age-old conception of an immortal mother who unites herself with a mortal father. She is perennially the same, but from the man the generations multiply themselves into infinity. Ever the same Great Mother mates with ever new men.

Visible creation, the offspring of Mother Earth, shapes itself into the idea of the Progenitor. Adonis, the image of the annually decaying and resurgent world of nature, becomes "Papas," the only begetter of what he himself is. It is the same with Plutus. As Demeter's son, Plutus is the visible, created world which continually renews itself. But as Penia's husband he is its father and begetter. He is at once the riches teeming out of the womb

47

of the earth, and the bestower of riches; the object and the active potency, creator and creature, cause and effect. But the first earthly manifestation of masculine power takes the form of the son. From the son, we infer the father; the existence and nature of masculine power are evidenced only by the son. On this rests the subordination of the masculine principle to that of the mother. The man appears as creature, not as creator; as effect, not cause. The reverse is true of the mother. She comes before the creature, appearing as cause, the prime giver of life, and not as an effect. She is not to be inferred from the creature, but is known in her own right. In a word, the woman first exists as a mother, and the man first exists as a son.[10]

Man then comes forth from woman by a miraculous metamorphosis of nature, which repeats itself in the birth of every male child. In the son, the mother appears transformed into the father. The he-goat, however, is merely Aphrodite's attribute, subject to her and intended for her usage. (The daughter-sons of Entoria in Eratosthenes' poem *Erigone*, quoted by Plutarch, have a similar meaning.) When a man is born of woman's womb, the mother herself marvels at the new apparition. For she recognizes in the form of her son, the very image of that fecundating power to which she owes her motherhood. Her eyes linger with delight upon his limbs. Man becomes her plaything, the goat is her mount, the phallus her constant companion. Cybele the Mother overshadows Attis, Virbius is dwarfed by Diana, Phaeton by Aphrodite. Everywhere the material, feminine, natural principle has the advantage; it takes the masculine principle, which is secondary and subsists only in perishable form as an ever-changing epiphenomenon, into its lap, as Demeter took the cista.[11]

The young men whom the Mother selects for her lovers may impregnate her, they may even be fertility gods, but the fact remains that they are only phallic consorts of the Great Mother, drones serving the queen bee, who are killed off as soon as they have performed their duty of fecundation.

For this reason these youthful companion gods always appear in the form of dwarfs. The pygmies who were worshiped in Cyprus, Egypt, and Phoenicia—all territories of the Great Mother —display their phallic character just like the Dioscuri, the Cabiri, and the Dactyls, including even the figure of Harpocrates. The attendant serpent—apart from its numinous nature—is likewise a symbol of the fertilizing phallus. That is why the Great Mother

[10] Bachofen, op. cit., Vol. II, pp. 356–58.
[11] Ibid., p. 359.

is so often connected with snakes. Not only in Creto-Mycenaean culture and its Greek offshoots, but as far back as Egypt, Phoenicia, and Babylon and similarly in the Bible story of Paradise, the snake is the companion of woman.

In Ur and in Erech they found, in the lowest layer of excavations, primitive representations of very old cult images of the Mother Goddess with her child, both having the heads of snakes.[12] The uroboric form of the oldest Mother Goddess is the snake, mistress of the earth, of the depths and the underworld, which is why the child who is still attached to her is a snake like herself. Both become humanized in the course of time, but retain the snake's head. Then the lines of development diverge. The fully human end-figure, the human Madonna with the human child, has her forerunner in figures of the human mother with her companion snake in the form of a child or a phallus, as well as in figures of the human child with the big snake.

The uroboros as a ring-snake, for instance the Babylonian Tiamat and Chaos Serpent, or the Leviathan who, as the ocean, "twines his girdle of waves about the lands," [13] later divides, or is divided, into two.

When the Great Mother assumes human form, the masculine part of the uroboros—the snakelike phallus-demon—appears beside her as the residuum of the originally bisexual nature of the uroboros.

Now it is characteristic that the phallic youths, the vegetation deities, are not fertility deities only; as something sprung up from the earth, they are the vegetation itself. Their existence makes the earth fruitful, but as soon as they have reached maturity they must be killed, mown down and harvested. The Great Mother with the ear of corn, her corn son, is an archetype whose power extends as far as the mysteries of Eleusis, the Christian Madonna, and the wheaten Host in which the wheaten

[12] Kaiser Wilhelm II, *Studien zur Gorgo;* Childe, *New Light on the Most Ancient East*, Pl. XIIIc.

[13] Gunkel, *Schöpfung und Chaos*, p. 46.

49

body of the son is eaten. The youths who belong to the Great Mother are gods of spring who must be put to death in order to be lamented by the Great Mother and reborn.

All lovers of Mother Goddesses have certain features in common: they are all youths whose beauty and loveliness are as striking as their narcissism. They are delicate blossoms, symbolized by the myths as anemones, narcissi, hyacinths, or violets, which we, with our markedly masculine-patriarchal mentality, would more readily associate with young girls. The only thing we can say about these youths, whatever their names may be, is that they please the amorous goddess by their physical beauty. Apart from that they are, in contrast to the heroic figures of mythology, devoid of strength and character, lacking all individuality and initiative. They are, in every sense of the word, obliging boys whose narcissistic self-attraction is obvious (*illus. 14*).

The myth of Narcissus makes it quite clear that this is an attraction to one's own body. Especially characteristic of this adolescent stage is the narcissistic accentuation of the phallus as the epitome of the body and the narcissistic personality.

The cult of phallic fertility, like the phallic sexual orgy, is everywhere typical of the Great Mother. Fertility festivals and rites of spring are sacred to the youthful phallus and its rampant sexuality. Or rather, this would be better formulated the other way round: the phallus of the young god is sacred to the Great Mother. For originally she was not concerned with the youth at all, but with the phallus of which he is the bearer.[14] Only later, with secondary personalization, is the primary sacrament of fertility with its gruesome castration rites replaced by the love motif. Then, instead of an impersonal and suprapersonal ritual cosmically guaranteeing the fertility of the earth for the community, we have myths relating to human beings. Only then

---

[14] The earliest representation of such a fertility festival may well be the neolithic picture at Cogul, Spain (Hoernes, *Urgeschichte der bildenden Kunst in Europa,* pl. on p. 154, and p. 678), showing nine women dancing round a phallus-bearing youth. The number 9, if not accidental, further emphasizes the fertility character.

do we hear tales about the adventures of gods and goddesses with mortals, and the line finally ends with the romantic novel and the love story which are better suited to the personalistic psychology of modern times.

The grim contrast between these orgiastic feasts in which the youth and his phallus play the central part, and the subsequent ritual castration and killing, defines archetypally the situation of the adolescent ego under the dominance of the Great Mother. Although this situation is an historical and cultural one, it must be understood in terms of the psychological evolution of the ego. The relation of son-lover to Great Mother is an archetypal situation which is operative even today, and the overcoming of it is the precondition for any further development of ego consciousness.

Those flower-like boys are not sufficiently strong to resist and break the power of the Great Mother. They are more pets than lovers. The goddess, full of desire, chooses the boys for herself and rouses their sexuality. The initiative never comes from them; they are always the victims, dying like adorable flowers. The youth has at this stage no masculinity, no consciousness, no higher spiritual ego. He is narcissistically identified with his own male body and its distinguishing mark, the phallus. Not only does the Mother Goddess love him simply for his phallus, and, in castrating him, take possession of it to make herself fruitful, but he too is identified with the phallus and his fate is a phallic fate.

All these youths, with their weak egos and no personality, only have a collective fate, not a fate of their own; they are not yet individuals and so they have no individual existence, only a ritual one. Nor is the Mother Goddess related to an individual, but only to the youth as an archetypal figure.

Even rebirth through the Great Mother, her healing and positive aspect, is in this sense "unrelated." It is not an ego, much less a self or a personality, that is reborn and knows itself to be reborn; rebirth is a cosmic occurrence, anonymous and universal like "life." From the point of view of the Earth Mother or Great

Mother, all vegetation is the same, every newborn creature is a mother's darling who remains one and the same in every spring and in every birth, just as she remains one and the same. But this only means that for her the newborn is a reborn, and every beloved the same, the one beloved. And when the goddess ritually unites herself with every fertility king, with father, son, and grandchild, or with each of her archpriests, these are always one and the same for her, because for her sexual union means only one thing, no matter who the bearer of the phallus may be, which is the only thing that does matter. Similarly, in her priestesses, the sacred prostitutes, she is a multiple womb, but in reality she always remains herself, the one Goddess.

The Great Mother is a virgin, too, in a sense other than that intended by the patriarchate, which later misunderstood her as the symbol of chastity. Precisely in virtue of her fruitfulness, she is a virgin, that is, unrelated and not dependent upon any man.[15] In Sanskrit, "independent woman" is a synonym for a harlot. Hence the woman who is unattached to a man is not only a universal feminine type but a sacral type in antiquity. The Amazon is unattached in her independence, but so is the woman who represents and is responsible for the fertility of the earth. She is the mother of all that has been born or will be born; but only in a brief access of passion, if at all, does she burn for the male, who is simply a means to an end, the bearer of the phallus. All phallus cults—and they are invariably solemnized by women—harp on the same thing: the anonymous power of the fertilizing agent, the phallus that stands by itself. The human element, the individual, is merely the bearer—the passing and interchangeable bearer—of that which does not pass away and cannot be interchanged because it is ever the self-same phallus.

Accordingly, the fertility goddess is both mother and virgin, the hetaera who belongs to no man but is ready to give herself to any man. She is there for anybody who, like herself, stands in the service of fertility. By turning to her womb, he serves her,

[15] Harding, *Woman's Mysteries.*

the sacred representative of the great fertility principle. The "bridal veil" must be understood in this sense, as the symbol of *kedesha,* the harlot. She is "unknown," i.e., anonymous. To be "unveiled" means to be naked, but this is only another form of anonymity. Always the goddess, the transpersonal, is the real and operative factor.

The personal incarnation of this goddess, i.e., the particular woman, is of no consequence. For the man she is a *kedesha,* a holy one (*kadosh* = holy), the goddess who stirs up the deeper layers of his being in sexuality. Yoni and lingam, female and male, are two principles which come together beyond the person, in holiness, where the personal is shed away and remains insignificant.

The youths, who personify the spring, belong to the Great Mother. They are her bondslaves, her property, because they are the sons she has born. Consequently the chosen ministers and priests of the Mother Goddess are eunuchs. They have sacrificed the thing that is for her the most important—the phallus. Hence the phenomeon of castration associated with this stage appears here for the first time in its proper sense, because specifically related to the genital organ. The castration threat makes its appearance with the Great Mother and is deadly. For her, loving, dying, and being emasculated are the same thing. Only the priests, at least in later times, escape being put to death because, by castrating themselves, they have voluntarily submitted to a symbolical death for her sake (*illus. 15*).[16]

[16] In order to avoid misunderstandings let it be emphasized once and for all that wherever in our discussion we speak of castration we mean a symbolic castration, and never a personalistic castration complex acquired in childhood and having concretistic reference to the male genitalia.

The stage of the son-lover and of his relation to the Great Mother has a phallic accent; that is, the activity of the adolescent is symbolized by the phallus and his world is ruled by fertility ritual. Hence the dangers that threaten his destruction are associated with the symbolism of a castration that was often carried out in the actual ritual. But castration symbolism must be understood in a general sense, even when its terminology is derived from the phallic adolescent phase. It is found as much in the prephallic stages as in the later, postphallic, masculine and heroic stages. Again, the blinding that occurs at a later phase is a symbolic castration. Negative castration symbolism is typical of the hostility of the unconscious to the ego and consciousness, but is closely associated with the positive

An essential characteristic of this adolescent ego stage is that the female, under the aspect of the Great Mother, is experienced as having a negative fascination. Two features are especially common and well marked: the first is the bloody and savage nature of the great Mother Goddess, the second is her power as a sorceress and a witch.

Worshiped from Egypt to India, from Greece and Asia Minor to darkest Africa, the Great Mother was always regarded as a goddess of the chase and of war; her rites were bloody, her festivals orgiastic. All these features are essentially interconnected. This "blood layer" deep down in the great Earth Mother only makes it more understandable why the youths she loves should fear castration.

The womb of the earth clamors for fertilization, and blood sacrifices and corpses are the food she likes best. This is the terrible aspect, the deadly side of the earth's character. In the earliest fertility cults, the gory fragments of the sacrificial victim were handed round as precious gifts and offered up to the earth, in order to make her fruitful. These human sacrifices for fertility occur all the world over quite independently of one another, in the rites of America and in the Eastern Mediterranean, in Asia and in northern Europe. Everywhere blood plays a leading part in fertility ritual and human sacrifice. The great terrestrial law that there can be no life without death was early understood, and still earlier represented in ritual, to mean that a strengthening of life can only be bought at the cost of sacrificial death. But the word "bought" is really a late and spurious rationalization. Slaughter and sacrifice, dismemberment and offerings of blood, are magical guarantees of earthly fertility. We misunderstand these rites if we call them cruel. For the early cultures, and even for the victims themselves, this sequence of events was necessary and self-evident.

---

symbol of sacrifice, which stands for an active offering up of the ego to the unconscious. Both symbols—castration and sacrifice—are united in the archetype of surrender, which can be active and passive, positive and negative, and rules the ego's relation to the self in the various stages of development.

The basic phenomenon behind woman's connection with blood and fertility is in all likelihood the cessation of the menstrual flow during pregnancy, by which means, in the archaic view, the embryo was built up.[17] This intuitively sensed connection underlies the relationship between blood and fertility. Blood means fruitfulness and life, just as the shedding of blood means loss of life and death. Consequently the shedding of blood was originally a sacred act, whether it was the blood of a wild beast, a domestic animal, or a man. The earth must drink blood if she is to be fertile, and therefore libations of blood are offered up to increase her power. But the mistress of the blood zone is woman. She has the blood magic that makes life grow. Hence the same goddess is very often the mistress of fertility, of war (*illus. 16*), and of hunting.

The ambivalent character of the great Mother Goddess, if we disregard India, is seen most clearly in Egypt, where the great goddesses—be they called Neith or Hathor, Bast or Mut—are not only nourishing goddesses who give and sustain life, but goddesses of savagery, blood-lust, and destruction.

Neith, the heavenly cow and first birth-giver, "the mother who bore the sun, who gave birth before birth was," and of whom Erman finds it remarkable that "in ancient times she was especially honored by women," [18] was a goddess of war and led the charge in battle. This same Neith, invoked to adjudicate in the dispute about Horus, says threateningly, "Or I shall wax wroth and the heavens shall fall upon the earth." [19]

Similarly Hathor, the cow and giver of milk, is the mother. She, too, is the mother of the sun, is especially honored by women, and is the goddess of love and destiny. Dancing, singing, the clashing sistrum, the rattling of necklaces and the beating of hand drums, pertain to her festivities and bear witness to her provocative, orgiastic nature. She is a war goddess, or rather the bloodthirsty, frenzied despoiler of mankind. "As thou truly

---

[17] This view prevailed throughout the ancient world and is even found in late stages of culture, e.g., in Jewish legend and Hindu literature.

[18] Erman, *Die Religion der Ägypter*, p. 33.

[19] Ibid., p. 77.

livest, I have prevailed over men, and it was comforting to my heart," [20] she says, when sent forth to bring judgment upon men. So drunken with blood was she that the gods, in order to save the human race from total destruction, had to prepare quantities of red beer which she mistook for blood. "Then she drank of it, and it tasted good, and she returned home drunken and knew not men."

She is identified with the friendly cat-goddess Bast, who in her terrible form is the lion-goddess Sekhmet. So it is not at all remarkable, as Kees thinks,[21] that the worship of the lion should have prevailed throughout Upper Egypt. The lion is the most beautiful and the most obvious symbol for the lacerating character of the great female deity.

Sekhmet, too, is a goddess of battles, belching fire. As the friendly Bast, her rites are celebrated with dancing, music, and the sistrum, but in her paw she holds a lion's head "as if to show that this terrible head suited her equally well." [22]

In this connection we might mention the legend of the lion-goddess Tefnut, who has to be brought back to Egypt from the desert. Thoth, the god of wisdom, undertakes this task. When he upbraids her and says how desolate Egypt is at having been abandoned by her in her rage, she begins to weep "like a cloud-burst," but suddenly her weeping turns to wrath and she changes into a lion. "Her mane smoked with fire, her back had the color of blood, her countenance glowed like the sun, her eyes shone with fire." [23]

Again, Ta-urt, a huge pregnant monster rearing up on its hind legs, whose cult dates from prehistoric times,[24] is depicted as a hippopotamus with a crocodile's back, lion's feet, and human hands (*illus. 17*). She is the protectress of women in childbirth, and of nursing mothers, though her aspect as the Terrible Mother is plain enough. Later, as Hesamut, she was correlated

[20] Roeder, *Urkunden zur Religion des alten Aegypten*, p. 143.
[21] Kees, *Götterglaube*, p. 7.
[22] Erman, op. cit., p. 34.
[23] Ibid., p. 67.
[24] Kees, *Götterglaube*, p. 13.

56

with the constellation of the Bear, whose maternal characteristics are well known.

Blood also plays a decisive part in feminine taboos, which from earliest times until far into the patriarchal cultures and religions have caused men to turn away from all feminine matters as though from something numinous. The blood of menstruation, defloration, and birth proves to men that women have a natural connection with this sphere. But in the background there is a dim knowledge of the blood affinity of the Great Mother who, as chthonic mistress of life and death, demands blood and appears to be dependent upon the shedding of blood.

We know from prehistoric times the role played by the divine kings, who had either to kill themselves or be killed when their powers failed and they could no longer personally guarantee fertility. This whole corpus of rites, whose significance and wide distribution have been described by Frazer, is dedicated to the Great Mother and serves her fertility. If, in Africa today, the sacred king is rainmaker, rain, and vegetation in one,[25] he was so from the very beginning as the son-lover of the Great Mother. Frazer says:

There is some reason to think that in early times Adonis was sometimes personated by a living man who died a violent death in the character of the god.[26]

That is an understatement, for everything points to the fact that in ancient times a human victim, whether god, king, or priest, was *always* offered up to ensure the fertility of the earth.

Originally the victim was the male, the fertilizing agent, since fertilization is only possible through libations of blood in which life is stored. The female earth needs the fertilizing blood-seed of the male.

Here, as nowhere else, we can see the meaning of the female deity. The emotional, passionate nature of the female in wild abandon is a terrible thing for man and his consciousness. The dangerous side of woman's lasciviousness, although suppressed,

[25] Seligman, *Egypt and Negro Africa*, p. 33.
[26] *The Golden Bough* (abridged edn., 1951), p. 394.

misunderstood, and minimized in patriarchal times, was still a living experience in earlier ages. Deep down in the evolutionary stratum of adolescence, the fear of it still dwells in every man and works like a poison wherever a false conscious attitude represses this layer of reality into the unconscious.

Mythology, however, tells us that woman's wildness and blood lust are subordinated to a higher natural law, that of fertility. The orgiastic element does not occur only in the sex festivals, which are fertility festivals. Women also celebrated orgiastic rites amongst themselves. These rites, often known to us only from the later mysteries, mostly revolved round the orgiastic dismemberment of a sacred animal or animal deity, whose bloody portions were devoured and whose death served the fertility of woman and consequently of the earth.

Death and dismemberment or castration are the fate of the phallus-bearing, youthful god. Both are clearly visible in myth and ritual, and both are associated with bloody orgies in the cult of the Great Mother. Dismemberment of the corpse of the Seasonal King and the burial of his parts are an age-old piece of fertility magic. But only when we view the *disjecta membra* as a unity can we grasp the original meaning. The preservation of the phallus and its embalming as a guarantor of fertility are the other side of the ritual. They supplement the castration, and together with it form a symbolic whole.

Behind the archetype of the terrible Earth Mother looms the experience of death, when the earth takes back her progeny as the dead, divides and dissolves them in order to make herself fruitful. This experience has been preserved in the rites of the Terrible Mother, who, in her earth projection, becomes the flesh eater and finally the sarcophagus—the last vestige of man's age-old and long-practiced fertility cults.

Castration, death, and dismemberment on this level are all equivalent. They are correlated with the decay of vegetation, with harvesting, and the felling of trees. Castration and tree-felling, closely associated in myth, are symbolically identical. Both are found in the Attis myth of the Phrygian Cybele, in the

58

myth of the Syrian Astarte and the Ephesian Artemis, and in the Bata fairy tale of the Osiris cycle. The meaning of certain parallel features, e.g., the fact that Attis emasculates himself under a pine, changes into a pine, is hanged on a pine, and is felled as a pine, cannot be elucidated here.

The sacerdotal sacrifice of hair is likewise a symbol of emasculation, just as, conversely, a rich growth of hair is taken to be a sign of enhanced virility. The sacrifice of men's hair is an ancient mark of priesthood (*illus. 15*), from the baldness of Egyptian hierophants to the tonsure of Catholic priests and Buddhist monks. Notwithstanding the great disparities of religious views, hairlessness is always associated with sexual abstinence and celibacy, i.e., with symbolic self-castration. The shaving of the head played this part officially in the cult of the Great Mother, by no means only as a token of mourning for Adonis, so that here again, felling the tree, harvesting the grain, the decay of vegetation, cutting the hair, and castration are all identical. The equivalent in woman is the sacrifice of her chastity. By surrendering himself, the devotee becomes the property of the Great Mother and is finally transformed into her. The priests of Gades (modern Cadiz), like the priests of Isis, were shaved, and, in some way not known to us, barbers were among the attendants of Astarte.[27]

In the use of women's clothing, known to have been worn by the Galli, the castrated priests of the Great Mother in Syria, Crete, Ephesus, etc., and preserved in the dress of the Catholic priests today, the sacrifice is carried to the point of identification (*illus. 15*). Not only is the male sacrificed to the Great Mother, but he becomes her representative, a female wearing her dress. Whether he sacrifices his masculinity in castration or in male prostitution is only a variant. The eunuchs are, as priests, also sacred prostitutes, for the *kedeshim*, like the *kedeshoth* or female sacred prostitutes, are representatives of the goddess whose orgiastic sexual character excels her fertility character. Since these castrated priests play a leading role in the cults of

[27] Pietschmann, *Geschichte der Phönizier.*

59

the Bronze Age in Syria, Asia Minor, and even in Mesopotamia, we find the same presuppositions at work in all the territories of the Great Mother.[28]

Death, castration, and dismemberment are the dangers that threaten the youthful lover, but they do not adequately characterize his relationship to the Great Mother. Were she terrible only, and a death-goddess, her resplendent image would lack something that makes her perhaps even more terrible, and yet at the same time infinitely desirable. For she is also the goddess who drives mad and fascinates, the seducer and bringer of delight, the sovereign enchantress. The fascination of sex and the drunken orgy culminating in unconsciousness and death are inextricably combined in her.

Whereas uroboric incest meant dissolution and extinction, because it had a total and not a genital character, incest on the adolescent level is genital and restricted absolutely to the genitalia. The Great Mother has become all womb, the young lover all phallus, and the whole procedure remains entirely on the sexual level.

Hence the phallus and the phallic cult go together with the sexuality of the adolescent stage, and the deadly aspect of this stage likewise appears as the slaying of the phallus, i.e., as castration. The orgiastic character of the Adonis, Attis, and Tammuz cults, not to speak of the Dionysian, is all part of this sexuality. The young lover experiences an orgy of sex and in the orgasm the ego dissolves, is transcended in death. On this level, orgasm and death go together, just as do orgasm and castration.

For the youthful god, with his feebly developed ego, the positive and negative aspects of sexuality are dangerously close to one another. When, intoxicated, he surrenders his ego and returns to the womb of the Great Mother, regressing to the pre-ego state, he is not consummating the beatific uroboric incest of the earliest stage, but the death ecstasy of sexual incest belonging to a later stage, whose motto is: *post coitum omne animal triste*. Sexuality here means losing the ego and being over-

[28] Albright, *From the Stone Age to Christianity*.

60

powered by the female, which is a typical, or rather archetypal, experience in puberty. Because sex is experienced as the all-powerful transpersonal phallus and womb, the ego perishes and succumbs to the supreme fascination of the nonego. The Mother is still too great, the seat of the unconscious still too near, for the ego to resist the surge of the blood.[29]

The Terrible Mother is an enchantress who confuses the senses and drives men out of their minds. No adolescent can withstand her; he is offered up to her as a phallus. Either this is taken by force or else, overpowered by the Great Mother, the frenzied youths mutilate themselves and offer up the phallus to her as a sacrifice.

Madness is a dismemberment of the individual, just as the dismemberment of the body in fertility magic symbolizes dissolution of the personality.

Since the dissolution of personality and individual consciousness pertains to the sphere of the Mother Goddess, insanity is an ever-recurrent symptom of possession by her or by her representatives. For—and in this lies her magical and fearful power—the youth burns with desire even when threatened with death, even when the consummation of his desire is attended by castration. The Great Mother is therefore the sorceress who transforms men into animals—Circe, mistress of wild beasts, who sacrifices the male and rends him. Indeed, the male serves her as an animal and no more, for she rules the animal world of the instincts which ministers to her and to her fertility. This explains the theriomorphic male consorts of the Great Mother, her priests and victims. And that is why, for example, the male votaries of the Great Goddess who prostituted themselves in her name were called *kelabim*,[30] "dogs," and wore women's clothing.

[29] It is a characteristic fact that the rites of initiation in puberty always begin at this point: masculine solidarity helps to depotentiate the Great Mother. The orgiastic element has a different meaning in feminine psychology at this stage, but we cannot enter into this question here.

[30] Pietschmann, op. cit., p. 233. Although other investigators (A. Jeremias, *Das Alte Testament im Lichte des Alten Orients;* F. Jeremias, "Semitische Völker in Vorderasien," in Chantepie de la Saussaye, *Lehrbuch der Religionsgeschichte*)

For the Great Mother, the divine youth means happiness, glory, and fertility, but she remains eternally unfaithful to him and brings him nothing but misfortune. Well might Gilgamesh reply to the seductive wiles of Ishtar (*illus. 16*), as she "raised an eye to the beauty of Gilgamesh":

> [What am I to give] thee, that I may take thee in marriage?
> [Should I give oil] for the body, and clothing?
> [Should I give] bread and victuals?
> [. . .] food fit for divinity,
> [. . .] drink fit for royalty.
> [. . . .]
> [. . . if I] take thee in marriage?
> [Thou art but a brazier which goes out] in the cold;
> A back door [which does not] keep out blast and windstorm;
> A palace which crushes the valiant [. . .];
> A turban whose cover [. . .];
> Pitch which [soils] its bearers;
> A waterskin which [soaks through] its bearer;
> Limestone which [springs] the stone rampart;
> Jasper [which . . .] enemy land;
> A shoe which [pinches the foot] of its owner!
> Which lover didst thou love forever?
> Which of thy shepherds pleased [thee for all time]?
> Come, and I will na[me for thee] thy lovers:
>
> Of . . . [. . .] . . .
> For Tammuz, the lover of thy youth,
> Thou hast ordained wailing year after year.
> Having loved the dappled shepherd bird,
> Thou smotest him, breaking his wing.
> In the groves he sits, crying "My wing!"
> Then thou lovedst a lion, perfect in strength;
> Seven pits and seven thou didst dig for him.
> Then a stallion thou lovedst, famed in battle;
> The whip, the spur, and the lash thou ordainedst for him.
> Thou decreedst for him to gallop seven leagues,
> Thou decreedst for him the muddied to drink;
> For his mother, Silili, thou ordainedst wailing!

---

do not connect this word with *kelev*, "dog," but conjecture "priest," the reference to dog sacrifices in Isaiah 66:3 makes the canine form of the priests not improbable.

Then thou lovedst the keeper of the herd,
Who ash cakes ever did heap up for thee;
Yet thou smotest him, turning him into a wolf,
So that his own herd boys drive him off,
And his dogs bite his thighs.
Then thou lovedst Ishullanu, thy father's gardener,
Who baskets of dates ever did bring to thee,
And daily did brighten thy table.
Thine eyes raised at him, thou didst go to him:
"O my Ishullanu, let us taste of thy vigor!
Put forth thy 'hand' and touch our 'modesty'!"
Ishullanu said to thee:
"What dost thou want with me?
Has my mother not baked, have I not eaten,
That I should taste the food of offense and curses?
Does reed-work afford cover against the cold?"
As thou heardst this his talk,
Thou smotest him and turn[edst] him into a spider.
Thou placedst him in the midst of . . [.];
He cannot go up . . . nor can he come down . . .
If thou shouldst love me, thou wouldst [treat me] like them.[31]

The stronger the masculine ego consciousness becomes, the more it is aware of the emasculating, bewitching, deadly, and stupefying nature of the Great Goddess.

Domains of the Terrible Mother

In order to illustrate the main features of the archetype of the Great and Terrible Mother and her son-lover, we shall take as an example the great myth of Osiris and Isis (*illus. 18*). The patriarchal version of this myth shows clear traces of the transition from matriarchate to patriarchate, and despite the editorial rearrangement and alteration of the material, it is still possible for us to hear the original accents. The myth has also been preserved as the oldest fairy tale in the world's literature, namely, as the story of Bata. In spite of the secondary personalizations

[31] "The Epic of Gilgamesh," trans. by E. A. Speiser, in *Ancient Near Eastern Texts*, ed. by Pritchard, p. 84.

which are inevitable in the passage from myth to fairy tale, this story likewise preserves in clear and interpretable form the relationships and symbols which disclose the original meaning.

In the myth, Isis, Nephthys, Set, and Osiris form a quaternity of two brothers and two sisters. Even in the womb, Isis and Osiris cleave together, and in its final phase the myth represents Isis as the positive symbol of conjugal and motherly love. But, besides her characteristics as a sister-wife, Isis also preserves something magical and maternal in her relations with Osiris. For, when the latter is done to death and dismembered by his enemy and brother, Set, it is his sister-wife, Isis, who brings about his rebirth, thus proving herself to be, at the same time, the mother of her brother-husband. In later developments of the myth, she largely discards the character of the Great Mother and assumes that of the wife. Nevertheless Isis, who seeks, mourns, finds, recognizes, and brings her dead husband to birth again, is still the great goddess adored by youths, whose rites are everywhere typified by this sequence of death, mourning, search, recovery, and rebirth.

It is an essential function of the "good" Isis to give up her matriarchal dominance, which was such an obvious feature in the original matriarchate of Egyptian Queens. Typical of this surrender, and of the transition to the patriarchal system, is Isis' struggle to get the legitimacy of her son Horus recognized by the gods. Whereas in the "uterine system," as Moret calls it,[32] a son is always the son of his mother, Isis fights for the recognition of the paternity of Osiris for Horus, who is to take over from him the paternal inheritance of the patriarchate. On this inheritance was based the lineage of the Egyptian Pharaohs, each of whom styled himself "Son of Horus." Osiris is "he who establishes justice over the two lands; he leaves the son in his father's place." [33]

One remarkable, and evidently somewhat incongruous, feature has been preserved which belies the good character of Isis

[32] Moret, *The Nile and Egyptian Civilization*, p. 96.
[33] Ibid., p. 98.

64

12. Diana of Ephesus

Rome, 2nd century A.D.

13. Mater Matuta

Etruria, 5th century B.C.

14. Aphrodite and Anchises (?)

Bronze relief from Paramythia, Greece, 4th century B.C.

15. Sacrificing priest of Magna Mater

Relief, Rome, 1st century B.C.

16. Ishtar as a goddess of war

Seal relief of King Anu-Banini, Hazar-Geri, Babylonia, 2500–2000 B.C.

17. The hippopotamus goddess Ta-urt, holding before her
the Sa symbol of protection

Egypt, Ptolemaic period, 332–30 B.C.

18. The King before Isis

Egypt, Temple of Seti I, Abydos, 14th–13th century B.C.

19. Rangda, female demon

Mask from Bali

as wife and mother. Horus resumes his father's struggle against the murderer Set, and in this he is encouraged by Isis. But when Set is struck by the spear of Isis, he cries out to her for pity, saying:

"Would you take up arms against his [Horus's] mother's brother?" Her heart felt compassion and she cried to the spear: "Leave him, leave him! See, he is my brother by the same mother." And the spear left him. Then the majesty of Horus was incensed against his mother Isis, like an Upper Egyptian panther. And she fled before him on this day, when the battle was appointed against the troublemaker Set. And Horus cut off the head of Isis. But Thoth by his magic changed it and set it upon her again, who was now called the "First of the Cows." [34]

It is characteristic that Set, in accusing his sister Isis, should say that he is after all her brother by the same mother and that therefore she should not love the "strange man" more than she loves him.[35] This strange man is either Osiris, who is here regarded not as the brother of Isis but as her husband, or else, as Erman thinks, he is her own son Horus. That is to say, Set's point of view is purely matriarchal, deriving from the age of exogamy, when the son went away and the maternal uncle was and remained the head of the family. The patriarchal as opposed to the matriarchal point of view is classically formulated by one of the gods in the dispute about the legitimacy of Horus: "Should the office be given to the mother's brother, while yet there is a son of her body?" Contrast with this Set's plea: "Will you give the office to my little brother, so long as I, his big brother, am there?" [36]

So Isis has evidently regressed, slipped back into the brother-sister relationship, which, as we know from Bachofen, had priority over the husband-wife relationship. Isis defends her brother Set because he is brother to her by her own mother, even though he has murdered her husband Osiris and cut him to pieces. Horus, as his father's avenger, makes himself guilty of matricide. The problem of the *Oresteia*, which we shall be dealing with

[34] Kees, *Aegypten*, p. 35.
[35] Erman, *Religion*, p. 80.
[36] Ibid., p. 77.

later as an example of the son's conflicting loyalties to father and mother, crops up here in connection with Isis, whose essential function lies in forming a bridge from the matriarchal to the patriarchal order of society.

A further trace of the originally "terrible" character of Isis can be seen in the strange fact that when Isis intervenes in the battle between Horus and Set, her spear first strikes her son Horus; this is a mistake which she instantly repairs. The terrible side of Isis is apparent in several other subsidiary traits, and although these do not belong to the authentic Isis-Osiris drama, they are nevertheless extremely significant. During her search for Osiris, she becomes nurse to "Queen Astarte" in Byblos. There she endeavors to make the Queen's child immortal by laying it in the fire, an attempt which fails. The King's younger son dies at the sight of her violent sobbing as she throws herself upon the coffin of Osiris, and the elder son she takes back with her to Egypt. When the boy catches her in the act of kissing, amid her tears, the face of the dead Osiris, she wrathfully turns upon him such a terrible look that he dies of fright on the spot.[37] This clear proof of her witchcraft is tucked away, as a subsidiary detail, in the clandestine destruction of the children of Astarte, Queen of Byblos—with whom, however, Isis is always identified. The good Egyptian Isis, the "exemplary" mother of Horus, stands side by side with the Terrible Mother, who in Byblos slays her children, the children of Astarte.

Astarte and one of her doubles, Anath, were both worshiped as Isis in the sanctuary at Phylae, which proves the affinity of the two goddesses.[38] The figure of Astarte-Anath corresponds to the matriarchal Isis, who is associated with her brother Set. And in the litigation about Horus, Anath is handed over to Set by way of "indemnity." [39] When the patriarchal development of Isis into a good wife and mother is complete, her terrible matriarchal aspect is delegated to Horus' maternal uncle Set.

[37] Ibid., p. 85.
[38] Ibid., p. 150.
[39] Ibid., p. 177.

Another striking fact is that Horus begets his four sons by his mother Isis. This cnly repeats what happens everywhere in the territory of the Great Mother. For all generations of men, she remains the One.

The terrible side of Isis is also revealed in the circumstance that the Osiris who is reborn with her help remains castrated. His member was never discovered; it was swallowed by a fish. Dismemberment and castration are no longer performed by Isis, but are taken over by Set. The result, however, is the same.

It is further to be noted that Isis conceives Horus, the Harpocrates of the Greeks, by the dead Osiris. That this son-god should be begotten by Osiris after his death is a somewhat baffling feature. The symbolism recurs in the story of Bata, whose wife is made pregnant by a splinter of the felled Bata tree. It becomes more intelligible if we realize that the fecundation of the Great Mother presupposes the death of the male, and that the Earth Mother can only be made fruitful by death, killing, castration, and sacrifice.

The Horus-child begotten by the dead Osiris is represented, on the one hand, as weak in the legs, and, on the other hand, ithyphallically. He holds his finger to his mouth, which is supposed to indicate sucking. Generally he is seated in the center of a flower, and his distinguishing mark is a long curling lock of hair, besides which he carries the cornucopia and the urn. He symbolizes the very young sun and his significance is undoubtedly phallic. The ithyphallus, the finger, and the lock of hair are evidence of this. At the same time, he has feminine attributes and is what we might call a true mother's darling. Even when, curiously enough, he is disguised as an old man, he carries a basket. This Harpocrates stands for the infantile stage of existence in the uroboros; he is the suckling, caught in the maternal coil. His father is a wind spirit, the dead Osiris, and thus he belongs to the matriarchal stage of the uroboros, where there is no personal father, but only the great Isis.

The dismemberment of Osiris and the theft of his phallus, later attributed to Set, are the most ancient portions of the fertility ritual. Isis compensates for this by replacing the missing member with a wooden phallus and is thereupon impregnated by the dead Osiris. We can reconstruct the ritual thus: While the torn limbs of Osiris, scattered over the fields, guarantee the year's fertility, the phallus is missing. For Osiris is robbed of his phallus, which is embalmed and preserved until the next resurrection feast of fertility. But it was from this embalmed phallus that Isis conceives the child Horus. Hence, for this Horus, as well as for Horus the sun-god, it is more significant that Isis was his mother than that Osiris was his father.

The fact that the Queen of Byblos was identified with the cow-headed Hathor, and that Isis got her cow's head by betraying Horus and Osiris, completes the picture. The Book of the Dead contains reminders of the terrible Isis, when it speaks of the "slaughtering knife with which Isis cut off a piece of flesh from Horus," [40] and of the "chopper of Isis." [41] Again, when we are told that Horus destroyed "the water-flood of his mother," [42] this only confirms her devouring character.

We find the same thing in Hathor. She appears as a hippopotamus and as a cow. The hippopotamus was originally sacred to Set, but the Osiris myth relates how it passed over to the Osiris-Horus faction. Here, too, it is a question of overcoming the Great and Terrible Mother in the guise of the pregnant hippopotamus, and of her transformation into the good mother, the cow.

Only when Horus, as the son of his father, beheads the terrible Isis, Set's sister, is her dreadful aspect destroyed and transformed. Thoth, the god of wisdom, then endows her with the cow's head, symbol of the good mother, and she becomes Hathor. As such she is the good mother and dutiful wife of the patriarchal age. Her power is delegated to her son Horus, heir of Osiris, and through him to the patriarchal Pharaohs of Egypt; her terrible side is repressed into the unconscious.

[40] Budge, The Book of the Dead, Ch. 153a.
[41] Ibid., Ch. 153b.
[42] Ibid., Ch. 138.

THE CREATION MYTH: *The Great Mother*

Evidence for this repression can be found in another of Egypt's mythological figures. Beside the scales in which, at the Judgment of the Dead, the hearts are weighed, there sits the monster Amam or Am-mit, "devourer of the dead." Those of the dead who have not passed the test are eaten by this "female monster" [43] and are extinguished for good. This monster has a very remarkable shape: "Her forepart a crocodile, her hindpart a hippopotamus, and her middle a lion." [44]

Ta-urt,[45] too, is a combination of hippopotamus, crocodile, and lioness; only here the marks of the lion-goddess Sekhmet are more strongly emphasized. Thus the devourer of the dead is the Terrible Mother of death and the underworld, though not in her splendid original form. She is "repressed" and crouches beside the judgment scales like a horror. As Erman says,[46] she was "not a subject that popular fancy cared to pursue."

Further confirmation of this is provided by the Book of the Dead, where it says of Amam, here represented as the god of the dead,

He maketh it to come to pass that the cedar trees grow not, that the acacia trees bring not forth.[47]

The Terrible Mother could not be better described than in these words, if we remember that the cedar and the acacia are, symbolically, very intimately connected with Osiris, whose life and everlastingness they represent.

The terrible aspect of Isis is further borne out by the Story of the Two Brothers, whose connection with the Isis-Osiris myth is generally recognized and has been authenticated by the latest excavations in Byblos.[48]

We shall briefly enumerate the motifs which connect the Osiris myth with the story of Bata. The dead Osiris, whom Isis

[43] Budge, *British Museum, Guide to the First, Second, and Third Egyptian Rooms*, p. 70.
[44] Budge, *The Book of the Dead*, p. 33.
[45] Ibid., p. 135.
[46] Erman, *Religion*, p. 229.
[47] Budge, *The Book of the Dead*, p. 461.
[48] Virolleaud, "Ischtar, Isis, Astarte" and "Anat–Astarte."

seeks, was found at Byblos in Lebanon, and he was found more-over as a tree; that is, he was enclosed in a tree trunk. From there he was brought back to Egypt. The principal symbol of Osiris is the *"djed* pillar," a tree fetish, itself sufficiently remark-able in treeless Egypt; and in Byblos, too, a tree, wrapped in linen and anointed, was worshiped as the "wood of Isis." [49] The importation of trees from Lebanon was one of the essential con-ditions for Egyptian culture, and above all for the cult of the dead. We hear of Egyptian tributes to the Queen of Byblos as far back as 2800 B.C. Unquestionably, the close ties between the Egyptian and the Syrian centers of culture go back even further.

The phallic tree fetish, as a symbol of the youthful lover, is known to us from numerous myths. To an even greater extent than the harvesting of the grain, signifying the death of the son born of the Earth Mother, the felling of trees was a ritual act. The mighty strength of this son, in his tree form, made the sac-rifice even more significant and impressive. We have already discussed the slaying and hanging of son-lover-priests on trees, and noted that their castration must be equated with tree-felling.[50] The correctness of our view is now corroborated by the fact that the reverse process, the erection of the Osirian *djed* pillar in the coronation ceremonies at the Sed festival, sym-bolizes the renewal of Pharaoh's strength.

The Story of the Two Brothers has for its setting the Valley of Cedars near Byblos. The heroine, the wife of Bata's elder brother, tries to seduce Bata. This is the old Joseph motif. Bata resists her blandishments; the wife accuses him before her hus-band, who thereupon tries to kill his younger brother. Bata, as a sign of his innocence, castrates himself. The gods now create a wonderful wife as a companion for the castrated Bata. Bata warns her—and this is a remarkable feature—about the dangers of the sea, saying, "Go not forth, lest the sea fetch you away. I cannot protect you from the sea, for I am a woman like you." [51]

[49] Erman, op. cit., p. 85.
[50] Frazer, *The Golden Bough*, Ch. XXVIII.
[51] "The Tale of the Two Brothers," in Erman, *Literature*, p. 156 (modified).

This warning about the sea is exceedingly interesting. We recall that the phallus of Osiris was swallowed by a fish, of a kind which the Egyptians regarded as sacred and not to be eaten.[52] The excavations at ancient Ugarit (now Ras Shamra, Syria) have made Astarte, Mistress of the Sea, as familiar to us as the foam-born Aphrodite. Always the primal ocean—"the waters of the deep" of Jewish legend—is the territorial waters of the Terrible Mother. For instance, the child-eating Lilith, the adversary of man, who refuses to submit to Adam, withdraws to a place called the "gorge of the sea." [53] Bata's wife is in danger of being swept away by the waves, i.e., of being overpowered by her negative Astarte character. Astarte had originally the form of a fish, in her Atargatis aspect. As Derceto, too, Astarte resembled a fish or water sprite, and in many of the myths she plunges into her native element.

In the Bata tale, the very thing that Bata fears and that no

[52] The word for "abomination" was a fish sign. Kees (*Götterglaube*, p. 63) says: "In the Old Kingdom the pictogram for this epitome of ritual impurity was, in the majority of cases, the so-called bynni fish, or else a barbel-bynni, which in all likelihood corresponds to the lepidotus of the ancients, hence to the type of fish that was most commonly held to be sacred."

It is significant that in most of the early fish cults the central figures were female deities and that male deities were the exception. This is proved by pictures of fishes surmounted by the crown of Hathor.

The oxyrhynchus fish was both abhorred and venerated. It was supposed to have eaten the phallus of Osiris and to have sprung from his wounds. Strabo (XVII, 818) states that the lepidotus and the oxyrhynchus were both venerated among the Egyptians. As Kees says, the Roman records of a fish guild in Fayum prove the correctness of this statement.

The piscine form of Osiris in Abydos confirms that the basic meaning of the maternal element is the fish-containing sea. The animating and fertilizing power of water can also be represented phallically as a fish. The fish is both the phallus and the child. The maternal uroboros appears as the sea in the image of the Syrian goddess who is portrayed as the "house of fishes." And the Graeco-Boeotian Great Mother, the Artemis of Iolcus (*The Cambridge Ancient History,* Vol. of Plates I, p. 196a), who was mistress of wild beasts in the three realms, wears a dress clearly characterized as the watery realm, by having on it a large fish.

The good mother is the water that cushions the fetus; she is the life-giving fish-mother, whether this fish be the child, the fertilizing male, or a living individual. Equally, as the Terrible Mother, she is the destructive waters of the devouring deep, the flood, and the waters of the abyss.

[53] Bin Gorion, *Sagen der Juden,* Vol. I, "Die Urzeit," p. 325; Scholem, *Ein Kapital aus dem Sohar,* p. 77; Scheftelowitz, *Alt-palästinischer Bauernglaube.*

poor, womanish eunuch could ward off naturally happens. His wife becomes the wife of the Egyptian king, and she causes the cedar, which is identified with Bata, whose "heart reposed on its flower," to be hewn down. The dead Bata, however, is resuscitated by his brother and comes to Egypt as a bull. Once more he is slain, and from the drops of his blood grow sycamore trees, which are likewise felled at the behest of the wife. But this time, Bata enters his wife's mouth as a splinter of wood from the tree, and she is made pregnant. In this way, he is born again as his own son by the Terrible Mother, is adopted by the King of Ethiopia, and finally becomes King of Egypt. On his accession to the throne as the patriarch, he kills his wife, who was also his sister, and makes his brother the Crown Prince.

We cannot concern ourselves here with the motif of the two brothers or with the motif of self-propagation, nor yet with the extent to which this fairy tale belongs to the later stage of the fight with the dragon and conflict with the male principle. We would only point out its connection with the Osiris myth and with the figure of the Terrible Mother who lurks behind Isis, the good wife and mother.

Bata is the son-lover of the Great Mother, as we would expect from the cultural sphere to which Byblos belongs. The Joseph motif, the tree-felling, the self-castration, the animal form of the victim, who is sacrificed as a bull, the blood-sacrifice as the fertility principle that causes the trees to grow, only to be hewn down again—all this is familiar. Everywhere the female is "terrible"; she is the seducer, the instrument of castration, cause of the two tree-fellings and of the death of the bull. But, despite everything, she is not terrible only; she is also the fruitful mother goddess, who is impregnated by the splinter of wood in order to bring forth the seduced, slain, and sacrificed Bata as her son.

Osiris, like Bata, has the form of a tree and a bull. The felled tree is his emblem, and not only was the cedar in fact imported into Egypt from Byblos, but the myth expressly relates that Osiris was found by Isis in Byblos in the form of a tree and was brought to Egypt from there. The whole myth clearly associates Osiris as a vegetation deity with the figures of Adonis, Attis, and Tammuz. Even his cult is that of the dying and resurgent god.[54]

But the power of the maternal uroboros is, as we have seen, already on the wane in Isis. The figure of the terrible Astarte, goddess of Byblos, clearly portrayed in the Bata fairy tale, is succeeded by Isis, the good mother; but by her side there appears the negative figure of Set, the masculine principle and twin brother, who takes over the role of the killer. Whereas in the Attis legend the negative-masculine side of the androgynous, uroboric Mother Goddess only appears as the boar who kills Attis, in the Osiris myth this figure is an independent entity and proves to be inimical not only to Osiris but, in the end, to Isis as well.

The story of Bata represents the terrible nature of the Great Mother as the nature of the female in general. But with the passing of the matriarchal reign of Egyptian Queens and the rise of the patriarchal Horus, the sun-god, under the Pharaohs, Isis gradually became merged with the archetype of the Good Mother, who presided over the patriarchal family (*illus. 18*). Her magical nature, as regeneratrix of her own brother and husband, was thrust into the background.

Important corroboration of all this is furnished by the recently discovered Canaanite myths, which were brought to light during the excavations at Ras Shamra. We shall mention only such features as pertain to the symbolism of the uroboros and the Great Mother.

Albright[55] has ascertained that the Canaanite religion, in comparison with the religions of its neighbors, remained relatively primitive and aboriginal. As an example, he cites the fact that the relations of the divinities to one another, and even their sex, varied; and he further mentions the tendency of Canaanite mythology to bring opposites together, so that, for instance, the god of death and destruction is also the god of life and healing,

---

[54] See infra, pp. 225 f., for a different interpretation.
[55] *Archaeology and the Religion of Israel*, p. 71.

just as the goddess Anath is the destroyer and, at the same time, the goddess of life and propagation. The uroboric coincidence of opposites is expressed in this juxtaposition of positive and negative features, of masculine and feminine attributes.

The three goddesses Asherah, Anath, and Ashtaroth are simply three different, but indistinct, manifestations of the archetypal Great Mother. Asherah is the enemy of the hero Baal and mother of the monsters of the desert who cause his death, and at the same time she is the enemy of Anath, Baal's sister-goddess. But here too, as with Isis, mother-beloved and sister, destroyer and helper, are inseparable aspects. The archetype has not yet split up into the firm outlines of distinct goddesses.

Like Isis, Anath resuscitates her dead brother-husband and vanquishes the evil brother Mot-Set. In Ashtaroth, whose name Albright translates as "sheep-breeder," we can recognize the primordial figure of Rahel, the mother sheep. But Ashtaroth and Anath are at the same time virgins and mothers of the peoples, "the great goddesses who conceive, but do not bear, i.e., the goddesses who are perennially fruitful without ever losing their virginity; they are therefore both mother goddesses and divine courtesans." Besides that, all three of them are sinister goddesses of sex and war, whose bloodthirstiness rivals even that of Hathor and the Hindu Kali. The later picture of the naked goddess galloping on a horse and brandishing a lance is vividly sketched in the Baal epic. After she had slaughtered the race of men, "the blood was so deep that she waded in it up to her knees, nay, up to her neck. Under her feet were human heads; above her, human hands flew like locusts; in her sensuous delight she decorated herself with suspended heads and attached hands to her girdle." Her joy at the butchery is described in ever more sadistic language: "Her liver swelled with laughter, her heart was full of joy, the liver of Anath was full of exultation." [56]

As with all goddesses of this type, blood is dew and rain for the earth, which must drink blood in order to be fruitful. In Ashtaroth, we can also recognize the primordial image of the

[56] Ibid., p. 77.

Mistress of the Sea; she is the earlier and more savage form of the sea goddess Aphrodite, and in one Egyptian fairy tale,[57] the gods, threatened by the sea, bring the Syrian Astarte to Egypt so that she may be pacified by veneration.

Not only are birth and death linked together in Canaanite mythology, but the original hermaphroditic form of the uroboros reappears in the relation between the masculine morning star, Astar or Attar, and the feminine evening star, the Ishtar of Mesopotamia.[58] Androgyny in a deity is a primitive characteristic, and so, too, is the combination of virginity and fertility in goddesses, and of fertility and castration in gods. The masculine traits of the female still coexist side by side with the feminine traits of the male. If the goddess holds the lily, the feminine symbol, in one hand and the snake, the masculine symbol, in the other, this is entirely in keeping with the fact that the eunuchs who serve her are male prostitutes, dancers, and priests.[59] In Canaan, therefore, we find all the features of the canon which is determined by the uroboric figure of the Great Mother and by the incomplete differentiation of the masculine principle.

Creto-Mycenaean culture is likewise a typical domain of the Great Mother; the same groups of symbolic and ritual characteristics recur as are to be met with in Egypt and in Canaan, in Phoenicia, Babylonia, Assyria, and in the Near Eastern cultures generally, among the Hittites as well as among the Indians. Aegean culture forms a link between Egypt and Libya on the one side, and Greece and Asia Minor on the other. For us it is of no consequence how the currents of culture flowed historically, because the purity of the archetypal figure is of far greater importance to our theme than the question of priority.

We have to rely chiefly on pictorial representations of the Creto-Mycenaean religion, for the texts are as yet undeciphered; but here again the comparative interpretation of the symbols

[57] Erman, *Literature,* pp. 169 f.
[58] Albright, *Stone Age.*
[59] Ibid., p. 178.

proves its value and leads us to the archetype of the Great Mother. Creto-Aegean culture is dominated by the figure of the Great Mother as a nature goddess; originally she was worshiped in caves, and her priests were women. She was mistress of the mountains and of wild animals. Snakes and underworld creatures were sacred to her, but birds, too, symbolized her presence. The dove especially was her attribute, and she still remained a dove-goddess, both as Aphrodite and as Mary (dove of the Holy Ghost). Her cult evidently dates back to the Stone Age, as is indicated by the fur garments that were worn in the ritual. Her Great Mother character is revealed in the dress of the goddess and of her priestesses, and in the women's costume generally, which left the breasts exposed; it is also evident in the numerous representations of animal mothers that have survived to our own day. The mythological meaning of these faïence paintings of cows with calves, and she-goats with kids,[60] is obviously connected with the myths that have been handed down to us from Greece via Crete. We have already mentioned that the youthful Zeus was the Cretan Zeus child who was suckled by a goat, cow, bitch, or sow, these being the representatives of Gaea, the Earth Mother, in whose charge he was placed.[61]

Central to the great Cretan fertility cult is the bull, the male instrument of fertility and also its victim. He is the chief protagonist in the hunts and festival games; his is the blood of the offerings; his head and horns are, besides the double ax, or labrys (the sacred sacrificial implement [62]), a typical symbol in Cretan shrines. This bull symbolizes the youthful god, son-lover of the Great Mother who, as the Europa of Greek mythology, reigned in Crete. She is the consort of the Cretan bull, in which form Zeus ravished her.

Just as Eshmun emasculated himself with the labrys in order

[60] The cow and calf symbolism is found very early in Egypt, where the ensign of the 12th nome, the seat of Isis, displays a cow with her calf (Kees, *Götterglaube*, p. 76).

[61] Nilsson, in Chantepie de la Saussaye, *Lehrbuch*, Vol. II, p. 297.

[62] Merezhkovski, *The Secret of the West*, pp. 288, 416.

to escape from Astronoë, otherwise known as Astarte-Aphrodite, so the Titans killed Zagreus-Dionysus with the labrys.[63] It is the instrument of sacramental castration, with which the bull, who later acted as a substitute for Dionysus, was sacrificed. Its neolithic form is still preserved in the flint knives with which the Galli of Asia Minor unmanned themselves, and also in the flint knife attributed to Set. In later times, the sacrifice, castration, and dismemberment were no longer performed on a human victim, but on an animal. Boar, bull, and goat stand for the gods Dionysus, Zagreus, Osiris, Tammuz, etc. The decapitation of the bull subsequently replaced the sacrifice of the phallus, and in the same way his horns became phallic symbols. In Egypt the head of the sacred Osiris-Apis bull was not allowed to be eaten, but was thrown into the Nile; and this is consistent with the myth, which relates that the phallus of Osiris disappeared in the Nile after his dismemberment. The connection between phallus and head is of the utmost significance in the mythological stages of conscious development.[64] It is sufficient here to say that each can stand for the other and that, characteristically, the bull's head symbolizes the human phallus. This substitution is the more understandable when one knows that the bull still appears as an archetypal sexuality and fertility symbol in modern dreams.

There is plenty of support for our statement that in Crete, too, the fertility ritual was originally performed between the Great Mother and her son-lover, and culminated in his sacrifice, but was subsequently replaced by the sacrifice of a bull. The individual details only acquire meaning when fitted into the picture as a whole, namely, the archetypal dominance of the Great Mother. As everywhere, the Great Mother goddess of Crete, the Demeter of the Greeks, is, as mistress of the underworld, also a goddess of death.[65] The dead, named by Plutarch *"demetrioi,"* are her property; her earthly womb is the womb of death, but

[63] Glotz, *The Aegean Civilization*, p. 75.
[64] See infra, pp. 158 f.
[65] Picard, "Die Grosse Mutter von Kreta bis Eleusis."

77

yet it is the lap of fertility from which all life springs.

The equation of Tammuz, Attis, Adonis, Eshmun, etc., with the Cretan Zeus is further supported by the remark attributed to Theodore of Mopsuestia:

The Cretans used to say of Zeus that he was a prince and was ripped up by a wild boar, and he was buried.[66]

The boar is a typical symbol of the doomed son-lover, and the killing of the boar is a mythological representation of his sacrifice to the Great Mother. On an Etruscan bronze relief, the Great Mother is depicted in her original form as Gorgo, strangling lions with both arms and spreading her legs wide in the attitude of ritual exhibitionism.[67] The same fragment also shows the boar hunt as we know it in Cretan paintings and in Greece at the time of the Cretan overlordship.

The killing of the boar is the oldest symbol we know for the killing of the Great Mother's son-lover. Here the goddess of fertility is a sow, and this is equally true of Isis, and later of Demeter in Eleusis. When the sow-goddess is ousted by the cow, and Hathor-Isis, for instance, appears instead of the porcine Isis, who was still associated with a porcine Set, then the boar is likewise replaced by the bull.

As we have seen, harvesting and tree-felling are the equivalents of death, dismemberment, and castration in the fertility ritual; and in Crete the breaking off of branches and fruit appeared to occupy an important place in the rites, together with an orgiastic sacred dance and a lamentation.[68] The canon of the later Adonis festivals, for which the priests wore women's garments, is thus established. Furthermore, the ritual renewal of the Cretan kingship, which had to follow after every "great year" of eight years' duration, offers close parallels to the Sed festival of renewal among the Egyptians.

Just as the renewal of kingship is to be interpreted as a late

[66] Cited by Cook, *Zeus*, Vol. I, p. 157, n. 3; after him, by Merezhkovski, op. cit., p. 280.

[67] Hausenstein, *Die Bildnerei der Etrusker*, illustrs. 2, 3.

[68] *The Cambridge Ancient History*, Vol. of Plates I, 200b.

substitute for the original sacrifice of the annual king, so, too, in Crete we can follow the road leading from his castration and yearly death to the substitution of a human and eventually an animal victim, and, last of all, to the festival of renewal, when the kingly power was ritually restored. The human sacrifices to the Minotaur, the bull-king of Crete, which according to the Greek legend originally consisted in a tribute of seven youths and maidens, can probably be explained in this manner, likewise the passion evinced by Queen Pasiphaë, mother of the Minotaur, for the bull.

From Egypt, Africa, and Asia, and even from Scandinavia, the evidence accumulates that human sacrifice guaranteed and prolonged the king's strength.[69] In Crete, as in Egypt, the rising patriarchate, with its concentration of power in the hands of the king and his nobles, evidently broke the sacred suzerainty of the mother-goddess. In the process, the yearly kingship came to be replaced by one that had at first to prolong its life by combat, but later it became an unbroken kingship which sacralized its continuity by means of vicarious sacrifices and yearly rites of renewal and regeneration.

We have shown that the Creto-Mycenaean area of Great Mother worship links up with Asia Minor, Libya, and Egypt, but its links with Greek myth and legendary history now appear in quite a new light. The historical accuracy of the myths proves itself yet again; doubts as to their veracity derive from an age which had lost all knowledge of Aegean culture. Once more Bachofen was the only one to have recognized, with his myth-piercing eye, the true content of Cretan culture from the historical records, even before the actual material of Aegean civilization had been unearthed.

From Europa and her associations with the bull, with the Cretan and Dodonaean Zeus, and with Dionysus, mythology derives the whole gloomy Cretan dynasty: Minos, Rhadamanthus, and Sarpedon. Her brother was Cadmus, whose history in Greece we have yet to trace. Both were children of Agenor, king

[69] Frazer, *The Golden Bough*, Ch. XXIV.

of Phoenicia, who had among his ancestors Libya, daughter of Epaphus, and Io his mother, the wandering milk-white moon-cow of Mycenae. In Egypt, Epaphus was worshiped as the bull Apis, and Io as Isis.

Libya, Egypt, Phoenicia, Crete, Mycenae, Greece—the historical connection between them is formulated as a genealogy. In the same way, we can recognize the symbolical and mythological sequence: the white moon-cow, Mycenaean Io, is the Egyptian Isis and the Cretan Europa, while associated with them are the Cretan Zeus-Dionysus bull, the Egyptian bull Apis, and the Minotaur.

Equally significant is the history of Cadmus, the legendary brother of Europa, who came from Phoenicia to found the city of Thebes. To him Herodotus attributes the transmission of the Osiris-Dionysus mysteries from Egypt to Pythagoras; in other words, Herodotus traces the origin of the late Greek mysteries and their Pythagorean and Orphic forerunners back to Egypt via Phoenicia. He also connects the Dodonaean Zeus, the phallic Hermes, and the pre-Grecian or Pelasgian cult of the Cabiri at Samothrace with the Osiris of Egypt and the Ammon of Libya. Earlier these connections were denied by science, but today they are obvious, since the cultural continuity that extended from Libya and Egypt, via Canaanite Phoenicia and Crete, to Greece is supported by a wealth of factual evidence.

Cadmus, founder of Thebes, is in league with Athene, but stands in an extremely ambivalent relationship to Aphrodite and her husband Ares. He slays the chthonic dragon, son of Ares, but marries Harmonia, daughter of Ares and Aphrodite. The cow with the moon sickle who leads him from Delphi, founded by the Cretans, to the site where Thebes is to be built, and whom he there sacrifices, is the ancient mother and moon-goddess of pre-Grecian days. She rules his life and that of his children, and proves more powerful than his helper Athene.[70]

[70] For an important contribution to genealogical interpretation see Philippson's "Genealogie als mythische Form" in *Untersuchungen über den griechischen Mythos*.

It is the ancient cow-goddess Aphrodite whose image breaks through in the daughters of Cadmus, and in them is manifested the terrible mythological power of the Mother Goddess. One of his daughters is Semele, mother of Dionysus, who remains a god-bearing goddess even though, as the mortal paramour of Zeus, she perishes in his lightning. The second daughter is Ino. In a fit of madness, she throws herself into the sea, together with her son Melicertes. Melicertes belongs to the cycle of son-lover gods who are lost, slain, mourned, and worshiped with orgiastic rites. The third daughter is Agave, mother of Pentheus; she too is a terrible mother, for she kills and tears her son to pieces in the madness of the orgy and bears off his bloody head in triumph. Pentheus himself becomes Dionysus-Zagreus, the dismembered god whom he tried to resist. The fourth daughter is Autonoë, mother of Actaeon, the young huntsman who unwittingly beheld the virginal Artemis in her nakedness, and, seized with terror, fled before her in the shape of a stag, only to be torn to pieces by his own hounds. Once more, animal transformation, dismemberment, and death. The virginal Artemis, goddess of the woods, is a pre-Grecian form of the Terrible Mother goddess, as is also the Artemis of Ephesus, Boeotia, etc.

Such are the daughters of Cadmus, and in all of them we see the dread sway of the terrible Aphrodite. Cadmus' only son is Polydorus, his grandson is Laïus, and his great-grandson—Oedipus. Even in the grandchild, the mother-son relationship leads to catastrophe. Only with him is this fatal bond between Great Mother and son-lover finally broken.

Europa and Cadmus form one tributary of the mythological stream that rises in Libya (Io) and reaches Greece via Phoenicia. The other tributary, also rising in Libya, leads to the Danaïdes and to Argos. Argos, an important area of Cretan culture in Greece, is associated in legend with Danaüs, who introduced the cult of Apollo Lykeios. According to Herodotus,[71] his daughters, the Danaïdes, brought the feast of Demeter, the Thesmophoria, to Greece from Egypt. The Thesmophoria and

[71] Book II.

its mysteries were a fertility festival, the central feature of which was a pit representing the womb of the Earth Mother. Into this womb-pit offerings were thrown, namely, pine cones, the phalli of the tree-son, and live pigs, these being the offspring of the gravid Earth Mother, the sow. The pit was infested with snakes, the constant companions of the Great Mother, who are always associated with her Gorgonesque womb. The noisome remains of the pigs were then fetched up again and, in accordance with the age-old fertility rites, solemnly rent asunder and spread over the fields.

Bachofen has shown convincingly that the Danaïdes, by killing the bridegrooms whom they have been forced to accept, belong to the sphere of the "emancipated" virgin-mother. Hypermnestra is the only one who, contrary to their mutual agreement, does not kill her husband, and with her the love relationship in mythology begins to be a matter for personal decision. Accordingly, she becomes the first mother of a line of heroes like Perseus and Herakles, who break the negative power of the Great Mother and establish a masculine culture. Both these belong to the type of hero fathered by a male deity and further assisted by Athene. The Perseus myth is the myth of the hero who conquers the symbol of matriarchal domination in the Libyan Gorgon, as Theseus does later in the case of the Minotaur.

Thus, in Io's descendants, though not in this branch of mythology alone, the conflict between the patriarchal and the matriarchal world is represented as epic history and personalized as family history in the Greek hero myths. Unquestionably, the scientific study of history and religion today would be satisfied with a reduction to ethnological groupings; but from a psychological standpoint, which has in mind the development of human consciousness, the supersession of the stage of the Great Mother and her son-lover by a new mythological stage is not a fortuitous historical occurrence, but a necessary psychological one. To correlate the new stage with a definite race or national group is impossible, so far as we can see at present. For side by side with the overcoming of the mother archetype in the Greco-

Indogermanic sphere of culture stands its no less radical counter-part in the Hebraic-Semitic sphere.

The conquest of the mother archetype has its proper place in the myth of the hero, and we shall be giving an account of it later. For the present, we have to examine more closely the stage of the Great Mother and her dominance over the son-lover.

The mythological and historical connection between the Cretan-Aegean sphere and Greece is evident in other figures of Greek myth. Hecate, the dread goddess, is the mother of the man-eating Empusa and the lamias who suck the blood of young men and devour their flesh. But this triple-bodied, uroboric Hecate, mistress of the three realms—sky, earth, and underworld —is the teacher of Circe and Medea in the arts of magic and destruction. To her is attributed the power to enchant and change men into animals, and to smite with madness, which gift belongs to her as to all moon-goddesses. The mysteries of the Great Mother were celebrated by women, peaceably enough in Eleusis, but in a sanguinary manner in the cult of Dionysus; and the orgiastic rending of goat and bull, with the eating of the bloody fragments as a symbolic act of fertilization, extends from Osiris to Dionysus-Zagreus and Orpheus, Pentheus, and Actaeon. As the Orphic saying has it, "The victim must be torn asunder and devoured." [72] The mother goddess is the mistress of wild animals, whether she appears as Tauropolos, the bull-grappler, in Crete and in Asia Minor, strangler of snakes, birds, and lions, or as a Circe who enslaves the men she has changed into beasts.

That the worship of the Earth and Death Goddess is often associated with swampy districts has been interpreted by Bachofen as symbolic of the dank level of existence on which, uroborically speaking, the dragon lives, devouring her progeny as soon as she has produced them. War, flagellation, blood offerings, and hunting are but the milder forms of her worship. The Great Mother in this character is not found only in prehistoric times. She rules over the Eleusinian mysteries of a later day,

[72] Merezhkovski, op. cit., p. 514.

and Euripides still knows Demeter as the wrathful goddess, riding in a chariot drawn by lions, to the accompaniment of Bacchic rattles, drums, cymbals, and flutes. She is shadowy enough to stand very near to the Asiatic Artemis and Cybele, and also to the Egyptian goddesses. Artemis Orthia of Sparta required human sacrifices and the whipping of boys; human sacrifices were likewise required by the Taurian Artemis; and the Alphaic Artemis was worshiped by women with nocturnal dancing, for which they smeared their faces with mud.

No "barbaric" goddesses are here being adored with "sensual" and "Asiatic" practices; all these things are merely the deeper-lying strata of Great Mother worship. She is the goddess of love, having power over the fruitfulness of earth, men, cattle, and crops; she also presides over all birth, and is thus, at one and the same time, goddess of destiny, wisdom, death, and the underworld. Everywhere her rites are frenzied and orgiastic; as mistress of wild animals, she rules all male creatures, who, in the form of the bull and the lion, bear aloft her throne.

There are numerous representations of these goddesses displaying their genitals in ritual exhibitionism,[73] both in India and in Canaan, as, for instance, the Egyptian Isis or the Demeter and Baubo of the Greeks. The naked goddess who "slumbers on the ground and abandons herself to love" is an early version of the Great Mother, and still earlier versions are to be seen in the monstrous female idols of neolithic times. Her attribute is the pig, a highly prolific animal; and upon it, or upon a basket—a female symbol like the cornucopia—the goddess sits with splayed legs, even in the supreme mystery of Eleusis.[74]

[73] Picard, "Die Ephesia von Anatolien"; cf. also Pietschmann, *Geschichte der Phönizier,* p. 228.

[74] Picard, "Die Grosse Mutter von Kreta bis Eleusis." It is extremely probable that the mouse, known to have been worshiped by the Phoenicians, the heathen neighbors of the Jews, on account of its high reproduction rate, which it shares with the pig, was a sacred fertility animal. Frazer has drawn attention to the passage in Isaiah (66:17) where it is said that the Israelites secretly celebrated a heathen feast at which pigs and mice were eaten. The reference is obviously to Canaanite practices connected with the cult of the Mother Goddess. This is borne out by the fact that images of mice are represented near the hand of the

The pig, as a primitive emblem of the Great Mother, occurs not only as a fertility symbol, but is also to be found in the very earliest phase as a cosmic projection:

The heretical image of the sky-woman as a sow, which shows the star-children going into her mouth in the manner of a sow eating her young, is to be found in a linguistically very early dramatic text preserved in the false tomb of Seti I, in the temple of Osiris at Abydos.[75]

Isis, like Nut, the Kore Kosmu,[76] appears as a "white sow," [77] and the head of the old god Set has been interpreted as that of a pig.[78] In Troy, Schliemann found the figure of a pig dotted with stars,[79] evidently representing the sky-woman as a sow, and the cult of the sow as a mother-goddess has left numerous traces.

Probably the most primitive and most ancient of the pig associations is with the female genitals, which even in Greek and Latin were called "pig," though the association can be traced back still further in the primitive name for the cowrie shell.[80] The image of Isis sitting with wide-open legs on a pig carries the line, via Crete and Asia Minor, to Greece. Speaking of Crete, where King Minos was suckled by a sow, Farnel says:

The Cretans consider this animal sacred and will not taste of its flesh; and the men of Praesos perform secret rites with the sow, making her the first offering of the sacrifice.[81]

The fact that the Syrians of Hierapolis could, in Lucian's day, discuss the sanctity or nonsanctity of the pig is merely a sign of ignorance and decadence. Its sanctity is attested not only by

---

goddess of Carthage, acknowledged to be a Great Mother (A. Jeremias, op. cit.). The negative side of the mouse lies in its being a carrier of bubonic plague, as indicated in the Iliad, Herodotus, and the Old Testament.

[75] Kees, *Götterglaube*, p. 42.
[76] Ibid., p. 6.
[77] Metternich stele, in Roeder, *Urkunden*, p. 90.
[78] Budge and Hall, *Introductory Guide to the Egyptian Collections in the British Museum*, p. 130.
[79] G. E. Smith, *The Evolution of the Dragon*, p. 216.
[80] Ibid.
[81] *Cults of the Greek States*, Vol. I, p. 37.

the bas-relief of the mother-sow that was found at Byblos [82] and probably belongs to the Adonis cult, but even more by the Phoenician custom of not eating pork and of sacrificing pigs at the anniversary of the death of Adonis. Frazer [83] has demonstrated the identity of Attis, Adonis, and Osiris and their identification with the pig. Wherever the eating of pork is forbidden and the pig is held to be unclean, we may be sure of its originally sacred character. The association of pigs with fertility and sexual symbolism lingers on into our own day, where sexual matters are still negatively described as "swinishness."

Kerényi has drawn attention to the connection of the pig as the "uterine animal" of the earth with Demeter and Eleusis.[84] It is important to remember that when Eleusis was permitted to make its own coinage, the pig was chosen as a symbol of the mysteries.[85]

The great feast of Aphrodite at Argos, when women appeared as men, and men as women wearing veils, was called the "Hysteria" after the pig sacrifices associated with it.

In the celebration of these anniversaries, the priestesses of Aphrodite worked themselves up into a wild state of frenzy, and the term Hysteria became identified with the state of emotional derangement associated with such orgies. . . . The word Hysteria was used in the same sense as Aphrodisia, that is, as a synonym for the festivals of the goddess.[86]

We might also mention that it is Aphrodite in her original character of Great Mother who sends the "Aphrodisia mania."

Not only does this emphasize the connection of the Great Mother archetype with sexuality and "hysteria," but it is even more significant that the hermaphroditic festival with its interchange of sex and clothing was called the "Hybristica." The repudiation of the hybrid, uroboric state by patriarchal Greece

---

82 Renan, *Mission de Phénicie*, pl. 31; Pietschmann, op. cit., p. 219 n.
83 *The Golden Bough*, p. 546.
84 Kerényi, "Kore," p. 119 (Torchbooks edn.). The author's exclusive concern with Greek mythology, however, prevents him from laying sufficient stress on the archetypal character of this phenomenon.
85 Smith, *The Evolution of the Dragon*, p. 153.
86 In Hastings, *Encyclopaedia of Religion and Ethics*, s.v. "Aphrodisia."

is characteristically expressed in this designation, which is conjectured to be cognate with *hybris* ("wantonness," "outrage").

The pig, then, symbolizes the female, the fruitful and receptive womb. As the "uterine animal," it belongs to the earth, the gaping pit, which, in the Thesmophoria, is fertilized by pig sacrifices.

Among the symbols of the devouring chasm we must count the womb in its frightening aspect, the numinous heads of the Gorgon and the Medusa, the woman with beard and phallus, and the male-eating spider. The open womb is the devouring symbol of the uroboric mother, especially when connected with phallic symbols. The gnashing mouth of the Medusa with its boar's tusks betrays these features most plainly, while the protruding tongue is obviously connected with the phallus. The snapping—i.e., castrating—womb appears as the jaws of hell, and the serpents writhing round the Medusa's head are not personalistic—pubic hairs—but aggressive phallic elements characterizing the fearful aspect of the uroboric womb.[86a] The spider can be classified among this group of symbols, not only because it devours the male after coitus, but because it symbolizes the female in general, who spreads nets for the unwary male.

This dangerous aspect is much enhanced by the element of weaving, as we find it in the Weird Sisters who spin the thread of life, or the Norns who weave the web of the world in which every man born of woman is entangled. Finally, we come to the veil of Maya, denounced by male and female alike as "illusion," the engulfing void, Pandora's Box.

Wherever the harmful character of the Great Mother predominates or is equal to her positive and creative side, and

[86a] Compare the dance-masks of the Balinese goddess Rangda (*illus. 19*), "the blood-thirsty, child-eating . . . witch-widow mistress of black magic." According to Covarrubias (*Island of Bali*, pp. 326 ff.), Rangda (whose name means "widow") is represented as a monstrous old woman, naked, striped black and white, with fantastically pendulous breasts ringed by black fur. Her long hair reaches to her feet, and through it one sees the bulging eyes, twisted fangs, and long red, flame-tipped tongue of the mask. "She wore white gloves with immense claws and in her right hand she held the cloth with which she hid her horrible face to approach her unsuspecting victims." And compare the Gorgon (*illus. 25*).

87

wherever her destructive side—the phallic element—appears to-gether with her fruitful womb, the uroboros is still operative in the background. In all these cases, the adolescent stage of the ego has not been overcome, nor has the ego yet made itself in-dependent of the unconscious.

Relations between Son-Lover and Great Mother

We can distinguish several stages in the youthful lover's rela-tion to the Great Mother.

The earliest is marked by a natural surrender to fate, to the power of the mother or uroboros. At this stage, suffering and sorrow remain anonymous; the young flower-like gods of vege-tation, doomed to die, are still close to the stage of the sacrificed child. Implicit in this stage is the pious hope of the natural crea-ture that he, like nature, will be reborn through the Great Mother, out of the fullness of her grace, with no activity or merit on his part. It is the stage of complete impotence against the uroboric mother and the overwhelming power of fate, as we still find it in Greek tragedy and particularly in the figure of Oedipus. Masculinity and consciousness have not yet won to independence, and uroboric incest has given way to the matri-archal incest of adolescence. The death ecstasy of sexual incest is symptomatic of an adolescent ego not yet strong enough to resist the forces symbolized by the Great Mother.

The transition to the next stage is formed by the "strugglers." In them, fear of the Great Mother is the first sign of centrover-sion, self-formation, and ego stability. This fear expresses itself in various forms of flight and resistance. The primary expression of flight, which is still completely under the dominance of the Great Mother, is self-castration and suicide (Attis, Eshmun, Bata, etc.). Here the attitude of defiance, the refusal to love, leads, nevertheless, to the very thing the Terrible Mother wants, namely, the offering of the phallus, though the offering is made in a negative sense. The youths who flee in terror and madness from the demands of the Great Mother betray, in the act of self-castration, their abiding fixation to the central symbol of the Great Mother cult, the phallus; and this they offer up to her, albeit with denial in their consciousness and a protesting ego.

This turning away from the Great Mother as an expression of centroversion can clearly be seen in the figures of Narcissus, Pentheus, and Hippolytus. All three resist the fiery loves of the great goddesses, but are punished by them or by their representatives. In the case of Narcissus, who rejects love and then becomes fatally infatuated with his own reflection, the turning toward oneself and away from the all-consuming object with its importunate demands is obvious enough. But it is not sufficient to give exclusive prominence to this accentuation and love of one's own body. The tendency of an ego consciousness that is becoming aware of itself, the tendency of all self-consciousness, all reflection, to see itself as in a mirror, is a necessary and essential feature at this stage. Self-formation and self-realization begin in earnest when human consciousness develops into self-consciousness. Self-reflection is as characteristic of the pubertal phase of humanity as it is of the pubertal phase of the individual. It is a necessary phase of human knowledge, and it is only persistence in this phase that has fatal effects. The breaking of the Great Mother fixation through self-reflection is not a symbol of autoeroticism, but of centroversion.

The nymphs who vainly pursue Narcissus with their love are simply aphrodisiac forces in personalized form, and to resist them is equivalent to resisting the Great Mother. Elsewhere we shall examine the significance of the fragmentation of archetypes for the development of consciousness. In the Greek myths we can see how this fragmentation proceeds. The terrible aspect of the Great Mother is almost wholly repressed and only fleeting glimpses of it can be caught behind the seductive figure of Aphrodite. And Aphrodite herself no longer appears in her suprapersonal majesty; she is split up and personalized in the form of nymphs, sirens, water sprites, and dryads, or else she appears as the mother, stepmother, or the beloved, as Helen or Phaedra.

This is not to say that the process always follows a perfectly clear course in the history of religion. Our starting point is the archetype and its relation to consciousness. Chronologically, however, nymphs—that is, partial aspects of the archetype—can appear just as easily before the historical worship of the mother archetype as afterwards. Structurally they remain partial aspects of the archetype and are psychic fragmentations of it, even though the historian can point to a nymph cult that is antecedent to the cult of the Great Mother. In the collective unconscious all archetypes are contemporaneous and exist side by side. Only with the development of consciousness do we come to a graduated hierarchy within the collective unconscious itself. (See Part II.)

Narcissus, seduced by his own reflection, is really a victim of Aphrodite, the Great Mother. He succumbs to her fatal law. His ego system is overpowered by the terrible instinctive force of love over which she presides. The fact that she borrows his reflection to effect the seduction only makes her the more treacherous.

Pentheus is another of these "strugglers" who cannot successfully accomplish the heroic act of liberation. Although his struggles are directed against Dionysus, the fate meted out to him for his sins shows that his true enemy is the Great Mother. That Dionysus has affinities with the orgiastic worship of the Great Mother and with her son-lovers, Osiris, Adonis, Tammuz, etc., is well known. We cannot go into the problematical figure of Semele, the mother of Dionysus, but Bachofen correlates Dionysus with the Great Mother and modern research confirms him in this:

Dionysus was worshiped at Delphi as the infant or cupid in the winnowing basket. His is a chthonic cult with the moon-goddess Semele as Earth Mother. Since he originated in Thrace and settled in Asia Minor, there becoming merged with the Magna Mater cult, it is probable . . . that a widespread primordial cult pertaining to the original pre-Grecian religion lives on in him.[87]

The heroic King Pentheus, so proud of his rationality, tries with the help of his mother, next of kin to Dionysus, to oppose the orgies, but both are overwhelmed by the Dionysian frenzy. He suffers the fate of all the Great Mother's victims: seized by madness, he dons women's clothing and joins in the orgies, whereupon his mother, raving mad, mistakes him for a lion and tears him to pieces. She then carries home his gory head in triumph—a reminder of the original act of castration which attended the dismemberment of the corpse. In this way, his mother, against the dictates of her conscious mind, turns into the Great Mother, while the son, despite the resistance put up by his ego, becomes her son-lover. Madness, the change into women's clothing and then into an animal, dismemberment, and castration—the whole archetypal destiny is here fulfilled; Pentheus, hiding in the top of a pine tree, becomes Dionysus-Attis, and his mother the Magna Mater.

The figure of Hippolytus takes its place alongside that of Pentheus and Narcissus. From love of Artemis, from chastity and love of his own self, he scorns Aphrodite by scorning the love of his stepmother Phaedra, and on the orders of his father and with the help of the god Poseidon he is dragged to death by his own horses.

We cannot enter here into the deeper conflict which rages in Hippolytus, between love for his mother, Queen of the Amazons, and for his stepmother, sister of Ariadne, and which accounts for his resistance to Phaedra and his devotion to Artemis. We shall only give a brief analysis of the myth so far as is relevant to our theme. Because of secondary personalization, the myth as dramatized by Euripides has become a personal fate overlaid with personalistic detail. But it is still transparent enough to be interpreted back to its origins.

The scorned Aphrodite and the scorned stepmother go together. They represent the Great Mother who amorously

[87] Bernoulli, in Bachofen, *Urreligion*, Vol. II, p. 74.

pursues the son and kills him when he resists. Hippolytus is bound to the virgin Artemis—not the original mother-virgin, but Artemis as a spiritual figure, the "girl friend" who resembles Athene.

Hippolytus himself is at the stage of critical resistance to the Great Mother, already conscious of himself as a young man struggling for autonomy and independence. This is evident from his repudiation of the Great Mother's advances and of her phallic, orgiastic sexuality. His "chastity," however, means far more than a rejection of sex; it signifies the coming to consciousness of the "higher" masculinity as opposed to the "lower" phallic variety. On the subjective level, it is the conscious realization of the "solar" masculinity which Bachofen contrasts with "chthonic" masculinity. This higher masculinity is correlated with light, the sun, the eye, and consciousness.

Hippolytus' love for Artemis and for the chastity of nature is negatively characterized by his father as "virtuous pride" and "self-adoration." [88] It is quite in keeping with these traits that Hippolytus belongs to what we would call a youth society. We shall concern ourselves later with the strengthening of the masculine principle through male friendships and also with the significance of the "spiritual" sister for the development of masculine consciousness. In Hippolytus, however, the defiance of youth ends in tragedy. Interpreted personalistically, this means that Aphrodite takes her revenge; the slanderous accusations of the stepmother he has scorned are believed by his father Theseus; she kills herself, and the father curses his son. Mechanically Poseidon must grant the wish he gave Theseus, and put Hippolytus to death. This rather senseless story of an Aphrodite intrigue, not in the least tragic to our way of thinking, is seen to have a very different content when psychologically interpreted.

No more than Oedipus could hold out against heroic incest with his mother can Hippolytus keep up an attitude of defiance. The power of the Great Mother, the madness of love sent by Aphrodite, is stronger than his conscious ego resistance. He is

[88] Euripides, *Hippolytus*, V, 1064 and 1080.

dragged by his own horses—that is to say, he falls victim to the world of his instincts, of whose subjugation he was so proud. The horses—characteristically enough, they are mares—fulfill the deadly will of Aphrodite. When one knows how the Great Mother wreaks her vengeance in the myths, one can see the story in its proper setting. The self-mutilation and suicide of Attis, Eshmun, and Bata; Narcissus dying of self-attraction; Actaeon, like so many other youths, changed into an animal and torn to pieces; all this hangs together. And whether it be Aithon burning in the fires of his own passion, or Daphnis languishing in insatiable desire because he does not love the girl Aphrodite sends him; whether we interpret the dragging to death of Hippolytus as madness, love, or retribution—in every case the central fact is the vengeance of the Great Mother, the overpowering of the ego by subterranean forces.

Characteristically, too, Poseidon, even if only indirectly, is an instrument in the hand of Aphrodite, behind whose loveliness lurks the Terrible Mother. It is Poseidon who sends the monstrous bull from the sea, which drives the horses of Hippolytus mad and makes them drag their master. Once again we encounter the phallic figure of the Earth-Shaker and lord of the deep, companion of the Great Mother. Aphrodite seeks vengeance because Hippolytus, in the growing pride of ego consciousness, "despises" her and declares that she is "the lowest among the heavenly ones." [89] We have already met this development in the plaint of Gilgamesh against Ishtar. But in contrast to the figure of Hippolytus—a very negative hero—Gilgamesh, with his more powerfully developed masculinity, is a real hero. Supported by his friend Engidu, he lives the hero's life completely detached from the Great Mother, whereas Hippolytus remains unconsciously bound to her, although he defies and denies her with his conscious mind.

The youth struggling for self-consciousness now begins, in so far as he is an individual, to have a personal fate, and for him the Great Mother becomes the deadly and unfaithful mother.

[89] Ibid., 13.

She selects one young man after another to love and destroy. In this way she becomes "the harlot." The sacred prostitute—which is what the Great Mother really is, as the vessel of fertility—takes on the negative character of the fickle jade and destroyer. With this, the great revaluation of the feminine begins, its conversion into the negative, thereafter carried to extremes in the patriarchal religions of the West. The growth of self-consciousness and the strengthening of masculinity thrust the image of the Great Mother into the background; the patriarchal society splits it up, and while only the picture of the good Mother is retained in consciousness, her terrible aspect is relegated to the unconscious.[90]

The result of this fragmentation is that it is no longer the Great Mother who is the killer, but a hostile animal, for instance, a boar or bear, with the lamenting figure of the good mother ranged alongside. Bachofen [91] has shown that the bear is a mother symbol, and he has stressed its identity with Cybele. We know today that the bear as a mother symbol belongs to the common stock of archetypes and is to be found in Europe and Asia equally.[92] Bachofen has also shown that the later substitution of the lion for the bear coincides with the supersession of the mother cult by the father cult.[93] The circle is completed by Winckler's evidence that, in astrology, the sun-god sets in the constellation of the Great Bear, also called the Boar.[94] Since

[90] The splitting of the Great Mother into a conscious "good" mother and an unconscious "evil" one is a basic phenomenon in the psychology of neurosis. The situation then is that consciously the neurotic has a "good relation" to the mother, but in the gingerbread house of this love there is hidden the witch, who gobbles up little children and grants them, as a reward, a passive, irresponsible existence without an ego. Analysis then uncovers the companion picture of the Terrible Mother, an awe-inspiring figure who with threats and intimidations puts a ban on sexuality. The results are masturbation, real or symbolic impotence, self-castration, suicide, etc. It makes no difference whether the picture of the Terrible Mother remains unconscious or is projected; in either case the very idea of coitus, of any connection with the female, will activate the fear of castration.

[91] *Urreligion*, Vol. I, pp. 138 ff. (concerning his "Der Bär in den Religionen des Altertums," 1863).

[92] Breysig, *Die Völker ewiger Urzeit.*

[93] Frobenius, *Kulturgeschichte Afrikas*, pp. 85 f.

[94] Winckler, "Himmels- und Weltenbild der Babylonier."

94

astrological images are projections of psychic images, we find the same connections here as in mythology. In later developments, therefore, the figure of the Great Mother splits into a negative half, represented by an animal, and a positive half having human form.

Attis and the Cretan Zeus are both killed by a boar, a variant of the castration motif, which is also linked with the taboo on the eating of pork in the Attis cult and with the swine-figure of the Great Mother. The father-significance of the boar as an avenger sent by a jealous father deity is a late importation. The father plays no role at this stage of the young god doomed to die. Indeed the divine youth is, without knowing it, his own father in another form; there is as yet no paternal progenitor other than the son himself. The reign of the maternal uroboros is characterized by the fact that the "masculine" features, later attributed to the father, are still integral parts of the uroboric nature of the Great Mother. The solitary tooth of the Graeae, and the other obviously masculine elements associated with Weird Sisters, hags, and witches, might be mentioned here. Just as beard and phallus are parts of her androgynous nature, so she is the sow that farrows and the boar that kills.

The emergence of the male killer in the cycle of Great Mother myths is an evolutionary advance, for it means that the son has gained a greater measure of independence. To begin with, the boar is part of the uroboros, but in the end he becomes part of the son himself. The boar is then the equivalent of the self-destruction which the myth represents as self-castration. No paternal character attaches as yet to the male killer; he is merely a symbol of the destructive tendency which turns against itself in the act of self-sacrifice. This dichotomy can be seen in the motif of the hostile twin brothers, the archetype of self-division. Frazer and Jeremias [95] have both amply proved that the hero and the beast that kills him are very often identical, though they offer no explanation of this fact.

The motif of hostile twin brothers belongs to the symbolism

[95] A. Jeremias, *Handbuch der altorientalischen Geisteskultur*, p. 265.

of the Great Mother. It appears when the male attains to self-consciousness by dividing himself into two opposing elements, one destructive and the other creative.

The stage of the strugglers marks the separation of the conscious ego from the unconscious, but the ego is not yet stable enough to push on to the separation of the First Parents and the victorious struggle of the hero. As we have emphasized, centroversion manifests itself negatively at first, in the guise of fear, flight, defiance, and resistance. This negative attitude of the ego, however, is not yet directed against the object, the Great Mother, as it is with the hero, but turns against itself in self-destruction, self-mutilation, and suicide.

In the myth of Narcissus, the ego, seeking to break the power of the unconscious through self-reflection, succumbs to a catastrophic self-love. His suicidal death by drowning symbolizes the dissolution of ego consciousness, and the same thing is repeated in modern times in young suicides like Weininger and Seidel. Seidel's book *Bewusstsein als Verhängnis* and the work of the misogynist Weininger bear the clear imprint of having been written by lovers of the Great Mother. They are fatally fascinated by her, and even in the futile resistance they put up they are fulfilling their archetypal fate.[95a]

The archetypal situation of the struggling and reluctant lover plays an important part in the psychology of suicide among modern neurotics, and also has a legitimate place in the psychology of puberty, of which the strugglers are the archetypal representatives. The negation, the self-denial, the *Weltschmerz*, the accumulated suicidal leanings of this period, are all appropriate here, and so is the fascination—at once enticing and dangerous—which emanates from the female. The close of puberty

[95a] [Otto Weininger, born in Vienna in 1880, shot himself there in 1903. His principal work, *Sex and Character* (English trans., 1906), asserts the spiritual and moral inferiority of women. See Abrahamsen's *The Mind and Death of a Genius* for a full account of Weininger. Alfred Seidel's *Bewusstsein als Verhängnis* ("Consciousness as Destiny") was published at Bonn in 1927, having been edited posthumously. Seidel, born in 1895, killed himself in 1924. —EDITOR.]

is marked by the successful fight of the hero, as the rites of initiation testify. The youths who die by their own hand in puberty represent all those who succumb to the dangers of this fight, who cannot make the grade and perish in the trials of initiation, which still take place today as always, but in the unconscious. Their self-destruction and tragic self-division are nevertheless heroic. The strugglers might be described as negative, doomed heroes. The male killer at work behind the destructive tendency is still, although the ego does not know it, the instrument of the Great Mother, and the boar that kills Adonis is, as it were, the Gorgon's tusk become independent; but, for all that, an ego that kills itself is more active, more independent and individual, than the sad resignation of the languishing lover.

In the separation of the male antagonist from the male-female uroboros, and in the splitting of the Great Mother into a good mother and her destructive male consort, we can already discern a certain differentiation of consciousness and a breaking down of the archetype. This separation and the consequent emergence of the twin-brother conflict mark an important stage on the way to the final dissolution of the uroboros, separation of the World Parents, and consolidation of ego consciousness.

Once again let us consider the primordial, mythological images that portray this event. Just as the motif of the twins is a determining factor in the Egyptian myth of Osiris and Set and plays an equally decisive part in Canaanite mythology, where it appears as the struggle between Baal and Mot, Resheph and Shalman—so we find it, with personalistic variations, in the Bible story of Jacob and Esau, and in the Jewish legends.

It is interesting to note that there actually exists a pictorial representation of this group of symbols, to which Albright has drawn attention:

A cult-stand of about the twelfth century B.C. from Beth-shan [Palestine] shows a remarkable tableau in relief: a nude goddess holds two doves in her arms as she sits with legs apart to show her sex; below her are two male deities with arms interlocked in a struggle (?), with a dove at the feet of one of them; toward them from below creeps a serpent and from one side advances a lion.[96]

The struggle between snake and lion—a life-and-death struggle—has also been preserved in the much later Mithraism, and the meaning is the same. This religion, being patriarchal, introduced certain variations; but in the cult-images of the bull sacrifice we find, below the bull, the same two animals, snake and lion, symbolizing night and day, heaven and earth. The whole is flanked by the representatives of life and death, two youths with torches, one upraised, the other lowered. The womb of the Great Mother in which the opposites were originally contained appears here only in symbolic form, as the krater, guarantor of rebirth, and the two animals are shown hastening toward it. A masculine religion like Mithraism no longer tolerated direct representation of a female deity.

Unfortunately we cannot, in the present context, show how the archetypes are as operative today, in the unconscious, as they ever were in the projections of mythology. We should only note that the primordial image from Beth-shan unconsciously crops up in the work of a modern writer, Robert Louis Stevenson, where it still retains the meaning it had thousands of years ago. In his *Dr. Jekyll and Mr. Hyde*, a recapitulation in modern personalistic form of the mythological struggle between the twin brothers Set and Osiris,[97] Stevenson's Dr. Jekyll makes the following entry in his diary. The passage forms the theme of the whole story:

It was the curse of mankind that these incongruous fagots were thus bound together, that in the agonized womb of consciousness [98] these polar twins should be continuously struggling. How then were they dissociated.

Up to the present, the last conscious realization of this psychological problem is to be found in the psychoanalysis of Freud, who postulated the opposition of a life instinct and a death instinct in the unconscious. The problem also reappears as the

[96] Albright, *From the Stone Age to Christianity*, p. 178.
[97] [The same theme occurs in Stevenson's *Master of Ballantrae.*—TRANS.]
[98] Meaning the unconscious.

98

principle of opposites in Jung's analytical psychology. Here, then, we have the same psychic archetype—the twin brothers locked in a life-and-death struggle in the womb of the Great Mother—as a myth, a pictorial image, a theme in a short story, and a psychological concept.

We shall sum up the significance of this problem for the development of masculinity when we come to examine the difference between the "Terrible Male" and the "Terrible Father." [99] Here we can only say that, as a consequence of the male's no longer being confronted with the superior power of the Great Mother, but with another male hostile to him, a conflict situation develops in which self-defense becomes possible for the first time.

This psychological development corresponds to a change in the original fertility ritual that forms the background of these myths.[100] In the beginning, the young fertility king was killed, his corpse cut up and spread over the fields, and his phallus was mummified as a guarantee of the next year's crops. Whether the female representative of the Earth Goddess was sacrificed at the same time is questionable, but in the beginning she probably was. With the rise of the mother deity, however, her representative, the Earth Queen, remained alive in order to celebrate her annual marriage with the young king. In later times, the sacrifice seems to have been replaced by a combat. The annual king consolidated his position and was permitted to fight for his life in combat with the next claimant. If defeated, he was sacrificed as the old year; if victorious, then his opponent died in his stead. Later, when the matriarchate changed into a patriarchate, a rite of renewal was celebrated annually or at set intervals, and the king was kept alive because the vicarious human or animal sacrifices at the feast, which was known in Egypt as the "Erection of the Venerable Djed," rendered his death unnecessary. The development thus runs parallel to that which originally took place with the Queen-Goddess.

[99] See infra, pp. 185 ff.
[100] Lord Raglan, *Jocasta's Crime*, p. 122.

99

We shall see the final stage of the struggle between ego consciousness and the unconscious when, at a later phase of development, the female is excluded by the patriarchate as a mere vessel, and the male, by reproducing himself, becomes the agent of his own rebirth.

During the transition stage, however, the regenerative force, the creative magic of the mother, continues to exist side by side with the masculine principle. It makes whole and new, reduces the broken pieces to unity, gives new form and new life to the corruptible, and leads beyond death. But the nucleus of masculine personality remains unaffected by the regenerative force of the mother. It does not perish, seeming to have foreknowledge of rebirth. It is as though some remnant, akin to the "little Luz bone" [101] of Jewish legend, could not be destroyed by death and harbored in itself the power to effect its own resurrection. In contrast to the deadly uroboric incest, where the embryonic ego dissolves like salt in water, the fortified ego launches forth into a life beyond death. Although this life is bestowed by the mother, it is at the same time mysteriously conditioned by the residual ego nucleus. As one of the hymns of the Rig-Veda says:

Creep into the earth, the mother,
Into the broad, roomy, most holy earth!
Soft as wool is the earth to the wise.
May she guard thee on the next lap of the journey.
Arch thy broad back, press not downwards,
Open thyself easily, let him in lightly;
As a mother her son with the hem of her garment,
So cover him over, O earth. [102]

Death is not the end, but a crossing over. It is a fallow period, but also the refuge afforded by the mother. The dying ego does not rejoice when it finds itself "back again" in the mother and no longer in existence; it shoots its life-will beyond death and passes through it into the next lap of the journey, into the new.

[101] [The last bone of the spine (os coccygis), believed to be indestructible and the seat of the body's resurrection. Cf. the sacrum of Osiris, which composes part of the djed pillar, infra, p. 231.—TRANS.]

[102] Hymns of the Rig-Veda 10. 18. 45, trans. from Geldner, Vedismus und Brahmanismus, p. 70.

This development, where death is not the predestined end, and the mortality of the individual not the only aspect of life, is, however, no longer accomplished in the old setting, i.e., in the relation of the youthful lover to the Great Mother. The masculine principle is now strong enough to have reached consciousness of itself. Ego consciousness is no longer the satellite son of the maternal uroboros, chained to the almighty unconscious, but has become truly independent and capable of standing alone.

With this we reach the next stage in the evolution of consciousness, namely, the separation of the World Parents, or the principle of opposites.

III

THE SEPARATION OF THE WORLD
PARENTS: THE PRINCIPLE OF OPPOSITES

RANGI AND PAPA, the heaven and the earth, were regarded as the source from which all things, gods, and men originated. There was darkness, for these two still clung together, not yet having been rent apart; and the children begotten by them were ever thinking what the difference between darkness and light might be. They knew that beings had multiplied and increased, and yet light had never broken upon them, but ever darkness continued. Hence these sayings were found in the old *karakia:* "There was darkness from the first division of time, to the tenth, to the hundredth, to the thousandth"—that is, for a vast space of time; and each of these divisions of time was regarded as a being, and each was termed Po, and it was because of them that there was yet no bright world of light, but darkness only for the beings which then existed.

At last, worn out with the oppression of darkness, the beings begotten by Rangi and Papa consulted among themselves, saying, "Let us determine what we shall do with Rangi and Papa; whether it would be better to slay them, or to rend them apart." Then spoke Tu-matauenga, the fiercest of the sons of Rangi and Papa, "It is well; let us slay them."

Then spoke Tane-mahuta, the father of forests and of all things inhabiting the forests, or that are constructed of trees, "Nay, not so. It is better to rend them apart, and to let Rangi stand far above us, and Papa lie beneath our feet. Let Rangi become as a stranger to us, but the earth remain close to us as a nursing mother."

To this proposal the brothers consented, with the exception of Tawhiri-matea, the father of winds and storms; and he, fearing that his kingdom was about to be overthrown, grieved at the thought of the parents being torn apart.

Hence, also, these sayings of old are found in the *karakia:* "The Po, the Po, the light, the light, the seeking, the searching, in chaos, in chaos," these signifying how the offspring of Rangi and Papa sought for some way of dealing with their parents, so that human beings might increase and live. So also the saying: "The multitude, the length," signifying the multitude of their thoughts and the length of time they considered. . . .

Their plans having been agreed to, Rongo-ma-Tane, the god and father of cultivated food, arose, that he might rend Rangi and Papa; he struggled, but he did not rend them apart. Next Tangaroa, the god of fish and reptiles, arose, that he might rend apart Rangi and Papa; he also struggled, but he did not rend them apart. Next Haumia-tikitiki, the god and father of food that springs without cultivation, arose and struggled, but quite ineffectually. Then Tu-matauenga, the god and father of fierce human beings, arose and struggled, but he too struggled ineffectually.

Then at last Tane-mahuta, the god and father of forests, of birds, and of insects, arose and struggled with his parents; in vain with hands and arms he strove to rend them apart. He paused; firmly he planted his head on his mother Papa, the earth, and his feet he raised up against his father Rangi, the sky; he strained his back and his limbs in a mighty effort. Now were rent apart Rangi and Papa, and with reproaches and groans of woe they cried aloud: "Wherefore do you thus slay your parents? Why commit so dark a crime as to slay us, to rend us, your parents, apart?" But Tane-mahuta paused not; he regarded not their cries and their groans; far, far beneath him he pressed down Papa, the earth; far, far above him he thrust up Rangi, the sky. Hence the saying of old time: "It was the fiercest thrusting of Tane which tore the heaven from the earth, so that they were rent apart, and darkness was made manifest, and light made manifest also." [1]

This Maori creation myth contains all the elements of the stage in the evolution of human consciousness which follows that of uroboric dominance. The separation of the World Parents, the splitting off of opposites from unity, the creation of heaven and earth, above and below, day and night, light and darkness—the deed that is a monstrous misdeed and a sin—all the features that occur in isolation in numerous other myths are here molded into a unity.

Speaking of this separation of the World Parents, Frazer says:

It is a common belief of primitive peoples that sky and earth were originally joined together, the sky either lying flat on the earth or being raised so little above it that there was not room between them for people to walk upright. Where such beliefs prevail, the present elevation of the sky above the earth is often ascribed to the might of some god or hero, who gave the firmament such a shove that it shot up and has remained up above ever since.[2]

[1] Andersen, *Myths and Legends of the Polynesians*, pp. 367–68.
[2] *The Worship of Nature*, p. 26.

103

Elsewhere Frazer interprets the castration of the primordial father as the separation of the World Parents. In this we see a reference to the original uroboric situation where heaven and earth are known as "the two mothers."

Again and again we come back to the basic symbol, light, which is central to the creation myths. This light, the symbol of consciousness and illumination, is the prime object of the cosmogonies of all peoples. Accordingly, "in the creation legends of nearly all peoples and religions, the process of creation merges with the coming of the light."[3] As the Maori text says: "The light, the light, the seeking, the searching, in chaos, in chaos."

Only in the light of consciousness can man know. And this act of cognition, of conscious discrimination, sunders the world into opposites, for experience of the world is only possible through opposites. Once more we must emphasize that the symbolism of the myths, which helps us to understand the corresponding human stages, is not philosophy or speculation. The work of art also, the dream in all its meaningfulness, rises up in the same way from the depths of the psyche and yields its meaning to the discerning interpreter, though often enough it is not grasped spontaneously by the artist or dreamer himself. Similarly, the mythical form of expression is a naïve demonstration of the psychic processes going on in humanity, although humanity itself may experience and transmit the myth as something entirely different. We know that in all probability a ritual, i.e., some ceremony or course of action, always precedes the formulation of the myth, and it is obvious that action must come before knowledge, the unconscious deed before the spoken content. Our formulations are therefore abstract summaries—otherwise we could not hope to survey the diversity of the material before us—and not statements such as primitive man could have made consciously about himself. Not until we have familiarized ourselves with the dominant images which direct the

[3] Cassirer, *The Philosophy of Symbolic Forms*, trans. Manheim, Vol. II, p. 96.

course of human development shall we be able to understand the variants and sidelines which cluster round the main track.

Consciousness = deliverance: that is the watchword inscribed above all man's efforts to deliver himself from the embrace of the primordial uroboric dragon. Once the ego sets itself up as center and establishes itself in its own right as ego consciousness, the original situation is forcibly broken down. We can see what this self-identification of the waking human personality with the ego really means only when we remember the contrasted state of *participation mystique* ruled by uroboric unconsciousness. Trite as it seems to us, the logical statement of identity—"I am I"—the fundamental statement of consciousness, is in reality a tremendous achievement. This act, whereby an ego is posited and the personality identified with that ego— however fallacious that identification may later prove to be— alone creates the possibility of a self-orienting consciousness. In this connection we would again quote that passage from the Upanishads:

In the beginning this world was Soul (Atman) alone in the form of a person. Looking around, he saw nothing else than himself. He said first: "I am." . . . He was, indeed, as large as a woman and a man closely embraced. He caused that self to fall (*pat*) into two pieces. Therefrom arose a husband (*pati*) and a wife (*patni*).[4]

If, as we saw earlier, existence in the uroboros was existence in *participation mystique,* this also means that no ego center had as yet developed to relate the world to itself and itself to the world. Instead, man was all things at once, and his capacity for change was well-nigh universal. He was at one and the same time part of his group, a "Red Cockatoo," [5] and an embodied ancestral spirit. Everything inside was outside, that is to say, all his ideas came to him from outside, as commands from a spirit or magician or "medicine bird." But also, everything outside

[4] Brihadaranyaka Upanishad 1. 4. 1–3, trans. by Hume, *The Thirteen Principal Upanishads.*

[5] A well-known example of *participation mystique* between man and animal, cited by von den Steinen, *Unter den Naturvölkern Zentral-Brasiliens,* p. 58.

was inside. Between the hunted animal and the will of the hunter there existed a magical, mystical rapport, just as it existed between the healing of the wound and the weapon that made it, since the wound deteriorated if the weapon were heated. This lack of differentiation was precisely what constituted the weakness and defenselessness of the ego, which in its turn reinforced the participation. Thus, in the beginning, everything was double and had a double meaning, as we have seen from the intermingling of male and female, good and bad, in the uroboros. But life in the uroboros meant being linked at the same time, at the deepest level, with the unconscious and with nature, between which there subsisted a fluid continuum that coursed through man like a current of life. He was caught up in this circuit flowing from the unconscious to the world and from the world back to the unconscious, and its tidal motion buffeted him to and fro in the alternating rhythm of life to which he was exposed without knowing it. Differentiation of the ego, separation of the World Parents, and dismemberment of the primordial dragon set man free as a son and expose him to the light, and only then is he born as a personality with a stable ego.

In man's original world picture, world unity was unimpaired. The uroboros was alive in everything. Everything was pregnant with meaning, or could at least become so. In this world continuum, single patches of life became visible here and there through their ever-changing capacity to evoke wonder and impress themselves as mana-charged contents. This "impressionability" was universal—that is to say, every part of the world was capable of making an impression, everything was potentially "holy" or, more accurately speaking, could turn out to be astonishing and thus charged with mana.

The world begins only with the coming of light (*illus. 20*), which constellates the opposition between heaven and earth as the basic symbol of all other opposites. Before that, there reigns the "illimitable darkness," as is said in the Maori myth. With the rising of the sun or—in the language of ancient Egypt—the creation of the firmament, which divides the upper from the

20. Michelangelo: *God Dividing Light and Darkness*

Detail from the Sistine Chapel, Rome

21. The separation of Heaven and Earth:
Nut lifted above Geb by Shu

Drawing after an Egyptian coffin

lower, mankind's day begins, and the universe becomes visible with all its contents.

In relation to man and his ego, the creation of light and the birth of the sun are bound up with the separation of the World Parents and the positive and negative consequences which ensue for the hero who separates them.

There are, however, other accounts of the creation as an unrelated, cosmic phenomenon, a stage in the evolution of the world itself. But even in the version we shall now quote, taken from the Upanishads, we can see the personal agency at work behind the evolutionary process, though in this text it is not accentuated.

> The sun is brahma—this is the teaching. Here is the explanation:
> In the beginning, this world was nonbeing. This nonbeing became being. It developed. It turned into an egg. It lay there for a year. It burst asunder. One part of the eggshell was of silver, the other part was of gold.
> The silver part is the earth, the golden part is the sky. . . .
> What was born of it, is yonder sun. When it was born there were shouts and hurrahs, all beings and all desires rose up to greet it. Therefore at its rising and at its every return, there are shouts and hurrahs, all beings and all desires rise up to greet it.[6]

Cassirer has shown, with ample supporting material, how the opposition between light and darkness has informed the spiritual world of all peoples and molded it into shape. The sacred world order and the sacred space—precinct or sanctuary—were "oriented" by this opposition.[7] Not only man's theology, religion, and ritual, but the legal and economic orders that later grew out of them, the formation of the state and the whole pattern of secular life, down to the notion of property and its symbolism, are derived from this act of discrimination and the setting of boundaries made possible by the coming of light.

World-building, city-building, the layout of temples, the Roman military encampment, and the spatial symbolism of the Christian Church are all reflections of the original mythology

[6] Chhandogya Upanishad 3. 19. 1–3 (based on Hume and Deussen translations).
[7] *The Philosophy of Symbolic Forms.*

of space, which, beginning with the opposition between light and darkness, classifies and arranges the world in a continuous series of opposites.

Space only came into being when, as the Egyptian myth puts it, the god of the air, Shu, parted the sky from the earth by stepping between them (*illus. 21*). Only then, as a result of his light-creating and space-creating intervention, was there heaven above and earth below, back and front, left and right— in other words, only then was space organized with reference to an ego.

Originally there were no abstract spatial components; they all possessed a magical reference to the body, had a mythical, emotional character, and were associated with gods, colors, meanings, allusions.[8] Gradually, with the growth of consciousness, things and places were organized into an abstract system and differentiated from one another; but originally thing and place belonged together in a continuum and were fluidly related to an ever-changing ego. In this inchoate state there was no distinction between I and You, inside and outside, or between men and things, just as there was no clear dividing line between man and the animals, man and man, man and the world. Everything participated in everything else, lived in the same undivided and overlapping state in the world of the unconscious as in the world of dreams. Indeed, in the fabric of images and symbolic presences woven by dreams, a reflection of this early situation still lives on in us, pointing to the original promiscuity of human life.

Not only space but time and the passage of time are oriented by the mythical space picture, and this formative capacity to orient oneself by the sequence of light and darkness, thus widening the scope of consciousness and one's grasp of reality, extends from the phasal organization of primitive society, with its division into age groups, to the modern "psychology of life's stages." In practically all cultures, therefore, the division of the world into four, and the opposition of day and night, play an extremely important part. Because light, consciousness, and cul-

[8] Danzel, *Magie und Geheimwissenschaft*, pp. 31 f.

ture are made possible only by the separation of the World Parents, the original uroboros dragon often appears as the chaos dragon. From the standpoint of the orderly light-and-day world of consciousness, all that existed before was night, darkness, chaos, tohubohu. The inward as well as the outward development of culture begins with the coming of light and the separation of the World Parents. Not only do day and night, back and front, upper and lower, inside and outside, I and You, male and female, grow out of this development of opposites and differentiate themselves from the original promiscuity, but opposites like "sacred" and "profane," "good" and "evil," are now assigned their place in the world.

The embedding of the germinal ego in the uroboros corresponds sociologically to the state in which collective ideas prevailed, and the group and group consciousness were dominant. In this state the ego was not an autonomous, individualized entity with a knowledge, morality, volition, and activity of its own; it functioned solely as part of the group, and the group with its superordinate power was the only real subject.

The emancipation of the ego, when the "son" establishes itself as an ego and separates the World Parents, is accomplished on several different levels.

The fact that, at the beginning of conscious development, everything is still interfused, and that each archetypal stage of transformation such as the separation of the World Parents always reveals to us different levels of action, with different effects and values, makes the task of presentation extraordinarily difficult.

The experience of "being different," which is the primary fact of nascent ego consciousness and which occurs in the dawnlight of discrimination, divides the world into subject and object; orientation in time and space succeeds man's vague existence in the dim mists of prehistory and constitutes his early history.

Besides disentangling itself from its fusion with nature and the group, the ego, having now opposed itself to the nonego as another datum of experience, begins simultaneously to constellate its independence of nature as independence of the body.

Later we shall have to come back to the question of how the ego and consciousness experience their own reality by distinguishing themselves from the body. This is one of the fundamental facts of the human mind and its discovery of itself as something distinct from nature. Early man is in the same case as the infant and small child: his body and his "inside" are part of an alien world. The acquisition of voluntary muscular movement, i.e., the fact that the ego discovers, in its own "person," that its conscious will can control the body, may well be the basic experience at the root of all magic. The ego, having its seat, as it were, in the head, in the cerebral cortex, and experiencing the nether regions of the body as something strange to it, an alien reality, gradually begins to recognize that essential portions of this nether corporeal world are subject to its will and volition. It discovers that the "sovereign power of thought" is a real and actual fact: the hand in front of my face, and the foot lower down, do what I will. The obviousness of these facts should not blind us to the enormous impression which this very early discovery must make, and unquestionably has made, on every infantile ego nucleus. If technics are an extension of the "tool" as a means for dominating the world around us, then the tool in its turn is nothing but an extension of the voluntary musculature. Man's will to dominate nature is but an extension and projection of that fundamental experience of the ego's potential power over the body, discovered in the voluntariness of muscular movement.

Opposition between ego and body is, as we have said, an original condition. Containment in the uroboros and its supremacy over the ego mean, on the bodily level, that ego and consciousness are at the outset continually at the mercy of the instincts, impulses, sensations, and reactions deriving from the world of the body. To begin with, this ego, existing first as a point and then as an island, knows nothing of itself and consequently nothing of its difference. As it grows stronger, it detaches itself more and more from the world of the body. This leads finally, as we know, to a state of systematized ego consciousness where the entire bodily realm is to a large extent unconscious, and the conscious system is split off from the body as the representative of unconscious processes. Though the split is not in effect so drastic as this, the illusion of it is so powerful and so real for the ego that the body region and the unconscious can only be rediscovered with a great effort. In yoga, for instance, a strenuous attempt is made to reconnect the conscious mind with the unconscious bodily processes. This exercise may, if overdone, lead to illness, but in itself it is quite sensible.

In the beginning, the realm of ego consciousness and the spiritual and psychic realm are indissolubly united with the body. Instinct and volition are as little divided as instinct and consciousness. Even in modern man, depth psychology has found that the division which has resulted between these two spheres in the course of cultural development—for their mutual tensions constitute what we call culture—is largely an illusion. The activity of instinct lies behind actions which the ego coordinates with its sphere of decision and volition, and to an even higher degree instincts and archetypes are at the back of our conscious attitudes and orientations. But, whereas in modern man there is at any rate the possibility of decision and conscious orientation, the psychology of archaic man and of the child is marked by a mingling of these spheres. Volitions, moods, emotions, instincts, and somatic reactions are still for all practical purposes fused together. The same applies to the original ambivalence of affects, which are later resolved into antithetical positions. Love and hate, joy and sorrow, pleasure and pain, attraction and repulsion, yes and no, are at first juxtaposed and interfused, and do not possess the antithetical character they subsequently appear to have.

Depth psychology has made the discovery that even today the opposites lie closer together and are more intimately connected than their actual degree of separation would lead one to suppose. Not only in the neurotic, but in the normal person too, the poles are hard side by side; pleasure turns to pain, hate to love, sorrow to joy, far more readily than we would expect. This

111

can be seen most clearly in children. Laughing and crying, starting a thing and then stopping it, liking and disliking, follow fast
on one another's heels. No position is fixed, and none is a flat
contradiction of its opposite, but both exist peaceably side by
side and are realized in closest succession. Influences stream in
and out from all sides; environment, ego, and interior world,
objective tendencies, consciousness, and bodily tendencies operate simultaneously, and all the while no ego worth mentioning,
or only a very diminutive ego, arranges, centers, accepts and
rejects.

It is the same with the pair of opposites male and female.
Man's original hermaphroditic disposition is still largely conserved in the child. Without the disturbing influences from outside which foster the visible manifestation of sexual differences
at an early date, children would just be children; and actively
masculine features are in fact as common and effective in girls
as are passively feminine ones in boys. It is only cultural influences, whose differentiating tendencies govern the child's early
upbringing, that lead to an identification of the ego with the
monosexual tendencies of the personality and to the suppression, or repression, of one's congenital contrasexuality. (See
Part II.)

The split between inside and outside in archaic man and the
child is no more complete than that between good and evil. The
fancied playmate is real and unreal at once, like everything else,
and the image in the dream as real as the reality outside. Here
the true "Reality of the Soul" [9] still holds sway, that versatile
make-believe of which the wizardry of art and fairy tale is a reflection. Here each of us can be all things, and so-called external
reality has not yet made us forget the equally powerful reality
within.

Yet whereas the child's world is entirely governed by these
laws, in the world of archaic man only certain portions of his
reality have remained childish and original in this sense. There
is a world reality besides, where he masters his surroundings

[9] [Reference to Jung's volume *Wirklichkeit der Seele*.—TRANS.]

112

rationally and practically, organizes and elaborates; in other words, has the sort of culture we find intensified in modern man.

Nor, as we have said, is the division between good and evil present in the beginning. Man and world have not yet been divided into pure and impure, good and bad; there is at most the difference between that which works, is pregnant with mana and loaded with taboo, and that which does not work. But what works is pre-eminent, beyond good and evil. Whatever works is powerful, be it black or white, or both, simultaneously or by turns. The consciousness of archaic man is no more discriminating than a child's. There are good magicians and bad magicians, but their range of action seems far more important than the goodness or badness of the act. What we find so difficult to understand is the credulous intensity of this level of existence, where seeming evil is accepted as readily as good, and there is, apparently, not even the beginning of what man subsequently claims to experience and recognize as a moral world order.

Within the original uroboric unity there were numerous organic and symbolic layers lying close together, which only became distinct and visible at the stage of separation. This confirms Jung's view of the polyvalence of a developmentally early constitution, and hence of the infantile constitution. In later stages different layers of symbols detach themselves from the original promiscuity and confront the ego. World and nature, the unconscious and the body, the group and the family, are all different systems of relationship which, as independent parts separated off from the ego and from one another, now exert a variety of effects and build up a multiplicity of systems operating together with the ego. But this unfolding of position and counterposition only partly describes the situation that has arisen at the stage of the separation of the World Parents.

The transition from the uroboros to the adolescent stage was characterized by the emergence of fear and the death feeling, because the ego, not yet invested with full authority, felt the supremacy of the uroboros as an overwhelming danger. This change of emotional tonality must be emphasized at all phases of conscious development, and its presence as an undertone indicates emotional components whose significance has still to be discussed.

We have already seen, when dealing with the adolescent, how the change from passivity to activity at first took the form of resistance, defiance, and a self-division which, at that stage, led to self-destruction. Similarly, at the stage of the son who separates the World Parents, and its equivalent the fight with the dragon, there is not only a change of content but a changed level of emotionality.

The action of the ego in separating the World Parents is a struggle, a creative act, and in later sections devoted to the fight with the dragon we shall give prominence to this aspect, and also to the decisive change of personality that follows from this resolve to overcome the danger.

For the moment, however, we shall concern ourselves with the other aspect of this deed: the fact that it is experienced as guilt, and moreover as original guilt, a fall. But first we have to discuss the emotional situation, and to understand that this deed, though it manifests itself as the coming of light, and as the creation of the world and of consciousness, is vitiated by a sense of suffering and loss so strong as almost to offset the creative gain.

Through the heroic act of world creation and division of opposites, the ego steps forth from the magic circle of the uroboros and finds itself in a state of loneliness and discord. With the emergence of the fully fledged ego, the paradisal situation is abolished; the infantile condition, in which life was regulated by something ampler and more embracing, is at an end, and with it the natural dependence on that ample embrace. We may think of this paradisal situation in terms of religion, and say that everything was controlled by God; or we may formulate it ethically, and say that everything was still good and that evil had not yet come into the world. Other myths dwell on the "effortlessness" of the Golden Age, when nature was bountiful,

114

and toil, suffering, and pain did not exist; others stress the "ever-lastingness," the deathlessness, of such an existence.

The factor common to all these early stages is that psychologically they tell us something about a pre-ego stage when there was no division into a conscious and an unconscious world. To that extent all these stages are pre-individual and collective. There was no feeling of loneliness, which is the necessary concomitant of egohood and particularly of an ego conscious of its own existence.

Ego consciousness not only brings a sense of loneliness; it also introduces suffering, toil, trouble, evil, sickness, and death into man's life as soon as these are perceived by an ego. By discovering itself, the lonely ego simultaneously perceives the negative and relates to it, so that it at once establishes a connection between these two facts, taking its own genesis as guilt, and suffering, sickness, and death as condign punishment. The whole life feeling of primitive man is haunted by the negative influences all around him, and at the same time by the consciousness that he is to blame for everything negative that befalls. This is as much as to say that for primitive man chance does not exist; everything negative comes from the infringement of a taboo, even though the infringement be unconscious. His *Weltanschauung*, or his conception of cause and effect, is for the most part emotionally colored, because based on a life feeling that has been profoundly disturbed by the growth of ego consciousness. Gone is the original uroboric life feeling, for the more differentiated and self-related his ego consciousness becomes, the more it feels its own pettiness and impotence, with the result that dependence on the powers that be becomes the dominant feeling. The torpor of the animal, but also, as Rilke says, its "open" gaze, is now lost.

> And yet within the warm and watchful beast
> is weight and care of some great melancholy.
> For, to the beast as well, there always clings
> what often overwhelms us—memory,
> as though the goal to which we strive had once

> been nearer and more trustful, and its contact
> immeasurably tender. All is distance here;
> there it was breath. Compared with that first home
> the second seems a hybrid thing and windy.
> O rapture of the little creature which
> stays ever in the womb that brought it forth!
> Joy of the gnat that on its wedding day
> is womb-enspasmed still—for womb is all.

But for the creature that has become an ego, only the "other" counts:

> This is called fate: this being opposite
> and being ever more in opposition.[10]

This being opposite and no longer contained in the womb is the dark feeling that pervades consciousness wherever the ego finds itself isolated and alone.

It is the mark of man to be pitted against the world, it is his sorrow and his specialty; for what at first seems loss turns out a positive gain. But not only that; on a higher level there falls to man, and to man alone, the essential mark of "relatedness," because he, as an individual, enters into relations with an object, be it another man, a thing, the world, his own soul, or God. He then becomes part of a higher and qualitatively different unity, which is no longer the pre-egoid unity of uroboric containment, but an alliance in which the ego, or rather the self, the totality of the individual, is preserved intact. But this new unity is likewise based on the "opposition" that came into the world with the separation of the World Parents and the dawning of ego consciousness.

Only with the separation of the World Parents was the world made dual, as is said in the Jewish midrash. This separation is due to the fundamental cleavage into a conscious portion of the personality, whose center is the ego, and a far greater unconscious portion. The partition also causes a modification of the ambivalence principle. Whereas, originally, the opposites could function side by side without undue strain and without exclud-

[10] Rainer Maria Rilke, Eighth Elegy.

ing one another, now, with the development and elaboration of the opposition between conscious and unconscious, they fly apart. That is to say, it is no longer possible for an object to be loved and hated at the same time. Ego and consciousness identify themselves in principle with one side of the opposition and leave the other in the unconscious, either preventing it from coming up at all, i.e., consciously suppressing it, or else repressing it, i.e., eliminating it from consciousness without being aware of doing so. Only deep psychological analysis can then discover the unconscious counterposition. But so long as the ego at the prepsychological level is unaware of this, it remains oblivious of the other side, and consequently loses the wholeness and completeness of its world picture.

This loss of wholeness and of total unconscious integration with the world is experienced as the primary loss; it is the original deprivation which occurs at the very outset of the ego's evolution.

We could call this primary loss the primary castration. It must be emphasized, however, that primary castration, in contrast to castration on the matriarchal level, has no genital reference. In the former case the separation and loss is like being cut off from a larger context; on the personalistic level, for instance, it is felt as separation from the mother's body. It is a self-imposed loss, a severance accomplished by the ego itself but nevertheless experienced as loss and guilt. This self-liberation is a severing of the umbilical cord, not a mutilation; but with it the greater unity, the mother-child identity within the uroboros, is shattered for good.

The threat of matriarchal castration impends over an ego that has not yet broken its tie with the Great Mother, and we showed how, for such an ego, self-loss was symbolically identical with loss of the penis. But the primary loss at the stage of the separation of the World Parents concerns a complete individual who makes himself independent by this very act. Here the loss has an emotional coloring, is expressed in guilt feelings, and has its source in the loss of *participation mystique*.

117

The sloughing off of the bisexual uroboros can have either a paternal or a maternal accent, and may be felt as a severance from the father-god or from the paradisal mother situation, or both.

Primary castration is correlated with original sin and the loss of paradise. In the Judaeo-Christian sphere of culture the old mythological motifs were consciously modified and reinterpreted, so that we find only vestiges of the myth of the separation of the World Parents. Nor does the literature contain anything more than a faint echo of the Babylonian version, where the divine hero Marduk cuts up the serpent Tiamat, Mother of Chaos, and builds the world from the pieces. In accordance with the Hebrew conception of God and the world, the moral element now occupies the foreground, knowledge of good and evil is accounted a sin, and relinquishment of the pristine uroboric state is degraded to a punitive expulsion from paradise.

The theme is not, however, confined to non-Greek cultures. Among the pre-Socratics, Anaximander held that the principle of original guilt is cosmic. In this sense is interpreted his saying:

The origin of all things is the Boundless. And into that from which they arise they pass away once more, as is meet; for they make reparation and satisfaction to one another for their injustice according to the ordering of time.[10a]

The original unity of the world and God is supposed to have been cleft asunder by some prehuman guilt, and the world born of this rupture must accordingly suffer punishment. The same principle runs through Orphism and Pythagoreanism.

In the view of the Gnostics this feeling of privation became the driving force of the world process, though they introduced a highly paradoxical twist, the reasons for which cannot be analyzed more closely here. On account of this complex feeling of loss, existence in the world meant being alone and cut off; man was utterly forsaken, abandoned to the alien element. His original pleromatic home, from which was derived the part worthy

[10a] Trans. by Burnet, in *Early Greek Philosophy*, p. 52.

of redemption, is clearly uroboric, although too much stress is laid on the spirit-pneuma aspect. The fundamental dualistic conception, in Gnosticism, of a higher spiritual part and a lower material part presupposes the separation of the World Parents. Despite that, the pleroma has the uroboric character of completeness, wholeness, undifferentiatedness, wisdom, primordiality, etc., except that here the uroboros has more of a masculine and paternal nature, with feminine Sophia features shining through, in contrast to the maternal uroboros where the transpicuous features are masculine. Consequently, in Gnosticism, the way of salvation lies in heightening consciousness and returning to the transcendent spirit, with loss of the unconscious side; whereas uroboric salvation through the Great Mother demands the abandonment of the conscious principle and a homecoming to the unconscious.

How powerful these basic archetypal images of the psyche are can be seen from the cabala more clearly than from any other cultural phenomenon. Judaism has always tried to eliminate the mythologizing tendency and the whole realm of the psyche in favor of consciousness and morality. But in the esoteric doctrines of the cabala, which is the hidden, pulsing lifeblood of Judaism, a compensatory countermovement persisted underground. Not only does the cabala reveal a large number of archetypal dominants, but, through them, it has had an important effect on the development and history of Judaism.

Thus, in a treatise on the doctrine of evil in the Lurian cabala, we read:

Man is not only the end purpose of creation, nor is his dominion limited to this world alone, but on him depends the perfection of the higher worlds and of God himself.

This saying, emphasizing as it does the distinctly anthropocentric standpoint of the cabala, forms the basis of the following declaration:

In the view of the cabala, original sin consisted essentially in this: that damage was done to the Deity. Concerning the nature of this damage there

119

are various views. The most widely accepted is that the First Man, Adam Kadmon, made a division between King and Queen, and that he sundered the Shekinah from union with her spouse, and from the whole hierarchy of the Sephiroth.[11]

Here we have the old archetype of the separation of the World Parents, but in a state of purity unknown even to the Gnostics, by whom the cabala may conceivably have been influenced. Generally speaking, the influence of Gnosticism seems highly questionable in those numerous passages where archetypal formulations and images occur in the cabalistic writings, as for instance in Nathan of Gaza, the disciple and inspirer of Sabbatai Zebi.[12] We must resign ourselves to the fact that this influence, like the migration theory, is secondary, and we shall have to substitute for it Jung's discovery, since confirmed by all depth-psychological analysis, that archetypal images are operative in every man and appear spontaneously whenever the layer of the collective unconscious is activated.

In the great religions, the primal deed, the separation of the World Parents, is theologized. An attempt is made to rationalize and moralize the undeniable sense of deficiency that attaches to the emancipated ego. Interpreted as sin, apostasy, rebellion, disobedience, this emancipation is in reality the fundamental liberating act of man which releases him from the yoke of the unconscious and establishes him as an ego, a conscious individual. But because this act, like every act and every liberation, entails sacrifice and suffering, the decision to take such a step is all the more momentous.

The separation of the World Parents is not merely an interruption of the original cohabitation, and a destruction of the perfect cosmic state symbolized by the uroboros. This in itself, or in conjunction with what we have called the primary loss, would be enough to induce a feeling of original guilt, precisely because the uroboric state is by nature a state of wholeness, embracing the world and man. The decisive thing, however, is

[11] Tishby, "The Doctrine of Evil and the 'Klipah' in the Lurian Cabala."
[12] Scholem, *Major Trends in Jewish Mysticism*, pp. 283 f.

that this separation is not experienced only as passive suffering and loss, but also as an actively destructive deed. It is symbolically identical with killing, sacrifice, dismemberment, and castration.

Now it is a very striking fact that what was done to the youthful lover by the maternal uroboros is at this point done to the uroboros itself. In mythology it happens just as often that the son-god castrates the father-god as that he cuts up the primordial dragon and builds the world from it. Mutilation—a theme which also occurs in alchemy—is the condition of all creation. So here we come upon two archetypal motifs that belong absolutely together and appear in all creation myths. Without the slaying of the old parents, their dismemberment and neutralization, there can be no beginning. We shall have to examine at some length this problem of parental murder. Obviously it entails a genuine and necessary guilt.

The emancipation of the youthful lover from the uroboros begins with an act which was shown to be a negative act, an act of destruction. Its psychological interpretation then enabled us to understand the symbolical nature of the "masculinity" which lies at the root of all consciousness.

We described the adolescent's advance towards independence and liberation as "self-division." To become conscious of oneself, to be conscious at all, begins with saying "no" to the uroboros, to the Great Mother, to the unconscious. And when we scrutinize the acts upon which consciousness and the ego are built up, we must admit that to begin with they are all negative acts. To discriminate, to distinguish, to mark off, to isolate oneself from the surrounding context—these are the basic acts of consciousness. Indeed, experimentation as *the* scientific method is a typical example of this process: a natural connection is broken down and something is isolated and analyzed, for the motto of all consciousness is *determinatio est negatio*. As against the tendency of the unconscious to combine and melt down, to say to everything *"tat tvam asi"*—"that art thou"— consciousness strikes back with the reply "I am *not* that."

121

Ego formation can only proceed by way of distinction from the nonego and consciousness only emerge where it detaches itself from what is unconscious; and the individual only arrives at individuation when he marks himself off from the anonymous collective.

The breakdown of the uroboric initial state leads to differentiation in duality, decombination of the original ambivalence, division of the hermaphroditic constitution, and the splitting of the world into subject and object, inside and outside, and to the creation of good and evil, which are only discriminated with the expulsion from the uroboric Garden of Paradise where the opposites lie down together. Naturally enough, as soon as man becomes conscious and acquires an ego, he feels himself a divided being, since he also possesses a formidable other side which resists the process of becoming conscious. That is, he finds himself in doubt, and so long as his ego remains immature, this doubt may drive him to desperation and even to suicide, which always means a murder of the ego and a self-mutilation that culminates with his death in the Great Mother.

Until it has finally consolidated itself and is able to stand on its own feet, which, as we shall see, is only possible after the successful fight with the dragon, the adolescent ego remains insecure. Its insecurity derives from the internal split into two opposed psychic systems, and of these the conscious system, with which the ego identifies itself, is still feeble, undeveloped, and somewhat hazy about the meaning of its specific principle. This inner insecurity, taking the form, as we have said, of doubt, produces two complementary phenomena that are characteristic of the adolescent phase. The first is narcissism with its excessive egocentricity, self-complacency, and self-absorption; the other is *Weltschmerz*.

Narcissism is a necessary transitional phase during the consolidation of the ego. The emancipation of ego consciousness from thralldom to the unconscious leads, like all emancipation, to an exaggeration of one's own position and importance. The "puberty of ego consciousness" is accompanied by a depreciation of the place from which one came—the unconscious. This deflation of the unconscious tends in the same direction as secondary personalization and the exhaustion of emotional components (cf. Part II). The meaning of all these processes lies in strengthening the principle of ego consciousness. But the danger inherent in this line of development is exaggerated self-importance, a megalomaniac ego consciousness which thinks itself independent of everything, and which begins by devaluing and repressing the unconscious and ends by denying it altogether. Overvaluation of the ego, as a symptom of immature consciousness, is compensated by a depressive self-destruction which, in the form of *Weltschmerz* and self-hatred, often culminates in suicide, all these being characteristic symptoms of puberty.

An analysis of this state discloses a feeling of guilt whose source is transpersonal; i.e., it goes back beyond the entanglements of the personalistic "family romance." The heinous deed of separating the World Parents appears as original guilt. But— and this is the important thing—it is in a sense the World Parents, the unconscious itself, which makes the accusation, and not the ego. As a representative of the ancient law, the uroboric unconscious struggles hard to prevent the emancipation of her son, consciousness, and so once again we find ourselves back in the orbit of the Terrible Mother who wants to destroy the son. So long as the conscious ego bows down before this accusation and accepts the death sentence, it is behaving like the son-lover and, like him, will end in self-destruction.

It is very different when the son turns the tables upon the Terrible Mother and adopts her destructive attitude, directing it not against himself but against her. This process is represented mythologically in the fight with the dragon. Summing up the change of personality which we shall be examining later as a consequence of this fight, we can say that the process corresponds psychologically to the formation of the conscious, "higher ego" of the hero, and to the raising of the buried treasure, Knowledge. Nevertheless the ego is bound to feel its aggression as guilt, because killing, dismemberment, castration, and sacrifice remain guilt even though they serve the necessary purpose of vanquishing such an enemy as the uroboros dragon.

This destruction is closely associated with the act of eating and assimilation, and is often represented as such. The formation of consciousness goes hand-in-hand with a fragmentation of the world continuum into separate objects, parts, figures, which can only then be assimilated, taken in, introjected, made conscious—in a word, "eaten." When the sun-hero, having been swallowed by the dragon of darkness, cuts out its heart and eats it, he is taking into himself the essence of this object. Consequently aggression, destruction, dismemberment, and killing are intimately associated with the corresponding bodily functions of eating, chewing, biting, and particularly with the symbolism of the teeth as instruments of these activities, all of which are essential for the formation of an independent ego. In this lies the deeper meaning of aggression during the early phases of development. Far from being sadistic, it is a positive and indispensable preparation for the assimilation of the world.

But, precisely because of its elemental bond with the world of nature, the primitive mind has always regarded killing, even the destruction of animals and plants, as an outrage upon the world order that cried out for expiation. The spirits of the slain take their revenge unless propitiated. Fear of the vengeance of the powers that be for the separation of the World Parents and for man's criminal emancipation from the power of the divine uroboros, this is the feeling of dread and guilt, this the original sin, with which the history of mankind opens.

The struggle against this fear, against the danger of being swallowed up again in the initial chaos through a regression that undoes the work of emancipation, is enacted in all its modulations in the fight with the dragon. Not until then will the ego and consciousness be firmly established. The son of the World Parents has to prove himself a hero in this fight; the ego, newborn and helpless, has to transform itself into a procreator and conqueror. The victorious hero stands for a new beginning, the beginning of creation, but a creation which is the work of man and which we call culture, as opposed to natural creation which is given to man at the outset and overshadows his beginnings.

As we have already pointed out, it is consistent with the conscious-unconscious structure of the opposites that the unconscious should be regarded as predominantly feminine, and consciousness as predominantly masculine. This correlation is self-evident, because the unconscious, alike in its capacity to bring to birth and to destroy through absorption, has feminine affinities. The feminine is conceived mythologically under the aspect of this archetype; uroboros and Great Mother are both feminine dominants, and all the psychic constellations over which they rule are under the dominance of the unconscious. Conversely, its opposite, the system of ego consciousness, is masculine. With it are associated the qualities of volition, decision, and activity as contrasted with the determinism and blind "drives" of the preconscious, egoless state.

The development of ego consciousness, as we have sketched it, consisted in its gradual emancipation from the overpowering embrace of the unconscious, which was exerted to the full by the uroboros and to a lesser degree by the Great Mother. Observing the process more closely, we found that its central features were the growing independence of masculinity, originally present only in the germ, and the systematization of ego consciousness, of which, in the early history of mankind as in early infancy, only the smallest beginnings could be detected.[13]

---

[13] Later we shall have to examine how far the feminine dominants, uroboros and Great Mother, differ as to the role they play in the psychology of men and women respectively. The conscious ego system which we have described as "masculine"—a term dictated not by caprice but by mythology—is equally present in woman, and its development is just as important for her culture as it is for a man's. Conversely the "feminine" system of the unconscious is also present in man, and, as in the case of woman, it determines his natural existence and his relation to the creative background. But here we must point to an essential difference in the structure of male and female which has never been sufficiently emphasized. Man experiences the "masculine" structure of his conscious as peculiarly his own, and the "feminine" unconscious as something alien to him, whereas woman feels at home in her unconscious and out of her element in consciousness.

125

The stage of separation of the World Parents which initiates the independence of the ego and consciousness by giving rise to the principle of opposites is therefore also the stage of increasing masculinity. Ego consciousness stands in manly opposition to the feminine unconscious. This strengthening of consciousness is borne out by the laying down of taboos and of moral attitudes which delimit the conscious from the unconscious by substituting knowing action for unwitting impulse. The meaning of ritual, irrespective of the useful effects which primitive man expects from it, lies precisely in strengthening the conscious system. The magical forms by means of which archaic man comes to terms with his surroundings are, all other considerations apart, anthropocentric systems of world domination. In his rituals he makes himself the responsible center of the cosmos; on him depends the rising of the sun, the fertility of crops, and all the doings of the gods. These projections and the various procedures by which the Great Individuals distinguish themselves from the herd as chiefs, medicine men, or divine kings, and the demons, spirits, and gods are crystallized out from a welter of indeterminate "powers," we know to be expressions of a centering process that imposes order upon the chaos of unconscious events and leads to the possibility of conscious action. Although nature and the unconscious are ordinarily experienced by primitive man as a field of unseen forces which leave no room for chance, life remains chaotic for the germinal ego, dark and impenetrable, so long as no orientation is possible with regard to these forces. But orientation comes through ritual, through the subjugation of the world by magic, which imposes world order. Even though this order is different from the kind we impose, the connection between our conscious order and the magical order of early man can be proved at all points. The important thing is that consciousness as the acting center precedes consciousness as the cognitive center, in the same way as ritual precedes myth, or magic ceremonial and ethical action precede the scientific view of the world and anthropological knowledge.

126

The center common to conscious action through the will and to conscious knowledge through cognition is, however, the ego. From being acted upon by external forces, it develops slowly into the agent, just as it ascends from the state of being over-powered by revealed knowledge into the light of conscious knowledge. Once again, this process is first accomplished not in the collective parts of the group, but only in the great, i.e., differentiated, individuals who are the representative bearers of the group's consciousness. They are the institutional fore-runners and leaders whom the group follows. The ritual marriage between fructifier and earth goddess, between king and queen, becomes the model for all marriages between members of the collective. The immortal soul of the divine king Osiris becomes the immortal soul of each and every Egyptian, even as Christ the Saviour becomes the Christ-soul of every Christian, the self within us. In the same way, the function of the chief, which is to will and to decide, becomes the model for all sub-sequent acts of free will in the ego of the individual; and the law-making function, originally attributed to God and later to the mana personality, has in modern man become his inner court of conscience.

We shall be discussing this process of introjection later, but for the moment we shall formulate the masculinization of con-sciousness and its theoretic importance thus: through the mas-culinization and emancipation of ego consciousness the ego be-comes the "hero." The story of the hero, as set forth in the myths, is the history of this self-emancipation of the ego, struggling to free itself from the power of the unconscious and to hold its own against overwhelming odds.

B. The Hero Myth

Nature subdues nature.

I

THE BIRTH OF THE HERO

WITH THE HERO MYTH we enter upon a new phase of stadial development. A radical shift in the center of gravity has occurred. In all creation myths the dominant feature was the cosmic quality of the myth, its universality; but now the myth focuses attention upon the world as the center of the universe, the spot upon which man stands. This means, in terms of stadial development, not only that man's ego consciousness has achieved independence, but that his total personality has detached itself from the natural context of the surrounding world and the unconscious. Although the separation of the World Parents is, strictly speaking, an integral part of the hero myth, the developments which, at that stage, could only be represented in cosmic symbols now enter the phase of humanization and personality formation. Thus the hero is the archetypal forerunner of mankind in general. His fate is the pattern in accordance with which the masses of humanity must live, and always have lived, however haltingly and distantly; and however short of the ideal man they have fallen, the stages of the hero myth have become constituent elements in the personal development of every individual.

The process of masculinization finally crystallizes out at this point and proves to be decisive for the structure of ego consciousness. With the birth of the hero the primordial struggle begins—the struggle with the First Parents. This problem, in personal and transpersonal form, dominates the hero's whole existence, his birth, his fight with the dragon, and his transformation. By gaining possession of the masculine and feminine sides of himself, which are not to be thought of as "paternal" and "maternal," and building up an inner core of personality

131

in whose structure the old and the new stages are integrated, the hero completes a pattern of development which is collectively embodied in the mythological projections of the hero myth, and has also left individual traces in the growth of human personality (Part II).

❖   ❖   ❖

The real significance of the dragon fight, or rather of that part of it which is concerned with the slaying of the World Parents, can only be understood when we have looked more deeply into the nature of the hero. The nature of the hero, however, is closely connected with his birth and with the problem of his dual parentage.

The fact that the hero has two fathers or two mothers is a central feature in the canon of the hero myth. Besides his personal father there is a "higher," that is to say an archetypal, father figure, and similarly an archetypal mother figure appears beside the personal mother. This double descent, with its contrasted personal and suprapersonal parental figures, constellates the drama of the hero's life. An important part of the analysis of the dragon fight has already been set forth in Jung's *Psychology of the Unconscious;* [1] but the early form of this work requires that the problem it broaches be corrected, supplemented, and systematized from the standpoint of the later developments of analytical psychology.

The ambiguity of the problem of the First Parents, with its dual and even contradictory meanings, has brought confusion into our analytical procedures right down to the present day. The final laying of the ghost which, in the form of the Oedipus complex, haunts our Western minds must be made the basis for any genuine understanding of the psychic phenomena we are concerned with here. These phenomena are fundamental so far

[1] [The author cites the original version, *Wandlungen und Symbole der Libido* (trans. as *Psychology of the Unconscious*), because the 1952 revision, *Symbole der Wandlung,* had not been published when he wrote. The original version is therefore also cited here, although the (very considerably) revised version is now available in German, as *Symbole der Wandlung,* and in English, as *Symbols of Transformation.* See bibliography.—TRANS.]

as the future psychological development of Western man is concerned, and hence they also affect his ethical and religious development.

As A. Jeremias [2] has pointed out and amply proved, the essence of the mythological canon of the hero-redeemer is that he is fatherless or motherless, that one of the parents is often divine, and that the hero's mother is frequently the Mother Goddess herself or else betrothed to a god.

These mothers are virgin mothers, which is not to say that what psychoanalysis has attempted to read into this fact is necessarily correct.[2a] As everywhere in the ancient world, virginity simply means not belonging to any man personally; virginity is in essence sacred, not because it is a state of physical inviolateness, but because it is a state of psychic openness to God. We have seen that virginity was an essential aspect of the Great Mother, of her creative power, which is not dependent on any personal mate. But there is also a procreative masculine element at work in her. At the uroboric level this element is anonymous; later it becomes subordinated to the Great Mother as phallic energy, and still later it appears by her side as her consort. Finally, in the patriarchal world, she is dethroned by her prince consort and is herself subordinated.[3] But always she retains her archetypal effectiveness.

The hero's birth is expressly attributed to a virgin. The virgin and the leviathan which the hero has to conquer (*illus. 22 and 23*) are two aspects of the mother archetype: beside the dark and terrible mother there stands another, bright and beneficent. And just as the fearful dragon aspect of the Great Mother, the "Old Woman of the West," is, as an archetypal image of humanity, eternal, so the friendly aspect, the bountiful, immortally

---

[2] *Handbuch der altorientalischen Geisteskultur*, pp. 205 f. The mythological material is supplemented and supported by ethnological data. Belief in the virgin birth of the hero, as Briffault (*The Mothers*, Vol. II, p. 450) has shown, is world-wide, prevailing in North and South America, Polynesia, Asia, Europe, and Africa.

[2a] Rank, *The Myth of the Birth of the Hero.*

[3] Przyluski, "Ursprünge und Entwicklung des Kultes der Mutter-Göttin."

beautiful Virgin Mother of the sun-hero has its eternal archetype in the "Maid of the East," regardless of the changeover from matriarchate to patriarchate.[4]

The *kedeshoth*, like all the virgin mothers of heroes down to the Virgin Mary, are typical examples of identification with the female deity—Ashtaroth, for instance—who, in the embrace of the male, is willing to surrender only to something suprapersonal, to the god and nothing but the god. The peculiarity of feminine psychology that manifests itself here will have to be discussed in another place. In the present context, only its relation to the transpersonal is of importance. Consequently, besides the virgin mothers, there are other mothers for whom the men are mere ciphers, as Joseph was for Mary, or who only appear as the mortal fathers of a mortal twin. Whether the procreating deity appears as a monster or as the Dove of the Holy Ghost, and whether Zeus is transmogrified into lightning, a golden shower (*illus. 24*), or an animal, is of no consequence. Always the important thing about the hero's birth is that its extraordinary, suprahuman, or nonhuman nature proceeds from something extraordinary, suprahuman, or nonhuman—in other words, he is believed to have been begotten by a demon or a divinity. At the same time the utter absorption of the mother in the experience of birth, and especially the birth of a hero, forms the essence of the myth. Her astonishment at having given birth to something extraordinary is only an intensification of the birth experience as such—an intensification, in particular, of the miracle that a female is able to produce a male out of herself. This miracle was, as we know, originally ascribed by primitive woman to the *numinosum*, to the wind or the ancestral spirits. It is a prepatriarchal experience that antedates the time when procreation was felt to be causally connected with sexual inter-

---

[4] Cf. Drews, *Die Marienmythe*, for a wealth of material. But when Drews derives the birth of the sun-hero from the constellation Virgo, which rises in the east on December 24 at the lowest point of the winter solstice, he is confusing cause and effect. The designation of this constellation with the name Virgo is only a projection of the virgin archetype upon the heavens. It was called Virgo because in it the sun-hero is born every year as the sun.

course and hence with a man. Woman's primary experience of birth is matriarchal. It is not the man who is father to the child: the miracle of procreation springs from God. Thus the matriarchal phase is ruled, not by a personal father, but by a suprapersonal progenitor or power. The creative energy of woman comes alive in the miracle of birth, by virtue of which she becomes the "Great Mother" and "Earth Goddess." At the same time, it is precisely at this deepest and most archaic level that the virgin mother and bride of God is a living reality. Briffault has shown how impossible it is to understand the early history of mankind from the patriarchal standpoint, which is a late product of development bringing with it numerous revaluations. Accordingly, the primordial images which represent the mothers of heroes as virgins betrothed to a deity embody essential elements of woman's prepatriarchal experience. This early matriarchal stage can be recognized most easily from the modifications of the hero myth in its later patriarchal form. Whereas, to begin with, the Great Mother was the only true creator—like Isis who regenerates the dead Osiris (*illus. 29*)—later she is impregnated by a suprapersonal and divine progenitor. As we have seen, this god first appears in the old fertility ritual as the deified King, gradually strengthening his position until he finally becomes the patriarchal God-King. The earliest matriarchal stage is to be found in Egypt, at the Feast of Edfu,[5] where, to the accompaniment of orgies, the solemn "consummation of the embrace of Horus" led to the immediate conception of the young Horus King. Here begetter and begotten are still one, as we found to be the case in the domain of the Great Mother. The figure of the virgin bride of God has an analogy in the Luxor festival, where the royal priestess of Hathor joins herself, in an age-old predynastic ritual, to the sun-god for the production of the divine son. Later, in patriarchal times, this role was taken over by the king, representing the sun-god. The double nature of god and king is clearly expressed in the words:

[5] Blackman, "Myth and Ritual in Ancient Egypt," in Hooke, *Myth and Ritual*, p. 34.

"They found her as she slept in the beauty of the palace." After the word "they" Blackman adds, in parentheses, "the combination of god and king." The double nature of the father is reproduced in the Horus son he begets, who is "the son of his father and yet at the same time a son of the supreme God." [6]

This dual structure of the hero reappears in the archetypal motif of the Twin Brothers, one mortal, the other immortal, the most obvious instance being the Greek myth of the Dioscuri. Their mother, in the same night, conceived the immortal son in the embrace of Zeus and the mortal son in the embrace of her husband Tyndarus. Again, Herakles was begotten by Zeus, and his twin brother by Amphitryon. We are also told that the mother of Theseus was impregnated in the same night by Poseidon and by King Aegeus. There are countless other heroes who are the sons of mortal mothers and immortal gods. Besides Herakles and the Dioscuri, we would only mention as examples Perseus, Ion, and Romulus, Buddha, Karna, and Zoroaster.[7] It is evident that in all these cases the experience of the hero's dual nature, which became a factor of such extraordinary historical importance, no longer derives exclusively from woman's own experience of birth.

In the first place it is mankind itself, the collective, to whom the hero, just because he deviates from the human norm, appears as a hero and a divinely begotten being. Secondly, the idea of the hero's intrinsically dual nature derives from his own experience of himself. He is a human being like the others, mortal and collective like them, yet at the same time he feels himself a stranger to the community. He discovers within himself something which, although it "belongs" to him and is as it were part of him, he can only describe as strange, unusual, godlike. In the process of being exalted above the common level, in his heroic capacity as doer, seer, and creator, he feels himself like one "inspired," altogether extraordinary and the son of a god. Thus, through his difference from others, the hero experi-

[6] Erman, *Religion*, p. 53.
[7] Rank, op. cit.

ences his suprapersonal progenitor as quite different from his personal earthly father with whom he shares his corporal and collective nature. From this point of view we can also understand the doubling of the mother figure. The feminine correlate of the hero's divine progenitor is no longer the "personal mother," but likewise a suprapersonal figure. The mother responsible for his existence as a hero is the virgin mother to whom the god appeared. She too is a "spiritual" figure with transpersonal characteristics. She exists side by side with the personal mother who bore him in the body and, whether as animal or nurse, suckled him. Thus both the parental figures are there twice over for the hero, personally and transpersonally. Their confusion with one another, and particularly the projection of the transpersonal image upon the personal parents, is an abiding source of problems in childhood.

The transpersonal archetype can appear in three forms: as the bountiful and nourishing Earth Mother, as the Virgin Mother whom the god impregnates, and as the guardian of the soul's treasure. In the myths this ambiguity is often expressed as the conflict between nurse and princess, etc. In the case of the father figure the situation is more complicated, because an archetypal Earth Father seldom appears in patriarchal times. For reasons still to be examined, the personal father generally turns up as an "obstructive" figure alongside the divine progenitor. The virgin mother, however, who gives birth to the hero after being impregnated by a god, is a spiritual-feminine figure who opens herself to heaven. She has many forms, ranging from the innocent virgin who is overwhelmed by the heavenly messenger and the young girl who receives the god in an ecstasy of longing, to the sorrowful figure of Sophia, who gives birth to the divine son, the Logos, knowing that he is sent by God and that the hero's fate is suffering.

The birth of the hero and his fight with the dragon only become intelligible if the significance of masculinity has been understood. Only with the hero myth does the ego really come into its own as the bearer of masculinity, and for this reason we must make clear the symbolic nature of this masculinity. Such a clarification is essential if we are to distinguish the "masculine" from the "paternal," which is all the more necessary because the errors of psychoanalysis, with its false interpretation of the so-called Oedipus complex and of the totem mythology derived therefrom, have caused the greatest confusion.

The awakening ego experiences its masculinity, i.e., its increasingly active self-consciousness, as good and bad at once. It is thrust out from the maternal matrix, and it finds itself by distinguishing itself from this matrix. In the sociological sense too, the male, once he grows up and becomes independent, is thrust out from the matrix to the degree that he experiences and accentuates his own difference and singularity. It is one of the fundamental experiences of the male that sooner or later he must experience the matrix, with which he originally lived in *participation mystique,* as the "You," the nonego, something different and strange. Here as everywhere in this fundamental survey of conscious development, we must shake off the prejudice of the patriarchal family situation. The original situation of the human group is prepatriarchal, if we wish to avoid the somewhat dubious term matriarchal.

Even among animals we frequently find that the young generation of males is driven off and that the mother stays with the young females.[8] The original matriarchal family group of mothers and children presupposes from the start that the young male will have a strong propensity to roam. Even if he stays within the matriarchal group, he will associate with other males to form a hunter and fighter group which is co-ordinated with the feminine center of the matriarchate. This masculine group is necessarily mobile and enterprising; moreover, in the situation of constant danger in which it finds itself, it has an added inducement to develop its consciousness. Here already, perhaps, is fostered the contrast between the psychology of male groups and the matriarchal psychology of the female.

The matriarchal group with its mass-emotionality between

[8] Briffault, *The Mothers,* Vol. I, p. 122.

mothers and children, its stronger local ties and its greater inertia, is to a large extent bound to nature and the instincts. Menstruation, pregnancy, and lactation periods activate the instinctual side and strengthen woman's vegetative nature, as the psychology of modern woman still shows. In addition, there is the powerful earth-tie which arises with the development of gardening and agriculture by women, and the dependence of these arts upon the natural rhythm. The strengthening of *participation mystique* as a consequence of the matriarchal group living all huddled together in caves, houses, and villages also plays its part. All these factors reinforce the submergence in the unconscious which is a characteristic feature of the female group.

The male group, on the other hand, given to roaming, hunting, and making war, is a nomadic fighter group long before the domestication of animals produced the roving bands of cattlemen, even when the group is domiciled about a matriarchal family nucleus.

The matriarchal system of exogamy hinders the formation of male groups, because the men are obliged to marry outside their tribe and thus get dispersed, having to live matrilocally, as strangers in the wife's tribe.[9] The man is an alien in the clan into which he has married, but as a member of his own clan he is alienated from his place of residence. That is to say, when, as was originally always the case, he lives matrilocally, in his wife's place of residence, he is a tolerated stranger; but in his native place of residence, where his rights are still valid, he lives only occasionally. The autonomy of the female group is, as Briffault has shown, strengthened by this institution, since the line runs from grandmother to mother and from mother to daughter, while the formation of male groups is broken down. What Preuss says is therefore true of the male group, particularly if the nuclear group in the community is a matriarchal continuum of mothers, women, and children:

[9] Ibid., p. 251.

We must therefore conclude that brothers, as integral parts of a whole composed of parents and children, are at the outset in constant danger of succumbing to feminine influence, unless they can break free by holding themselves absolutely aloof. . . . All members of the exogamous group find themselves in this position.[10]

This is probably one of the reasons why men's societies came into being. In the course of time the male group steadily gains in strength, and political, military, and economic considerations eventually lead to organized male groups in the nascent city and state. Within these groups the cultivation of friendships is more important than rivalry, and more stress is laid on male similarity, and on dissimilarity from the female, than on mutual jealousies.

The youth group, made up of young men who are all contemporaries, is the place where the male really discovers himself for the first time. When he feels himself a stranger among women and at home among men, we have the sociological situation that corresponds to the self-discovery of ego consciousness. But "masculine," as we have said, is in no way identical with "father," least of all with a personal father figure, which cannot be supposed to have been very effective in the prepatriarchal family. The old women, the mothers-in-law and the mothers, stand at the head of the female group; and, as with many animals, a self-contained unit is formed to which everything belongs, including the boys up to a certain age. Exogamous admission to this group, by emphasizing the alien character of the male, exposes him to the influence of the evil mother-in-law, who is always the object of a powerful taboo, but not to the influence of any masculine authority.

In its original form, as a system of alliances among members of different age groups, the male group was organized on a strictly hierarchical basis. The rites that induct a man from one age group to another were accordingly rites of initiation. Everywhere these men's societies are of the greatest importance, not only for the development of masculinity and of the

[10] Preuss, *Die geistige Kultur der Naturvölker,* p. 73.

man's consciousness of himself, but for the development of culture as a whole.

This horizontal organization of age groups obviates personal conflict in the sense of a hostile father-son relationship, because the terms "father" and "son" connote group characteristics and not personal relations. The older men are "fathers," the young men "sons," and this collective group-solidarity is paramount. Conflicts, so far as they exist at all, are between the age groups and have a collective and archetypal, rather than a personal and individual, character. The initiations enable the young men to rise up in the scale and to perform various functions within the group. The trials of endurance are tests of the virility and stability of the ego; they are not to be taken personalistically as the "vengeance of the old" upon the young, any more than our matriculation is the vengeance of old men upon the rising generation, but merely a certificate of maturity for entry into the collective. In almost all cases, age brings an increase in power and importance based on the increased knowledge gained through successive initiations, so that the old men have little cause for resentment.

Male societies, secret societies, and friendly societies originated in matriarchal conditions. They are the natural complement to the supremacy of the matriarchate.[11] The self-experience of the ego, recognizing its specific affinity with the world of men and its distinction from the feminine matrix, marks a decisive stage in its development and is the precondition of independence. The initiation into the men's house, where the ego becomes conscious of itself, is a "mystery," vouchsafing a secret knowledge that always gravitates round the "higher masculinity." The higher masculinity here in point has no phallic or chthonic accent; its content is not, as in many initiations of young girls, sexuality, but its counterpole, spirit, which appears together with light, the sun, the head, and the eye as symbols of

---

[11] Even today we almost always find, in cases of male homosexuality, a matriarchal psychology where the Great Mother is unconsciously in the ascendant.

141

consciousness. This spirit is what is accentuated, and into it the initiations lead.

The men are ranked with the fathers, with the elders who are the "bulwark of law and order," [12] and hence with a world system which we may call, symbolically, "heaven," because it stands at the opposite pole to the feminine earth. The system embraces the whole sacrosanct and magical world order, down to the law and reality of the state. "Heaven" in this sense is not the abode of a deity, or a celestial locality; it simply denotes the spiritual pneuma principle which, in masculine cultures, gives birth not only to the patriarchal God, but to scientific philosophy as well. We use the symbolical expression "heaven" in order to characterize this complex realm in its entirety before it came to be differentiated, using for this purpose a comprehensive term in keeping with the mythological symbolism of early times.[13] It is immaterial whether this "heaven" is an indeterminate mass of "powers" or is animated by definite figures—spirits, ancestors, totem animals, gods. All these are representatives of the masculine spirit and the world of men, and they communicate themselves with or without violence to the neophyte on his expulsion from the maternal world. In the initiation rites, therefore, the young men are as it were swallowed up by the tutelary spirit of this masculine world and are reborn as children of the spirit rather than of the mother; they are sons of heaven, not just sons of earth. This spiritual rebirth signifies the birth of the "higher man" who, even on the primitive level, is associated with consciousness, the ego, and will power. Hence the fundamental correlation between heaven and masculinity. Therein lies the "higher activity" of conscious action, conscious knowledge, and conscious creation as distinct from the blind drive of unconscious forces. And precisely because the male group, in accordance not only with its "nature" but also with its sociological and psychological trends, requires the individual

[12] Goldenweiser, *Anthropology*, p. 409.

[13] Where, as in Egypt, we find a sky goddess and an earth god, Bachofen has correctly diagnosed a dominance of the Great Mother. The masculine principle, as yet undeveloped, lies dormant within her.

to act independently as a responsible ego, initiation into the men's society is always bound up with the testing and strengthening of consciousness, with what—mythologically speaking— one might call the "generation of the higher masculinity."

Fire and other symbols of wakefulness and alertness play an important part in the rites of initiation, where the young men have to "watch and wake," i.e., learn to overcome the body and the inertia of the unconscious by fighting against tiredness. Keeping awake and the endurance of fear, hunger, and pain go together as essential elements in fortifying the ego and schooling the will. Also, instruction and initiation into the traditional lore are as much part of the rites as the proofs of will power that have to be given. The criterion of manliness is an undaunted will, the ready ability to defend the ego and consciousness should need arise, and to master one's unconscious impulses and childish fears. Even today the initiation rites of puberty still have the character of an initiation into the secret world of the masculine spirit. Whether this spirit lies hidden in the stock of ancestral myths, in the laws and ordinances of the collective, or in the sacraments of religion, is all one. They are all expressions, differing in rank and degree, of the same masculine spirit which is the specific property of the male group.

This is the reason why women are forbidden, on pain of death, to be present at the initiations, and why they were originally excluded from the places of worship in all world-religions. The man's world, representing "heaven," stands for law and tradition, for the gods of aforetime, so far as they were masculine gods. It is no accident that all human culture, and not Western civilization alone, is masculine in character, from Greece and the Judaeo-Christian sphere of culture to Islam and India. Although woman's share in this culture is invisible and largely unconscious, we should not underestimate its significance and scope. The masculine trend, however, is towards greater co-ordination of spirit, ego, consciousness, and will. Because man discovers his true self in consciousness, and is a stranger to himself in the unconscious, which he must inevitably

143

experience as feminine, the development of masculine culture means development of consciousness.

Historically speaking, it seems to us that the phenomenon of totemism is of great importance for the development of "heaven" and the spiritual world of man. For this phenomenon, even though it originated in the matriarchal epoch, is specifically masculine in spirit.

Identification with the procreative spiritual principle is an extraordinarily important factor in the lives of primitives. Here, too, Freud made a vital discovery, though he distorted and misunderstood something even more vital. The totem is indeed partly a father, but it never has a personal character, let alone that of the personal father. On the contrary, the whole point of the ritual is that the procreative spirit should be experienced as something remote and different, and yet as "belonging." That is why the totem is very often an animal, but it can also be a plant, or even a thing. Although the soul of the primitive is much closer to "things" than we are, he can only establish identity with them by means of magical rites. His ritual induction into the spiritual world of the ancestral totem with the aid of the transforming mask indicates that the transpersonal *numinosum* ought to be experienced as the source from which he, as an initiate, derives his being. That is the meaning of all rituals where the purely personal has to be transcended. The initiations of puberty, like all initiations, aim at producing something suprapersonal, namely that part of the individual which is transpersonal and collective. Hence the production of this part is a second birth, a new generation through the masculine spirit, and is accompanied by the inculcation of secret doctrines, ancestral knowledge, and cosmic lore, in order to sever all ties with the purely familial existence of the immature.

The male group is the birthplace not only of consciousness and of the "higher masculinity," but of individuality and the hero. We have referred more than once to the connection of centroversion with the development of the ego. The tendency towards wholeness which centroversion represents functions

22. Jonah in the whale

From the Khludoff Psalter, Byzantine,
late 9th century

Raven

23. The hero Raven in the whale

Drawing by a Haida Indian, Pacific Northwest coast, late 19th century

24. Danaë and the shower of gold

*From a red-figure calyx krater, by the Triptolemos
painter, Attic, early 5th century* B.C.

25. Perseus slaying the Gorgon, with Hermes

After a black-figure jug by Amasis, Attic, 6th century B.C.

26. Perseus and Andromeda

Pompeian wall painting, 1st century A.D., *probably after a picture
by Nikas, an Athenian of the late 4th century* B.C.

quite unconsciously in the earliest phase, but in the formative phase it manifests itself as a group tendency. This group wholeness is no longer entirely unconscious; it is experienced through projection upon the totem. The totem is an indefinable quantity to which the various parts of the group stand in a participatory relationship; in other words, they are unconsciously identical with it. On the other hand, there exists also a link running back over the generations: the totem is an ancestor, but more in the sense of a spiritual founder than a progenitor. Primarily he is a *numinosum,* a transpersonal, spiritual being. He is transpersonal because, although an animal, a plant, or whatever else, he is such not as an individual entity, not as a person, but as an idea, a species; that is to say, on the primitive level he is a spirit that has mana, works magic and is taboo, and must be approached with considerable ceremony.

This totemic being forms the basis of a whole, a totem community which is not so much a natural biological unit as a spiritual or psychic structure. It is already an association or a brotherhood in the modern sense, that is, a sort of spiritual collective. The totem and the social order depending from it are totally different from the matriarchal group, which is a true biological unit, whereas these are "founded" and have come into being through a spiritual act.

We know that among the North American Indians, but not among them alone, the essential content of initiation is the acquisition of an individual "guardian spirit." [14] This spirit, who may be lodged in an animal or a thing, introduces into the life of the initiate who experiences him a whole sequence of ritual obligations and observances, and plays a decisive role among all shamans, priests, and prophetic figures in primitive societies and throughout the classical world. This universal phenomenon is the expression of a "personal revelation" of God, which can occur at all levels and take any number of forms. The growth of totemism is to be regarded as a missionary religion of a primitive kind, for we may suppose that the individual who has

[14] Goldenweiser, op. cit., p. 242.

been granted the vision of a spirit in the initiation rites will form a group with others of like mind, whom he draws with him into communion with the spirit. This mode of group formation can be seen at work to this day in the founding of sects; and the initiation ceremonies of primitives, the mystery religions of the ancient world, and the great institutional religions all arise in the same way. In totemism, the early form of institutional religion, the founder is the priest-prophet; he enjoys primary intercourse with his individual spirit and hands on its cult. As the myths tell us over and over again, he is the hero in the annals of his totem, and the spiritual ancestor.

He and the totem belong together, and this is particularly true from the standpoint of the community which later groups itself round them. The hero and founder as the personal, experiencing ego, and the totem experienced by him as a spiritual being, belong together not only in the psychological sense in which the spiritual "self" appears in some form to the ego, but for the community also these two figures always coincide. Thus Moses, for example, acquires the features of Jehovah, and the God of Love is worshiped in the figure of Christ. The sacred formula "I and the Father are one" always subsists psychologically between the ego and the transpersonal manifestation it experiences, whether this manifestation takes the form of an animal, a spirit, or a father figure.

Hence the spirit totem and the ancestor to whom it first appeared often merge in the figure of the spiritual "Founding Father," where the word "founding" is to be taken literally, as denoting a spiritual creator or originator. That this founding is inspirational can be seen from the description and analysis of every initiation rite and every totemistic ceremony.

The spiritual collective as we find it in all initiations and all secret societies, sects, mysteries, and religions is essentially masculine and, despite its communal character, essentially individual in the sense that each man is initiated as an individual and undergoes a unique experience that stamps his individuality. This individual accent and the elect character of the group stand in marked contrast to the matriarchal group, where the archetype of the Great Mother and the corresponding stage of consciousness are dominant. The opposed group of male societies and secret organizations is dominated by the archetype of the hero and by the dragon-fight mythology, which represents the next stage of conscious development. The male collective is the source of all the taboos, laws, and institutions that are destined to break the dominance of the uroboros and Great Mother. Heaven, the father, and the spirit go hand in hand with masculinity and represent the victory of the patriarchate over the matriarchate. This is not to say that the matriarchate knows no law; but the law by which it is informed is the law of instinct, of unconscious, natural functioning, and this law subserves the propagation, preservation, and evolution of the species rather than the development of the single individual. As the masculine ego consciousness increases in strength, the biological weakness of the female group of pregnant or nursing mothers, children, etc., tends to heighten the power consciousness of the protective fighter group. The situation of the males fortifies the ego and consciousness, just as that of the females fortifies the instinct and the group. Hunting and war are conducive to the development of an individual ego capable of acting responsibly in a dangerous situation, and equally conducive to the development of the leader principle. Whether the leader is chosen to cope with a given situation, say for the specific purpose of canoe-building or for a hunting expedition, or to act as the permanent leader, the situation of leader and led is bound to arise sooner or later in the male group, even when this is still co-ordinated with a matriarchal nucleus.

With the emergence and stabilization of leadership the group becomes further individualized. Not only is the leader set up as a hero, but the figures of spiritual progenitor, creator-god, ancestor, ideal leader, etc. begin to crystallize out from the mistiness of the primitive totem-image. It is a characteristic of the "god in the background"—a very early figure in the history of religion—that he is regarded not as a forefather, but more as

147

the father who is the "author of all things." He is a spiritual figure not primarily connected with nature; he belongs to the primordial age, to the dawn of history, and steps out of it to bring culture and salvation to mankind. He is timeless in the sense that he does not enter into time, but dwells in the background of time, in the primordial time that regulates our earthly chronology. Characteristic, too, is his relation to history and morality; for, as the tribal ancestor, he is directly related to the medicine men and the elders, the representatives of authority, power, wisdom, and esoteric knowledge.[15]

This creator figure is a numinous projection from whom is derived the God-King figure of the hero. Generally speaking, the hero appears as the son of a god, if he is not the god himself. The creator-god is, as a figure, identical with the mythological "heaven," namely the masculine, spiritual, supreme, uroboric background, though "heavenly" is not to be taken as identical with a heavenly god. The fusion of the ancestor with the creator-god and the culture hero is due to this process of personalization, which gives form to the unformed.

Not until the hero identifies himself with what we have called the masculine "heaven" can he enter upon his fight with the dragon. The identification culminates in the feeling that he is the son of God, embodying in himself the whole mightiness of heaven. This is as much as to say that all heroes are god-begotten. Heavenly succor, the feeling of being rooted up aloft in the father divinity, who is not just head of the family but a creative spirit, alone makes possible the fight with the dragon of the Great Mother. Representing and upholding this spiritual world in the face of the dragon, the hero becomes the liberator and savior, the innovator and bringer of wisdom and culture.

Jung has demonstrated that the hero's incest implements his rebirth, that only as one twice-born is he the hero, and that conversely anyone who has suffered the double birth must be regarded as a hero. It is not only among primitives that rebirth is the sole object of the initiation rites. As one initiated into the

[15] Van der Leeuw, *Religion in Essence and Manifestation*, Ch. 20.

mysteries every Gnostic, every Indian Brahman, and every baptized Christian is a man reborn. For, by submitting to heroic incest and entering into the devouring maw of the unconscious, the ego is changed in its essential nature and is reborn "another."

The transformation of the hero through the dragon fight is a transfiguration, a glorification, indeed an apotheosis, the central feature of which is the birth of a higher mode of personality. This qualitative and essential change is what distinguishes the hero from the normal person. As we have said, mythology represents the hero as having two fathers: a personal father who does not count or is the father of the carnal lower man, of the mortal part; and a heavenly father who is the father of the heroic part, of the higher man, who is "extraordinary" and immortal.

Hence the archetype of the hero myth is often a sun myth or even a moon myth. Glorification means deification. The hero is the sun or moon, i.e., a divinity. As a mere mortal, he is in reality the son of a purely personal father, but as the hero he is the son of a god and is identified, or identifies himself, with him.

Perhaps the earliest historical example of this is to be found, once again, in the Egyptian Pharaoh. The kings of Egypt were on their fathers' side sons of Horus, the heirs of Osiris, and, as the kingship developed, they were identified not only with Osiris, the moon, but with Ra, the sun. The king styled himself "the god Horus." People spoke of him as "God," and this is not, as Erman thinks, a "fine phrase" merely, but a symbolic fact which degenerated into a phrase only in modern times, with the "divine right of kings."

In the same way the king was called "the living sun" and "the living image of God upon earth." As early as the Fourth Dynasty the king was at the same time the son of Ra. This also belonged to his stock of titles.

The expression goes back to the idea, which we also find in other places and in other epochs, that the king, although outwardly the son of his father, is simultaneously a son of the supreme God.[16]

[16] Erman, *Religion*, p. 53.

Modern man's failure to understand this phenomenon of "double fatherhood," also displayed by the psychoanalysts, is painfully evident in Erman, who adds in conclusion: "Naturally we, with our limited understanding, must not seek to fathom how such a thing can be possible."

Thus the "enlightened" comment of an investigator nearly two thousand years after the birth of Christ. The phenomenon of psychic duality plainly expressed in Egyptian ritual and formulated theologically thousands of years later in the famous dialogue between Nicodemus and Christ [17] is still alive today in the not uncommon feeling that one is a "child of God," although a son or daughter of Mr. X. The dual parentage evidently corresponds to some duality in human nature, here represented by the hero.

The mother and father archetypes originally appeared in connection with the hero and his fate, i.e., someone who was extraordinary and unique. But here again, as was once the case with the immortality of Osiris, the *hieros gamos,* etc., what was unique and symbolic later becomes the common property of the collective. With the progressive individualization of humanity and its emergence from the inchoate state of *participation mystique* the ego of each man takes on clearer definition; but, in the process, the individual becomes the hero and has in his turn to exemplify the myth of the dragon fight.

It must be emphasized yet again that the mythological fate of the hero portrays the archetypal fate of the ego and of all conscious development. It serves as a model for the subsequent development of the collective, and its stages are recapitulated in the development of every child.

If, in the course of our exposition, we "personify," speaking for example of the hero's own experience, or describing a mythological situation from the feminine point of view, it is to be understood that we are speaking figuratively and in abbreviated form. Our retrospective psychological interpretation corresponds to no point of view consciously maintained in earlier

[17] John, Ch. 3.

times; it is the conscious elaboration of contents that were once extrapolated in mythological projections, unconsciously and symbolically. These symbols, however, can be interpreted as psychic contents, and from this we can read the psychic situation which underlies the production of such symbols.

The slaying of the mother is no less relevant to a consideration of the hero and his dual parentage than the slaying of the father, for, besides a suprapersonal father, he must also acquire a suprapersonal mother.

THE SLAYING OF THE MOTHER

ONCE the uroboros has divided into a pair of opposites, namely the World Parents, and the "son" has placed himself between them, thereby establishing his masculinity, the first stage of his emancipation is successfully accomplished. The ego, standing in the center between the World Parents, has challenged both sides of the uroboros, and by this hostile act has ranged both the upper and lower principles against him. He is now faced with what we have termed the dragon fight, a militant struggle with these contrary forces. Only the outcome of this struggle will reveal whether the emancipation is really successful, and whether he has finally shaken off the tenacious grip of the uroboros.

Turning to this fight with the dragon, a basic type in all mythologies, we must first distinguish the various stages of battle and its components. The numerous possible ways of interpreting this key theme of the unconscious must invite our caution. Contrary interpretations hang together as different stages within a basic situation, and only in the unity of all these interpretations will the true picture be disclosed.

The dragon fight has three main components: the hero, the dragon, and the treasure. By vanquishing the dragon the hero gains the treasure, which is the end product of the process symbolized by the fight.

The nature of this treasure, variously known as the "treasure hard to attain," the captive, the pearl of great price, the water of life, or the herb of immortality, will be dealt with later. At present we are faced with the fundamental question: what does the symbol of the dragon mean?

As Jung[1] has already established, though without taking it sufficiently into account in his own interpretation, this dragon bears all the marks of the uroboros. It is masculine and feminine at once. The fight with the dragon is thus the fight with the First Parents, a fight in which the murders of both father and mother, but not of one alone, have their ritually prescribed place. The dragon fight forms a central chapter in the evolution of mankind as of the individual, and, in the personal development of the child, it is connected with events and processes which psychoanalysis knows as the Oedipus complex, and which we call the problem of the First Parents.

Freud's father-murder theory, which Rank[2] has tried to elaborate, combines the following features in a systematic unity: The family romance, so far as it revolves round the boy, culminates in the son's incestuous longings for the mother, which are thwarted by the hostile father. The hero is the lad who kills his father and marries his mother. The hero myth thus becomes a mere fantasy for the direct or indirect fulfillment of this wishful idea. The theory is supported—or, to be more accurate, is overlaid—by Freud's illogical and anthropologically impossible hypothesis of a gorilla father. A formidable apelike patriarch makes off with his sons' women and is eventually done to death by the brotherly band. Heroism consists in liquidating your father. Freud takes all this as the literal truth, and from it he derives totemism and the basic features of culture and religion. Here as everywhere, Freud, with his personalistic bias, has misinterpreted something very important. Nevertheless the killing of the father remains an essential element of the dragon fight, though it is not the most essential, let alone the key to the whole history of mankind.

While Rank takes a bigoted stand upon Freudian theory, Jung gives a very different answer to this problem in his early work, *Psychology of the Unconscious*. He arrives at two conclusions which are, in our opinion, final. He shows, first, that the hero's

[1] *Symbols of Transformation [=Psychology of the Unconscious]*.
[2] *The Myth of the Birth of the Hero*.

153

fight is the fight with a mother who cannot be regarded as a personal figure in the family romance. Behind the personal figure of the mother there stands, as is evident from the symbology, what Jung was later to call the mother archetype. Jung was able to prove the transpersonal significance of the hero's fight because he did not make the personal family aspect of modern man the starting point of human development, but rather the development of the libido and its transformations. In this transformation process the hero's fight plays an eternal and fundamental part in overcoming the inertia of the libido, which is symbolized by the encircling mother-dragon, i.e., the unconscious.

Jung's second conclusion, the significance of which has not yet been generally accepted in psychology, demonstrates that the hero's "incest" is a regenerative incest. Victory over the mother, frequently taking the form of actual entry into her, i.e., incest, brings about a rebirth. The incest produces a transformation of personality which alone makes the hero a hero, that is, a higher and ideal representative of mankind.

The present study, which is based on Jung's discoveries, attempts to distinguish the individual types of dragon fight and its different stages, and in this way to correct and combine the two opposing theories of Freud and Jung. In his *Psychology of the Unconscious,* Jung was still so much under the influence of Freud's father theory that his interpretations have to be corrected and recast in the light of his later discoveries.

The conquest or killing of the mother forms one stratum in the myth of the dragon fight. The successful masculinization of the ego finds expression in its combativeness and readiness to expose itself to the danger which the dragon symbolizes. The ego's identification with masculine consciousness produces the psychic cleavage which drives it into opposing the dragon of the unconscious. This struggle is variously represented as the entry into the cave, the descent to the underworld, or as being swallowed— i.e., incest with the mother. This is shown most clearly in the hero myths which take the form of sun myths; here the swallowing of the hero by the dragon—night, sea, underworld—corresponds to the sun's nocturnal journey, from which it emerges victoriously after having conquered the darkness (*illus. 22 and 23*).[2a]

All reductive interpretations assert that being swallowed is identical with castration, with fear of the dragon and fear of the father, who prevents incest with the mother. That is to say, incest with the mother is in itself desirable, but is made terrible by this fear of the father. The mother is supposed to be a positive object of desire, and the father the real obstacle. This interpretation is erroneous, because incest and the fear of castration are already apparent at the stage when no father is operative, much less a jealous father.

The question goes deeper than that and touches a more primordial level. Fear of the dragon does not correspond to fear of the father, but to something far more elemental, namely the male's fear of the female in general. The hero's incest is incest with the Great and Terrible Mother, who is by nature terrible and does not become terrible indirectly through the intervention of a third party. It is true that the dragon also symbolizes the hero's fear, but the dragon is sufficiently terrible without any surplus fear being added. The descent into the abyss, into the sea or the dark cave, has terrors enough without the bogey of a father to bar the way. The bisexual structure of the uroboric dragon shows that the Great Mother possesses masculine, but not paternal, features. The aggressive and destructive features of the Great Mother—her function as a killer, for example—can be distinguished as masculine, and among her attributes we also find phallic symbols, as Jung has already pointed out. This is especially evident in the case of Hecate's attributes: key, whip, snake, dagger, and torch;[3] they are masculine, but are not on that account paternal symbols.

When the eunuch priests of the Great Mother perform their castrations and sacrifices, they are portraying her terrible

---

[2a] Raven, the typical hero among the Indians of northwestern America, conquers the whale after being swallowed by him.

[3] Jung, *Symbols of Transformation*, index, s.v.

character; but it is impossible to see these emasculated priests as father figures. The phallic figures who are better equipped to serve in this capacity are always subordinate; the Great Mother controls and uses them, and this fact contradicts their independent significance as father figures. The aggressive and destructive elements in the Great Mother can also appear symbolically and ritually as separate figures detached from her, in the form of attendants, priests, animals, etc. Warrior groups given to masculine orgies, such as the Curetes, often belong to the sphere of the Great Mother, and so do the phallic consorts who execute her destructive will. At a still later stage, among the matriarchally governed Indians of North America, we find that the chiefs are executively dependent upon the Old Mother. In this category we would also have to include not only the boar that kills the youthful god, but the maternal uncle as the instrument of the authority complex directed, for instance, against Isis' son, Horus. Even the phallic-chthonic sea-god Poseidon and his brood of monsters belong by nature to the domain of the Great Mother, and not to that of the Great and Terrible Father.

Later, however, when the patriarchate has succeeded to the Great Mother's sovereignty, the role of the Terrible Father is projected upon the masculine representatives of her terrible aspect, especially when it is in the interests of patriarchial development to repress that aspect and to bring the figure of the "good mother" to the fore.

The two forms of incest which we have studied so far were essentially passive: uroboric incest, in which the germinal ego was extinguished, and matriarchal incest, in which the son was seduced by the mother and the incest ended in matriarchal castration. But what distinguishes the hero is an active incest, the deliberate, conscious exposure of himself to the dangerous influence of the female, and the overcoming of man's immemorial fear of woman. To overcome fear of castration is to overcome fear of the mother's power which, for man, is associated with the danger of castration.

This brings us to a question of considerable diagnostic, therapeutic, and theoretical importance. The differentiation of the various archetypal stages enables us to decide what form of incest we are dealing with and what is the position of the ego and consciousness—in a word, what the developmental situation is in each individual case. In his *Psychology of the Unconscious,* Jung was still so much under the spell of Freud that he failed to recognize the archetypal differences in this situation, and consequently simplified the problem of the hero by treating it reductively.

The feminine element in the androgynous son-lover,[4] which Jung derives from regression to the mother, is, on the contrary, entirely original, as the androgyne's structurally undifferentiated disposition shows, and is not caused by the regression of an already developed masculinity. This disposition originates at a deeper level where the Great Mother is still dominant and masculinity not yet firmly established; hence there is no "renunciation of masculinity," it is simply that this masculinity has not so far achieved any independence at all. Admittedly the self-castration by which the adolescent sacrifices his masculinity is regressive, but it is only a partial regression, or we could say more accurately that his development has been nipped in the bud.

The effeminate nature of the adolescent is an intermediate stage, which can also be regarded as an intersexual stage. The interpretation of the priest or prophet as such an intermediate type [5] is psychologically correct, though not correct biologically. We have to distinguish between the adult ego's creative connection with the Great Mother and one in which the ego is not yet able to throw off her supremacy.

But what, the reader may ask, does castration mean at this stage of heroic incest? Is it not a misleading generalization of neurotic psychology to speak of the male's immemorial fear of the female?

For the ego and the male, the female is synonymous with the

[4] Ibid.
[5] Carpenter, *Intermediate Types among Primitive Folk.*

unconscious and the nonego, hence with darkness, nothingness, the void, the bottomless pit. In Jung's words:

. . . it should be remarked that *emptiness* is a great feminine secret. It is something absolutely alien to man; the chasm, the unplumbed depths, the *yin*.[6]

Mother, womb, the pit, and hell are all identical. The womb of the female is the place of origin from whence one came, and so every female is, as a womb, the primordial womb of the Great Mother of all origination, the womb of the unconscious. She threatens the ego with the danger of self-noughting, of self-loss —in other words, with death and castration. We have seen that the narcissistic nature of the phallus-obsessed adolescent constellates a connection between sexuality and the fear of castration. The death of the phallus in the female is symbolically equated with castration by the Great Mother, and in psychological terms this means the ego's dissolution in the unconscious.

But the masculinity and ego of the hero are no longer identical with the phallus and sexuality. On this level, another part of the body erects itself symbolically as the "higher phallus" or the "higher masculinity": the head, symbol of consciousness, with the eye for its ruling organ—and with this the ego now identifies itself.

The danger which threatens the "upper" principle symbolized by head and eye is closely connected with the help extended to the hero by what we called "heaven." Even before the dragon fight has begun, this higher part is already developed and active. In the mythological sense this proves his divine parentage and his hero's birth; psychologically it indicates his readiness to face the dragon like a hero and not like the lower, normal man.

This upper part of his nature is confirmed and finally brought to birth if the struggle is victorious, but is threatened with extinction in the event of defeat.

There is no need for us to demonstrate here that the head and the eye occur everywhere as symbols of the masculine and spiritual side of consciousness, of "heaven" and sun. The

[6] "Psychological Aspects of the Mother Archetype," p. 98.

breath and Logos groups also belong to this canon of symbols, where higher masculinity is distinguished from the lower masculinity of the phallic stage. It is therefore correct to interpret beheading and blinding as castration, but the castration occurs above, not below. This does not imply an "upwards displacement," from which point of view "losing one's head" would be identical with impotence—an equation that is true neither mythologically nor symbolically nor psychologically. There are "upper" eunuchs as well as "lower" eunuchs, and the devotees of the phallus are just as likely to be eunuchs in the upper regions as the highbrows are in the lower. Only the combination of both zones produces a whole masculinity. Here again Bachofen grasped the essence of the problem with his distinction between chthonic and solar masculinity.

The corresponding symbolism is to be found in the story of Samson, a secondarily personalized myth or, as happens equally often, a secondarily mythologized hero story.

As in numerous other places in the Old Testament, the gist of the story is Jehovah's struggle with the Canaanite-Philistine Astarte principle. The main outlines are clear enough: Samson is dedicated to Jehovah, but his instincts succumb to the wiles of Delilah-Astarte. Thereupon his fate is sealed, which means the cutting of his hair, blinding, and loss of the Jehovah power.

The castration takes the form of loss of the hair, and this is all the more significant because the worshipers of Jehovah and opponents of the Astarte principle may never cut their hair. Further, the loss of hair and strength relates to the archetypal stage of the sun hero who is castrated and devoured.

The second element is the blinding. Once again it is an "upper" as distinct from a "lower" castration. Upper castration, or loss of the Jehovah power, leads to the hero's captivity among the Philistines, in the realm of Astarte. He lingers in the underworld, where he must "tread the mill." Jeremias [7] has pointed out that the treading of the mill is a religious motif. This is confirmed by the reference to the temple of Dagon in which Samson is held

[7] A. Jeremias, *Das Alte Testament im Licht des alten Orients*, p. 678.

a prisoner, for Dagon is the corn god of the Canaanites, a vegetation deity like Osiris. Dagon is the father of Baal,[8] but all the
territories of this Jehovah-hating Baal are subject to the rule of
the Great Mother of the Canaanites. Samson's captivity is therefore an expression of the servitude of the conquered male under
the Great Mother, just as were the labors of Herakles under
Omphale, when he wore women's clothes—another well-known
symbol of enslavement to the Great Mother, to whom we must
also attribute the mill as a symbol of fertility.[9]

Enslavement to the Astarte world is finally overcome by a
resurgence of the victorious hero's solar power. Samson breaks
the pillars of Dagon's temple, and in his sacrificial death the old
Jehovah power of the Nazarite is restored. With the collapse
of the temple and Samson's self-renewal in death, Jehovah
triumphs over his enemies and over the Astarte principle.

The hero's fight is always concerned with the threat to the
spiritual, masculine principle from the uroboric dragon, and
with the danger of being swallowed by the maternal unconscious.
The most widely disseminated archetype of the dragon fight is
the sun myth, where the hero is swallowed every evening by the
nocturnal sea monster dwelling in the west, and who then grap-
ples with its double, so to speak—the dragon whom he en-
counters in this uterine cavern. He is then reborn in the east as
the victorious sun, the *sol invictus;* or rather, by hacking his way
out of the monster, he accomplishes his own rebirth. In this
sequence of danger, battle, and victory, the light—whose significance for consciousness we have repeatedly stressed—is the
central symbol of the hero's reality. The hero is always a light-
bringer and emissary of the light. At the nethermost point of
the night sea journey, when the sun hero journeys through the
underworld and must survive the fight with the dragon, the new
sun is kindled at midnight and the hero conquers the darkness.
At this same lowest point of the year Christ is born as the shining Redeemer, as the light of the year and light of the world,

[8] Albright, *Archaeology*, p. 74.
[9] Silberer, *Problems of Mysticism and Its Symbolism*, pp. 97 ff.

and is worshiped with the Christmas tree at the winter solstice. The new light and the victory are symbolized by the illumination and transfiguration of the head, crowned and decked with an aureole. Even though the deeper meaning of this symbolism will only become clear to us later, it is evident that the hero's victory brings with it a new spiritual status, a new knowledge, and an alteration of consciousness.

In the mystery religions, too, the neophyte has to endure the perils of the underworld, pass through the seven portals—a very early feature, found even in Ishtar's descent into hell—or spend the twelve night hours in the dark hemisphere, as described by Apuleius in his account of the Isis mysteries. The mysteries culminate in a deification, which in the Isis mysteries means identification with the sun god. The initiate receives the crown of life, the supreme illumination; his head is hallowed by the light and anointed with glory.

Wundt [10] characterizes the heroic age as the "predominance of individual personality." This, he says, is what the hero represents; in fact he derives the divine figure from the hero, seeing in God only an intensified hero figure. Even though this view is not altogether correct, there is nevertheless a connection between the hero as bearer of the ego, with its power to discipline the will and mold the personality, and the formative phase in which the gods are crystallized out from a mass of impersonal forces. The development of the conscious system, having as its center an ego which breaks away from the despotic rule of the unconscious, is prefigured in the hero myth.

The unconscious forces of this now obsolete psychic stage thereupon deploy themselves against the ego-hero as fearsome monsters and dragons, demons and unclean spirits, who threaten to swallow him up again. The Terrible Mother, the all-inclusive symbol of this devouring aspect of the unconscious, is therefore the Great Mother of all monsters. All dangerous affects and impulses, all the evils which come up from the unconscious and overwhelm the ego with their dynamism, are her progeny. This

[10] *Elements of Folk Psychology,* pp. 281 f.

is precisely what is meant when Goya uses, as a motto for his *Caprichos*, "The dream of reason breeds monsters," or when, in Greek mythology, Hecate, the primeval and all-powerful goddess, appears as the mother of the man-eating Empusa and of the lamias who devour the flesh of boys. She is the archenemy of the hero who, as horseman or knight, tames the horse of unconscious instinct, or, as Michael, destroys the dragon. He is the bringer of light, form, and order out of the monstrous, pullulating chaos of Mother Nature.

One of the first figures we encounter in our investigation of the hero myth is the hero whose name has become a byword in modern psychology and who has been so calamitously misinterpreted: Oedipus. He is the type of hero whose fight with the dragon is only partially successful. His tragic fate is eloquent of this abortive attempt and can only be understood from the transpersonal standpoint here adopted.

There are three fateful points in the myth of Oedipus which must be borne in mind if we are to give him his rightful place in the evolution of human consciousness: firstly, the victory over the Sphinx; secondly, the incest with the mother; thirdly, the murder of the father.

Oedipus becomes a hero and dragon slayer because he vanquishes the Sphinx. This Sphinx is the age-old foe, the dragon of the abyss, representing the might of the Earth Mother in her uroboric aspect. She is the Great Mother whose deadly law runs in the fatherless earth, threatening destruction upon all men who cannot answer her question. The fatal riddle she propounds, and whose answer is "Man," can only be solved by the hero. He alone answers fate by conquering it, and he conquers because, in his answer, fate itself is answered. This heroic answer, which makes him truly a man, is the victory of the spirit, man's triumph over chaos. Thus, by conquering the Sphinx, Oedipus becomes a hero and dragon slayer, and as such he commits incest with his mother, like every hero. The hero's incest and the conquering of the Sphinx are identical, two sides of the same process. By conquering his terror of the female, by entering into the womb, the abyss, the peril of the unconscious, he weds himself triumphantly with the Great Mother who castrates the young men, and with the Sphinx who destroys them. His heroism transforms him into a fully grown male, independent enough to overcome the power of the female and—what is more important—to reproduce a new being in her.

Here, where the youth becomes the man, and active incest becomes reproductive incest, the male unites with his female opposite and brings to birth a new thing, the third: a synthesis arises in which for the first time male and female are equilibrated in a whole. The hero is not only conqueror of the mother; he also kills her terrible female aspect so as to liberate the fruitful and bountiful aspect.

If we follow up this line of thought and disregard for the present the meaning of the father-murder, we can see why Oedipus was only half a hero, and why the real deed of the hero remained only half accomplished: though Oedipus conquers the Sphinx, he commits incest with his mother, and murders his father, unconsciously.

He has no knowledge of what he has done, and when he finds out, he is unable to look his own deed, the deed of the hero, in the face. Consequently he is overtaken by the fate that overtakes all those for whom the Eternal Feminine reverts to the Great Mother: he regresses to the stage of the son, and suffers the fate of the son-lover. He performs the act of self-castration by putting out his own eyes. Even if we discount Bachofen's interpretation, which sees in the clasp used for the blinding a symbol of the old matriarchal system, the fact remains that he uses as an instrument an article belonging to his wife and mother. The blinding is no longer a puzzle for us. It signifies the destruction of the higher masculinity, of the very thing that characterizes the hero; and this form of spiritual self-castration cancels out all that was gained by his victory over the Sphinx. The masculine progression of the hero is thrown back by the old shock, the fear of the Great Mother which seizes him after the deed. He becomes the victim of the Sphinx he had conquered.

In Sophocles' *Oedipus at Colonus,* the old man finds rest and deliverance at last in the grove of the Erinyes, representatives of the ancient mother power, and his path is rounded out to the full uroboric circle. His end crowns his tragic life with lofty, mystical solemnity. Blind and infirm, he vanishes mysteriously into the bowels of the earth, guided by Theseus, the ideal hero of a later age, who refused to succumb to his stepmother, the sorceress Medea. The Great Earth Mother takes Oedipus, the Swell-foot, her phallic son, back into herself. His grave becomes a sanctuary.

He is one of the great human figures whose agony and suffering lead to more gracious and civilized behavior, who, still embedded in the old order of which they are the products, stand there as its last great victims, and at the same time as the founders of a new age.[11]

It is no accident that the story of Oedipus' origins lacks all the characteristic marks of the hero's birth which connect him with a divinity. The story as we have it in Sophocles is no heroic tragedy, but the glorification of a fate beyond the control of man, in the hands of dispassionate gods. The drama contains traces of the early matriarchal epoch when the human and the divine had not yet come together, and the ego's dependence on the powers that be was paramount. The dominance of the Great Mother appears here, with a philosophical coloring, as total dependence upon fate. All such pessimistic systems are thinly veiled expositions of the Great Mother's ascendency over the ego and consciousness.

To the hero, the clutching Earth Mother appears as a dragon to be overcome. In the first part of the dragon fight she twines herself about the son and seeks to hold him fast as an embryo, by preventing him from being born or by making him the eternal babe in arms and mother's darling. She is the deadly uroboric mother, the abyss in the West, the kingdom of the dead, the underworld, the devouring maw of the earth, into which, weary and submissive, the ordinary mortal sinks to his death in the dissolution of uroboric or matriarchal incest. The devouring is

[11] Bachofen, *Mutterrecht,* Vol. 2, p. 442.

often represented as a preliminary defeat in the dragon fight. Even in a typical victor myth like that of the Babylonian hero Marduk, there is a phase of captivity and defeat during his struggle with the monster Tiamat.[12] This phase is the necessary prelude to rebirth.

If, however, the hero succeeds in being a hero, if he proves his higher origin and his filiation to the divine forefather, then, like the sun hero, he enters into the Terrible Mother of fear and danger, and emerges covered in glory from the belly of the whale, or from the Augean stables, or from the uterine cavern of the earth. The slaying of the mother and identification with the father-god go together. If, through active incest, the hero penetrates into the dark, maternal, chthonic side, he can only do so by virtue of his kinship with "heaven," his filiation to God. By hacking his way out of the darkness he is reborn as the hero in the image of God, but, at the same time, as the son of the god-impregnated virgin and of the regenerative Good Mother.

Whereas the first half of the night, when the westering sun descends into the belly of the whale, is dark and devouring, the second half is bright and bountiful, for out of it the sun-hero climbs to the eastward, reborn. Midnight decides whether the sun will be born again as the hero, to shed new light on a world renewed, or whether he will be castrated and devoured by the Terrible Mother, who kills him by destroying the heavenly part that makes him a hero. He then remains in the darkness, a captive. Not only does he find himself grown fast to the rocks of the underworld like Theseus, or chained to the crag like Prometheus, or nailed to the cross like Jesus, but the world remains without a hero, and there is born, as Ernst Barlach says in his drama,[13] a "dead day."

We shall discuss this drama, whose mythological symbolism is profounder than that of most classical tragedies, in some detail, because in it the symbolism of the dragon fight reappears in a modern writer.

[12] Gadd, "Babylonian Myth and Ritual," in Hooke, *Myth and Ritual,* p. 59.
[13] *Der Tote Tag* (1912).

The basic theme of the work is the mother's resistance to the growth and development of her son. He has always lived with her, but now he threatens to go away. This mythical mother conceived her son by the sun-god who, on taking his departure, said he would return when the child had become a man, and would see how well she had brought him up. We then meet the blind personal father, the husband of our Great Mother. He understands that the son is a hero, a god's son, and, with the help of his wife's familiar spirit, he tries to make the hero's fate and its necessity apparent to her and the boy. This familiar is a motherless spirit, visible only to the divine eyes of the son. He tells the son: "It is rumored that your mother has a grown-up baby in her house," and adds, "Men come from men." But the mother silences him. The words "enough mother, too little father" and "a man is kin to the father, and a nurse that speaks to him of the father feeds him better than a mother who keeps silent" are as poisonous to her ears as her husband's remark that their son is a hero. The blind personal father then says, "Perhaps he is stuck fast in the world like a bird breaking from the egg. With his eyes he lives in the other world, and it has need of him," and "gods' sons are no mothers' darlings." To this the mother answers, "My son is no hero, I need no hero son," crying, "The world's good is death to the mother!" But the son has dreamt that his father appeared to him, like "a man having a sun for his head," and in the dream he rode the sun steed of his future that his father gave him. Already this horse, named "Herzhorn," which "has wind in his belly" and "snuffs the sun," stands in the stable and gladdens the boy's heart. The invisible conflict sways round the existence or nonexistence of this horse.

The blind father then tries to interpret the world to the son. He tells him about the images of the future which can and must come forth from the night, and how the hero must rouse them from their slumber in order to give the world a better face. He speaks of the truth, of the sun that "was, is, and shall be," trying to rouse up the son who is not his own. But to all this the mother replies impassively, "Son's future is mother's past," and

"The hero must first bury his mother." Then the son begins to understand: "Perhaps the life we live is also the life of the gods," but the mother denies him his right to a future, lest the child grow away from her. So one night she secretly kills the sun-horse and by this murder destroys the future, both of her son and of the world. What now comes is the "dead day," or as the mother says with half-unconscious irony, "Just a little boy born of the night, a newborn thing without light or consciousness." In despair the son cries out, "But nobody can be anybody else; nobody else can be what I am—nobody but me!" But the mother slaps his face and tells him he is to remain his mother's son and not have an ego.

Still not suspecting that his mother murdered the horse, the son grows up in the knowledge that he is not like the familiar spirit who was begotten of one parent only. So he has no hope that he could ever be reborn through the mother alone: "No mother begot me alone, so she cannot give me back the life which she has not given me alone." He complains that he lacks a father, alleging that he needs his father's bodily presence and example, and rails against his "invisibility." The son, brought up on the earthly wisdom of the mother, that one cannot "live by the bread that is baked in dreams," is thereupon scolded by the familiar spirit, a father's son with no mother, and told, "You bed-wetter, my father's dreams would have shown me my heritage, without my father's example. The body does not help; it must cleave to the spirit." So the son is torn between the ele-mental parents above and below. He hears "the sun roaring above the mist" and "the great heart of the earth hammering in the depths," and laments, "From high and low the echoes battle for my ears!" Transfixed between mother and father, he twice calls out to his father. But his third call drifts back—to the mother. As he once again breaks away from her, she curses him and kills herself. Now he must decide. Rejecting the fatal knife of self-destruction, he says, "Father would not do it either," only to follow his mother with the words: "Mother's way suits me better after all."

The mother has killed his horse and so castrated her son. There came a dead day, a day without sun. His denial of father-god, identical with self-mutilation, ends in suicide. The mother's curse, counteracted by no paternal blessing, is fulfilled. He obeys the mother who bore him and he dies by her curse, an accursed mother's son.

This drama is a myth of early times. It enacts the history of men between the epoch of the Great Mother and the intermediate stage of the dragon fight, whose protagonist in antiquity is Oedipus—Oedipus the vanquished, not the victor.

The next stage is dramatically presented in the *Oresteia*. It describes the victory of the son, who becomes a matricide in order to avenge his father, and who introduces the new age of the patriarchate with the help of the paternal-solar principle. We use the word "patriarchate" in Bachofen's sense, to signify the predominantly masculine world of spirit, sun, consciousness, and ego. In the matriarchate, on the other hand, the unconscious reigns supreme, and the predominant feature here is a preconscious, prelogical, and preindividual way of thinking and feeling.[14]

In the *Oresteia* the son stands squarely on the side of the father. Liberation from the mother has gone a stage further. Just as in Indian mythology Rama, at the behest of his father, beheads his mother with an ax,[15] so in the *Oresteia*, and again with variations in *Hamlet*, the spirit of the father is the impelling force that compasses the death of the sinful mother. Here, identification with the father is so complete that the maternal principle can be killed even when it appears, not in the symbolic form of a dragon, but as the real mother—and killed precisely because this principle has sinned against the father principle.[16]

As a defense against the mother-world of vengeful Furies who hound down the matricide with intent to kill him, Orestes has

[14] In this sense the matriarchate always precedes the patriarchate, and with reference to a whole group of neurotics we can still speak of a matriarchal psychology which must be replaced by the psychology of the patriarchate.

[15] Zimmer, *Maya, der Indische Mythos*, pp. 219 f.

[16] Heyer, "Erinnyen und Eumeniden."

for his ally the world of light. Apollo and Athene help him to obtain justice, and justice in this case means the setting up of a new law opposed to the old matriarchal law which knows no forgiveness for the inexpiable crime of mother-murder. His cause is espoused by the goddess Athene, who herself was not born of woman, but sprang from the head of Zeus, and whose nature, therefore, is profoundly inimical to the chthonic-feminine element in every mother and every woman born of a mother. This Athene aspect of woman is bound up with the psychological significance of the anima-sister.[17] It is this same virginal quality which comes to the aid of the hero in his fight with the mother-dragon, and helps him to overcome his terror of the Erinys face of the feminine unconscious.

[17] Van der Leeuw, *Religion in Essence and Manifestation.*

III

THE SLAYING OF THE FATHER

B UT IF THE FIGHT with the dragon means incest with the mother, what does the slaying of the father mean, particularly in view of the fact that we described the dragon fight and mother incest as prepatriarchal, i.e., not bound to a patriarchal form of society or to the patriarchal family? If the dragon does not, as Freud and the early Jung thought, symbolize fear of the father who bars the way to the mother, but rather the mother herself in all her fearfulness, then we must explain why the hero's fight is connected with the murder of the father.

The dangers of the unconscious, its rending, destroying, devouring, and castrating character, confront the hero as monsters, prodigies, beasts, giants, and so forth, which he has to conquer. An analysis of these figures shows that they are bisexual like the uroboros, possessing masculine and feminine symbolic qualities. Accordingly the hero has *both* the First Parents against him and must overcome the masculine as well as the feminine part of the uroboros. To reduce all these figures to a father figure is an arbitrary and dogmatic violation of the facts. The situation of the hero presupposes very much more complicated "parental relationships" than the simplification of the Freudian family romance would allow. The type of hero represented, for instance, by Herakles, who is helped by his father and persecuted by his wicked stepmother, cannot be interpreted according to the same scheme that fits the Oedipus myth.

Before we can interpret the murder of the father there must be a fundamental clarification of the father principle.

The structure of the "father," whether personal or transpersonal, is two-sided like that of the mother: positive and negative. In mythology there stands beside the creative, positive father the destructive, negative father, and both father images are as alive in the soul of modern man as they were in the projections of mythology.

There is, however, between the ego's relation to the father and father image and its relation to the mother and mother image a difference whose significance for masculine and feminine psychology must not be underestimated. In relation to the ego, the mother image has both a productive and a destructive aspect, but over and above that, it preserves a certain immutability and eternality. Although it is two-faced and can assume many shapes, for the ego and consciousness it always remains the world of the origin, the world of the unconscious. In general, therefore, the mother represents the instinctual side of life, which, compared with the changing positions of the ego and consciousness, proves to be constant and relatively unalterable, whether it be good or bad, helpful and productive, or hurtful and terrible. Whereas man's ego and his consciousness have changed to an extraordinary degree during the last six thousand years, the unconscious, the Mother, is a psychic structure that would seem to be fixed eternally and almost unalterably. Even when the mother image takes on the character of the spiritual mother, Sophia, it retains its unchangingness, for it is an embodiment of the everlasting and all-embracing, the healing, sustaining, loving, and saving principle. It is eternal in a sense quite different from that in which the father image is eternal. The transformations and developments in the creative background are, in unconscious symbolism, always correlated with masculine mobility and dynamism as expressed in the Logos-son. In comparison with him, the mover and the moved, Sophia is the maternally quiescent. This is clearly revealed in modern psychology, where the significance of the personal mother is eclipsed by the mother archetype to a far greater degree than is the case with the personal father. The mother image is less conditioned by the temporal and cultural pattern.

On the other hand, besides the archetypal image of the father, the personal father image also has a significance, though it is

171

conditioned less by his individual person than by the character of the culture and the changing cultural values which he represents. There is a broad resemblance between the mother figures of primitive, classical, medieval, and modern times; they remain embedded in nature. But the father figure changes with the culture he represents. Although in this case, too, there is in the background an indefinite archetypal figure of a spiritual father or creator god, it is an empty form; it is only filled out by the father figures that vary with the development of culture. As Van der Leeuw says:

When, for example, the myths call God the "Father," they do so, not on a given paternal basis, but because they set up a father figure to which every given father figure has to adjust itself.[1]

The male collective, which bodies forth the archetypal father figure through the creation of myths, imparts to the visible form of the archetype a critical stamp and coloring determined by the cultural situation. Our contention, that there is an essential difference between the father image and the mother image, confirms and supplements in a most surprising way one of Jung's central discoveries, namely the anima psychology of man and the animus psychology of woman.[2] The empirical fact, which has hitherto been extremely difficult to explain, that the woman's unconscious is inhabited by a multiplicity of masculine spirit-animus figures, contrasted with the single, Janus-faced soul-anima figure in the unconscious of man, now becomes more intelligible. The cultural diversity of what we have termed "heaven," that is to say, the numerous father-husband images known to humanity, has left a deposit in the unconscious experience of woman, just as is the case with the uniform mother-wife image in the unconscious experience of man.

In prepatriarchal conditions the men and the elders stand for "heaven," and they transmit the collective cultural heritage of their day and generation. "The fathers" are the representatives of law and order, from the earliest taboos to the most

[1] Van der Leeuw, *Religion in Essence and Manifestation.*
[2] "The Relations between the Ego and the Unconscious."

modern juridical systems; they hand down the highest values of civilization, whereas the mothers control the highest, i.e., deepest, values of life and nature. The world of the fathers is thus the world of collective values; it is historical and related to the fluctuating level of conscious and cultural development within the group. The prevailing system of cultural values, i.e., the canon of values which gives a culture its peculiar physiognomy and its stability, has its roots in the fathers, the grown men who represent and reinforce the religious, ethical, political, and social structure of the collective.

These fathers are the guardians of masculinity and the supervisors of all education. That is to say, their existence is not merely symbolical; as pillars of the institutions that embody the cultural canon, they preside over the upbringing of each individual and certify his coming of age. It makes no difference how this cultural canon is constituted, whether its laws and taboos be those of a tribe of head-hunters or of a Christian nation. Always the fathers see to it that the current values are impressed upon the young people, and that only those who have identified themselves with those values are included among the adults. The advocacy of the canon of values inherited from the fathers and enforced by education manifests itself in the psychic structure of the individual as "conscience."

This paternal authority, whose necessity for culture and the development of consciousness is beyond dispute, differs from the maternal authority in that it is essentially relative, being conditioned by its day and generation, and not having the absolute character of the maternal authority.

In normal times, when culture is stable and the paternal canon remains in force for generations, the father-son relationship consists in handing down these values to the son and impressing them upon him, after he has passed the tests of initiation in puberty. Such times, and the psychology that goes with them, are distinguished by the fact that there is no father-son problem, or only the barest suggestion of one. We must not be deceived by the different experience of our own "extraordinary" age. The monotonous sameness of fathers and sons is the rule in a stable culture. This sameness only means that the paternal canon of rites and institutions which make the youth an adult and the father an elder holds undisputed sway, so that the young man undergoes his prescribed transition to adulthood just as naturally as the father undergoes his to old age.

There is, however, one exception to this, and the exception is the creative individual—the hero. As Barlach says, the hero has to "awaken the sleeping images of the future which can and must come forth from the night, in order to give the world a new and better face." This necessarily makes him a breaker of the old law. He is the enemy of the old ruling system, of the old cultural values and the existing court of conscience, and so he necessarily comes into conflict with the fathers and their spokesman, the personal father.

In this conflict the "inner voice," the command of the trans-personal father or father archetype who wants the world to change, collides with the personal father who speaks for the old law. We know this conflict best from the Bible story of Jehovah's command to Abraham: "Get thee out of thy country, and from thy kindred, and from thy father's house, unto a land that I will show thee" (Genesis 12:1), which the midrash [3] interprets as meaning that Abraham is to destroy the gods of his father. The message of Jesus is only an extension of the same conflict, and it repeats itself in every revolution. Whether the new picture of God and the world conflicts with an old picture, or with the personal father, is unimportant, for the father always represents the old order and hence also the old picture current in his cultural canon.

If we keep to Rank's summing up of the situation, we can begin with two statements. The first avers that the hero is the child of aristocratic parents, generally a king's son—which incidentally is only partly true, because a large number of heroes and redeemers are of "lowly" origin—and the second, that the father always receives a warning. In addition to this, there are

[3] Bin Gorion, *Sagen der Juden*, Vol. II, "Die Erzväter," XI.

the extraordinary circumstances of the hero's birth, the fact that he is begotten by a god and born of a virgin. What the symbols and myths tell us about the essential nature of the hero can now be understood. The virgin mother, connected directly with the god who engenders the new order, but only indirectly with the husband, gives birth to the hero who is destined to bring that new order into being and destroy the old. For this reason the hero is frequently "exposed" with his mother, because a prophecy declares that her child will take over the rulership from the old king.[4]

The hero's descent from the reigning family is symbolic of the struggle for the system of rulership, for that is what the struggle is really about. A significant deviation from the general mythological pattern is the story of Moses, which Freud[5] tried in vain to interpret along reductive lines.

In general the hero child is cast out from the unfriendly reigning house by the father-king, only to be triumphantly reinstated later on. In the Moses story the situation is somewhat different. Firstly, he is not a king's son but a foundling. Secondly, although Pharaoh, the mythological terrible father, is as anxious as ever to have the hero-child assassinated—slaying of the first-born— not only does he not succeed in this, but Jehovah, the transpersonal father, with the help of Pharaoh's daughter and in contradiction to the mythological pattern, brings the redeemer child back into the alien system of rulership, which he should have overthrown and from which he was to have been expelled. In this Hebrew variant, the relationship to the personal father— Amram—is preserved in a positive sense, but only as a side issue. The real reason why Jehovah's protégé is installed in the household of the god-king Pharaoh, is to bring out the transpersonal meaning of the conflict, already apparent in the hero's birth.

We find an analogous situation in the myth of Herakles, although this is derived from a different sphere of culture and

---

[4] Rank, *The Myth of the Birth of the Hero*. Cf. A. Jeremias, whose legitimate transpersonal interpretations are personalized by Rank and reduced to absurdity.
[5] *Moses and Monotheism*.

another level of being. Here the wicked father-king, Eurystheus, who is in league with the goddess Hera, the jealous stepmother, imposes the labors which the hero performs with the aid of his divine father Zeus.

It is precisely the persecutions and dangers heaped upon him by the hateful father figure that make him a hero. The obstacles put in his way by the old patriarchal system become inner incentives to heroism, and, so far as the killing of the father is concerned, Rank is quite right when he says that "the heroism lies in overcoming the father, who instigated the hero's exposure and set him the tasks." It is equally right to say that the hero, "by solving the tasks which the father imposed with intent to destroy him, develops from a dissatisfied son into a socially valuable reformer, a conqueror of man-eating monsters that ravage the countryside, an inventor, a founder of cities, and bringer of culture." But only if we take the transpersonal background into account do we arrive at an interpretation which does justice to the hero as a maker of human history, and which sees in the hero myth a great prototypal event honored by all mankind.

It is no uxorious gorilla father who, as paterfamilias, drives out his sons "to protect himself from the violence of his offspring, fast growing up and thirsting for power"; no wicked king packs off his son to slay the monster, which is himself, as the nonsensical psychoanalytical interpretation would have us believe. No, the dragon fight as we now see it presents a very different picture.

Two father and two mother figures have to be borne in mind. The "wicked king" or personal father figure, representing the old ruling system, sends the hero forth to fight the monster— Sphinx, witches, giants, wild beasts, etc.—hoping that it will prove his undoing. This fight is the struggle with the uroboric Great Mother, with the unconscious, to which the hero may easily succumb because it is the seat of the ego's anxiety and holds the threat of impotence. With the help of his divine father, however, the hero succeeds in vanquishing the monster. His higher nature and noble birth are victorious, and are them-

176

selves proven in the victory. The ruin wished upon him by the negative father redounds to his glory and to the negative father's own ruin. Thus, the old king's expulsion of the son, the hero's fight, and the killing of the father hang together in a meaningful way. They form a necessary canon of events which, in symbol and in fact, are presupposed by the very existence of the hero, who, as the bringer of the new, has to destroy the old.

At his side there stands the good mother in the shape of his own mother and the sisterly virgin, either fused together or as two separate figures. The divine father may intervene in the critical situations as a helper, or he may remain waiting in the wings. Waiting, because only if the hero stands the test will he prove his genuine sonship, just as Horus could only be recognized as the true son of Osiris after he had overthrown Set. Thus waiting and testing, the divine father may easily be confused with the negative father, for the father who sends forth his son into danger is an ambiguous figure with personal and impersonal characteristics.

But always the hero, as bringer of the new, is the instrument of a new manifestation of the father-god. In him the patriarchal gods struggle against the Great Mother, the invaders' gods against the indigenous gods, Jehovah against the gods of the heathen. Basically it is a struggle between two god images or sets of gods, the old father-god defending himself against the new son-god, and the old polytheistic system resisting usurpation by the new monotheism, as is exemplified by the archetypal wars of the gods.

The picture becomes more complicated when the hero ceases to be an instrument of the gods and begins to play his own independent part as a human being; and when he finally becomes, in modern man, a battleground for suprapersonal forces, where the human ego pits itself against the deity. As breaker of the old law, man becomes the opponent of the old system and the bringer of the new, which he confers upon mankind against the will of the old deity. The most typical example of this is the Promethean theft of fire; another is the story of Paradise as interpreted by the Gnostics. Here, Jehovah is the vengeful old god, while Adam, in league with Eve and the serpent, is the hero who imparts the new knowledge to mankind. But he is also the son of a new father-god, the redeemer who brings the new system to birth. As in all gnostic systems, he is the son of the higher unknown deity and must take upon himself the struggle with the old.

At this point we must make an attempt to sort out, into separate layers, the hero's experience of the "Terrible Male."

The hero, as we have said, fights the androgynous figure of the uroboros. In the cosmic projection of celestial battles we find, at the outset, the battle between light and darkness, where darkness is associated with a number of symbolic components, and light is always identified with the hero, whether he be a moon, sun, or star hero. The devouring darkness, however, can appear in feminine form, as Tiamat, chaos, etc., just as easily as in the masculine form of a monster like Set or the Fenris-wolf.

Thus all child-eating father figures stand for the masculine aspect of the uroboros and the masculine-negative side of the First Parents. In these figures the accent falls primarily on the devouring force, i.e., the uterine cavern. Even when they later appear in the patriarchate as genuine Terrible Father figures, e.g., Cronus or Moloch, their uroboric character is transparent so long as the symbolism of eating is in the foreground and hence their propinquity to the Great Mother.

Similarly, the phallic-chthonic earth and sea divinities are, as Bachofen has rightly discerned, simply satellites of the Great Mother. For Hippolytus, the Great Mother is Aphrodite, for Perseus, she is the Medusa, and in both myths Poseidon, although he appears as an independent god, remains the instrument of the Great Mother's destructive will.

The earlier stage in which we met the languishing figure of the adolescent, the hero of ego consciousness, and which we described as being under the dominance of the Great Mother, really comprises two stages: the first, when the doomed and sorrowful hero succumbs to the Great Mother; the second, when his resistance increases and he finds himself in a hopeless situation of conflict. The second stage of mounting resistance corresponds to a narcissistic turning away from the Great Mother, and it is this point that the passive fate of being castrated and driven mad is superseded by active self-castration and suicide.

The young hero's growing masculinity now experiences the destructive side of the Great Mother as something masculine. It is her murderous satellites, with whom are connected the destructive elements stone and iron,[6] who carry out the sacrifice of the adolescent son. In mythology this side manifests itself as a dark homicidal male force, a savage animal, in particular the boar, which is akin to the sow, symbol of the Great Mother, but later it manifests itself as her masculine warrior consort or as the priest who performs the castration. The male's experience of himself, his sacrifice as a male by another male in the old fertility rites, for instance, begins at this point. When, with growing self-awareness, he experiences his relation to an opponent, and the sacrificed realizes his identity with the sacrificiant, and vice versa, the hitherto cosmic opposition of light and darkness is experienced as an opposition between human or divine twins, and the long succession of fraternal feuds in mythology opens with the squabbles between Osiris and Set, Baal and Mot.[7]

The earliest stage of the twin-brother conflict, based on the natural periodic rhythm of summer and winter, day and night, life and death, is still entirely under the dominance of the Great Mother. The dark, negative death force of the male is experienced as her destructive instrument, just as sociologically and mythologically Set, the maternal uncle of Horus, is the instrument of the hostile executive power of the matriarchate.

As masculine self-consciousness grows stronger, the stage

[6] Cf. the connection between Set, the brother of Isis, and the flint knife; or between Mars, Aphrodite's lover, and iron.

[7] Rank (*Psychoanalytische Beiträge zur Mythenforschung*, p. 374), like all Freudians, simply substitutes for the problem of the twins the conflict between elder brother and younger brother and then between father and son, in order to reduce the whole thing to the Oedipus complex again. The historical and psychological stages here in question must be kept apart and not interpreted personalistically.

179

of matriarchy is followed by that of division. Symptomatic of this transition period is the twin-brother motif in mythology, which expresses the mutual affinity of opposites. This division turns destructively against itself in self-mutilation and suicide. As we saw, in uroboric and matriarchal castration the will of the Great Mother was paramount. But the centroversion tendency which underlies the ego-hero's struggle for self-preservation and which first takes the form of anxiety, advances beyond the passive, narcissistic stage and turns into resistance, defiance, and aggression directed against the Great Mother, as illustrated mythologically in the story of Hippolytus. The destruction of an ego system hostile to the unconscious, symbolized in the myths as persecution, dismemberment, and madness, presupposes an ego that has attained a relatively high degree of autonomy and maturity. The fact that, for the Great Mother, father and son are nothing but the fertilizing phallus can also be formulated from the masculine standpoint by saying that victor and victim are always the same: the triumphant sacrificer himself becomes a future sacrifice. Consciousness of the bond between the male opponents is the beginning of masculine self-consciousness. This is not to say that the sacrificer and the sacrificed develop "personal" feelings for one another. Since the processes described are transpersonal, we are only permitted to draw conclusions from typical events. One such typical event is that the subordinate male group in the matriarchate gradually experiences and asserts its independence and no longer allows itself to be made the tool of rituals inimical to it. The development of masculine self-consciousness is both the cause and the product of this self-discovery, and gradually male enmities are replaced by male friendships.

Accentuation of the man-to-man relationship eventually leads to the overthrow of the matriarchate by patriarchal rulers. Just as in Sparta, with its late matriarchal conditions, a strongly marked masculine relationship is to be observed among pairs of young warriors, so, at a much earlier date, we find the same thing in the Gilgamesh Epic and numerous other hero myths.

The countless male friendships in Greek mythology vindicate themselves, like that between Gilgamesh and Engidu, in the hero's fight with the Great Mother dragon.

The principle of opposites which formerly divided the hostile brothers has now become the principle of brotherhood. These friendly alliances often exist between unequal brothers who, despite the fact that one is mortal and the other immortal, must be regarded as twins. We recall in connection with the hero's birth that very often the immortal twin and his mortal brother were both begotten in the same night by different fathers. These two parts now combine. In every case the man-to-man relationship strengthens consciousness and invigorates the ego principle, no matter whether the alliance appears psychologically as the combination of ego and shadow, or the combination of ego and self. That is to say, on one level the ego's assimilation of the earthly shadow-brother, i.e., its instinctual, destructive, and self-destroying side, is more evident, while on another it is the alliance of the earthly ego with its immortal twin brother, the self.

In contrast to the passive, self-absorbed, and narcissistic resistance to the mother, the fleeting defiance and self-destruction, this strengthening of masculine consciousness leads the ego to pit itself against the supremacy of the matriarchate, a process that can be followed out sociologically as well as psychologically. Sociologically the advance is from matrilocal-matriarchal marriage to patrilocal-matriarchal marriage, and finally to patriarchal marriage. The depotentiation of the female can be seen most clearly in the status of woman. At first, as the birth-giver, she had complete control over her child; there was no father to contend with, particularly while the connection between the sexual act and birth remained unrecognized. Later the father was a stranger institutionally excluded from exercising authority over the children. In the patriarchate, on the other hand, the father who begets the child is its master, and woman is only the vessel, the birth-passage, the nurse. We have a corresponding psychological process when, with the strengthening of

181

masculinity and ego consciousness, the fight with the mother dragon becomes the hero's, i.e., the ego's, struggle for self-liberation. In this struggle the union of the hero with the masculine "heaven" brings about a self-regeneration in which the male reproduces himself without the aid of a female.

The rise of the patriarchate brings with it a revaluation. The matriarchate, representing the supremacy of the unconscious, now becomes negative. Consequently the mother assumes the character of dragon and Terrible Mother. She is the old order that has to be surpassed. In her stead there appears the elder brother, the maternal uncle, bearer of the authority complex in the matriarchate, as we find it in the conflict between Set and Horus.

The conflict between maternal uncle and son is eventually replaced by that between father and son. This development shows very clearly how the archetypal link between the bad old order and the "enemy" changes with the different stages of consciousness and is projected upon different carriers, but still continues to exist as such, because archetypal. For the hero who represents the new consciousness, the hostile dragon is the old order, the obsolete psychic stage which threatens to swallow him up again. The most comprehensive and earliest form of this is the Terrible Mother; she is followed by the authoritarian male representative of the matriarchate, the maternal uncle; he is followed by the unfriendly old king, and only then do we get the father.

The killing of the father in mythology is part of the problem of the First Parents and is not to be derived from the personal parents, much less from the son's sexual fixation to the mother. The conjectured originality of the patriarchal family is, as Briffault has rightly seen, a psychological residue caused by excessive reliance upon Biblical research.[8] With the refutation of this conjecture, the father-murder theory collapses, and with it the

[8] Briffault (*The Mothers*, Vol. I, p. 201) has demonstrated that the beginnings of society are not to be found in the patriarchal family but in the matriarchal family, and that the psychology of anthropoid apes provides no evidence for an originally patriarchal family.

Oedipus complex and the anthropological proofs which Freud attempted in *Totem and Taboo*.

Mythology makes it clear that Horus was positive to his father and negative to his maternal uncle Set, in whom, as we know, all authority was invested in the matriarchal family. This confirms Malinowski's findings [9] that, in primitive societies founded upon matriarchal law, there is a wish to kill, not the father, but the mother's brother, who "represents discipline, authority, and executive power within the family." The intention to kill, or rather the ambivalence underlying it, is therefore in no sense sexually based and does not aim at possession of the mother.

The boy's relation to the father who possesses the mother sexually is, if anything, tender. But against the maternal uncle, for whom the mother was sexually and in all other respects taboo from earliest childhood, there is nevertheless a death wish. And if in these cultures the sexually tabooed sister is unconsciously desired, she is as much taboo for the maternal uncle as for the boy himself, so that the motive of sexual jealousy breaks down in the case of the sister as well.

Why, then, the death wish? Because the maternal uncle is the carrier of what we named "heaven," which stands for masculinity. Malinowski says of this maternal uncle that he brings "duty, prohibition, and coercion" into the children's lives. "He wields the power, he is idealized, and to him the mother and children are subject." Through him the boy acquires ideas like "social ambition, fame, pride of birth, and feelings for his tribe, hope of future riches, and social position." It is against this authority who stands for collective law that the boy's death wish is directed,[10] whether because his infantile side feels this authority to be overbearing or his heroic side feels it to be restrictive. It is through the maternal uncle, therefore, that the collectively determined superego component of the father archetype—conscience—is experienced. His killing has nothing and can have

[9] *Mutterrechtliche Familie und Ödipus-Komplex; The Father in Primitive Psychology;* etc.
[10] Aldrich, *The Primitive Mind and Modern Civilization,* p. 6.

nothing to do with rivalry for the mother, because no such rivalry exists. (We appreciate that the term "father archetype" is colored by our own patriarchal culture, but we retain it nevertheless because it helps to make our meaning clear.)

This resounding defeat for psychoanalytical theory is particularly instructive in that it shows up the psychoanalyst's habit of making a spurious universal principle out of late personalistic phenomena. But it is also significant because it proves the importance of transpersonal factors such as the authoritarian side of the father archetype. The transpersonal factor is projected upon different objects, sometimes upon the maternal uncle and sometimes upon the father, according to the sociological and historical situation. But in every case there must be an encounter with the carrier of this factor, for without the murder of the "father" no development of consciousness and personality is possible.

With the accession to power of the male there also follows an intensified rivalry among the male groups, which grows in proportion to the expansion of individual villages, tribes, and states, and the accumulation of property. Primitive culture is characterized by a rigid isolation of separate groups, sometimes carried to such grotesque length that different tribes inhabiting the same island do not know one another and remain in a state of xenophobia that is prehistoric. The spread of civilization creates increasing cross-connections and cross-conflicts. So begins man's political life, which is almost always identical with the rise of the patriarchate; and with it there comes another shift in the principle of opposites, namely, the masculine opposition between young and old, although originally this was in no sense identical with the father-son conflict.

Originally, at the sacrifice of the seasonal king in fertility ritual, the representative of the old year or year-cycle was just as young as the new king who succeeded him after his death. Only by virtue of his identification with the year was he symbolically old and therefore doomed to die. The lamentation which even in quite late times was followed, without any pause, by resur-

184

rection testifies to the ritual nature of this sacrifice. It also disproves the naturalistic explanation that the vegetation was killed by the summer heat and rose again in the spring. That would be to assume that between death and resurrection there lay a period of drought and wintertime—a spell of some duration, which is not at all the case. On the contrary the resurrection—originally that of the new king—followed immediately upon the death of the old. The conflict between the two kings was only a symbolical and not a factual conflict between old and young. Later, during the transition to the patriarchate, the annual king, or the secular king who reigned for a few years, was replaced by a king who had the right to defend his life in battle. The king, renewed annually or at longer intervals, had as his deputy a seasonal king who was sacrificed, though this was later superseded by the sacrifice of an animal. In this way the permanent king, whose vitality represented the fertility of the group, could now really grow old and become feeble, and was expected to survive the fight with his deputy or with anyone who challenged him. So long as he was victorious he remained king. If conquered, he was sacrificed and the victor succeeded him.

Only with the institution of the permanent king as described by Frazer, therefore, does there arise any conflict between old and young, the permanent king representing the old, and his opponent the young. This early stage of the patriarchate was of great importance for the hero myth, because then and then only does the conflict arise between the old king and the young hero. The mythological element—the conflict between stepfather and hero—is not a disguise for a conflict between the personal father and son. Again and again we see from ancient history that the founding of dynasties by heroes and the overthrow of old kings and old dynasties are historical realities. The underlying principle of opposites, even when it appears in symbolical form, is much earlier than the patriarchal family and cannot be derived from or reduced to it.

The Terrible Male who has to be killed and whose final form is the Terrible Father has, then, an antecedent history, which

185

is not the case with the Terrible Mother. This confirms our hypothesis of the constant nature of the mother archetype and the cultural complexion of the father archetype. Compared with the uniform frightfulness of the mother dragon, the father dragon is a culturally stratified structure. From this angle also she is nature, he is culture. The Terrible Male, like the Terrible Female, is always old and evil and to be overthrown—at any rate for the hero, whose task it is to achieve something out of the common. The Terrible Male, however, functions not only as a principle that disintegrates consciousness, but even more as one that fixes it in a wrong direction. It is he who prevents the continued development of the ego and upholds the old system of consciousness. He is the destructive instrument of the matriarchate, as its henchman; he is its authority, as the maternal uncle; he is the negative force of self-destruction and the will to regression, as the twin; and finally he is the authority of the patriarchate, as the Terrible Father.

The Terrible Father appears to the hero in two transpersonal figures: as the phallic Earth Father and the frightening Spirit Father. The Earth Father, lord of all chthonic forces, belongs psychologically to the realm of the Great Mother. He manifests himself most commonly as the overwhelming aggressiveness of phallic instinct or as a destructive monster. But whenever the ego is overwhelmed by the sexual, aggressive, or power instincts of the male, or by any other form of instinct, we can see the dominance of the Great Mother. For she is the instinctual ruler of the unconscious, mistress of animals, and the phallic Terrible Father is only her satellite, not a masculine principle of equal weight.

But the other side of the Terrible Father, who thwarts the son and hinders his self-development, is spiritual rather than phallic. Just as in Barlach's *Der Tote Tag* the terrible Earth Mother prevents her son from becoming a hero and thus "castrates" him, so there is a Terrible Father who castrates the son by not letting him achieve self-fulfillment and victory. Once again, this father is transpersonal. He acts, as it were, like a spiritual system which, from beyond and above, captures and destroys the son's consciousness. This spiritual system appears as the binding force of the old law, the old religion, the old morality, the old order; as conscience, convention, tradition, or any other spiritual phenomenon that seizes hold of the son and obstructs his progress into the future. Any content that functions through its emotional dynamisms, such as the paralyzing grip of inertia or an invasion by instinct, belongs to the sphere of the mother, to nature. But all contents capable of conscious realization, a value, an idea, a moral canon, or some other spiritual force, are related to the father-, never to the mother-system.

Patriarchal castration has two forms: captivity and possession. In captivity, the ego remains totally dependent upon the father as the representative of collective norms—that is, it identifies with the lower father and thus loses its connection with the creative powers. It remains bound by traditional morality and conscience, and, as though castrated by convention, loses the higher half of its dual nature.

The other form of patriarchal castration is identification with the father-god. This leads to the possessed state of heavenly inflation, "annihilation through the spirit." Here too the ego-hero loses consciousness of his dual nature by losing touch with his earthly part.

Behind patriarchal castration through inflation there looms the devouring figure of the uroboros, combining in itself the voracity of the male and of the female. In the vortex of the divine pleroma the paternal and maternal aspects of the uroboros fuse into one. Annihilation through the spirit, i.e., through the Heavenly Father, and annihilation through the unconscious, i.e., through the Earth Mother, are identical, as the study of every psychosis teaches. The collective spiritual forces are as much parts of the uroboros as the collective instinctual forces pulling in the opposite direction.

Annihilation through the spirit is a motif that occurs as early as the Babylonian Etana myth, where the hero is borne up to heaven by an eagle and crashes to earth. (Here the unattainable

187

heaven is related to the mother goddess Ishtar who, uroborically speaking, is heaven and earth at once.) The same mythological situation is repeated in Icarus, who flies too near the sun, and in Bellerophon, who attempts to reach heaven on the winged horse Pegasus, but crashes to earth, and goes mad. The hybris of Theseus and other heroes depicts a similar constellation. Just because he is begotten by God the hero must be "devout" and fully conscious of what he is doing. If he acts in the arrogance of egomania, which the Greeks called hybris, and does not reverence the *numinosum* against which he strives, then his deeds will infallibly come to nought. To fly too high and fall, to go too deep and get stuck, these are alike symptoms of an overvaluation of the ego that ends in disaster, death, or madness. An overweening contempt for the transpersonal powers above and below means falling victim to them, whether the hero crashes to earth like Etana, or plunges into the sea like Icarus, or sticks fast to the underworld like Theseus, or is chained to the rock like Prometheus, or does penance like the Titans.

Patriarchal castration, involving as it must the sacrifice of man's earthly side, leads no less than matriarchal castration to the sacrifice of the phallus. This is yet another indication of the mysterious identity of the paternal with the maternal uroboros. Consequently castration symbols often occur in those who are overpowered by the spirit, for example in gnosis and the mystery religions. In the gnostic Attis-cult hymn,[11] Attis is identified with Adonis, Osiris, Hermes, Adamas, Corybas, and Papas, it being said of all of them that they are the "corpse, God, and barren." The element already encountered in the "strugglers" against the matriarchate reappears here, namely self-castration as an act of defiance against the Great Mother. The gnostic strugglers are possessed by the Spirit Father. Fascinated, they succumb to patriarchal castration and thus to the uroboric pleroma, which proves to be the Great Mother and the very thing they were trying to resist. They are overtaken by the same fate as the strugglers in the myth.

[11] Leisegang, *Die Gnosis*, pp. 129 f.

Nevertheless, patriarchal castration has a somewhat different coloring. Whereas matriarchal castration is orgiastic, the other tends toward asceticism. As with all extremes, the two forms overlap. For instance, certain gnostic sects indulged in sexual orgies, but these were nullified in a typically gnostic manner. The orgy, being an ecstatic phenomenon, was related to the Spirit Father, while at the same time the fertility principle attributed to the mother deity or the demiurge was negated to the point of systematic abortion and child-murder.

Fathers' sons are the parallels of the mothers' sons already discussed. They owe their impotence to patriarchal castration, for which, when it takes the form of "captivity," we could coin the term "Isaac complex." Abraham is prepared to offer up his son Isaac, who trusts him implicitly. We shall not consider the religious and psychological situation of Abraham, because here we are solely concerned with that of the son. Two symptoms are characteristic. The first, clearly indicated in the Bible, is Isaac's utter reliance upon his father, whom he follows in all things without ever standing on his own feet. The second is the peculiar nature of his religious experience, i.e., of that part of his personality which is able to stand alone and which experiences God as *"pachad Yizchak"*—Isaac's fear and trembling.[12]

In all such cases of impotence and excessive respect for the law, "conscience," or the authority of the old collective father, drowns the "inner voice" which announces the new manifestation of the Divine. Just as with mothers' sons the father-god is eclipsed by the Terrible Mother, and they themselves are unconsciously held fast in the womb and cut off from the creative, solar side of life, so, for the fathers' sons, the hero-bearing goddess is blotted out by the Terrible Father. They

[12] Even if philological research should prove that *pachad* means "kinship" and that the interpretation "dread" is wrong, the latter enjoys general acceptance and as such is effective. (Cf. Albright, *Stone Age*, for the "kinship" interpretation.)

Isaac's father-son psychology is characteristic of the Jew, in whom it is still found to this day as the Isaac complex. For him the law and the old order serve as a refuge from the demands of reality. The law becomes "Abraham's bosom," and the Torah a sort of masculine spiritual womb from whose clutches nothing new can be born.

live entirely on the conscious plane and are incarcerated in a kind of spiritual uterus that never allows them to reach the fruitful feminine side of themselves, the creative unconscious. In this way they are castrated like the mothers' sons. The heroism that has been stifled in them manifests itself as sterile conservatism and a reactionary identification with the father, which lacks the living, dialectical struggle between the generations.

The reverse side of this father complex—which by no means implies liberation from it—is to be found in the "eternal son," the permanent revolutionary. He identifies himself with the dragon-slaying hero, but is totally unconscious of his divine sonship. The absence of father identification prevents the eternal youth from ever obtaining his kingdom. His refusal to become a father and to assume power seems to him a guarantee of perpetual youth, for to assume power is to accept the fact that it must be passed on to a future son and ruler. The individualist is essentially nonarchetypal—that is to say, the eternal revolutionary, as he grows older, turns out to be a neurotic who is not prepared to "be his age" and accept his limitations. To negate the Isaac complex is not to get beyond it.

Thus the hero's task in fighting the dragon is not merely to overcome the mother, but the father also. The conflict is never personal, but is always transpersonal. Even where the personal parents play a part—and in practice they always do so—their personal share is relatively small, while that of the transpersonal parental imagos acting through them is enormously important. When we examine the history of the individual, we find that the personal reality of the parents is not only distorted but may sometimes be completely inverted if the archetypal canon demands it. Even Freud observed with astonishment that a prohibition may be obstinately attributed to the parent who never expressed any such thing.[13] Time and again it happens that, aside from the secondary personalization which always conveys a false picture to the ego, the operative factors are the transpersonal components of the unconscious.

[13] "From the History of an Infantile Neurosis."

The ego's encounter with these transpersonal factors alone creates personality and builds up its "authorities." [14] For this the hero serves as a model; his deeds and his sufferings illustrate what will later fall to the lot of every individual. The formation of the personality is symbolically portrayed in his life—he is the first "personality," and his example is followed by all who become personalities.

The three basic elements in the hero myth were the hero, the dragon, and the treasure. The nature of the hero was made clear in the chapter dealing with his birth, and that of the dragon in the chapters on the slaying of the mother and father. It still remains to analyze the third element, the goal of the dragon fight.

This goal, whether it be the beloved, the maiden in distress, or the "treasure hard to attain," is intimately linked with what happens to the hero in the course of the fight.

Only in this struggle does the hero show himself a hero and change his nature; for whether he is the doer who redeems or the conqueror who liberates, what he transforms transforms him too. Therefore the third and last stage is the transformation myth. The nature and creation myths of the first stage, which led in the hero myth to the battle of the natures, culminate in the triumphal myth of transformation, of which it is written: "Nature rules over nature."

[14] See infra, pp. 349 ff.

C. The Transformation Myth

I. THE CAPTIVE AND THE TREASURE

II. TRANSFORMATION, OR OSIRIS

Nature rules over nature.

I

THE CAPTIVE AND THE TREASURE

THE MYTHOLOGICAL GOAL of the dragon fight is almost always the virgin, the captive, or, more generally, the "treasure hard to attain." It is to be noted that a purely material pile of gold, such as the hoard of the Nibelungs, is a late and degenerate form of the original motif. In the earliest mythologies, in ritual, in religion, and in mystical literature as well as in fairy tales, legend, and poetry, gold and precious stones, but particularly diamonds and pearls,[1] were originally symbolic carriers of immaterial values. Likewise the water of life, the healing herb, the elixir of immortality, the philosophers' stone, miracle rings and wishing rings, magic hoods and winged cloaks, are all symbols of the treasure.

There is one phenomenon which is of great importance in psychological interpretation, and this phenomenon we would call the typological dual focus of myth and symbol. This only means that it is the nature of myths and fairy tales to work in equal measure, though in different ways, upon contrary psychological types.[2] That is to say, the extravert as well as the introvert finds "himself" portrayed and addressed in the myth. For this reason the myth must be interpreted on the objective level for the extravert and on the subjective level for the introvert,[3] but both interpretations are necessary and meaningful.

To take an example, "the captive" on the objective level is to be understood as a real living woman. The problem of the man-woman relationship, its difficulties and its solutions, will

[1] Cf. Jung and Wilhelm, *The Secret of the Golden Flower;* Jonas, "Lied von der Perle," in *Gnosis und spätantiker Geist,* pp. 320 f.; Preuss, *Die geistige Kultur der Naturvölker,* p. 18; Jung, *Psychology and Alchemy,* fig. 61.
[2] Jung, *Psychological Types.*
[3] Jung, "On Psychic Energy."

then find its prototype in the myth, and so, as an external event, this motif can be understood by the naïvest intelligence. But in primitive times, when the question of a partner presented no such problem as it does for us moderns, the winning and setting free of the captive meant very much more. The fight for her was a form of encounter between male and female, but, like the First Mother and the First Father, this female is transpersonal and stands for a collective psychic element in mankind.

Thus, besides interpretation on the objective level, there is from the very beginning another, equally valid, interpretation which sees the captive as something within—namely the soul herself. The myths deal with the relation of the masculine ego to this soul, and with the adventures and perils of the fight and her final deliverance. So much prominence is given to the miraculous and unreal in the events leading up to the goal of the dragon fight that the events taking place in the psychic background—which, for the introvert, is the center of attention—must unquestionably have depicted themselves in the mythological symbolism.

Naturally the typologically different reactions, laying emphasis now on the psychic background and now on the world as an external object, always remain unconscious. The background events in the soul are projected outwards and are experienced through the object, as a synthetic unity compounded of external reality and the psychic activation of this reality. The myth and its symbolism, however, are characterized by a preponderance of the inner psychic element, which distinguishes the mythological event from the "factual" event.

Besides the dual focus of mythological motifs, psychological interpretation has also to consider the juxtaposition of personalistic and transpersonal factors. Not that the difference between a personalistic and a transpersonal interpretation is identical with the difference we have already indicated between the views of the extraverted and the introverted type. Both types can have archetypal experiences, just as both can be limited to the purely personalistic plane. For instance, the introvert can stick to the

personal contents of his consciousness, or of his personal unconscious, which are full of significance for him, while the extravert can experience the transpersonal nature of the world
through the object. Hence the "captive," as an interior quantity, can be experienced both personalistically and transpersonally on the subjective level, just as it can be experienced personalistically and transpersonally as an exterior feminine quantity.
A personalistic interpretation is no more identical with the
objective level than a transpersonal interpretation with the subjective level.

The myth, being a projection of the transpersonal collective
unconscious, depicts transpersonal events, and, whether interpreted objectively or subjectively, in no case is a personalistic
interpretation adequate. Moreover, the subjective interpretation which sees the myth as a transpersonal psychic event is, in
view of the myth's origins in the collective unconscious, much
fairer than an attempt to interpret it objectively, e.g., as a mete-
orological or astral event.

Consequently the hero myth is never concerned with the private history of an individual, but always with some prototypal
and transpersonal event of collective significance. Even quasi-
personal traits have an archetypal meaning, however much the
individual heroes, their fates and the goals of their respective
dragon fights may appear to differ from one another.

Again, even when we interpret the fight and its goal subjectively, as a process going on within the hero, it is really a transpersonal process. Although they appear as inner events, the
victory and transformation of the hero are valid for all mankind; they are held up for our contemplation, to be lived out
in our own lives, or at least re-experienced by us. While modern
historiography, with its personalistic bias, is inclined to represent the collective events in the life of nations and mankind as
being dependent upon the personalistic whims of monarchs and
leaders, the myth reflects the transpersonal reality behind the
singular events in the life of the hero.

In a large number of myths the goal of the hero's fight is the rescue of a captive from the power of a monster. This monster is archetypally a dragon, or, where archetypal and personalistic features are intermingled, a witch or a magician, or, personalistically, a wicked father or wicked mother.

So far we have tried to interpret the fight with the dragon as an encounter with the mother-father archetype. It remains to clarify the relation of the captive and the treasure to the guardian powers symbolized by the two-faced dragon, and to explain what the goal means to the hero himself.

In the end, the captive always marries the hero; union with her is the essential outcome of dragon fights all the world over. The old fertility myths and the rituals underlying all spring and new-year festivals form the cultic prototype of which the hero myth is a segment. The overcoming of monsters and enemies is the condition of the young hero king's triumphal union with the Earth Goddess, which magically restores the fertility of the year. The freeing and winning of the captive through the dragon fight is an offshoot of this old fertility ritual. We have already discussed the development of the hero's masculinity in his fight with the dragon, and the overpowering of the Terrible Mother with which it is identical. The freeing and winning of the captive form a further stage in the evolution of masculine consciousness.

The transformation which the male undergoes in the course of the dragon fight includes a change in his relation to the female, symbolically expressed in the liberation of the captive from the dragon's power. In other words, the feminine image extricates itself from the grip of the Terrible Mother, a process known in analytical psychology as the crystallization of the anima from the mother archetype.

The union of the adolescent son with the Great Mother is followed by a phase of development in which an adult male combines with a feminine partner of his own age and kind, in the *hieros gamos*. Only now is he mature enough to reproduce himself. He is no longer the tool of a superordinate Earth Mother, but, like a father, he assumes the care and responsi-

198

bility for his offspring, and, having established a permanent relationship with a woman, founds the family as the nucleus of all patriarchal culture, and beyond that the dynasty and the state.

With the freeing of the captive and the founding of a new kingdom, the patriarchal age comes into force. It is not yet patriarchal in the sense that the female is subjugated, only in the sense that the male exercises independent control over his children. Whether the woman shares this control or the man arrogates all the power to himself, as in the tyrannical form of patriarchy, is of secondary importance beside the fact that the autocratic rule of the mother over her offspring is now ended.

We spoke earlier of the male's immemorial fear of the female which appears as soon as he ceases to be childishly dependent upon the all-providing Good Mother and becomes a separate entity.[4] This separation is natural and necessary. That is to say, there are more inside tendencies aiming at self-emancipation than there are outside tendencies which require and enforce this emancipation. No baleful father figure robs the infant of its mother; even if this picture does occur, it is always the projection of an inner, "heavenly" authority who insists upon the self-emancipation of the ego, just as, in the shape of the father, it exhorts the hero to fight. The youth's fear of the devouring Great Mother and the infant's beatific surrender to the uroboric Good Mother are both elementary forms of the male's experience of the female; but they must not be the only ones if a real man-woman relationship is to develop. So long as the man loves only the bounteous mother in woman, he remains infantile. And if he fears woman as the castrating womb, he can never combine with it and reproduce himself. What the hero kills is only the terrible side of the female, and this he does in order to set free the fruitful and joyous side with which she joins herself to him.

This freeing of the positive feminine element and its separation from the terrifying image of the Great Mother mean the

[4] See supra, pp. 155, 158.

freeing of the captive and the slaying of the dragon in whose custody she languishes. The Great Mother, hitherto the sole and sovereign form in which woman was experienced, is killed and overthrown.

The foreshadowing of this process in mythology, the transformation of the Terrible Mother, has been described by Kees [5] under the motif of the "pacification of the beast of prey," [6] though he does not consider the connections with which we are concerned here. He writes:

The pacification of the untamed forces in the beast of prey, as we see it in the magical taming of the injurious powers of "poisonous" nature deities, and above all in the conquest of the Uraeus serpent as the royal diadem of Buto, is a very characteristic contribution of human thought in the historical epoch.

Actually the taming of terrible deities goes back to the prehistoric age of mythology, as when the Egyptian Hathor is mollified and her "wrath" averted with the help of dancing, music, and intoxicating liquor; or when Bast, the friendly form of the lion goddess Sekhmet, becomes the goddess of healing, and her priests become physicians. In Egyptian mythology, however, this development soon reaches a higher level:

Now the wonder came to pass that the brutal goddess laid aside her nature and, as the "good sister" of her divine partner, changed into a human woman.

Here the transformation of the terrible female still takes place on the divine plane, and characteristically enough it is Thoth, the god of wisdom, who undertakes to pacify Tefnut,[7] another terrible lion goddess. But in the hero myth, where the action passes to the human world, the task of transforming and freeing the female is assigned to the hero.

In the captive she no longer appears as a mighty, transpersonal archetype, but as a human creature, a partner with whom

[5] Der Götterglaube, pp. 134 ff.
[6] Kees, "Die Befriedigung des Raubtiers," pp. 56 f.
[7] Erman, Religion, pp. 66 f.

man can unite himself personally. More: she is something that cries out to be rescued, set free, and redeemed, and she demands that the man shall prove himself manly, not merely as the bearer of the phallic instrument of fertilization, but as a spiritual potency, a hero. She expects strength, cunning, resourcefulness, bravery, protection, and readiness to fight. Her demands upon her rescuer are many. They include the throwing open of dungeons, deliverance from deadly and magical powers both paternal and maternal, the hacking down of the thorny thickets and flaming hedges of inhibition and anxiety, liberation of the slumbering or enchained womanhood in her, the solution of riddles and guessing games in a battle of wits, and rescue from joyless depression. But always the captive to be set free is personal and hence a possible partner for the man, while the perils he has to overcome are transpersonal forces which, objectively speaking, bind the captive or, subjectively, hinder the hero's relation to her.

Besides these rescue myths and dragon-slaying myths there are others in which the hero kills the monster with the assistance of a friendly female figure. In this series the woman— Medea, Ariadne, Athene, for example—is actively hostile to the dragon of the devouring mother archetype. These myths show us the helpful, sisterly side of woman, standing shoulder to shoulder with the hero as his beloved, helpmate, and companion, or as the Eternal Feminine who leads him to redemption. Fairy tales lay particular stress on the sisterliness of these figures who succor the hero in his peril, touchingly ready to sacrifice themselves and to love him with their purely human love whose very differences complement his own. It is no accident that the many-sided figure of Isis was not only the wife of Osiris and the mother who bore him anew, but also his sister.

The sisterly side of a man-woman relationship is that part of it which stresses the common human element; consequently, it gives man a picture of woman that is closer to his ego and more friendly to his consciousness than the sexual side. It is a typical form of relationship, not a real one. Mother, sister, wife, and daughter are the four natural elements in any relationship between men and women. Not only do they differ typologically, but each has its legitimate place in the development—and mis-development—of the individual. In practice, however, these basic types may be mixed; for instance, maternal or conjugal traits may be involved in a man's relations with his sister. But the important thing is that the sister, the feminine soul-image who appears personally as Electra and transpersonally as Athene, is a spiritual being, representing the female as a separate, ego-conscious individual who is quite distinct from the feminine-collective aspect of the "Mothers."

Once the anima-sister side has been experienced through the rescue of the captive, the man-woman relationship can develop over the whole field of human culture. The freed captive is not merely a symbol of man's erotic relations in the narrow sense. The task of the hero is to free, through her, the living relation to the "you," to the world at large.

The primitive psychology of man is characterized by a tendency of the libido to activate incestuous family ties, which Jung has called "kinship libido." [8] That is to say, the original state of *participation mystique* in the uroboros expresses itself as the force of inertia that keeps man fixed in the oldest and most intimate of family ties. These family ties are personalistically projected to mother and sister; and the symbolic incest with them, straining back to the uroboros, is therefore marked by a "lower femininity" which binds the individual and his ego to the unconscious.

With the rescue of the captive the hero frees himself from bondage to the endogamous kinship libido and advances toward "exogamy": the conquest of a woman outside the family or tribe. This "heterogynous" aspect of the anima always has the character of "higher femininity," because the anima-sister, both as the captive awaiting deliverance and as the helper, is related

[8] Jung, "Psychology of the Transference," par. 431.

to the higher masculinity of the hero, i.e., to the activity of his ego consciousness.[9]

The experience of the captive and helper marks out, within the threatening, monstrous world of the unconscious presided over by the Mothers, a quiet space where the soul, the anima, can take shape as the feminine counterpart of the hero, and as the complement to his ego consciousness. Though the anima figure also has transpersonal characteristics, she is closer to the ego, and contact with her is not only possible, but is the source of all fruitfulness.

Familiarity with this "higher" aspect of woman helps man to overcome his terror of the fanged and castrating womb, the Gorgon who bars his way to the captive, i.e., prevents entry into the creative, receptive womb of a real woman.

Besides the figure of Sophia-Athene, the "Eternal Feminine," we also find that of the captive princess, who not only draws the hero "upward and on," but "into" herself, thus changing him from a callow youth into her lord and master. In this sense the captive—Ariadne, Andromeda, etc.—is primarily the beloved, Aphrodite. But this Aphrodite is no longer the primordial ocean symbolizing the Great Mother; she has been born out of it and she carries its marks in altered form. We cannot dwell on the numerous anima aspects of the captive princess and their relation to the Great Mother; suffice it to say that the hero unites himself with the woman he has set free, and founds his kingdom with her.

The rite of marriage derives from the part played by the king in the old fertility ritual. The union of the Earth Goddess with the god-king becomes the prototype of marriage, and only with the institution of this symbolic ritual did the act of sexual union, endlessly repeated for millions of years, begin to be understood consciously. It now became evident, as an ideal and in actual fact, that the hitherto unconscious union, previously regulated

[9] Needless to say, only this factor can constellate the higher femininity. So-called "spiritual" arguments which activate kinship libido and lead to incest belong to the sphere of the lower femininity, whereas sexual motives which lead to the dragon fight must be classed with the higher.

only by instinct, has a meaning. Its link with the transpersonal invests a mindless natural occurrence with the solemn significance of a ritual act.

Thus the hero's rescue of the captive corresponds to the discovery of a psychic world. This world is already of vast extent as the world of Eros, embracing everything that man has ever done for woman, everything that he has experienced and created for her sake. The world of art, of epic deeds, poesy, and song which revolves round the liberated captive spreads out like a virgin continent that has broken away from the world of the First Parents. Great tracts of human culture, and not of art alone, spring from this interplay and counterplay of the sexes, or rather, of masculine and feminine. But the symbolism associated with the rescue of the captive goes even further. For, with the liberation of the captive, a portion of the alien, hostile, feminine world of the unconscious enters into friendly alliance with the man's personality, if not actually with his consciousness.

Personality is built up largely by acts of introjection: contents that were before experienced outside are taken inside. Such "external objects," as well as being contents of the objective world without, i.e., things and persons, can also be contents of the psychic world of objects within. In this sense the liberation of the captive and the dismemberment of the dragon mean not merely an "analysis" of the unconscious, but its assimilation, resulting in the formation of the anima as one authority within the personality. (Cf. Part II.)

It is a tremendous step forward when a feminine, "sisterly" element—intangible but very real—can be added to the masculine ego consciousness as "my beloved" or "my soul." The word "my" separates off from the anonymous, hostile territory of the unconscious a region which is felt to be peculiarly "my" own, belonging to "my" particular personality. And although it is experienced as feminine and therefore "different," it has an elective affinity with the masculine ego which would have been unthinkable in connection with the Great Mother.

The dragon fight is correlated psychologically with different phases in the ontogenetic development of consciousness. The conditions of the fight, its aim and also the period in which it takes place, vary. It occurs during the childhood phase, during puberty, and at the change of consciousness in the second half of life, wherever in fact a rebirth or a reorientation of consciousness is indicated. For the captive is the "new" element whose liberation makes further development possible.

The tests of masculinity and the proofs of ego stability, will power, bravery, knowledge of "heaven," and so forth, which are demanded of the hero, have their historical equivalent in the rites of puberty. Just as the problem of the First Parents is resolved in the dragon fight, and is in turn succeeded by the hero's encounter with woman as his partner and his soul, so, through the initiation ceremony, the neophyte is detached from the parental sphere, and becomes a marriageable young man capable of founding a family. But what happens in myth and in history also happens in the individual, and on the basis of the same archetypal determinism. The central feature of puberty psychology is the syndrome of the dragon fight. Time and again the failure of the dragon fight, i.e., involvement in the problem of the First Parents, proves to be the central problem for neurotics during the first half of life and the cause of their inability to establish relations with a partner. The personal aspects of this situation, a small part of which has been formulated psychoanalytically as the personalistic Oedipus complex, are merely surface aspects of the conflict with the First Parents, i.e., with the parental archetypes. And in this process, not only the man, but, as will be shown elsewhere, the woman, too, has to "kill the parents" by overthrowing the tyranny of the parental archetypes. Only by killing the First Parents can a way be found out of the conflict into personal life.

To get stuck in this conflict and to yield to its fascination is characteristic of a large group of neurotics, and also of a certain spiritual type of man whose limitations lie precisely in his failure to master the feminine psyche in his fight with the dragon.

So long as the conflict with the First Parents occupies the

foreground, consciousness and ego remain rooted in the magic circle of this relationship. Although this circle is of almost infinite extent, and the struggle within it the struggle with the primary forces of life, the fact remains that the activity of the individual who confines himself to this primal circle is essentially negative in character. He is the victim of his own isolation and seclusion. People who get exclusively involved with these primary forces, the First Parents, remain "in the retort," as the alchemists say, and never reach the stage of the "red stone." The fact that they have failed to rescue and redeem the feminine side of themselves is often expressed psychologically in an intensive preoccupation with universals to the exclusion of the personal, human element. Their heroic and idealistic concern with humanity at large lacks the self-limitation of the lover, who is ready to cleave to the individual, and not to mankind and the universe alone.

All redeemer and savior figures whose victory stops short without rescuing the captive, without sacramentally uniting themselves with her, and therefore without having founded a kingdom, have something dubious about them from the psychological point of view. Their manifest lack of feminine relationship is compensated by an excessively strong unconscious tie to the Great Mother. The nonliberation of the captive expresses itself in the continued dominance of the Great Mother [10] under her deadly aspect, and the final result is alienation from the body and from the earth, hatred of life, and world negation.

Despite the extraordinary importance of the captive for conscious development, we do not find in the myths any particular characterization of her as an individual, nor would this be consistent with the nature of the anima.

It is only the captive's connection with the "treasure hard to attain," that reveals her nature, for the captive is herself the treasure, or is somehow related to it. The treasure is invested with magical properties: its finder obtains the power to make witchcraft, to fulfill wishes, to become invisible and invulner-

[10] See infra, p. 252.

able, to change his shape, to have revelations, to conquer space and time, to become immortal.

We constantly find it asserted that the magical treasure is merely the recrudescence of "infantile wishful thinking," and that the faculties thereby acquired are nothing but wishful ideas. It would seem to be a question of what Freud was later to call the "sovereign power of thought," an expression that has since become popular. By this he meant the alleged peculiarity of childish and primitive natures to believe that wishes and thoughts are effective, i.e., real. Here too Jung made discoveries of fundamental importance in his *Psychology of the Unconscious,* although at the time much of the material was taken in the narrow psychoanalytical sense and could only be rectified later in his *Psychological Types.* This applies in particular to introversion, the inward-turning of the libido, which requires an interpretation on the subjective level. But, before it was recognized that introversion and extraversion were equally legitimate attitude types, Jung himself interpreted introversion reductively and misunderstood it as an archaic and regressive phenomenon, i.e., as a relapse into a primitive mode of functioning.

This view is very much in evidence when Jung interprets "the precious thing hard to attain" as masturbation, particularly where the object of the hero's fight is the theft of fire.[11] It is at first not altogether clear why, if masturbation is the precious thing, it should be so very "hard" to attain, especially as psychoanalysis states that it is a perfectly natural stage in infantile sexuality. Such a statement borders on the paradoxical when the captive crops up in connection with this precious thing. All the same, psychoanalysis has grasped an essential aspect of the mythological situation. It was correct in seeing the facts as symbolic, but it interpreted them personalistically and therefore falsely. As the precious thing hard to obtain, masturbation is to be taken in connection with the theft of fire as a symbol of

11 *Symbols of Transformation,* p. 160.

creative generation,[12] in which sense it has remarkable correspondences with the production of fire by rubbing and also with immortality, rebirth, and self-discovery.[13] And indeed, if the liberation of the captive and the gaining of the treasure release a flood of productivity in the soul, causing the individual to feel himself, in this creative act, akin to the gods, then it is no wonder that mythology is so passionately concerned with the symbol of the treasure.

In dealing with the creation myths we pointed out that the childish question of "where life comes from" is bound up with the question of the parents and the nature of birth and generation. We found that personalistic interpretations and explanations which only take account of sexuality were inadequate, and this is true also in the present context. Just as the child is really asking about the "First Parents" of all that lives, so it is not a question here of masturbation, but of the creative and self-generating powers of the soul.

Mankind is not infantile and is not to be fobbed off with wishful thinking. Despite all the idiosyncrasies of human nature, a purely illusory sort of thinking, even in the case of primitive man, stands in flagrant contrast to his genius for adaptation and his sense of reality, to which we owe all the elementary inventions that make civilization possible.

To take an example, the magical connection between the ritual representation of the killing of an animal in paleolithic art and the killing of it in reality is not "real"—i.e., does not "work"—in the way in which primitive man possibly thought that it did work. We, with our logical mode of thinking, first understand this magical working in terms of causality, and then declare that no such causal connection exists. But primitive man experiences the magical effect differently, and more correctly. In any case, the effect of the pictorial killing upon the real animal is not the effect of "thought," so that to speak of the "sovereign power of thought" is exceedingly problematical. We can

[12] See supra, pp. 19 f.
[13] Jung, op. cit.

establish as a scientific fact that the rite is not likely to have any objective effect upon the animal; but that is not to say that the magic rite is therefore illusory, infantile, and mere wishful thinking.

The magical effect of the rite is factual enough, and in no sense illusory. Moreover it actually works out, just as primitive man supposes, in his hunting successes; only the effect does not proceed via the object but via the subject. The magical rite, like all magic and indeed every higher intention, including those of religion, acts upon the subject who practices the magic or the religion, by altering and enhancing his own ability to act. In this sense the outcome of the action, whether it be hunting, war, or whatever else, is in the highest degree objectively dependent upon the effect of the magic ritual. It was left for modern man to make the psychological discovery that the operative factor in magic is the "reality of the soul" and not the reality of the world. Originally the reality of the soul was projected outwards upon an external reality. Even today, prayers for victory are commonly regarded not as an inner alteration of the psyche but as an effort to influence God. In exactly the same way, hunting magic was experienced as an effort to influence the quarry, and not as an influencing of the hunter himself. In both cases our enlightened rationalism misunderstands the magic and prayer as illusory, in its scientific pride at having established that the object cannot be influenced. In both cases it is wrong. An effect that proceeds from an alteration in the subject is objective and real.

The reality of the soul is one of the basic and most immediate experiences of mankind; it permeates primitive man's whole view of life, naturally without his being aware that it is an inner experience. The animating principle of mana, the effect of magic, the magical efficacy of spirits, and the reality of collective ideas, dreams, and ordeals are all governed by the laws of this interior reality which modern depth psychology is trying to bring to the surface. We must not forget that the discovery of the objective, external world is a secondary phenomenon, the result of human consciousness endeavoring, with infinite labor and the help of the instruments and abstractions of modern science, to grasp the object as such, independently of the primary reality of man, which is the reality of the psyche. But early man relates himself above all to this primary reality of psychic dominants, archetypes, primordial images, instincts, and patterns of behavior. This reality is the object of his science, and his efforts to deal with it in his cults and rituals were just as successful in controlling and manipulating the inner forces of the unconscious as are modern man's efforts to control and manipulate the forces of the physical world.

This discovery of the reality of the psyche corresponds mythologically to the freeing of the captive and the unearthing of the treasure. The primordial creative powers of the psyche, which in the creation myths were projected upon the cosmos, are now experienced humanly, as part of man's personality, as his soul. Only now does the hero become humanized, and only through this act of liberation do the transpersonal processes of the unconscious become psychic processes within a human person.

By freeing the captive and raising the treasure, a man gains possession of his soul's treasures, which are not just "wishes," i.e., images of something he has not got but would like to have, but possibilities, i.e., images of something he could have and ought to have. The task of the hero, which is to "awaken those sleeping images that can and must come forth from the night, in order to give the world a better face," is far indeed from "masturbation." And yet it is a preoccupation with oneself, a case of letting the libido stream inward, without a partner—a kind of masturbatory self-fertilization in the uroboric manner, which alone makes possible the creative process of psychic palingenesis or self-birth.

The reality of all culture, our own included, consists in realizing these images which lie dormant in the psyche. All art, religion, science, and technology, everything that has ever been done, spoken, or thought, has its origin in this creative center. The self-generating power of the soul is man's true and final secret, by virtue of which he is made in the likeness of God the creator and distinguished from all other living things. These images, ideas, values, and potentialities of the treasure hidden in the unconscious are brought to birth and realized by the hero in his various guises—savior and man of action, seer and sage, founder and artist, inventor and discoverer, scientist and leader.

It seems to be a well-established fact that the problem of creation lies at the heart of the mythological canon which once prevailed throughout the Near East: everywhere the drama of the dying and resurgent god, enacted on New Year's Day by the king as the god's successor, was accompanied by a recitation of the current creation story.[14]

If we take this dramatic enactment of mythological events as a projection of the psychological processes going on in the hero, then the connection between creation, the New Year's ritual, and rebirth becomes self-evident. The question as to why mankind "reproduces" the natural process in his cults and rituals, so indefatigably, so passionately, and apparently so senselessly, can now be answered. If primitive man holds the rite responsible for the fruitfulness of the earth and postulates a magical connection between the two, we must surely ask: Why does he do this? How comes it that he apparently overlooks the self-evident fact that the vegetation continues to grow and that nature can get on perfectly well without him?

Man's magico-religious behavior, which anthropocentrically includes his own actions as an essential part of the natural process, is the fountainhead of all culture. It is not true to say that he "reproduces" nature; rather, by means of an analogous set of symbols, he produces in his own soul the same creative process which he finds outside himself in nature. This equation of creation inside with creation outside can be seen in the identification of the Great Individual who represents mankind or the group—e.g., the fertility king—with the creator-god. The hero is a bringer of culture, like the god with whom the king is identical. It is related of Osiris that he led the Egyptians out of the

---

[14] Hooke, *Myth and Ritual*, pp. 8 f.

state of savagery and cannibalism and gave them their laws, not only teaching them to honor the gods, but to plant corn, to gather fruit, and to cultivate the grape.[15] In other words, civilization and agriculture are attributed to him. But why precisely to him? Because he is not merely a fertility god in the sense that he controls natural growth. He is this too, but his creativeness includes that capacity without being limited to it.

Every culture-hero has achieved a synthesis between consciousness and the creative unconscious. He has found within himself the fruitful center, the point of renewal and rebirth which, in the New Year fertility festival, is identified with the creative divinity, and upon which the continued existence of the world depends. This is what the rite—and, through it, mankind— "means": about this knowledge of the creative point, of the buried treasure which is the water of life, immortality, fertility, and the after-life rolled into one, the aspirations of mankind unwearyingly revolve. The constellation of this point is not a "reproduction" of nature, but a genuine creation, and the symbolic recitation of the story of creation at the new year has its rightful place at this point.[16] The inner object of the ritual is not the natural process, but the control of nature through the corresponding creative element in man.

It is, however, impossible to find the treasure unless the hero has first found and redeemed his own soul, his own feminine counterpart which conceives and brings forth. This inner receptive side is, on the subjective level, the rescued captive, the virgin mother who conceives by the holy wind-ghost and who is at once man's inspiration, his beloved and mother, the enchantress and prophetess, just as the hero is her lover and father.

The fruitfulness of the Great Mother—in other words, the predominance of the collective unconscious—causes a flood of unconscious material to irrupt into the personality, sweeping it along and sometimes even annihilating it like an elemental force. But the fruitfulness of the hero who gains the captive is a human

---

[15] Frazer, *The Golden Bough* (abridged edn., 1951), p. 421.
[16] Hooke, op. cit., p. 3.

and cultural fruitfulness. From the union of the hero's ego consciousness with the creative side of the soul, when he "knows" and realizes both the world and the anima, there is begotten the true birth, the synthesis of both.

The symbolic marriage of ego-hero and anima, as well as being the precondition of fertility, offers a firm foundation on which the personality can stand and fight the dragon, whether this be the dragon of the world or of the unconscious. Hero and princess, ego and anima, man and woman pair off and form the personal center which, modeled on the First Parents and yet opposed to them, constitutes the proper human sphere of action. In this marriage, which in the oldest mythologies [17] was consummated at the New Year festival immediately after the defeat of the dragon, the hero is the embodiment of the "heaven" and father archetype, just as the fruitful side of the mother archetype is embodied in the rejuvenated and humanized figure of the rescued virgin. The liberation of the captive has the effect of releasing the virgin-wife, the young mother and partner, from her fusion with the uroboric mother, in whom dragon and virgin-mother were still one; but now they are finally differentiated from one another through the activated masculine consciousness of the hero (Part II).

After having discussed the symbol of the captive in all its ramifications, we shall sum up by taking the story of Perseus as a paradigm of the hero myth, for only now is it possible to understand the background and the symbolic meaning of all the mythological data.

Perseus was the child of Danaë, who conceived him by Zeus in a shower of golden rain (*illus. 24*). The "negative father" appears twice over in personal form. First as the grandfather, King Acrisius of Argos, who, because the oracle had prophesied that he would meet his death at the hands of his grandson, causes his daughter Danaë and her improvidently begotten child to be shut in a chest and cast into the sea. The second negative father figure is Polydectes, the "hospitable" ruler who marries Danaë and, to

[17] Ibid., p. 8.

get rid of Perseus, commands him to bring back the Gorgon's head.

Now the Gorgons are the daughters of Phorcys, the "Gray One," who, like his two sisters Keto ("the monstrous") and Eurybia ("the great in strength"), and his brother Thaumas ("the wonder-maker"), is a child of the deep, Pontos. All of them give birth to a terrifying and fabulous brood of monsters. The Gorgons, metallic-winged, serpent-haired and serpent-engirdled, tusked like boars, bearded and barbed, and with protruding tongues, are uroboric symbols of what we might justly call "the Infernal Feminine." Their sisters and guardians are the Graeae, whose name means fear and dread. They too, with their one eye and one tooth between them, are uroboric creatures who dwell on the uttermost confines of night and death, far to the westward, by the shores of the primeval ocean.

Perseus has Hermes and Athene on his side, the tutelary deities of wisdom and consciousness, with whose help he outwits the Graeae, contriving to learn from them the way to the nymphs. These beneficent sea-goddesses give him the helmet of invisibility that belongs to Hades, a pair of winged sandals, and a wallet. Hermes presents him with a sword, and Athene lends him her brazen shield for a mirror, in which he can see the Medusa's head reflected and so is able to kill her, for to look directly upon the Gorgon's features is to risk certain death by being instantly turned to stone (*illus. 25*).

We cannot enter more closely into this exceedingly interesting symbolism, except to say that intellect and spiritualization symbols play a most significant part. Flying, invisibility, and reflected sight form a homogeneous group, and to this we would add the wallet in which Perseus hides the Gorgon's head, thus making it invisible and harmless, as a symbol of repression.

Now, what is so very odd is the manner in which Perseus is represented in early Greek art.[18] The main feature is not, as one might think, the killing of the Gorgon, but the hero's headlong flight from the pursuing sisters. To our way of thinking it is

---

[18] Woodward, *Perseus: A Study in Greek Art and Legend.*

strange indeed to see the valiant Perseus depicted over and over again as a tearing fugitive.

Evidently the winged sandals, the helmet of invisibility, and the hiding-wallet are much more important to him than the death-dealing sword, and his fear greatly enhances the horrific aspect of the slain but ever-pursuing Gorgon. Once more we encounter the mythological prototype of Orestes pursued by the Furies, for, like him, Perseus becomes a hero because he has killed the Terrible Mother.

The uroboric character of the Gorgon can be adduced not only from the symbols but also from the history of religion. In connection with the Gorgonesque sculpture on the temple of Artemis in Corfu, dating from the sixth century, Woodward writes:

It may seem odd that this uncouth, grimacing figure should be given the place of honor on the temple pediment, but the idea behind it takes us back to a time long before these Gorgon-figures were identified with the creatures of the Perseus legend. With her attendant lions, she embodies the great Nature Spirit of primitive belief, who appears in early Asiatic and Ionian works of art as a goddess, with birds, lions, or snakes heraldically set on either side of her, the prototype of the Cybele of Phrygian worship and the Artemis of the Greeks. Here, through one aspect of her nature, she has become partly identified with Medusa.[19]

Without pausing to comment on this passage, we can take it that the identity of the Gorgon dispatched by Perseus, and the figure of the Great Mother who rules over wild animals, is proven, even for investigators not familiar with the real background of the myth.

The hero's flight and escape, then, testify very clearly to the overpowering character of the Great Mother. Despite the assistance of Hermes and Athene, despite the miraculous gifts bestowed on him by the nymphs, and despite the fact that he averts his face for the death stroke, he is barely man enough to kill her. (Note that the paralyzing and petrifying effect of the hideous death mask reappears as the "stickfast motif" [20] in the

[19] Ibid., p. 39.
[20] [See Coomaraswamy, "A Note on the Stickfast Motif."—TRANS.]

215

story of Theseus. Attempting to abduct Persephone from the underworld, he sticks fast to the rocks and is tormented by the Erinyes until Herakles comes to his rescue.) The power of the Great Mother is too overwhelming for any consciousness to tackle direct. Only by indirect means, when reflected in Athene's mirror, can the Gorgon be destroyed—in other words, only with the help of the patron goddess of consciousness, who, as the daughter of Zeus, stands for "heaven."

On his way back from killing the mother, Perseus frees Andromeda from a horrible sea monster that ravages the land and is about to devour the girl (*illus. 26*). This monster has been sent by Poseidon, who is referred to as "the Medusa's lover" [21] and is, as ruler of the ocean, himself the monster. He is the Terrible Father, and since he is the Medusa's lover, he is clearly related to the Great Mother as her invincible phallic consort. Again and again in his wrath he sends monsters to devastate the land and destroy the inhabitants; he is the dragon or bull who represents the destructive masculine side of the uroboros which has split off and became autonomous. The defeat of this monster is the task of the hero, whether he be called Bellerophon or Perseus, Theseus or Herakles.

Thus the sequence so typical of the hero myth is recapitulated in the story of Perseus: The killing of the transpersonal mother and father (the Medusa and the sea monster) precedes the rescue of the captive, Andromeda. His father a god and his mother the bride of a god, a personal father who hates him, then the killing of the transpersonal First Parents, and finally the liberation of the captive—these are the stages that mark the progress of the hero. But this path can only be trodden to its triumphal conclusion with the help of the divine father, whose agent here is Hermes, and with the help of Athene, whose spiritual character and hostility to the Great Mother we have already emphasized.[22]

[21] Woodward, op. cit., p. 74.

[22] Cf. supra, p. 169. Hermes, Athene, and Perseus represent the triple alliance of the self, Sophia, and the ego against the unconscious, i.e., the Medusa. This triad corresponds to the earlier triadic combination of Osiris, Isis, and Horus

The fact that Perseus then gives the Gorgon's head to Athene, and that she emblazons it upon her shield, crowns this whole development as the victory of Athene over the Great Mother, of the warrior aspect which is favorable to man and consciousness, and which we also met in the *Oresteia*. The most striking feature in the figure of Athene is the defeat of the old mother goddess by the new, feminine, spiritual principle. Athene still has all the characteristics of the great Cretan goddess. On numerous vase paintings she is surrounded by snakes; indeed the great snake is her constant companion right to the end. Likewise her emblem, the tree, and her appearance in the form of a bird betray her Cretan origins. But the primordial power of the female has been subdued by her; she now wears the Gorgon's head as a trophy upon her shield. From quite early times she had been the patron goddess of the ruler and was worshiped in his palace,[23] so that she came to symbolize the revolution which, in the patriarchal age, broke the power of the mother deity. Sprung from the head of Zeus, she is father-born and motherless in contrast to the mother-born, fatherless figures of ancient times; and in contrast, again, to the Terrible Mother's animosity toward all things masculine, she is the companion and helper of the masculine hero. This fellowship between man and woman is illustrated on a vase, dating from the second quarter of the sixth century B.C., which shows Perseus hurling stones at the monster. Andromeda is not, as is usually the case, chained and passive; she is standing beside Perseus as his helpmate.

Another symbolically important feature of the myth tells us that a winged horse, Pegasus, sprang from the decapitated trunk of the Gorgon. The horse belongs to the chthonic-phallic world and was said to be the offspring of Poseidon; he represents nature and instinct, which are all-powerful in half-human creatures like the centaurs. The sea horse sporting among the

---

against Set, which we shall examine in the next chapter. Athene stands for the hero's virgin-mother Sophia, whose earthly anima representative he sets free in Andromeda.

[23] Nilsson, in Chantepie de la Saussaye, *Lehrbuch*, Vol. II, p. 316.

white-crested breakers is a variant of the same motif. As the moved and moving element in the stormy sea of the unconscious, he is the destructive impulse; whereas in the horse as a domesticated animal nature is tamed and submissive. It is interesting to note that in an early picture of the slaying of the Medusa, from the seventh century B.C.,[24] she appears as a centaur.[25] This symbolism seems to be primordial and is the basis of the story that Pegasus sprang from the slain Medusa; the winged horse is set free when the centauress is destroyed by the winged man.

What the winged horse symbolizes is the freeing of libido from the Great Mother and its soaring flight, in other words, its spiritualization. It is with the help of this same Pegasus that Bellerophon performs his heroic deeds. He withstands the seductions of Antheia, who thereupon sends him forth to fight the Chimera and the Amazons. Again the symbolism points clearly enough to the victory of the masculine, conscious spirit over the powers of the matriarchate.

The profound psychological intuition of the myth is revealed even more strikingly in the fact that Pegasus, on being released from the Medusa, is credited with a creative work upon earth. We are told that, as the winged horse flew up to Zeus amid thunder and lightning, he struck the Fountain of the Muses from the ground. The archetypal affinity between horse and fountain is the same as that between natural impulse and creative fertilization. In Pegasus it takes the form of transformation and sublimation: the winged horse strikes the fountain of poesy from the earth. As we shall see later, this aspect of the Pegasus myth lies at the root of all creativity.

The destruction of the dragon means not only the liberation of the captive, but the ascent of libido. The process known in psychological theory as the crystallization of the anima from the mother archetype is dynamically portrayed in the myth of Pegasus. The soaring creative forces are set free by the death of

---

[24] Woodward, op. cit., Pl. 3a.

[25] For the connection between the Great Mother as Pheraea-Hecate-Demeter, the Medusa and the horse, see Philippson, *Thessalische Mythologie.*

the dragon. Pegasus is the libido which, as winged spiritual energy, carries the hero Bellerophon (also called Hipponoüs, "skilled with the horse") to victory, but he is also inward-flowing libido that wells forth as creative art. In neither case is the release of libido undirected; it rises up in the direction of spirit.

Thus, to put it abstractly, the hero Perseus espouses the spiritual side, he is the winged one, and the gods of the spirit are his allies in the fight with the unconscious. His foe is the uroboric Gorgon dwelling far to the West, in the land of death, flanked by her hideous sisters the Graeae, denizens of the deep. Perseus defeats the unconscious through the typical act of conscious realization. He would not be strong enough to gaze directly upon the petrifying face of the uroboros, so he raises its image to consciousness and kills it "by reflection." The treasure he gains is firstly Andromeda, the freed captive, and secondly Pegasus, the spiritual libido of the Gorgon, now released and transformed. Pegasus is therefore a spiritual and transcendent symbol in one. He combines the spirituality of the bird with the horse character of the Gorgon.

The development of personality proceeds in three different dimensions. The first is outward adaptation, to the world and things, otherwise known as extraversion; the second is inward adaptation, to the objective psyche and the archetypes, otherwise known as introversion. The third is centroversion, the self-formative or individuating tendency which proceeds within the psyche itself, independent of the other two attitudes and their development.

In the foregoing we have tried to show what the goal and content of the dragon fight—the captive and the treasure—meant for the extraverted and introverted attitude types. In conclusion we have to demonstrate their significance from the point of view of centroversion.

II

TRANSFORMATION, OR OSIRIS

THE AIM of the extraverted type of hero is action: he is the
founder, leader, and liberator whose deeds change the face
of the world. The introverted type is the culture-bringer, the
redeemer and savior who discovers the inner values, exalting
them as knowledge and wisdom, as a law and a faith, a work to
be accomplished and an example to be followed. The creative
act of raising the buried treasure is common to both types of
hero, and the prerequisite for this is union with the liberated
captive, who is as much the mother of the creative act as the
hero is its father.

The third type of hero does not seek to change the world
through his struggle with inside or outside, but to transform the
personality. Self-transformation is his true aim, and the liberating effect this has upon the world is only secondary. His self-
transformation may be held up as a human ideal, but his consciousness is not directed in the narrower sense to the collective;
for in him centroversion expresses a natural and fundamental
trend of the human psyche, which is operative from the very
beginning and which forms the basis not only of self-preservation, but of self-formation as well.

We have followed the birth of ego consciousness and of the
individual all through the archetypal stages whose climax was
reached in the hero's fight with the dragon. In this development
a constant increase of centroversion can be detected, tending
toward the consolidation of the ego and the stabilization of
consciousness. It gives rise to a standpoint, indeed a rallying
point, from which to combat the dangerous fascination of the
world and the unconscious—a fascination that lowers the level
of consciousness and disintegrates the personality. Both attitude

types, introversion as well as extraversion, can easily succumb to this danger. Centroversion, by building up the conscious ego and by strengthening the personality, tries to protect them and to counteract the danger of disintegration. In this sense, the growth of individuality and its development are mankind's answer to the "perils of the soul" that threaten from within, and to the "perils of the world" that threaten from without. Magic and religion, art, science, and technics are man's creative efforts to cope with this threat on two fronts. At the center of all these endeavors stands the creative individual as the hero, who in the name of the collective—even when he is a lonely figure standing out against it—molds it into shape by molding himself.

Before we examine the psychological side of this process, namely the formation of personality, we shall have to turn our attention to the myths which are its archetypal repositories.

Stability and indestructibility, the true goals of centroversion, have their mythological prototype in the conquest of death, in man's defenses against its power, for death is the primorial symbol of the decay and dissolution of the personality. Primitive man's refusal to recognize death as a natural occurrence, the immortalization of the king among the ancient Egyptians, ancestor worship, and the belief in the immortality of the soul in the great world-religions—all these are but different expressions of the same fundamental tendency in man to experience himself as imperishable and indestructible.

The best example of centroversion and its symbolism is to be found in ancient Egypt, in the cults and myths that cluster round the figure of Osiris. The story of Osiris is the first self-delineation of this process of personality transformation, whose counterpart is the visible emergence of the spiritual principle from the natural or biological principle. It is no accident that in the figure of Osiris we can see a matriarchal life-affirming world changing into a patriarchal one, where the accent falls on spirit. Thus the Osiris myth throws light on an important chapter in the early history of mankind, but it also furnishes the clue to a chief aspect of the hero myth, namely the transformation resulting from the fight with the dragon, and the relation of the hero son to the father figure.

Osiris is a many-sided figure, but in his most original form he is unquestionably a fertility god. We have seen how, in the matriarchal phase of fertility ritual, the Great Mother predominated, and how the bloody dismemberment of the young king guaranteed the earth's fertility. The regeneration of Osiris through Isis belongs to this stage. As we read in the Pyramid Texts:

Thy mother has come to thee, that thou mayst not perish away; the great modeler she is come, that thou mayst not perish away. She sets thy head in place for thee, she puts together thy limbs for thee; what she brings to thee is thy heart, is thy body. So dost thou become he who presides over his forerunners, thou givest command to thy ancestors and also thou makest thy house to prosper after thee, thou dost defend thy children from affliction.[1]

Or, in the lament of Isis for Osiris:

Come to thy house, come to thy house, thou pillar! Come to thy house, beautiful bull, Lord of men, Beloved, Lord of women.[2]

Although derived from a late papyrus, this is the age-old lament for the dead known as the "Maneros Lament," the lament for the loss of the "living phallus," which is why the symbol of the pillar, the *djed*, emblem of Osiris, is found in conjunction with the bull. The identification of Osiris with the ithyphallic Min was later transferred to Horus, but the significance of the chthonic Osiris, the beloved and Lord of women, is age-old. This same Osiris, as Horus the son of Isis, is called the "bull of his mother," just as in Heliopolis he is invoked as the "son of the white sow." [3] The lower Osiris belongs to the matriarchal sphere of fertility, and so in all probability did the *sem* priest who, with the leopard skin and long tail, was called the "pillar of his mother." [4]

[1] Spells 834 f., in Sethe, *Pyramidentexte.*
[2] Kees, *Aegypten,* p. 29.
[3] Metternich stele, in Roeder, *Urkunden,* p. 90.
[4] Budge, *Book of the Dead,* intro., p. c [100].

The signification of Osiris as the living phallus connects him with Mendes, another place where he was worshiped, and with the sacred goat. It is no accident that the cult assigned a special role to a certain queen whose image was set up in the temple and bore the name "Arsinoë Philadelphos, beloved of the goat." [5] The sexual union of the divine animal with one of the sacred priestesses was an ancient rite, so once more we find ourselves back in the old sphere of matriarchal fertility with its phallic deities.

This phase is ruled by the Earth Goddess and by Osiris as a corn god. The grain significance of fertility gods is widespread, likewise the analogy of their death and resurrection with the "corruption and resurrection" of the seed grain. In the coronation ceremony of the Egyptian kings the significance of the grain formed the most ancient element: Osiris, the grain, is "threshed" by his enemy Set:

Barley is placed on the threshing floor and trodden by oxen. The oxen represent the followers of Set and the barley Osiris who was thus cut in pieces. There is a play here on the words *i-t,* "barley," and *i-t,* "father," both 6CⲰT in Coptic. As the oxen were driven round the threshing floor, an act equated with Horus' smiting of the followers of Set, Horus says: "I have smitten for thee (Osiris) them that smote thee." The threshing over, the corn was carried away on the backs of asses. This symbolized the ascent of Osiris into heaven, supported by Set and his confederates.[6]

This interpretation of Blackman's is undoubtedly correct, at least as far as the last sentence about Osiris' resurrection. In the Book of the Dead, too, we find Set identified with the sacrificial oxen, but this identification, although predynastic, probably does not derive from the oldest level. The oldest may well be that in which Set, as well as Isis and Osiris, appears as a pig or boar.[7] Frazer has pointed out that originally the grain was trodden into the earth by swineherds; this would seem to be the

[5] Erman, *Religion,* pp. 362 f.
[6] Blackman, in Hooke, *Myth and Ritual,* p. 30.
[7] See supra, p. 85.

earliest form of the killing of Osiris by Set, while the threshing is perhaps the second form.[8]

As we have seen, Osiris is killed twice over by Set in the myth: firstly he is drowned in the Nile or shut up in a chest, and secondly he is hacked to pieces, the equivalent of threshing by being trodden underfoot.

The dismemberment of the corpse and the burial of its parts in the fields is the magical analogy of inseminating the earth with grain, a ritual that may have been connected with the original mode of interment practiced by the predynastic inhabitants of Egypt, who dismembered the dead body.[9]

Another characteristic of the matriarchal fertility rites has assumed the greatest significance. In all probability the phallus of the dismembered king was mummified as a symbol of male potency and preserved until the death of his successor. Frazer

[8] On account of the taboos surrounding it, the part played by the pig in Egypt is exceedingly obscure. The fact that no early representations of pigs treading the corn have been discovered does not prove that this operation was originally undertaken by sheep, and by pigs only in the New Kingdom. It is always possible that pigs were only represented in the New Kingdom because the taboo did not relax its hold until then. The association of the savage boar with the enemy and destroyer of the young god, who, as Attis, Adonis, Tammuz, and Osiris, was a corn god, seems to indicate that the pig played a negative role in the ritual. It is true that in the early coronation ceremonies oxen and asses took over the role of an enemy (Blackman, op. cit., p. 30), but in the Book of the Dead, Set still appears both as a boar and as an ox.

The suppression of Set, the boar, and the pig is consistent with the suppression of the Great Mother and all her rites and symbols. Whereas in the matriarchate the pig was a favored animal sacred to the great mother goddesses Isis, Demeter, Persephone, Bona Dea, and Freya, in the patriarchate it became the epitome of evil. The "great god" Set was still associated as a boar with Isis, the white sow. But, whereas the boar originally represented the wild, destructive, chthonic power of the Great Mother (A. Jeremias, *Das Alte Testament im Licht des Alten Orients*, p. 331), it now stood for Set in his role of the murderous maternal uncle, and finally became identified with everything evil.

The statement (Hall and Budge, *Guide to the Fourth, etc., Rooms*, p. 114) that pigs were thought to be extremely sacred and therefore unclean, and were on that account not eaten in Egypt until the Christian era, can hardly be reconciled with the fact that one of the princes who lived in the Eighteenth Dynasty possessed 1500 pigs and only 122 oxen (Erman and Ranke, *Aegypten und ägyptisches Leben*, p. 529). The economic importance of the pig in Egypt remains uncertain; it is possible that pigs, like fish, were the staple diet of the people but, being sacred and unclean, were not eaten in the best society.

[9] Budge, *Book of the Dead*, Intro., pp. xix and cxx.

224

has given numerous examples of the last vestiges of this ceremony, showing that the spirit of vegetation, in the shape of a
sheaf of grain or something similar, was preserved until the next
sowing or harvest and was regarded as a sacred object.[10] The
fertility king or his substitute—an animal, sheaf of grain, etc.—
suffers a double fate. In the first place he is killed and cut up,
but a portion of him, the sacred phallus, or the thing representing it, "remains." This remainder is stored "in" or "under" the
earth, like the seed or the corpse; its "descent" into the underworld is accompanied by a threnody for the dead. The descent,
or *katagogia* as it is called in the peasant festal calendar, corresponds to the hiding of grain in subterranean chambers [11] for
future sowing. Descent and entombment, therefore, are not
only identical with the burial of the dead and the insemination
of the earth, but amount to a rite for the "perpetuation of fertility." He who "remains" was originally represented by the
permanent mummified phallus of the slain fertility king, or by
corresponding phallic symbols which were preserved underground with the buried seed, i.e., with the dead, until the "resurrection festival" of the young grain.

From the very beginning, however, Osiris was not identical
with these young fertility gods. Very early stress was laid not
so much upon the transitoriness of the youthful figure as upon
his "everlasting" nature. Worshiped as vegetation, grain, and
in Byblos, as the tree, he is a god of fertility, earth, and nature,
thus combining in himself the characteristics of all the divine
sons of the Great Mother; but he is also water, sap, the Nile—in
other words, he is the animating principle of vegetation. Whereas
in the Gardens of Adonis, for instance, Adonis stands only for
growth, the ceremonial effigy of Osiris with stalks growing
out of him proves that he is more than the grain; he is in fact
the moisture and the prime cause whence the grain springs. He
is not just the god who dies to rise again; he is the god who does

---

[10] *The Golden Bough* (abridged edn., 1951), pp. 438 ff.
[11] Van der Leeuw, *Religion in Essence and Manifestation.*

not die, who remains for ever—a paradox indeed, for he is the "mummy with the long member." [12]

It can easily be shown that this cognomen expresses the essential nature of Osiris. It accords with certain peculiar features of the myth which have never been sufficiently emphasized, much less understood. The myth says that when the dismembered portions of Osiris were put together again, the phallus could not be found; that Isis replaced it by a wooden or cult phallus, and that she was made pregnant by the dead Osiris. So, although lacking a phallus, or equipped only with a wooden one, Osiris became the father of Horus—an exceedingly remarkable feature in a fertility god.

In all matriarchal fertility rites castration and fertilization, phallic worship and dismemberment, are interrelated parts of a symbolic canon. The problem of Osiris, however, goes deeper than that and demands interpretation on many more levels. To understand the fertility of Osiris only as the lower, phallic fertility of the earth, as water, as the fertilizing Nile, as the living verdure of vegetation, and as the grain, is to limit the range of his action; indeed the whole nature of Osiris lies in transcending this lower fertility.

The higher as opposed to the lower nature of Osiris can be conceived as a transformation, or as a new phase of his self-revelation. Both natures are connected with the same object, the cult phallus.

The death of the original fertility king led, as we saw, to two distinct ceremonies: the dismemberment of the body and the "induration" of the phallus. Dismemberment, sowing, and threshing are equivalent to destroying the personality and breaking down the living unit. Such was originally the fate meted out to the dead body of Osiris. The principle opposed to this found embodiment in the mummification of the phallus, to make it hard and everlasting; and the symbol of everlastingness is Osiris, "the mummy with the long member."

[12] "From the Prayers of One Unjustly Prosecuted," in Erman, *The Literature of the Ancient Egyptians*, p. 304.

This paradoxical double significance of Osiris, evidently present right from the beginning, forms the basis of his development in Egyptian religion. On the one hand, as the dismembered god, he is the bringer of fertility, the young king who passes away and returns; on the other hand, as the procreative mummy with the long member, he is everlasting and imperishable. Not only is he the living phallus, but he retains his potency even as the mummified phallus. As such he begets his son Horus and thus, as a spirit, as the dead man who "remains," his fertility is imbued with a higher meaning. In this mysterious symbol of the fertile dead, mankind has unconsciously stumbled on a vital factor which it projected outside itself, because no clearer formulation of it was then possible: the everlastingness and fruitfulness of the living spirit as opposed to the everlastingness and fruitfulness of nature.

The great antagonist of Osiris was symbolized by Set, the black boar, whose emblem is the primeval flint knife, the instrument of dismemberment and death. This Set is the epitome of darkness, evil, destructiveness; being twin brother to Osiris, he is the archetypal "antagonist," not only in the cosmic sense in which he stands for the "powers of darkness," but also in the historical sense, for he represents the matriarchate and the destructive side of Isis against which Osiris is fighting as founder of the partriarchate.

Dismemberment, whose symbols are the "knife of Set," the Apopis serpent and the whole demonic horde of scorpions, snakes, monsters, and gorillas, is the danger that threatens the dead.[13] It is the danger of psychophysical decay and extinction. The most vital parts of the Egyptian religion, and the whole of the Book of the Dead, are devoted to averting this danger.

Homage to thee, O my divine father Osiris, thou hast thy being with thy members. Thou didst not decay, thou didst not become worms, thou didst not diminish, thou didst not become corruption, thou didst not putrefy, and thou didst not turn into worms. I am the god Khepera, and my members shall have an everlasting existence. . . . I shall have my being; I shall

[13] Budge, op. cit., figs. to Chs. 28 and 149.

live; I shall germinate; I shall wake up in peace; I shall not putrefy; my intestines shall not perish; I shall not suffer injury; mine eye shall not decay; the form of my visage shall not disappear; mine ear shall not become deaf; my head shall not be separated from my neck; my tongue shall not be carried away; my hair shall not be cut off; my eyebrows shall not be shaved off; and no baleful injury shall come upon me. My body shall be stablished, and it shall neither fall into ruin nor be destroyed on this earth. [Ch. 44.]

The fundamental trend of centroversion—the conquest of death through everlastingness—finds its mythological and religious symbol in Osiris. Mummification, the preservation for all eternity of the body's shape, as the outward and visible sign of its unity—this gives living expression to the anti-Set principle of Osiris.

Osiris is the Self-Perfected, he who has overthrown Set and escaped the threat of dismemberment. Whereas on the matriarchal level he is reborn of the animating wind-breath through his mother-sister-spouse, or, in the Pyramid Texts, has his head restored to him by the Mother Goddess Mut as a symbol of unity,[14] he is finally worshiped precisely because he renews himself. We read in the Book of the Dead:

I have knit myself together; I have made myself whole and complete; I have renewed my youth; I am Osiris, the Lord of Eternity.[15]

The evident fact that the archaic custom of cutting up the corpse for burial was repudiated, indeed anathematized, by a later tribe of settlers is, as so often happens, only the historical reflection of a much deeper psychic change. Dismemberment of the dead is practiced only among primitive peoples who have no consciousness of personality, and for whom the deciding motive is their fear of revenants. In Egypt, however, the intensification of ego consciousness and the development of centroversion are particularly clear; in these circumstances dismemberment would obviously be regarded as the supreme danger, and the preservation of a man's bodily shape, through embalming, the supreme good. The mummified Osiris could become the legitimate exponent of this tendency because, even in the

14 Sakkara pyramids; cf. Budge, intro., p. cxx.
15 Ibid., Ch. 43.

earliest times when the matriarchal fertility cult held sway, he had been the bearer and representative of the cult phallus and, as such, he who "remains."

The earliest Osiris symbol is the *djed,* and his earliest place of worship, Dedu, the old Busiris on the Nile delta. The interpretation of the *djed* pillar has remained a puzzle to this day. Generally the *djed* is taken to represent a tree trunk with the stumps of branches projecting to either side at the top. In the cult, at all events, it was as bulky and heavy as a tree trunk, as can be seen very clearly from the illustrations of the erection of the *djed* at the festivals. Moreover the Osiris myth fully indicates that the *djed* pillar was a tree trunk. Isis fetched the body of Osiris from Byblos in Phoenicia, enclosed in a tree trunk which the king of that place, husband of "Queen Astarte," had used as a pillar in the hall of his court. Isis "cut the coffer out of the tree," [16] but the tree she wrapped in fine linen and anointed, and right down to Plutarch's day it was still worshiped in Byblos as the "wood of Isis." We have already discussed the tree cult in Byblos and its relation to Isis and Osiris, in connection with the son-lover and the Mother Goddess. Here we would only draw attention to the significance of timber for Egypt. The religious and cultural links between Egypt and Phoenicia are extremely ancient.[17]

Trees, and particularly very big trees like the cedars of Lebanon, offer a powerful contrast to the fleeting life of vegetation, which in a treeless land like Egypt comes and goes with the season. They are the things that endure, so it is understandable that in early times the tree became the symbol of the *djed,* signifying duration: for the tree is a fully grown thing that nevertheless endures. To the primitive Egyptian, wood symbolized organic, living duration as opposed to the inorganic, dead

[16] Frazer, op. cit., p. 423.

[17] If the unlikely proposition that Osiris was originally the Sumerian god Asar and reached Egypt via Mesopotamia (cf. Winlock, *Basreliefs from the Temple of Rameses I at Abydos,* p. 7 n) proves to be correct, then Byblos becomes even more important as a cultural crossroads. At the time of the matriarchal fertility cult Egypt seems to have been culturally dependent upon Byblos, as hinted by the myth when it says that Isis brought Osiris from Byblos to Egypt.

duration of stone and the ephemeral life of vegetation.[18] In the Canaanite sphere of culture centering upon Byblos, the tree trunk was sacred to the Great Mother, "Queen Astarte," in the form of a post with hewn-off lateral branches; [19] at all events it comes under the broad category of sacred trees and posts.

Another salient point is the identity of the tree trunk and the wooden sarcophagus, the most important item in the Egyptian rites for the dead.

The mythical entombment of Osiris in a tree coffin by his brother Set, and the Byblos episode, bring out his *djed* nature, both as a god in the form of a pillar, and as a mummy. But the mummy and the coffin are a means for making the corpse ever-lasting, and Osiris, whether as tree, pillar, or mummy, is identical with the wooden cult phallus which replaced the embalmed phallus of the seasonal King.

According to the Egyptian belief, which held that the dis-membered portions of Osiris were distributed among the various places of worship, the backbone was buried in Dedu; and in view of its articulated structure the *djed* pillar lends itself to such a conception. The pillar is composed of two segments. De-rived originally from the trunk of a tree, the upper segment, corresponding to the treetop with its four lateral branch stumps, finally came to be correlated with the neck and head region of Osiris, while the lower segment, corresponding to the trunk, was correlated with the backbone. Like many another Egyptian fetish, the *djed* pillar shows us very clearly how the original fig-ure became humanized. First it sprouted arms, as on the west wall of the temple at Abydos, then the eyes were painted in,[20] and finally the pillar was equated with the entire figure of Osiris.

In what manner the *djed* pillar arose has, so it seems to us,

[18] A. Jeremias, op. cit., fig. 125.

[19] Carpentry, too, as a sacred process, belongs to this canon. Wood, like milk and wine, was thought to be a life-principle of Horus-Osiris (cf. Blackman, op. cit., p. 30), and cedar oil with its preservative and hardening qualities played an important part in embalming. [The wood symbolism recurs in the story that Jesus was a carpenter: cf. Coomaraswamy, *The Bugbear of Literacy.*—TRANS.]

[20] Budge, op. cit., figs. to pp. 73, 77, 121.

been demonstrated with the utmost clarity by Budge.[21] From a comparison of the paintings he has established that it was formed by combining Osiris' sacrum, the lowest joint in the spinal column, with the tree trunk dedicated to the old god of Busiris, upon which it was erected: ౸ . The ordinary *djed* symbol is a stylization of this combination: ౹ .

Three components enter into conjunction here. The first is phallic, since the sacrum is "the lower part of the backbone of Osiris which was believed to form the seat of his virility." The second component is the aforesaid "duration." The fact that the sacrum, a bony structure, is used here instead of the phallus serves, like the pillar, to emphasize the character of "everlastingness." For this reason the *djed* symbol and the image of the tree with branch stumps could easily coalesce, both as regards their form and their content.

But the third and, for us, the most important factor is the "erection," i.e., the fact that the sacrum was set on the top of the tree trunk.

In this way the "everlasting begetter," the "erected" or "higher" phallus, becomes the head, which proves its character as a "spermatic" or spiritual symbol.[22] Like the solar phallus—another spiritual symbol—the "head" of the tree begets and brings forth in the tree birth; but neither the everlasting begetter nor the begotten stands for the "lower" principle; on the contrary they are "erected," that is, "raised up," as the ritual itself shows.[23]

Because the "sublimation," [24] the erection, and transformation of the lower principle into the higher was the most important component of the *djed* symbol, its upper segment was later identified with the head of Osiris.

I am Osiris, the Lord of the heads that live, mighty of breast and powerful of back, with a phallus which goeth to the remotest men and women. . . . I have become a spirit, I have been judged, I have become a divine being,

[21] Budge, *Guide to the Fourth, etc., Rooms,* p. 98.
[22] See infra, pp. 247 f.
[23] See infra, pp. 242 f.
[24] See infra, pp. 242, 248.

I have come, and I have avenged mine own body. I have taken up my seat by the divine birth-chamber of Osiris, and I have destroyed the sickness and suffering which were there. [*Book of the Dead*, Ch. 69.]

This reuniting of the head with the body, for the purpose of producing a whole figure and nullifying the dismemberment, is one of the main features of the Osiris cult. A chapter in the Book of the Dead is entitled "The Chapter of Not Letting the Head of a Man Be Cut Off from Him in the Underworld." [25] The restoring of the head was absolutely essential if Osiris was to be put together again,[26] and what we know of the mystery cult at Abydos confirms this. In the "reconstitution of the body of Osiris" we are told that "the crowning scene was erection of the backbone of Osiris and the placing of the head of the God upon it." [27] Thus the *djed* pillar symbolizes the reunited Osiris, the everlasting, who can say of himself: "I have made myself whole and complete."

This interpretation of the union of head and backbone in the *djed* is also confirmed by the prayer which had to be spoken while laying a golden *djed* upon the neck of the dead man:

Rise up, O Osiris, thou hast thy backbone, O Still Heart, thou hast the ligatures of thy neck and back, O Still Heart. Place thyself upon thy base.[28]

There are thus two determining motifs running through the Egyptian belief in a future life, both connected with Osiris. The first is perpetual duration, the preservation of the body's shape, and therefore of the personality, in the funeral rites by means of embalming, and by safeguarding the mummies in pyramids; the second is resurrection and transformation.

The figure of Osiris is from the very beginning bound up with the principle of ascension. The earliest picture of him shows him

[25] Budge, *Book of the Dead*, Ch. 43.
[26] See supra, p. 222.
[27] Budge, op. cit., intro. to Ch. 43.
[28] Ibid., Ch. 155. The dead man is promised that he shall become a perfected spiritual being, a *khu*, and that at the New Year festival he shall join the attendants of Osiris. This gives us an important clue to the significance of the *djed* pillar at the New Year festival, to be discussed later.

as "the God at the Top of the Staircase." [29] He is the ladder from earth to heaven, and those who could not be buried in Abydos itself tried at least to set up a stone there at the "staircase of the great God." [30] Budge writes:

This ladder is referred to in the Pyramid Texts. It was made originally for Osiris, who by means of it ascended into heaven. It was set up by Horus and Set, each of whom held one side while they assisted the God to mount it; in the tombs of the Ancient and Middle Empires several models of ladders have been found.[31]

Osiris the dismembered fertility god who overcomes his dismemberment, Lord of the Ascent and the Heavenly Ladder, is, on the cosmic level of mythology, the same as Osiris the Moon-God.

Briffault has put together a mass of material proving that the kingship of Osiris was originally of a lunar character.[32] This association is archetypal. In the matriarchate, the fertility-kingship of the adolescent lover is always connected with the moon, which is "quartered" and reborn, and thus guarantees fertility. It is, however, important to note how significantly the figure of Osiris rises above these matriarchal associations.

By ascending from earth to heaven [33] and conquering death and dismemberment, Osiris becomes the exemplar of transformation and resurrection. In the Book of the Dead, the dead man who is identified with Osiris says, "I set up a ladder to Heaven among the gods, and I am a divine being among them." His ascension and resurrection reflect a psychic transformation which is mythologically projected as the union of the lower, earthly Osiris with the higher, or the union of the dismembered but reconstituted body of Osiris with the higher "spiritual soul" and "spiritual body." This self-transformation, resurrection and sublimation, which is at once a union with the self, is described

[29] Petrie, *The Making of Egypt*, Pls. X, LII.
[30] Erman, *Religion*, p. 265.
[31] Op. cit., intro. to Ch. 98.
[32] *The Mothers*, Vol. II, pp. 778 f.
[33] Pyramid Texts, spells 472, 974, in Erman, *Religion*, p. 219.

as the union of Osiris, God of the Underworld, with the Sun-God, Ra.

The ascent of Osiris is depicted in the Book of the Dead [34] as the rising of the Horus Sun—signifying life—out of the *djed* pillar, and the pillar itself is shown placed between the twin mountain peaks of sunrise and sunset. The *djed* is therefore the "material body" that gives rise to the Sun Soul. On the other hand, at the Memphis festival the mummy was worshiped with a *djed* for its head; [35] in other words, it was worshiped as the whole body to which the head had been restored.

Dedu Busiris, the oldest shrine of Osiris, is situated in a nome whose emblem was of great importance for the development of Osiris symbolism. We can trace the development of the basic symbols as the Osiris cult moved from Busiris to Abydos. Osiris took over the symbols of the old reigning god Anzti, the original Lord of Busiris, which were the scourge and the scepter. The Anzti symbol consisted, besides these, in a body shaped like a post, or fasces, surmounted by a head with two ostrich plumes,[36] and it is clear that Osiris was able to assimilate both symbols, the fasces and the head.

The same thing happened when the Osiris religion assimilated the Abydos symbols. Here as well the old symbols, together with the local cult of the "First among the Western Ones," i.e., a god of the dead, accommodated themselves with the greatest ease to the nature of Osiris.

After Osiris had established himself in Abydos, the local emblem—likewise a fasces bearing a kind of head with two ostrich feathers and a sun—was equated with the Anzti symbol and the head of Osiris (*illus. 28*). An ancient model shows this Abydos pillar, surmounted by the head-relic with its sun and feathers, "planted in the mountain hieroglyph." [37]

The relation to the sun becomes all the stronger when we note that, at the foot of the Abydos emblem, the pillar is supported

[34] Budge, op. cit., pp. 55, 73, 77.
[35] Erman and Ranke, *Aegypten*, p. 318.
[36] Moret, *The Nile*, p. 58.
[37] Winlock, op. cit., p. 21.

on both sides by two lions, the *akeru*, symbolizing the morning and evening sun, yesterday and today. In the vignettes they are shown flanking both the rising and the setting sun.[38] The Osiris symbol in Abydos was—a fact overlooked by Winlock—the sinking sun; the local god was worshiped like Osiris as the "First among the Western Ones," that is, as the evening sun and god of the dead, and in later times Abydos was considered to be the place where the head of Osiris was buried.

If we now sum up this "syncretistic" development, we shall see that the symbolism is extremely significant. Osiris, Osiris' head, and Osiris the sun all go together, for sun and head reflect his spirituality. The head of Anzti, the Abydos head, and the head of Osiris are one. But since Abydos lies "to the west," it became the place where Osiris was worshiped as the evening sun and god of the dead, and where "the head of Osiris rests."

Osiris, however, is not just the sinking sun; the Abydos emblem is also held to symbolize the "Head Soul" of Ra, and his worshipers are depicted as Horus-headed and also as jackal-headed demons, indicating that they worship the morning as well as the evening sun.

Osiris has two shapes: he is the Western God of the Underworld, Ruler of the Dead, and equally he is the Everlasting, Lord of Heaven. Originally he was the Ruler of the Earth and the Underworld who reigned in the West, while Ra, the Lord of Heaven, reigned in the East, but before long these two figures came together in the double structure of Osiris, to form the double soul:

Thy material body liveth in Dedu (and in) Nif-Urtet and thy soul liveth in Heaven each day.[39]

The mythological statement about the double nature of Osiris, the unity of Osiris and Ra, corresponds to the psychological statement about the union of the heart-soul (*ba*), which is the transpersonal body-center, with the spiritual soul or subtle body (*khu*). In this union lies the mystery of Osiris:

[38] Budge, op cit., figs. on pp. 81 and 94.
[39] Ibid., p. 666.

I am the divine soul which dwelleth in the divine Twin Gods. Question: Who is this? Answer: It is Osiris. He goes to Dedu and findeth there the soul of Ra. Each god embraces the other and the divine Souls spring into being within the Divine Twin Gods.[40]

The same chapter contains other formulations of this double nature, such as:

Yesterday is Osiris and Today is Ra on the day when he shall destroy the enemies of Osiris and when he shall establish as prince and ruler his son Horus.

I know the god who dwelleth therein. Who then is this? It is Osiris or (as others say) Ra is his name, (or) it is the Phallus of Ra, wherewith he was united to himself.

Again in the "Book of Things Which Are and of Things Which Shall Be," we read:

Who then is this? It is Osiris; or (as others say) it is his dead body or (as others say) it is his filth. The things which are and the things which shall be are his dead body; or (as others say) they are eternity and everlastingness. Eternity is the day and everlastingness is the night.

The god who begets himself is depicted more particularly as the *khepri,* the scarab or dung beetle. Because he rolls a ball of dung before him, this beetle was venerated as the sun-moving principle. Even more significant is the fact that, his task completed, he buries the sun-ball in a hole in the ground and dies, and in the following spring the new beetle creeps out of the ball as the new sun, risen from under the earth. He is thus a symbol of the "Self-Begotten" and is deemed "Creator of the Gods." [41] Budge says:

He is a form of the rising sun and his seat is in the boat of the Sun-god. He is the god of matter which is at the point of passing from inertness into life, and also of the dead body from which a spiritual and glorified body is about to burst forth.[42]

[40] Ibid., Ch. 17.
[41] The self-renewing character of the *khepri* is of primary importance here. Whether, as Briffault thinks, an originally lunar significance has been transferred to the sun is irrelevant in this context.
[42] Op. cit., p. 4 n.

The *khepri* also symbolizes the Heart (*ab*). But Osiris, even though he is likened to the heart-soul which animates the body, and of which it is said "My Heart, my Mother," is something suprapersonal. The heart is shown in the shape of the self-begetting scarab; it is the seat of the powers of conscience which appear as the Assessors at the Judgment of the Dead, and, in the creation myth of Memphis, the creative organ par excellence: [43]

It is the Heart which makes all that results to come forth, and it is the tongue which repeats (expresses) the thought that the Heart created. . . . The demiurge who created all the gods and their *kas* is in his Heart.[44]

The hieroglyph for "thought" is written with the ideogram for "heart," which indicates that the heart-soul is a spiritual principle. At the same time it is the libido principle of all earthly life; hence the phallic form of Osiris, the he-goat or ram of Mendes (*ba*), is identified with the heart-soul (*ba*).

However, Osiris is not only the lower phallic principle, but the higher solar principle as well. He is the *benu* bird, the Greek phoenix:

Thou art the Great Phoenix that was born in the branches of the tree at the great House of Princes in Heliopolis.[45]

Self-renewal and tree-birth—the "higher" nativity—go together. The Osiris who is born of the tree is born of himself in the precise sense of one risen from his coffin, for Osiris, tree, and coffin are one and the same (*illus. 31*). Hence the tree-birth is identical with rebirth: Osiris is the sun rising out of the tree,[46] just as he is the sign of life rising out of the *djed* pillar. This vignette illustrates one of the oldest chapters in the Book of the Dead, the fourteenth, whose opening words sum up all the essential points in the mystery of Osiris:

I am Yesterday, Today, and Tomorrow, and I have the power to be born a second time; I am the divine hidden soul who created the gods.

[43] See supra, p. 20.
[44] Moret, op. cit., p. 376; Kees, op. cit., p. 11.
[45] Metternich stele, in Roeder, op. cit., p. 90.
[46] Budge, op. cit., fig. to p. 211.

The problem of death was originally solved by the simple device of regarding the next world as a continuation of this. The change in point of view that resulted in a spiritual instead of a materialistic answer to this question—a change also reflected in the transformation of Osiris—can be seen very clearly in a dialogue between the dead Osiris and Atum, a species of creator god. The latter says:

I have given glorification in place of water, air, and gratification of the senses, and a light heart in place of bread and beer.

And he ends with this promise:

Thou shalt exist for longer than a million million years, an era of millions. But I shall destroy all that I have created. The earth shall appear once more as the primeval ocean, as the flood of waters that was in the beginning. I am that which shall remain, together with Osiris, after I have changed myself back into a serpent, which no man knoweth, which no God seeth.[47]

Atum's answer passes beyond the next world; it is an eschatological answer that holds a promise of perpetuity even when the world has reverted to the uroboric state. "Together with Osiris"—this is a promise that the soul shall be the deathless companion of the creator. The identity of Osiris, the human soul, and the prime creative force amounts to identity with the creativity of godhead. In this sense, too, we can understand the mysterious saying of the dead man who describes his transformation into Osiris as an initiation into the mystery of metempsychosis:

I have entered in as a man of no understanding, and I shall come forth in the form of a strong spirit, and I shall look upon my form which shall be that of men and women for ever and ever.[48]

False theories abound, all trying to prove that the symbolic contents of this passage express a later spiritualization. But, characteristically enough, it does not belong to a late chapter at all; it is taken from an exceedingly solemn text that sums up

[47] Ibid., Ch. 175; Kees, op. cit., p. 27.
[48] Budge, op. cit., Ch. 64.

the essence of the Book of the Dead in a single chapter, the shorter version of which is ascribed to the First Dynasty.[49]

Osiris of the double soul, then, is the luminary of the Upper and Lower Worlds, the self-unifier, preserving and yet changing his shape, conqueror of death, the self-begotten, holder of the secret of resurrection and rebirth, through which the lower power is transformed into the higher.

The Pharaoh, too, in imitation of Osiris, is at his death changed into a spirit dwelling in heaven; [50] he undergoes an "Osirification" which consists in the union of his soul parts, and the first condition of this is the preservation of the mummy and its magical resuscitation. The whole purpose of the ritual in the Book of the Dead is to make the earthly body immortal by uniting the parts and preventing it from being dismembered.

Preservation of the body through embalming, its purification, also the purification of the *ka*, the ghost-soul belonging to the body, these are the preliminaries that lead up to the grand Osirian mystery, namely the germination [51] of the spiritual body

---

[49] It is immaterial whether we date the First Dynasty with Petrie, at 4300 B.C., or with Breasted, at 3400 B.C. In either case we are back at the beginning of the historical epoch.

[50] Pyramid Texts, spells 370–75, in Sethe, *Pyramidentexte*.

[51] A question which cannot be answered at present is whether the significance of grain in its many permutations, particularly as a symbol of spiritual transformation in the mystery religions, may not originally have been connected with the phenomenon of fermentation and the brewing of intoxicating liquor. For Osiris is not a corn god only, he is also a wine god; moreover the Feast of Epiphany, on January 6, when the changing of water into wine at the marriage of Cana is commemorated, is also the anniversary of the water-wine transformation performed by Osiris (Gressmann, *Tod und Auferstehung des Osiris*). Intoxicating spirits and fertility orgies were always associated with one another in the ancient world, and still are, in primitive societies. Indeed, the transformation of grain into spirit must have struck mankind everywhere as one of the most astonishing instances of natural change. The basis of the liquor, whether it be grain, rice, maize, tapioca, etc., is invariably a fruit of the earth, an "Earth Son" who occupies a central place in fertility ritual. Through its strange transformation this earthly product acquires an intoxicating spirit-character and becomes a sacrament, mediating revelation, wisdom, redemption. This age-old basis of the mystery is still transparent, not only in the Dionysian and Christian wine symbolism, but wherever sacramental intoxication plays a part. It would be surprising if the secret doctrines of transformation which flourished in the ancient world right down to the time of the alchemists were not connected with this elementary phenomenon. The *prima materia* as the dead body, its sublimation and the ascent of

from the mummified corpse.[52]

The heart-soul (*ba*), a human-headed falcon who is the life principle of the body and the mummy, is connected with the spiritual soul (*khu*),[53] which is the life principle of the spiritual body (*sahu*). Whereas the *khu* is immortal, its companion heart-soul is material and immaterial according to its pleasure. *Ba*, *khu*, and *khepri* (heart) are all co-ordinated.

Naturally these part souls or soul parts are mythological projections and cannot be defined more closely. The crucial task is their transformation and unification, resulting in the production of the deathless double being, Osiris-Ra; this is the "great work" which Osiris accomplishes, and which Pharaoh accomplishes after him.

The *ka* soul has a particularly important part to play in this process. It is extraordinarily difficult for us to understand what is meant by the *ka*, because the *ka* soul corresponds to no concept in our modern consciousness, and is an archetypal entity. The Egyptians conceived it as a man's double, as his genius or guardian angel, as his name and as that which nourished him; it was eternally youthful, for which reason "to die" was the same as *"aller vivre avec son 'ka'."* [54] Moret sums up its meaning in these words:

Sous ce nom de Ka il faut donc entendre non pas seulement le principe de vie du Pharaon, des dieux et des hommes, mais l'ensemble des forces vitales et la nourriture qui alimente, et sans laquelle dépérit tout ce qui existe dans l'univers.[55]

The same authority writes:

---

the spirit, liberation of the spirit from the body, transubstantiation, etc., are all processes which have their place in the mystery of intoxication and illustrate at the same time the spiritual history of the Earth or Corn Son, so that these images may well be the symbolic prototypes of spiritual transformation. Such associations, being archetypal, are not confined to the West; for instance in Mexico we find the same connection between the young corn god and intoxication, here represented by the pulque deities.

[52] Budge, op. cit., Chs. 83, 94, 154.
[53] Ibid., Intro., p. xii.
[54] Pyramid of Pepi I, in Moret, *Mystères Égyptiens.*
[55] Ibid., p. 210.

27. The hawk god Horus with King Nectanebo II
Egypt, 370 B.C.

28. Ramesses I sacrifices to Isis and to the Osiris head symbol
Egypt, Abydos, 14th–13th century B.C.

29. Osiris recalled to life by Isis

Egypt, Temple of Seti I, Abydos, 14th–13th century B.C.

30. The King before Osiris and Horus
Egypt, Temple of Seti I, Abydos, 14th–13th century B.C.

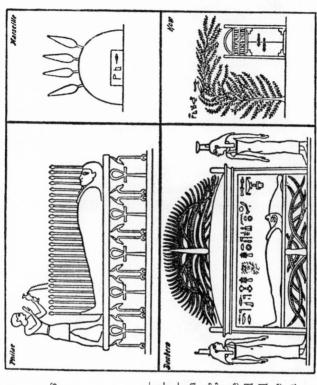

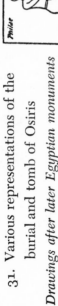

31. Various representations of the burial and tomb of Osiris

Drawings after later Egyptian monuments

Eduard Meyer's explanation of these representations (in *Ägypten zur Zeit der Pyramidenerbauer*, p. 19): "(Right, above) the grave-mound of Osiris, bearing his name and with stalks growing out; (below) the closed tomb, with the tree beside it, upon which sits Osiris' soul in heron form, as phoenix; (left, below) the corpse of the god in the coffin, supported and shaded by an immense tree, while Isis and Nephthys stand mourning nearby; (above) the corpse, sprouting grain and watered by a servant."

This *ka* is the father and the being which causes man to live, presides over the intellect and the moral forces, gives spiritual and physical life.[56]

It is connected with *kau*, "sustenance," and is therefore an elementary libido and life symbol:

From this essential and collective *ka*, a primordial substance living in heaven, the gods detach an individual *ka* for the king.

When the *ka* and the body are purified and united, the king—like Osiris before him and every individual after him—is "a complete being who achieves perfection."

The *ka* soul is therefore an archetypal prefiguration of what we know today as the "self"; in its union with the other soul parts, and in the transformation of personality thereby effected, we have the first historical example—in mythological projection —of the psychic process we call "individuation" or the "integration of the personality."

Through this union of soul parts the king becomes a *ba*, a heart-soul who dwells with the gods and possesses the breath of life; he is now an *akhu*, a perfect spiritual being:

The king is reborn in the glory of the eastern horizon *akhet*; and he who is born in the east becomes an *akh* (a glorious, shining one).[57]

The archetypal affinities between light, sun, spirit, and soul, all referring to Osiris and his transformation, have seldom been expressed more plainly.

Seen against this symbolical and mythological background, the actual content of the ritual will more readily yield up its meaning.

Our knowledge of the Osiris ritual derives from three sources: the Osiris festivals, in particular the "Erection of the Venerable Djed" on New Year's Day in Dedu Busiris; the coronation ceremonies; and the Sed festival of the Pharaohs, the purpose of which was to strengthen and renew the kingly power.

On more than one occasion we have pointed out the significance of Osiris for fertility, and his connection with the Great

[56] Moret, *The Nile*, p. 183.
[57] Ibid., p. 184.

Mother. This stage, however, had already been passed at the time when the Osiris ritual was celebrated in Dedu at the feast of the New Year; traces of the old seasonal kingship still lingered, but the dominant feature was the idea of "duration" which gave its name to the *djed* pillar and also to the city.

Following the eclipse of his moon character, Osiris came to embody in himself the whole year, as we can see from the 365 lights that accompanied the voyage of the thirty-four little papyrus boats down the Nile on All Soul's Day, the twenty-second of Khoiakh.[58] The wooden effigy of Osiris which had been buried in the ground the previous year was then dug up and, having been replaced by a new one, was laid upon boughs of sycamore,[59] as a symbol of the resurrection of the year and the birth of the sun from a tree. The erection of the *djed,* which is the main feature of the festivities, symbolizes the "resuscitation of Osiris," i.e., the coming to life of the dead, and not the resurrection of a young vegetation god.[60]

The festal calendar of Dendera says:

As for the last day of the fourth month of Akhet, the raising of the djed takes place in Busiris on that day of the burying of Osiris in the region of B'ḥ in the vault under the *iśd*-trees; for on that day the divine body of Osiris comes into him after the wrapping of Osiris.[61]

The New Year was celebrated on the day following this erection and resurrection; it was the anniversary of Horus of Edfu, also prescribed as the day on which the Egyptian king mounted the throne and on which the Sed feast was celebrated for the periodic renewal of Egyptian kingship.

The original interment of the old King of the Year at his death, and the enthronement of the new, are still perceptible in these ceremonies; the raising of the *djed* corresponds to the embalming of the phallus and the annual killing of the king in the old fertility ritual, as is apparent from the connection between the setting up of the *djed* and the new king's enthronement. In the

[58] Frazer, *The Golden Bough,* p. 436.
[59] Ibid.
[60] Blackman, op. cit., p. 21.
[61] Ibid., p. 21.

harvest festival, too, we find that the Horus king cuts a sheaf of grain, symbolizing the old vegetation spirit, with a sickle.

The connection between the Horus king's enthronement and the simultaneous resurrection of Osiris, however, reveals something else, which means more than just the supplanting of the old by the new. In the Osiris myth, the vestiges of the original conflict between the old and the new king, so evident in the fertility rites, are completely overgrown by a new psychic constellation in which the son has a positive relation to the father.

We have seen how the originally matriarchal figure of Isis, and the rites pertaining to her, were superseded by the rule of the Horus kings under the patriarchal protection of Osiris, of whom it was said that "he leaves the son in his father's place." Isis helps him in this: she conducts a lawsuit for the legitimacy of her son and of his claim to the throne, and gets the gods to recognize Horus' paternity, the basis of the patriarchate.

The supersession of the matriarchal by a patriarchal epoch is an archetypal process; that is to say, it is a universal and necessary phenomenon in the history of mankind. We interpret it in this sense, without respect to the possible and even probable overthrow of a predynastic matriarchal Egypt by patriarchal tribes owing allegiance to Horus, and without discussing the possible union of a late Horus sun cult with an earlier Osiris moon cult.

Moret has examined the decay of this matriarchal "uterine system." He speaks of an "evolution of society from the uterine system in which each woman of the clan believes herself impregnated by the totem, to the paternal system in which the husband is the true father," and he associates the transition from clan to family and from the supremacy of the community to that of the individual with this development. We have still to discuss the role of the god-king as the "Great Individual" who, with his heroic consciousness, breaks down the power of the Great Mother. (Cf. Appendices.)

Interestingly enough, traces of this shifting of the center of gravity can still be seen in Egyptian myth and ritual. The early capitals of Upper and Lower Egypt were cities where two Mother goddesses "of lasting splendor" had reigned from time immemorial: the vulture goddess Nekhbet of Nekhen in Upper Egypt, and the snake goddess Uatchet of Buto in Lower Egypt. In the Osiris myth the city of Buto has a sinister connection with death and dismemberment: Horus was killed there by a scorpion, a creature sacred to Isis, and it was there that the rediscovered body of Osiris was cut in pieces by Set.

Buto and Nekhen are twin cities, also known as Pe-Dep and Nekheb-Nekhen. It is significant that, in the north and south, the Horus cities and the mother cities lie facing one another on opposite banks of the river.

Traces of the age-old conflict between the patriarchal Horus and the ancient matriarchal rulers can still be seen in the ritual. For instance, in the ceremonial performance of the battle between Pe and Dep, Horus first is attacked, but the end shows his victorious incest with his mother, which proves him a hero.[62] Later, at the time of the historical Dynasties, the vulture and snake symbols of the vanquished female deities occur as emblems in the crown of the Horus kings, and their names form part of the fivefold royal title.

These patriarchal kings, the "sons of Horus" (*illus. 27*) who take over the inheritance of Osiris, necessarily become the avengers of their father and adversaries of the maternal uncle Set, Osiris' deadly enemy. Whether in consequence the role of an "elder Horus" devolves upon a "younger Horus" is of no importance here: the protection that Osiris extends to his son derives from their old battles with Set. In this struggle Horus strikes off Set's testicles; the wound that Horus receives in his eye heals, the dead Osiris is restored to life with the help of this same "eye of Horus," and Horus is thereupon invested with the symbols of power: two scepters in which Set's testicles are incorporated.[63] The restoration of Osiris is identical with his resurrection and

[62] Erman and Ranke, op. cit., p. 318.
[63] Blackman, op. cit., p. 32.

transformation, which make him the king of the spirits, and his son king of the earth.

Thus the enthronement and rulership of the son rest upon the spiritualization of the father. The raising of the dead man, which is symbolically identical with the erection of the *djed* pillar and the placing of the previous year's effigy of Osiris upon the sycamore branches, precedes both the enthronement of Horus and the Sed festival every time.

Any interpretation which assumes that these rites merely entreat the dead to help the living is quite inadequate. The close connection between the Osiris ritual, the coronation ceremonies, and the Sed festival makes such a general interpretation impossible.

One of the basic phenomena of totemism and of all initiation rites is that the totem or ancestor is reincarnated in the initiate, finding in him a new dwelling place and at the same time constituting his higher self. This result can be traced all the way from the sonship of the Horus hero and its connection with the apotheosis of his father Osiris to the Christian Incarnation and the phenomenon of individuation in modern man.

Between the son who regenerates himself as a hero, his divine parentage, and the rebirth of the dead father in the son there exists a fundamental relationship which was formulated as: "I and the Father are one." In Egypt this relationship was mythologically prefigured in the process to which we have repeatedly drawn attention: Horus, as the avenger of his father, becomes the supreme temporal ruler, but at the same time his earthly power is grounded in the spiritual authority exercised by Osiris.

The erection of the *djed* pillar occupies a central position in the enthronement of Horus and in the Sed festival: the succession of the Horus kings is based on this ritual, by which the right of succession of the son, who is always Horus, and the elevation of the father, who is always Osiris, are archetypally established as universal laws. As the generations succeed one another, and yet remain magically connected, the patriarchal line of fathers and sons is seen to rest upon the spiritual phenomenon of their identity, which transcends their differences. Every king was once Horus and becomes Osiris (*illus. 30*); every Osiris was once Horus. Horus and Osiris are one.

This identity is reinforced by the figure of Isis, who confronts both of them as mother, wife, and sister: mother, because she gives birth to Horus and awakens the dead Osiris to new life (*illus. 29*); wife, because she conceives Horus by Osiris, and the Horus sons by Horus; sister, because—if we equate the function of the sister with the role played by Athene in respect of Perseus and Orestes—she fights for the dynastic rights of the dead Osiris and the living Horus.

As son and heir, the Horus king reigns over the "earthly world" and represents its phallic fertility. The coronation ceremonies show how far he has become the permanent successor to the old fertility king. The original sacrifice of this king was replaced by a fight with his deputy; now the fight with evil falls to the lot of the hero and victorious king. The defeat of Set by Horus, which plays such an important part in the Edfu ritual [64] and in the coronation ceremonies, and again at the erection of the *djed* during the Sed festival, is the condition of the god-king's triumphant fertility. The identification of Horus with the phallic bull-god of Min and the creator-god Ptah, the victory of the corn god, the annexation of Set's testicles, the sacred marriage with Hathor in Edfu, and the ritual renewal of kingship at the harvest festival are all evidence of this fertility character.

It is now abundantly clear that the Horus king no longer acts the part of a temporary fertility king under the dominance of the Earth Mother; he has become the ever-fruitful patriarch who continually fertilizes the earth and reigns over its progeny.

His function has made itself independent of the natural rhythm which was given sacred expression in the old fertility ritual. But it achieved independence only because it found support in an authority that was itself independent of the natural process and its periodicity. The earthly king, like the divine

[64] Ibid., p. 33.

Horus son with whom he identified himself, needed a higher sanction, and this they both found in the spiritual principle of duration, the incorruptibility and everlastingness symbolized by Osiris.

In the matriarchate, death and resurrection occurred on the same earthly plane; death meant the cessation of fertility, and resurrection meant the reappearance of living vegetation. But both poles remained bound to the rhythm of nature.

With Osiris, however, resurrection means realizing his eternal and lasting essence, becoming a perfected soul, escaping from the flux of natural occurrence. The corollary of this is Horus' enthronement as the son of Osiris. As the son of Isis he would be no more than a fleeting god of vegetation, having his roots in the eternal but eternally changing nature of the Great Mother. Now, however, he is conjoined to the father, the everlasting and unchanging spiritual father who rules over the spirits. Like him, he lasts forever; he is at once his avenger, his heir, and the cause of his elevation. When the ladder of Osiris is raised up in the coronation ceremonies, and the erection of the *djed* and elevation of the old king usher in the crowning of Horus, this means that his power is grounded in the higher father and no longer in the lower mother.

We can now understand why it is the *dead* Osiris who begets Horus. This is a primitive, symbolical way of expressing spiritual generation. It is not an earthly generation: the father is the mummy with the long member or, as another image puts it, the scarab with the phallus, eternally potent.

And that, too, is why Osiris, when he rose from the dead, lacked a male organ. Isis replaced the missing phallus by a wooden cult phallus. The eunuch is, so to speak, a "spermatic" eunuch, a not uncommon symbol of spiritual generation which occurs again and again in the mystery religions and secret teachings.

The dead man who begets is a spirit ancestor. He is spermatic spirit, blowing where he listeth, invisible as the wind spirit. The collective unconscious, expressing itself through a modern psychotic,[65] and an Egyptian magic papyrus both agree that the seat of this pneumatic principle is the sun. The solar phallus is the source of the wind, they say. But the sun is Ra-Horus and Osiris combined.

The problem of creation and the allied problem of spirit found definitive symbolic formulation in the Osiris myth. "I and the father are one"—Osiris and Horus are, psychologically speaking, parts of a single personality.

The father without a phallus, or to be more accurate, with a spirit phallus, has his counterpart in the chthonic-phallic son: each depends on the other for his creative powers, but Horus addresses himself to the world and is the temporal ruler, while Osiris, the eternal power behind him, rules the spirits. Son and father together are the God of this world and the next. Their relation to one another is analogous to that between the ego and the self in psychology.

The symbolism that gravitates round the figure of Osiris embraces the most primitive levels of man's psychology as well as its highest reaches; it has its source in prehistoric burial customs, and it finally ends with projections of the process known today as integration. If we briefly review the different layers of symbolism which illustrate the transformation of human personality and man's growing awareness of this process, we shall see how clearly the trend of centroversion has been seeking to assert itself in mankind from the very beginning.

The most primitive layer is the recombination of the severed parts, the attempt to make durable and to preserve, but also to "elevate." This is seen in the raising up of the body of Osiris upon the tree, in the symbol of tree birth, the lifting of the buried effigy, the placing of the sacrum upon the tree in the *djed* symbol, and above all in the erection of the *djed* pillar. The *mystique* of erection and ascension is intimately connected with the mystery of wholeness and integration. Reunion of the divided parts, mummification and preservation of the body, form its basis, but

65 Jung, "The Structure of the Psyche," p. 150.

250

this primitive ritual soon passes over into the symbolism of ascent and transformation.

The union of body and head then becomes the union of the upper and lower Osiris and finally the union of Osiris and Ra. But this is equivalent to self-transformation, for Osiris unites himself with his Ra soul to form a perfect being. All this is archetypal when played out among the gods, but the process becomes humanized as soon as the role of Osiris is taken over by the Egyptian king who, as Horus, unites himself with Osiris. Once the king is included in the divine drama, mythological processes begin to reveal themselves as psychological ones. The process finally takes the form of psychic unification and psychic transformation, by which the discrete soul parts become integrated and the earthly Horus-ego aspect of the personality combines with the spiritual, divine self. The outcome of both processes— union and transformation on ever higher levels—is the conquest of death, which has always been the supreme goal even in the psychology of primitive man.

The patriarchal father-son relationship ousted the once dominant mother figure, Isis, in the religious, psychological, social, and political spheres. Vestiges of the original matriarchal rule still remained, but in historical times they were already overshadowed by the father-king. The investiture and enthronement of the son are based on the resurrection of Osiris and the defeat of his enemies. Horus' struggle with the principle of evil —Set—is, in a sense, the prototype of "God's holy war" which each of his sons has to wage.

With this, the ring closes and we come back to the hero myth and the dragon fight. Only, we must read the Osiris myth in such a way as to include Horus, the hero, as part of Osiris.

We have seen that certain elements of the hero myth belong essentially together. The hero is an ego hero; that is, he represents the struggles of consciousness and the ego against the unconscious. The masculinization and strengthening of the ego, apparent in the hero's martial deeds, enable him to overcome his fear of the dragon and give him courage to face the Terrible

Mother—Isis—and her henchman Set. The hero is the higher man, the "erected phallus," whose potency is expressed in head, eye, and sun symbols. His fight bears witness to his kinship with "heaven" and to his divine parentage, and sets up a dual relationship: on the one hand he needs the support of heaven in fighting the dragon, and, on the other, he has to fight it in order to prove himself worthy of such support. As one regenerated through the fight, the hero is ritually identical with the father-god, and is his incarnation. The reborn son is child of the divine father, father of himself, and, by fathering the rebirth of the father in himself, he also becomes his father's father.

Thus all the essential elements of the hero myth are to be found in the myth of Horus and Osiris. There is only one qualification, and that has to do with the patriarchal conquest of the Terrible Mother. The myth contains traces of the terrible Isis,[66] but the fact that Horus beheads her and commits incest with her in the Memphis festivities is clear proof that she has been overcome.[67] In general, however, her negative role is taken over by Set,[68] and Isis becomes the "good mother." [69]

In this way the hero myth develops into the myth of self-transformation, the myth of man's divine sonship which is latent in him from the beginning, but can only be realized through the heroic union of the ego (Horus) with the self (Osiris). This union had its first exponent in the mythical Horus, and then in the Egyptian kings who succeeded him (illus. 30). These were followed by individual Egyptians—though in their case identification with the king was a matter of primitive magic only—and finally, in the course of further spiritual development, the principle that man had an immortal soul became the inalienable property of every individual.

Everywhere the influence of the Osiris myth has been pro-

[66] See supra, pp. 64 f.
[67] Herodotus, Book II.
[68] See supra, p. 66.
[69] The feminine counterpart of the Horus-Osiris myth is the myth of Demeter and the Kore. The relevant material has been put together in Jung and Kerényi, *Essays on a Science of Mythology*.

digious. Traces of it are to be found in the classical mysteries,[70] in Gnosticism, Christianity, alchemy, mysticism, and even in modern times.

In some of the classical mystery religions there is evidence of initiation rites whose purpose it was to produce the higher masculinity, to transform the initiate into the higher man and so make him akin to, or identical with, God. For instance the *solificatio* of the Isis mysteries stresses identification with the sun god, while in certain others the aim is to achieve fellowship with God by means of *participation mystique*. The path varies, but whether the celebrant is seized with ecstasy and becomes "*entheos*," or is ritually regenerated, or takes God into his own body through communion with him, always the goal is the higher man, the attainment of his spiritual, heavenly part. As the Gnostics of a later day expressed it, the initiate becomes an "*ennoos*," one who possesses nous, or whom the nous possesses, a "*pneumatikos*." [71]

A common feature of these mysteries is castration, obviously symbolizing the mortification of lower masculinity in the interests of the higher. When, for example, this happens as a result of the celebrant identifying himself with Attis, or when we find, in the Adonis mysteries, that the couch upon which Adonis rests is strewn with lettuces,[72] food of the dead and plant of eunuchs which "drives out the generative forces," and that hemlock plays the same role in the Eleusinian mysteries, this only means that the sacrifice of lower masculinity is the precondition of spirituality.

All these ascetic trends are ruled by the uroboros and Great Mother principle, and form part of the *mystique* of the suffering son. Their ultimate goal is the mystic uroboric incest that hides behind castration.[73] In terms of stadial development, these

[70] Reitzenstein, *Hellenistische Mysterienreligionen,* pp. 75 f.
[71] Jung, "Concerning Rebirth."
[72] Merezhkovski, *The Secret of the West,* p. 288. In Egypt, however, lettuces were sacred to the Coptic Min on account of their aphrodisiac powers (cf. Kees, *Götterglaube,* p. 349).
[73] See supra, pp. 117 f.

mystery cults have either not yet reached the stage of the hero fight or have remained fixed at that level.

The aim of this fight is to combine the phallic-chthonic with the spiritual-heavenly masculinity, and the creative union with the anima in the *hieros gamos* is symptomatic of this. But, since in the mystery religions the fight with the dragon is conceived only as the fight with the mother dragon, representing the unconscious chthonic aspect, the inevitable result is identification with the spiritual father, so far as the dragon-fight situation is reached at all in the mystery religions. The failure of the fight with the father-dragon, the overwhelming force of spirit, leads to patriarchal castration, inflation, loss of the body in the ecstasy of ascension, and so to a world-negating mysticism. This phenomenon is particularly evident in Gnosticism and Gnostic Christianity. The infiltration of Iranian and Manichaean influences strengthens the martial component in the hero, but because he is still a Gnostic at heart, he remains hostile to the world, the body, materiality, and woman. Although there are certain elements in Gnosis that strive for a synthesis of opposites, these always fly apart in the end; the heavenly side of man triumphs and the earthly is sacrificed.

Behind the ecstatic afflatus of patriarchal castration there lurks the threat—and the fascination—of uroboric incest.[74] Uroboros and Great Mother are reactivated. That explains why the mysteries are almost always rebirth mysteries. But there is no active self-regeneration as in the hero myth: here the rebirth is passively experienced by one already dead. In the Phrygian mysteries, for example, the limbs of the dead man are put together again. The awakening of the dead, as a rebirth mystery,[75] is a very characteristic feature of religion everywhere, but it is important to note whether it is initiated by the mother deity, by the priest who represents the self, or by the ego. The situation as we find it in myth and ritual is that, simultaneously with the ego's experience of its death, a revivifying self appears in

[74] See supra, p. 187.
[75] Reitzenstein, op. cit., p. 252.

the form of a god. The hero myth is fulfilled only when the ego identifies with this self, in other words, when it realizes that the support of heaven at the moment of death means nothing less than to be begotten by a god and born anew. Only in this paradoxical situation, when the personality experiences dying as a simultaneous act of self-reproduction, will the twofold man be reborn as the total man.

Accordingly, in the Tibetan Book of the Dead, the dead and the dying are summoned to a visionary knowledge of this reproductive act. Likewise the widespread form of mystery in which the celebrant brings the god to life is an early mythological form of self-generation. Where, on the other hand, the celebrant undergoes a symbolical death, but the revivifying god is represented by a priest, there can be no full realization of the likeness between father and son. Already in the Hellenic mysteries we can see how symbolic contents which had once been acted out in the ritual performance of mythical events gradually turn inward, becoming first the sacred experience of the initiate, and finally processes within the individualized psyche.

This progressive interiorization is a symptom of the individualization and intensification of human consciousness, and this same principle, which first promoted the growth of personality, continues to govern the next phase of its development (Part II).

Historically speaking, however, the synthetic path of development—which includes the stage of the hero fight—was never followed in Christianity as it grew up under Gnostic influences, but only in alchemy, the cabala, and above all in Hasidism.

In alchemy, from which the term "uroboros" is borrowed, we discover all the archetypal stages and their symbolism down to the last detail, including even the symbol of Osiris as the basic symbol of the arcane substance, so that the whole process of alchemical change and sublimation can be interpreted as a transformation of Osiris.[76]

---

[76] Since alchemy actually originated in Egypt, it is not improbable that esoteric interpretations of the Osiris myth are among the foundations of the art. Osiris is one of the symbols for lead, and the transmutation of this into the solar gold of

Thus the archetypal stages of conscious development have their crowning symbol in the transfiguration of Osiris, an archaic, mythological form of the phenomenon which was destined to reappear thousands of years later as the process of individuation in modern man. But now there comes a new development. As though a Copernican revolution had taken place within the psyche, consciousness faces inward and becomes aware of the self, about which the ego revolves in a perpetual paradox of identity and nonidentity. The psychological process of assimilating the unconscious into our present-day consciousness begins at this point, and the consequent shifting of the center of gravity from the ego to the self signalizes the latest stage in the evolution of human consciousness.

Ra is the principal object of the "great work." Ascension and sublimation are just as characteristic of Osiris as his connection with Ra.

PART II

The Psychological Stages in the
Development of Personality

A. The Original Unity

(MYTHOLOGICAL STAGES:
UROBOROS AND GREAT MOTHER)

Centroversion and Ego Formation

THE SECOND PART of this work is an attempt to evaluate, in the light of analytical psychology, the processes whose mythological projection we described in the first part. We have now to demonstrate the significance of myth for modern Western man and to show how it has assisted the growth of his personality.

Besides summing up the psychological developments dealt with in the first part, we here put forward a piece of speculative "metapsychology" by way of supplementing and amplifying our theme. The fragmentariness and known limitations of our experience should not prevent us from trying to take temporary stock of the situation and to discover the unifying evolutionary aspect which alone will give our individual findings their proper place and value. This is merely one among many other possible and necessary aspects of analytical psychology; but we believe that the evolutionary aspect of the archetypal stages is of importance not only for the theory but also for the practice of psychotherapy. The stadial psychology we are seeking to outline offers more than a contribution to the psychology of individual personality; for the psychological approach to culture, which puts the humanistic significance of Jung's depth psychology in its proper setting, would not have been possible had not analytical psychology advanced beyond the personalistic sphere into collective psychology. Before the stadial development of the ego discussed in Part I is subjected to psychological interpretation, we must make a few introductory remarks about the concept of the ego, about the stages, and about our interpretative method.

Fundamental to analytical psychology is the theory of complexes, which recognizes the complex nature of the unconscious and defines complexes as "living units of the unconscious psyche." [1] It also recognizes the complex nature of the ego,

[1] Jung, "A Review of the Complex Theory," p. 101.

which, as the center of consciousness, forms the central complex in the psychic system.

This conception of the ego, substantiated by the psychological and psychopathological findings, is one of the distinctive features of analytical psychology:

The ego complex is a content of consciousness as well as a condition of consciousness, for a psychic element is conscious to me so far as it is related to the ego complex. But so far as the ego is only the center of my field of consciousness, it is not identical with the whole of my psyche, being merely one complex among other complexes.[2]

We have traced the development of this ego complex in mythology, and in so doing have familiarized ourselves with part of the history of consciousness in its mythological projection. The developmental changes in the relation between the ego and the unconscious were expressed mythologically in the different archetypal figures—uroboros, Great Mother, dragon, etc. —in which the unconscious presents itself to the ego, or which the ego constellates out of the unconscious. In taking the archetypal stages to be developmental stages of ego consciousness, we have interpreted the mythological figures of the child, the adolescent, and the hero as stages in the ego's own transformation. The ego complex, which is the central complex of the psyche, forms the theater for the events described in Part I.

Like every figure in a work of art—for instance, in a play or a novel—the mythological figure of the ego requires a dual interpretation, that is to say, a "structural" interpretation based on the nature of the figure itself, and what we might call for short a "genetic" interpretation which regards the figure as the expression and exponent of the psyche from which it springs.

Thus the structural interpretation of the Faust figure has to consider the characteristics and activities with which Faust is endowed in Goethe's drama, while the genetic interpretation has to take Faust as a part of Goethe's personality, a complex in his psyche. The two interpretations are mutually complementary. The structural—objective—interpretation seeks to em-

[2] Jung, *Psychological Types*, def. 16.

brace the whole span of the structure represented by the person of Faust, and then combine it with the genetic interpretation which recognizes that the Faust figure stands for the totality of Goethe's psychic situation, both conscious and unconscious, and for the whole history of his development. The fact that the poet's conscious mind uses extraneous material for the creative process, such as the existing story of Dr. Faustus, does not disprove the inner associations presupposed by the genetic interpretation, for the selection and modification of this material are decisive and typical of the psychic situation. Just as residues from the previous day are elaborated in dreams, so the existing literary, historical, and other material is worked up by the "editor" in the unconscious in order to assist the self-representation of the psyche, and, after being processed by the conscious mind of the creative artist, is finally assimilated to the inner situation which is seeking to project itself.

As in poetry, so in mythology, the figures must submit to the same dual interpretation. Our contention that the development of ego consciousness is depicted in myth is, however, complicated by the fact that while we take the myth literally and describe the experiences of the youthful lover, for example, "as if" he were a living figure, we must simultaneously interpret him as the symbolical representative of a definite ego stage in man's development.

These myth figures are archetypal projections of the collective unconscious; in other words, humanity is putting something outside itself in its myths, something of whose meaning it is not conscious.

Just as unconscious contents like dreams and fantasies tell us something about the psychic situation of the dreamer, so myths throw light on the human stage from which they originate and typify man's unconscious situation at that stage. In neither case is there any conscious knowledge of the situation projected, either in the conscious mind of the dreamer or in that of the mythmaker.

When we speak of the stages of conscious development, we

mean—as has doubtless been made clear in Part I—the archetypal stages, though at the same time we have repeatedly stressed their evolutionary and historical character. These stages, with their fluctuating degrees of ego consciousness, can be shown to be archetypal; that is, they work as an "eternal presence" in the psyche of modern man and form elements of his psychic structure. The constitutive character of these stages unfolds in the historical sequence of individual development, but it is very probable that the individual's psychic structure is itself built up on the historical sequence of human development as a whole. The concept of the stages can be taken as much in the "Platonic" as in the "Aristotelian" sense; as archetypal stages of the psyche's structure they are constituents of psychic development, but they are also the result and deposit of this development all through human history. This paradox, nevertheless, has a rational foundation, for although the archetype is a condition and constituent of psychic experience, man's experience can only become self-experience in the course of human history. He experiences the world through the archetypes, but the archetypes are themselves impressions of his unconscious experience of the world. The modifications of consciousness whose deposits are found in the mythological stages reflect an inner historical process which can be correlated with prehistoric and historical epochs. The correlation, however, is not absolute, only relative.

Flinders Petrie [3] established a system of what he called "sequence-dating" (abbreviated "s.d.") for the early history of Egypt, that is, sequences within which one can lay down a "before" and an "after" without knowing the temporal correlation. For instance, s.d. 30 comes before s.d. 77, though this does not tell us to what dated period we must assign s.d. 30 or 77, or how great an interval lies between them. Similarly, we have to make do with psychological sequence-dating in dealing with the archetypal stages. The uroboros comes "before" the stage of the Great Mother, and the Great Mother "before" the dragon fight; but an absolute correlation in time is impossible because

[3] *The Making of Egypt*, p. 8.

we have to consider the historical relativity of individual nations and cultures. Thus Creto-Mycenaean culture was, for the Greeks, the prehistoric Great Mother period, since in that culture her cult was dominant. Greek mythology is largely the dragon-fight mythology of a consciousness struggling for independence, and this struggle was decisive for the spiritual importance of Greece. But whereas in Greece this development falls roughly between 1500 and 500 B.C., the corresponding process in Egypt took place probably long before 3300. The development is already complete in the myth of Osiris and Horus, and the identification of the king with Osiris is proved as far back as the First Dynasty, which is not to say that it did not occur until then.

Two important consequences follow from the relativity of these stages and their occurrence at different periods in different cultures. Firstly, it proves their archetypal structure. The universality and necessity of their occurrence shows that there is a common psychic substructure which functions identically in all men. Secondly, it justifies our method of illustrating a particular stage by collecting and comparing data derived from different cultures and epochs. For instance, Frobenius has found that the cult of the Great Mother and ritual regicide play an important part among certain African tribes.[4] These near-contemporary examples are an illustration of, and a living commentary upon, age-old religious customs practiced in Egypt perhaps seven thousand years ago. Whether the archetypal symbolism appears spontaneously, or whether it is due to ancient Egyptian influences,[5] is irrelevant so far as concerns the actuality of the stages and their symbolism, and our use of material from different spheres of culture. Wherever archetypal symbolism occurs, mythological material is just as valuable for us as anthropological material. Hence our repeated references to Bachofen, for although his historical evaluation of mythology

[4] Frobenius, *Monumenta Africana*, Vol. VI, pp. 242 f.
[5] Seligman, *Egypt and Negro Africa*.

may be out of date, his interpretation of the symbols has been largely confirmed by modern depth psychology.

Our task is now to assess the archetypal stages of conscious development—as known from mythological projection—with a view to understanding their psychological significance for the formation and development of personality. We have seen that the earliest developments of the ego and consciousness occurred in and through the symbols of the uroboros and Great Mother, and could be registered from the ego's changing relations towards them. The psychological interpretation of these two initial archetypal stages and their symbolism is our first concern— that is, we have to trace the ego's development from the germ, and its relation to the unconscious.

The Ego Germ in the Original Uroboric Situation

Psychologically speaking, the uroboros, the initial archetypal stage which forms our point of departure, is a "borderline" experience, being individually and collectively prehistoric in the sense that history only begins with a subject who is capable of experiencing—in other words, when an ego and a consciousness are already present. The initial stage symbolized by the uroboros corresponds to a pre-ego stage, and just as this antedates human history, so also in the history of individual development it belongs to the stage of earliest childhood when an ego germ is just beginning to be. But in spite of the fact that this stage can only be experienced "on the border," its symptoms and symbolisms have an important effect upon wide areas of man's collective and individual life.

The original situation which is represented mythologically as the uroboros corresponds to the psychological stage in man's prehistory when the individual and the group, ego and unconscious, man and the world, were so indissolubly bound up with one another that the law of *participation mystique,* of unconscious identity, prevailed between them.

The essential fate of man, at least of the mature modern man, is enacted on three fronts which, although interconnected, are nonetheless clearly marked off from one another. The world as the outside world of extrahuman events, the community as the sphere of interhuman relationships, the psyche as the world of interior human experience—these are the three basic factors which govern human life, and man's creative encounter with each of them is decisive for the development of the individual. In the initial stage, however, these territories have not yet become separated from one another, neither man from the world, nor individual from the group, nor ego consciousness from the unconscious. Nor is the human world which is composed of individuals and the group in any way distinguished from what we call the external world of objects. Although we know the original condition of things only as a borderline experience, we can still describe its symptomatology because, with those parts of our psyche which are not our ego consciousness, we continue to participate in this archetypal stage.

This indivisibility of group, individual, and external world is found wherever psychic contents—contents, that is to say, which our present-day consciousness recognizes as psychic and which it therefore relegates to the world within us—are projected upon the world at large and are experienced as though they were outside ourselves. Contents of this kind are recognized readily enough as projections when they derive from earlier epochs, from alien spheres of culture, or from other people, but it becomes increasingly difficult for us to do so the more closely they approximate to the unconscious conditions of our own time, our own culture, and our own personality. The animism which endows trees with indwelling spirits, idols with divinity, holy places with wonder-working powers, or human beings with magical gifts is easily seen through; for us it is a transparent case of "projection." We know that trees, idols, holy places, and human beings are recognizable objects of the external world, into which early man projected his inner psychic contents. By recognizing them, we withdraw such "primitive projections," we diagnose them as autosuggestion or something of the sort, and thus the fusion effected by participation between man and the objects of the external world is nullified. But when it comes to experiencing God's intervention in world history, or the sanctity of the Fatherland symbolized by flag or king, or the devilish intentions of nations beyond the latest Iron Curtain, or even the bad character of those we dislike or the good character of those we love; when it comes to experiencing these as a projection, then our psychological powers of discernment incontinently fail us, not to mention the fact that we cannot lay our finger on the most blatant examples of all for the simple reason that they are entirely unconscious and belong to the preconceptions which we accept without question.

Man's original fusion with the world, with its landscape and its fauna, has its best-known anthropological expression in totemism, which regards a certain animal as an ancestor, a friend, or some kind of powerful and providential being. The sense of kinship felt by a human member of the totem for the totem animal and ancestor, and for all animals of that species, is carried to the point of identity. There is abundant evidence that such kinships are not just matters of belief, but matters of fact, i.e., psychological realities which sometimes result in telepathic hunting-magic, etc.[6] There is no doubt that early man's magical view of the world rests on identity relationships of this kind.

The same phenomenon of fusion as originally existed between man and the world also obtains between the individual and the group, or rather, between man as a member of a group, and the collective. History teaches that in the beginning the individual did not exist as an independent entity, but that the group dominated and did not allow the emancipation of a separate ego. We find this state in all departments of social and cultural life; everywhere at the outset there is an anonymous collectivity.

This original group unity does not imply the existence of an objective group psyche apart from its carriers, and no doubt individual differences were present among group members from

[6] Frobenius, *Kulturgeschichte Afrikas*, pp. 127 f.

the beginning, the individual being allowed certain limited areas of independence; [7] but the fact remains that in the initial state of affairs the individual was to a large extent integrated through the group. This integration was not necessarily anything mystical, as the rather nebulous term *participation mystique* might lead one to suppose. All it means is that, in the original group, the solidarity of the group members is to be conceived more on the analogy of an organ in relation to the body, or of a part in relation to the whole, than of a part in relation to the sum, and that the whole exercised a paramount effect, so that the ego could only free itself very slowly from the tyranny of the group. This late birth of the ego, consciousness, and the individual is an incontestable fact.[8]

Even though modern research has shown that the individual comes into conflict with the group very early in primitive society, it is nevertheless certain that the further back we go in human history, the rarer individuality becomes and the more undeveloped it is. Indeed, even today, psychological analysis still comes up against the dead weight of collectively unconscious, non-individual factors in the psychology of modern man. From these two facts alone it must be sufficiently evident that man was originally part of the collective psyche of his group and enjoyed

[7] See Appendix I.

[8] This remains true despite the modifications which the school of anthropology associated with the name of Malinowski has effected in our conception of the collective psyche among primitives (cf. Malinowski, *Crime and Custom in Savage Society*, p. 55). The discovery of the collective psyche and of the individual's submergence in it caused it to be overemphasized at first, and Malinowski's reference to the role played by the individual even in the early stages of social life is therefore important. He is right to lay stress on the dialectic between individual and group, but this does not impair the fundamental importance of the discoveries made by the Dürckheim school. What Lévy-Bruhl called *participation mystique* and prelogical thinking is identical with what Cassirer, in his attack on the Dürckheim school (Cassirer, *An Essay on Man*, pp. 79 f.), called the experience of the "oneness of life" and the "predominance of feeling." Prelogical thinking is not to be taken as an incapacity to think logically. Primitive man is quite capable of this, but, because his view of the world is determined unconsciously, it is not oriented toward the logic of conscious thinking. To the extent that modern man is unconscious, he too thinks prelogically, outside the categories prescribed by his conscious, i.e., scientific, world views (cf. Aldrich, *The Primitive Mind and Modern Civilization*, p. 66).

only the narrowest range of action as an individual. All the social, religious, and historical evidence points to the late birth of the individual from the collective and from the unconscious.[9]

The Copernican revolution signalized by the application of depth psychology to the problems here under discussion consists essentially in this: that it proceeds from the collective psyche of the group as the determining factor, and not from the individual ego and consciousness.

The cardinal discovery of transpersonal psychology is that the collective psyche, the deepest layer of the unconscious, is the living ground current from which is derived everything to do with a particularized ego possessing consciousness: upon this it is based, by this it is nourished, and without this it cannot exist. The group psyche—which, as we shall see later, is not to be confused with the mass psyche—is characterized by the primary preponderance of unconscious elements and components, and by the recession of individual consciousness. In saying this we must, however, emphasize that at this deep level it is not so much a question of recession, dissolution, or regression; it is rather that consciousness is still in abeyance, being not yet developed or only partially developed. Tardes' formula that "the social, like the hypnotic, state is only a form of dreaming" [10] is a neat summing up of the original group situation. Only, we must not regard our modern, waking consciousness as the obvious point of departure and then, on the analogy of hypnosis, take the *participation mystique* of the group psyche to be a limi-

[9] We must draw attention here to the somewhat unusual system that governs the arrangement of Part II. The development of the ego, the problem of centroversion, and the formation of personality are discussed in the main sections, while in the appendices an attempt is made to outline the individual's relations to the group, and the phenomena of projection and introjection operating between them. We thus have two sequences, which, although related and complementary, are yet worked out independently of one another. It is, however, impossible to carry through this line of demarcation in our account of the initial uroboric stage. To distinguish the psychological development of the individual from that of the group is already something of a problem, since the two are in ceaseless intercommunication; and in the earliest stage, when individual and group are indissolubly fused together, such a division is quite out of the question.

[10] Reiwald, *Vom Geist der Massen*, p. 133.

tation of this waking state. The reverse is true; the conscious
state is the late and uncommon phenomenon, and its complete
attainment is far more of a rarity than modern man so flatter-
ingly pretends, while the unconscious state is the original, basic,
psychic situation that is everywhere the rule.

Group unity in participation is still so widely prevalent, even
in modern man, that it is only through the ceaseless conscious
efforts of certain individuals of genius that we gradually become
aware of the psychic factors which, as the unconscious "cultural
pattern" we so blindly accept, regulate the life and death of each
one of us. Although enjoying a higher conscious development,
probably, than any previously attained by man, modern individuals, for all their conscious achievements, are still deeply embedded in the tissue of their group and its unconscious laws.

The fusion of the individual with the group can be seen in
small things as in great. For instance, one investigator describes
the state of possession among primitives, i.e., the seizure of the
personality by certain unconscious contents [11] which are believed to be spirits, as follows:

Though possession may often be induced voluntarily, it can sometimes
occur involuntarily. In the latter case members of the same family are frequently afflicted with similar symptoms.[12]

This emotional contagion is due to the unconscious fusion
with one another of all members of the family. Their identity is
the prime factor, although the very term "contagion" presupposes a state of separation which actually exists only in the
smallest degree. But so far as it does exist, as in the case of individualized Western man, it applies in the main, for reasons
still to be discussed, only to certain differences of conscious
structure. The emotionality of the group, on the other hand,
forms a layer of unconscious, psychic connective tissue which
generally has a far greater energy potential than the "individualized" consciousness.

The emotional bond between members of the collective has

[11] Jung, "The Psychological Foundations of Belief in Spirits," p. 301.
[12] Thurnwald, *Die eingeborenen Australiens und der Südseeinseln*, p. 30.

nothing to do with a conscious feeling-relationship or with love. It springs from a variety of sources which cannot be discussed here. Common descent from the same tribe, the sharing of a common life, and, above all, common experiences create emotional bonds even today, as we well know. Social, religious, aesthetic, and other collective experiences of whatever coloring —from the tribal head-hunt to the modern mass meeting—activate the unconscious emotional foundations of the group psyche. The individual has not yet broken loose from the emotional undercurrent, and any excitation of one part of the group can affect the whole, as a fever seizes upon all parts of the organism. The emotional fusion then sweeps away the still feebly developed differences of conscious structure in the individuals concerned and continually restores the original group unity. This phenomenon, taking the form of mass recollectivization,[13] still exerts a powerful influence upon the life of the individual in relation to the community.

In the early uroboric state there is a fusion both of man with the world and of the individual with the group. The basis of both phenomena is the nondifferentiation of ego consciousness from the unconscious—in other words, the incomplete separation of these two psychic systems.

When we speak of a psychic content being projected or introjected, meaning by this that it is experienced as something outside, but is then taken inside, we are postulating a clearly defined structure of personality for which an "outside" and an "inside" exist. In reality, however, the psyche began by being exteriorized to a very large extent. Projection presupposes that what is projected, i.e., actively put outside oneself, previously existed inside as something psychic. But the exteriority of a psyche content, contrasted with the idea of projection, implies the existence outside of something not originally to be found inside the personality. This exteriority of a content is its original condition; it means that the content was only recognized as belonging to the psyche at a later stage of consciousness. Only

[13] See Appendices.

from that point of view, therefore, can the exteriorized content be diagnosed as projected. For instance, so long as God is exteriorized, he acts as the "real God outside," though a later consciousness may then diagnose him as a projection of the God-image which dwells in the psyche.[14] The formation and development of human personality largely consists in "taking in"—introjecting—these exteriorized contents.

Among the basic phenomena characteristic of the uroboric existence of the group and the submersion of each part in the group psyche is the government of the group by the dominants of the collective unconscious, by the archetypes, and by instincts. The emotional tone of the group is determined by these same contents, and because their libido charge exceeds that of the individual's consciousness, their manifestation has a violent effect upon individuals and groups even today.

In connection with the submersion of the individual in the group and of ego consciousness in the unconscious, we would quote the following interesting observation from Trotter, concerning the herd:

The appropriate response by the individual is to an impulse received from the herd and not directly from the actual object of alarm. It seems to be in this way that the paralyzing emotion of fear is held back from the individual, while its effect can reach him only as the active and formidable passion of panic.[15]

Reiwald, from whose book we take this extract, comments:

The passivity of the individual in relation to the herd is to some extent a condition of the herd's activity.[16]

Though this teleological interpretation of Trotter's is somewhat questionable, since the individual can sometimes be stampeded into danger or death by collective reaction, the

---

[14] The concept of transpersonality is not to be confused with exteriorization. A content of the personality can, as part of the collective unconscious, be "transpersonal" in our sense of the word, since it does not ultimately derive from the personal ego-sphere or from the personal unconscious. A content of the personal unconscious, on the other hand, can easily be exteriorized.

[15] *Instincts of the Herd in Peace and War*, p. 115.

[16] Reiwald, op. cit.

phenomenon is sufficiently important in itself to merit attention. In the original situation each part is adjusted to the group rather than to the outside world, and its orientation is in reactive dependence upon the group. The relation to the outside world is in large measure actuated not directly by the individual, but by that imaginary entity the "group," whose incarnation is the leader or leading animal, and whose consciousness does duty for all parts of the group.[17]

Participation, as we know, also plays an important role in childhood, since the child is involved in the unconscious psychology of his parents.[18] Exactly the same uroboric situation then recurs on the ontogenetic plane that we have described on the collective plane.

In these circumstances, when consciousness is insufficiently differentiated from the unconscious, and the ego from the group, the group member finds himself as much at the mercy of group reactions as of unconscious constellations. The fact that he is preconscious and preindividual leads him to experience and react to the world in a way that is more collective than individual, and more mythological than rational. A mythological apperception of the world and an archetypal, instinctive mode of reaction are accordingly characteristic of the dawn man. The collective and the group members do not experience the world objectively, but mythologically, in archetypal images and symbols; and their reaction to it is archetypal, instinctive, and unconscious, not individual and conscious.

The unconscious reactions of group members when contained in their group invariably lead to the hypostatization of a group soul, a collective consciousness, or some such thing. This is justifiable enough, if we begin with the experience of the part who perceives the whole as a totality; in fact, we still speak of the

---

[17] That this same relationship still remains catastrophically in force in Western civilization is painfully obvious. Even today, the ruled are mostly supine members of the herd with no direct orientation of their own. The ruler, the State, etc., act as a substitute for individual consciousness and sweep us blindly into mass movements, wars, etc. See Appendices.

[18] Jung, "Analytical Psychology and Education"; Wickes, *The Inner World of Childhood*; Fordham, *The Life of Childhood*.

274

nation, the people, etc., in exactly the same way. And although this "nation" is an hypostasis, it is psychologically true and necessary to make such an hypostasis. For, as an effective whole, the nation is psychologically something more and other than the sum of its parts, and is always experienced as such by each part of the group. The more unconscious the whole of a man's personality is and the more germinal his ego, the more his experience of the whole will be projected upon the group. The ego germ and the group self are directly related, just as, conversely, individualization, ego development, and finally self-experience through individuation bring about the withdrawal of this projection. The more unindividualized people are, the stronger the projection of the self upon the group, and the stronger, too, the unconscious participations of group members among themselves. But, as the group becomes more individualized and the significance of the ego and of the individual increases, the more these interhuman relations must be made conscious and the unconscious participations broken down. In the uroboric situation, however, the ego is still germinal and consciousness has not yet developed into a system.

Development of the Ego out of the Uroboros

In the beginning, consciousness rises up like an island with whatever contents it then has, but soon sinks back again into the unconscious. There is in fact no continuity of consciousness. This state has often been reported of primitives, who, if they are not actively occupied with something, drowse off and are easily tired by conscious effort. Only with the progressive systematization of consciousness is there an increase of conscious continuity, a strengthening of the will, and a capacity for voluntary action, which in modern man are the hallmarks of ego consciousness. The stronger his consciousness the more he can do with it, and the weaker it is the more things "just happen." The uroboric state is unquestionably a "borderline" state.

It is in dreams that we most readily regress to the uroboric stage of the psyche, which like all the other bygone stages continues to exist in us and can at any moment be reactivated, provided that the level of consciousness falls, as during sleep, or as the result of some debility or illness or a lowering of consciousness otherwise induced.

When we plunge back into the world of dreams, our ego and our consciousness, being late products of human development, are broken down again. In our dreams we inhabit an interior world without being aware that we do so, for all the figures in the dream are the images, symbols, and projections of interior processes. Similarly the world of the dawn man is very largely an interior world experienced outside himself, a condition in which inside and outside are not discriminated from one another. The feeling of oneness with the universe, the ability of all contents to change shape and place, in accordance with the laws of similarity and symbolic affinity, the symbolic character of the world, and the symbolic meaning of all spatial dimensions —high and low, left and right, etc.—the significance of colors, and so forth, all this the world of dreams shares with the dawn period of mankind. Here as there, spiritual things take on "material" form, becoming symbols and objects. Light stands for illumination, clothes stand for personal qualities, and so on. Dreams can only be understood in terms of the psychology of the dawn period, which, as our dreams show, is still very much alive in us today.

The phase in which the ego germ is contained in the unconscious, like the embryo in the womb, when the ego has not yet appeared as a conscious complex and there is no tension between the ego system and the unconscious, is the phase we have designated as uroboric and pleromatic. Uroboric, because it is dominated by the symbol of the circular snake, standing for total nondifferentiation, everything issuing from everything and again entering into everything, depending on everything, and connecting with everything; pleromatic, because the ego germ still dwells in the pleroma, in the "fullness" of the unformed

God, and, as consciousness unborn, slumbers in the primordial egg, in the bliss of paradise. The later ego deems this pleromatic existence to be man's first felicity, for at this stage there is no suffering; suffering only comes into the world with the advent of the ego and ego experience.

The wakening ego is easily tired during this phase of early infancy, because poor in libido, and consequently the ego germ is still for the most part passive, having no real activity of its own, as this would presuppose an ego with expendable units of libido at its disposal, e.g., volition. So, to begin with, consciousness is mainly receptive, though even this receptivity is exhausting and leads to loss of consciousness through fatigue.

The ego's tendency to dissolve back into unconsciousness has been termed by us "uroboric incest." This regression—at the stage when the ego is still feeble and quite unconscious of itself —is pleasurable, as is shown by the positive character of the symbols during the uroboric phase, of which infancy and sleep are typical. "Pleasurable" in this context means the extinction of the incipient world of the ego and consciousness with all its tensions. Ego and consciousness, however, presuppose a tension between conscious and unconscious; and without the resultant energy-potential consciousness cannot live.

During this early phase all the experiences of the ego in relation to the unconscious are simultaneously pleasurable and painful. Uroboric incest is a typical instance of this. Even self-dissolution is a pleasurable experience, for while the solute— the ego—is weak, the solvent—which finds the dissolution pleasurable—is strong. Unconscious identity with the stronger solvent, the uroboric mother, brings a pleasure which must be called masochistic in its later, perverted form. The dissolvent sadism of the uroboros and the masochism of the dissolved ego germ coalesce in an ambivalent pleasure-pain feeling. The subject of this feeling is formless, because it is the unconscious psychic unity of uroboros and ego germ. This "death in ecstasy" is symbolized by the pleroma, the "fullness" known to the ego as a borderline experience, it being a matter of indifference whether the fullness—i.e., the collective unconscious—is interpreted as the bliss of paradise, the world of Platonic Ideas, or as the all-pervading void.

The stage of uroboric incest is the lowest and earliest phase in the ego's history. Regression to, and fixation at, this level occupy an important place in the life of the average person, and they play a decidedly negative role in the life of the neurotic and a decidedly positive one in the life of creative man. It depends on the intensity of consciousness and on the phase of development reached by the ego whether uroboric incest will be regressive and destructive or progressive and creative. Since the world of the uroboros is the world of origination and regeneration, from which life and the ego are eternally reborn like day from night, it follows that the uroboros has a creative value. For this reason many creation myths have as their emblem the uroboros: for while uroboric incest is the symbol of death, the maternal uroboros is the symbol of rebirth, of the nativity of the ego, and of the dawn of consciousness, the coming of light.

Reiwald has drawn attention in his book to a significant passage from Leonardo da Vinci:

Now you see that the hope and the desire of returning to the first state of chaos is like the moth to the light, and that the man who with constant longing awaits with joy each new springtime, each new summer, each new month and new year—deeming that the things he longs for are ever too late in coming—does not perceive that he is longing for his own destruction. But this desire is the very quintessence, the spirit of the elements, which finding itself imprisoned with the soul is ever longing to return from the human body to its giver. And you must know that this same longing is that quintessence, inseparable from nature, and that man is the image of the world.[19]

As the term "uroboric incest" makes clear, this longing for death is a symbolical expression for the tendency of the ego and consciousness to self-disintegration, a tendency with a profoundly erotic character. We saw in Part I how this incest reflects the activity of the maternal uroboros, of the Great Mother

[19] *The Literary Works of Leonardo da Vinci,* ed. by Richter, Vol. II, p. 242, §1162 ("Morals," from his manuscripts).

archetype, mother of life and death, whose figure is transpersonal and not reducible to the personal mother. The archetypal image of uroboric incest is eternally at work, and its effects extend from Leonardo and Goethe right down to our own day, when they found valid contemporary expression in a poem by D. H. Lawrence:

> . . . row, little soul, row on
> on the longest journey, towards the greatest goal.
>
> Neither straight nor crooked, neither here nor there
> but shadows folded on deeper shadows
> and deeper, to a core of sheer oblivion
> like the convolutions of a shadow-shell
> or deeper, like the foldings and involvings of a womb.
>
> Drift on, drift on, my soul, towards the most pure
> most dark oblivion.
> And at the penultimate porches, the dark-red mantle
> of the body's memories slips and is absorbed
> into the shell-like, womb-like convoluted shadow.
>
> And round the great final bend of unbroken dark
> the skirt of the spirit's experience has melted away
> the oars have gone from the boat, and the little dishes
> gone, gone, and the boat dissolves like pearl
> as the soul at last slips perfect into the goal, the core
> of sheer oblivion and of utter peace,
> the womb of silence in the living night.
>
> Ah peace, ah lovely peace, most lovely lapsing
> of this my soul into the plasm of peace.
>
> Oh lovely last, last lapse of death, into pure oblivion
> at the end of the longest journey
> peace, complete peace!
> But can it be that also it is procreation?
>
> Oh build your ship of death
> oh build it.
> Oh, nothing matters but the longest journey.[19a]

[19a] "The Ship of Death," a variant from MS. B, in the appendix of his *Last Poems*.

In spite of the death aspect it comprises, uroboric incest is not to be regarded as the basis of an instinctive tendency which could legitimately be termed the "death instinct."

The unconscious state is the primary and natural one, and the conscious state the product of an effort that uses up libido. There is in the psyche a force of inertia, a kind of psychic gravitation which tends to fall back into the original unconscious condition. In spite of its unconsciousness, however, this state is a state of life and not a state of death. It is just as ridiculous to speak of the death instinct of an apple that falls to the ground as to speak of the death instinct of the ego that falls into unconsciousness. The fact that the ego experiences this state as a symbolical death is due simply to this particular archetypal stage of conscious development, and no speculative scientific theory postulating a death instinct can be derived from such a state.[20]

The pull exerted by the great "mass" of the unconscious, i.e., by the collective unconscious with its powerful energy-charge, can only be overcome temporarily by a special performance on the part of the conscious system, though it can be modified and transformed by the building of certain mechanisms. On account of this inertia the child, particularly when he is small, tends, as investigators have shown, to persist in a given attitude and to experience any change—for instance an external stimulus or, later, a new situation, a command, etc.—as a shock, which brings fright, pain, or at least a feeling of uneasiness.

Even in its waking state our ego consciousness, which in any case forms only a segment of the total psyche, exhibits varying degrees of animation, ranging from reverie, partial attention, and a diffuse wakefulness to partial concentration upon something, intense concentration, and finally moments of general

[20] Uroboric incest is the sole psychological ground we have for postulating a "death instinct," and it is wrong to mix it up with aggressive and destructive tendencies. A deeper understanding, which is by no means only a pathological phenomenon, would prevent us from confusing it with a psychically nonexistent instinct "to break down all particulars and reduce them to the original inorganic state" (Freud, *Civilization and Its Discontents*). The "death instinct" of uroboric incest is not the "adversary of Eros," but one of his primordial forms.

and extreme alertness. The conscious system even of a healthy person is charged with libido only during certain periods of his life; in sleep it is practically or completely emptied of libido, and the degree of animation varies with age. The margin of conscious alertness in modern man is relatively narrow, the intensity of his active performance is limited, and illness, strain, old age, and all psychic disturbances take their toll of this alertness. It seems that the organ of consciousness is still at an early stage of development and relatively unstable.

At all events, a marked instability of the ego characterizes the psychological and historical dawn state whose emblem is the uroboros. The fusion of areas of consciousness which for us are more or less clearly defined leads, as it were, to a perpetual game of hide-and-seek with ourselves and to a confusion of ego positions. Emotional instability, ambivalent pleasure-pain reactions, the interchangeability of inside and outside, of individual and group—all these result in an insecurity for the ego which is intensified by the powerfully emotional and affective "vectors" of the unconscious.

It is in keeping with the paradoxical nature of symbolical language, which enables us at best to "circumscribe" rather than describe the "intangible core of meaning" [21] of an archetype, that the uroboros is, as a circle, not only the "perfect figure," but the symbol of chaos and amorphousness. It is the symbol of the pre-ego epoch, and hence of the prehistoric world. Before the beginning of history, mankind existed in a state of nameless amorphousness of which we know, and can know, very little, because at that period "the unconscious" ruled, as we say— hoping by this vague circumlocution to disguise our manifest ignorance of the facts. So long as an apperceptive ego consciousness is lacking, there can be no history; for history requires a "reflecting" consciousness, which by reflecting constitutes it. Hence the time before history must be indeterminate chaos and nondifferentiation.

[21] Jung, "The Psychology of the Child Archetype," p. 179.

The equivalent, on the religious plane, of this amorphous psyche is the indeterminate numen, the prime agency or substrate from whose matrix "the Divine" and the gods are subsequently crystallized out. Indeterminate agencies such as mana, orenda, or even what we call "dynamism" are typical of the pre-animistic period of universal psychization, where the psyche has not yet taken on definite shape, for in that condition it is still unassociated with the idea of an individualized soul, nor can it be derived from any such ideas. This vague, all-embracing force is the plane on which magic works, acting upon all things through the principle of correspondence and similarity. Logical contraries united in *participation mystique*—that is the law of this magical world where everything is full of holy workings. There is no hard and fast division of the holy from the unholy, the divine from the human, the human from the animal. The world is still bathed in a medium in which everything changes into everything and acts upon everything. Just as the still germinal nature of the ego causes the archetype of wholeness to be projected upon the group as the group self, so, surprisingly enough, the religious corollary of the most primitive human level is a primitive monotheism, for it is just here that we find the uroboros projected as a totality figure, i.e., as the primordial deity.

Thus, speaking of the "supreme deity," whose cult, however, was either "nonexistent or exceedingly small" and with whom no personal relations could be established, Preuss says:

In the majority of cases it was probably the night sky or the day sky, or the combination of both with their multitudinous phenomena all simulating life, that caused him to be apprehended as a personality,

and he goes on:

These ideas of God, through which many diverse phenomena are sensuously comprehended, must have arisen before the observation of details, such as the stars, which later became endowed with the properties of heaven.[22]

[22] Preuss, *Die geistige Kultur der Naturvölker*, p. 60.

282

This formulation is open to misunderstanding because the term "comprehended" might mean the rational activity of the ego. Only if "sensuous comprehension" is understood as the "configurational vision" of primitive man, is the description of the process correct. In the uroboric state there is a totality of indeterminate forces holding everything together and uniting it in participation. It is only as the configurational powers of consciousness increase and the ego becomes more clearly shaped that individual forms can be perceived:

The corn field is more strikingly significant than the single ear of corn, the sky more so than the stars, the human community more than the individual man.[23]

In the same way Preuss found that

the night sky and the day sky were apprehended in their totality earlier than the stars, because the totality could be grasped as a uniform being and the religious conceptions attaching to the stars often caused the latter to be confused with the heavens as a whole, so that man's thought was unable to break away from the total view.[24]

Equally,

the supremacy of the sun is later than that of the moon, which in its turn follows that of the night sky as a whole.[25]

Similarly the dark interior of the earth "which contains everything that appears on the earth's surface," and the earth itself with all its vegetation, are identified with the starry night sky, and only later is this taken to be an eagle equal to the sun.

Here the development is analogous to that of ego consciousness: it starts with an uroboric conception of wholeness and then proceeds to an increasingly powerful plastic configuration and differentiation of phenomena.

The original weakness of the individual ego—corresponding ontogenetically to the phase of childhood—makes it all the more dependent on the surrounding whole for the safety and security

[23] Ibid., p. 72.
[24] Ibid., p. 9.
[25] Ibid., p. 42.

which it cannot create for itself. This situation naturally intensifies the emotional ties with the group and the extrahuman world. The uroboros is constantly experienced afresh as the All-Sustainer and All-Container, that is, as the Great Mother. In this uroboric situation it is the "good" Great Mother and the "blessings of the matriarchate" that occupy the foreground, and not a primal fear.

Universal participation, exteriorization of psychic contents, and the presence of highly charged emotional components combine to produce, in the pleromatic phase, an undifferentiated feeling of oneness which unites the world, the group, and man in an almost bodily way. Although this "submersion in the unconscious" causes a certain disorientation of the ego and consciousness, it by no means unbalances the personality as a whole. The latter's orientation is that of a being surely guided by instinct and by the pattern of unconscious vectors, as is the unquestioned rule throughout the whole realm of extrahuman nature.

Millions of years of ancestral experience are stored up in the instinctive reactions of organic matter, and in the functions of the body there is incorporated a living knowledge, almost universal in scope, but not accompanied by any sort of consciousness. During the last few thousand years the human mind has laboriously made itself conscious, through its scientific knowledge of physics, chemistry, biology, endocrinology, and psychology, of some meager fragments of what the cells, functional systems, and organisms "knowingly" do in their adaptations and reactions. By reason of this incorporated knowledge the pleromatic phase of the uroboros is also intuited as one of primordial wisdom. The Great Mother has a wisdom infinitely superior to the ego, because the instincts and archetypes that speak through the collective unconscious represent the "wisdom of the species" and its will.

As we have seen, the uroboric phase is ruled by an ambivalent pleasure-pain feeling which attaches to all experiences that revert to the uroboric level or are overcome by it. In the case of

284

creative uroboric incest this feeling expresses itself in the ambivalent experience of rebirth through death, and in masochistic or sadistic fantasies when the incest is neurotic or psychotic. But in no circumstances does the Great Mother archetype of the collective unconscious represent the "locus of pleasure." To associate the unconscious only with the pleasure principle, as opposed to the reality principle, is proof of a depreciating tendency and corresponds to a conscious defense mechanism.

Impulses and instincts, archetypes and symbols, are far more adapted to reality and to the external world than consciousness in its early stages. No instinct—one has only to think of the nesting and rearing instinct—can possibly be adapted to a mere "wish-fulfilling" pleasure principle, for the instincts command a knowledge of reality infinitely superior to our conscious knowledge even today. Animal psychology provides countless examples of an absolutely baffling and inexplicable reality orientation to the surrounding world, to other animals, plants, the seasons, etc. This adaptation of instinct to environment is unconscious, but the wisdom of these instincts is real and in no sense determined by any kind of "wish" whatsoever.[26]

The real source of conflict between the individual and the unconscious lies in the fact that the unconscious represents the will of the species, of the collective, and not in the opposition of the pleasure and the reality principles, where the pleasure principle is supposedly associated with the unconscious and the reality principle with consciousness.

In the cosmic symbolism associated with the uroboros in creation mythology we find a symbolic self-portrayal of that early psychic phase when there is as yet no uniformly centered

[26] In human beings, too, the unconscious is almost always directly opposed to the "wishing" conscious mind and is seldom identical with it. Nor is it her pleasure-loving and wishful nature, but rather her collective character, that sets the Great Mother in opposition to ego consciousness. Wishful thinking is not a quality of a fantasy-spinning unconscious, but of the fantasy-spinning ego, so that a genuine fantasy may be gauged by whether it is "wish-conditioned" or not. If it is a wish-fantasy, it derives from consciousness or from the personal unconscious at most; if not, then the deeper layers of the unconscious have been activated in the imagination.

personality. The multiplicity of the world and the corresponding multiplicity of the unconscious reveal themselves in the light of evolving consciousness.

During the phase of the uroboric Great Mother, ego consciousness, so far as it is present, has not yet evolved its own system and has no independent existence. We can only imagine the earliest emergence of the elements of ego consciousness on the analogy of what happens today, when, at particular moments of emotional exaltation, or when the archetypes break through—that is, in certain extraordinary situations—there comes an illumination, a momentary uprising of consciousness, like the tip of an island breaking surface, a flash of revelation which interrupts the humdrum flow of unconscious existence. These isolated or habitual phenomena have always been regarded by primitives and by ourselves as characterizing the "Great Individual" who, as medicine man, seer, and prophet, or later as the man of genius, possesses a form of consciousness different from the average. Such men are recognized and esteemed as "godlike," and their insights, whether they take the form of visions, maxims, dreams, or revelations vouchsafed by an "apparition," lay the first foundations of culture.

In general, however, the course of human—and extrahuman—existence in this phase is directed by the unconscious. The unity of the psyche, which analytical psychology defines as the self, functions immediately and without reflection in the totality of a self-regulating and self-balancing psychophysical system. In other words, the tendency we call centroversion has a biological and organic prototype.

Centroversion in Organisms on the Uroboric Level

Centroversion is the innate tendency of a whole to create unity within its parts and to synthesize their differences in unified systems. The unity of the whole is maintained by compensatory processes controlled by centroversion, with whose help the whole becomes a self-creative, expanding system. At a later stage centroversion manifests itself as a directive center, with the ego as the center of consciousness and the self as the psychic center. During the prepsychic stage it functions as the entelechy principle in biology, and at this stage it would perhaps be better to call it the integrative tendency. The specific trend of centroversion only asserts itself during the formative stage, when a visible center appears in the ego or has to be postulated in the self. It operates unconsciously, as the integrating function of wholeness, in all organisms from the amoeba to man. For simplicity's sake we shall keep to the term "centroversion" even when dealing with the early stages, because integration itself proceeds from the totality of a centered, but invisible, system.

Centroversion expresses itself in an organism through its regulation of the whole and through its compensatory striving for balance and systematization. It promotes cellular aggregation and facilitates the harmonious working of different cell tissues, organs, and so forth. The very fact that the differentiated organization of the amoeba, for instance, forms a whole which is of a higher order than the metabolic processes of nutrition and excretion is an expression of centroversion on the uroboric level.

Manifesting itself in the infinitely varied and harmonious cooperation of organs and groups of organs in all higher organisms, the force of centroversion works unconsciously. In so far as an organism subjects all causal processes to its own system of purposive relationships, teleological orientation is a superordinate principle which belongs to the very nature of that organism and expresses its wholeness and unity. But we have, to the best of our knowledge, no grounds for co-ordinating this teleological principle with any conscious center. Incorporated knowledge and unconscious purposivity must be regarded as essential marks of every organism.

The more primitive the psychic level, the more it is identical with the bodily events which rule it. Even personal complexes, i.e., semiconscious "split offs" which belong to the upper layers of the personal unconscious and are affectively charged and

287

"feeling-toned," can evoke physical alterations in the circulatory system, in the respiration, blood pressure, and so on. Deeper-seated complexes and archetypes have their roots far down in the body's physiology and, on irrupting into consciousness, violently affect the whole of the personality, as is painfully evident in the extreme case of psychosis.[27]

Accordingly on the uroboric level, where the ego and consciousness are least developed, centroversion is bound up with a primitive body symbolism. The body stands for wholeness and unity in general, and its total reaction represents a genuine and creative totality. A sense of the body as a whole is the natural basis of the sense of personality. That the body and its changes are the unquestioned basis of what we call our personality can be seen from the fact that we still point to our bodies when we speak of "ourselves," and there is no doubt that the uniqueness of a man's body and the blending of hereditary factors in its constitution are the very foundation of individuality. This would explain early man's self-absorption in his body and his preoccupation with all the parts that belong to it and participate in it, e.g., hair, nails, excreta, etc., which, as much as his shadow, his breath, and his footprints are deemed to be essential and integral portions of his personality.

An instructive example of this "body-self" symbolism is furnished by the *churinga* of the Australian aborigines and the corresponding *ap* in New Guinea.

The *churinga* are pieces of wood or stone which are hidden away in special caves. The word *churinga* means "one's own hidden body." [28] It appears from the legends that the bodies of most of the totem ancestors changed into such *churinga*.

The *churinga* is regarded as a body common to this man and to his totemic ancestor [*iningukua*]. It associates the individual with his personal totemic ancestor, guarantees him the protection afforded by the *iningukua*.[28a]

[27] The body-soul ligature and the question of causality are beside the point here. We orientate ourselves "as if" the biological and the psychic were two aspects of an essentially unknown "thing-in-itself" or "process-in-itself."

[28] Thurnwald, op. cit., p. 3.

[28a] Lévy-Bruhl, *The "Soul" of the Primitive*, p. 188, citing Strehlow, Part II, p. 76.

The *churinga* is not the seat of life or of the soul, but as Lévy-Bruhl says:

The *churinga* is therefore a "double" of the individual, i.e. the individual himself. . . . The relation between a man and his *churinga* is expressed by the saying: *"nana unta mburka nama"*—this is thy body.[29]

In the same way the grandfather, when the young man has attained his majority, shows him the *churinga* with the words:

Here is your body, here is your second self.

The relation between self, second self, totem ancestor, and *churinga* is one of participation, of which Lévy-Bruhl rightly says that it comes very near to consubstantiality. The second self is the individual's guardian angel, but if made angry by neglect it can also be his enemy, causing illness, etc.

The *iningukua* accompanies him throughout life, warns him of the dangers threatening him and helps him to escape from them. He is a sort of tutelary deity or guardian angel. But, ought we to say perhaps, since the individual and his *iningukua* are but one, he is himself his own guardian?—Yes, for here participation does not imply that the two beings are altogether blended. No doubt in one aspect, the individual *is* the *iningukua*. But from another point of view, this *iningukua* is distinct from him. It lived before him, and will not die with him. Thus the individual participates in a being who is undoubtedly in him, who in certain characteristics differs from [him], and keeps him in a state of dependency.[30]

We have quoted this passage at such length because it is a classical example not only of Lévy-Bruhl's *participation mystique*, but also of the projection of what analytical psychology calls the self. That the self is here felt to be identical with the body and with the world of the ancestors makes the connection all the more significant. The totem ancestor represents the "ancestral experience within us," which is incorporated in the body and is at the same time the basis of our individuality. Note that this passage comes from a chapter entitled "The Immanence of the Group in the Individual"; that is to say, the group's totality,

[29] Lévy-Bruhl, p. 189, citing Strehlow, pp. 76–7.
[30] Lévy-Bruhl, p. 192.

which is identical with the common totem ancestor, is simultaneously included in the body and the self.

In New Guinea the name for the analogue of the Australian *churinga* is *ap*, "man"; [31] here too the individual is united with the collective and with the body, in the ancestral body common to both.

This original tie with the body as with something "peculiarly one's own" is the basis of all individual development. Later the ego relates to the body, to its superior powers, and to the unconscious—with which its processes are largely identified—in a different and even contrary way. As the higher principle working through the head and consciousness, the ego comes into conflict with the body, and this conflict sometimes leads to a neurotic, partial dissociation which, however, is only the product of a later overdifferentiation. But even then the body totality seems to stand in a relationship of identity and equality with the totality of the psyche, namely, the self. These two totality formations, or images of wholeness, are superordinate to the ego consciousness and regulate the individual systems—including ego consciousness—from a total standpoint of which the ego can become only partially conscious.

All this is in keeping with the uroboric state of perfection where body and psyche are identical. Psychologically, there are two sides to this basic situation, both of which we have summed up under the symbol of the "alimentary uroboros." There is, firstly, the unconscious "psychization" of the body and the consequent symbolic significance of its various parts and regions; secondly, a preponderance of metabolic symbolism. Whereas in its later developments centroversion promotes the formation of ego consciousness as its specific organ, in the uro-

[31] Thurnwald, op. cit., p. 16. [Sanskrit terminology also provides interesting parallels. The *atman*, as well as meaning the universal self of which the individual self partakes, could also mean "oneself" in the bodily sense, as is made quite clear in the amusing story of Indra's instruction by Prajapati, in Chhandogya Upanishad 8. 7–12. The same concrete bodily significance also attached to *purusha*, which, although later it denoted the "person" or "spirit" and ultimately came to have a philosophical value equal to that of the *atman*, originally meant "man," in the sense of his "ghost-soul," his shadow or double.—TRANS.]

boric phase, when ego consciousness has not yet been differentiated into a separate system, centroversion is still identified with the functioning of the body as a whole and with the unity of its organs. The metabolic symbolism of mutual exchange between body and world is paramount. The object of hunger, the food to be "taken in," is the world itself; while the other, productive side of the process is symbolized by "output," that is, evacuation. The dominant symbol is not the semen; in creation mythology, urine, dung, spit, sweat, and breath (and later, words) are all elementary symbols of the creative principle.

When we are informed that the most important foodstuffs on the Solomon Islands, taro and yams, arose from "Tantanu's excrement," [32] or that in the initiation ceremonies in New Guinea the neophytes are treated as newborn infants and may only eat food mixed with sperm,[33] and that the uninitiate, being ignorant of the creation myths, get no sperm to eat because they do not "appreciate and properly esteem the nourishing plants and animals," the explanation may be assumed to lie in the symbolic accentuation of the body, and the sanctification of everything pertaining to it, which are characteristic of the uroboric phase.

This dynamic process of exchange between body and world, symbolized by the alimentary uroboros, is in harmony with the animal world of instinct, where eating and being eaten are the sole expressions of life and of man's efforts to dominate nature. It remains the basis even of the highest stages of development, and is the precondition of the sexual stage. Sexuality and the prior differentiation into two sexes are late products in the scheme of evolution. The primary thing is reproduction by cell division, which causes organisms to proliferate into myriad-celled structures. But cell division as the primary means of propagation only takes place when the nutritional conditions are favorable, and is dependent upon them.

To have and to exercise power, to be strong and to gain in strength, all these tendencies pertain to the primordial sphere

[32] Thurnwald, op. cit., p. 28.
[33] Ibid., p. 33.

of the alimentary uroboros. They express themselves in the feeling of bodily well-being, in a physical performance which is primarily identical with a balanced metabolism, where the intake and output of matter—the biological prototypes of the introversion and extraversion of libido—are in equilibrium. The feeling of health, not when reflected in consciousness, but when unconsciously taken for granted, is fundamental to that *joie de vivre* which is a condition of ego formation. But even when unconscious, with no center in the ego, the psychic system represents a psychic assimilation of the world, traces of which have been deposited in the instincts.

The instincts of the collective unconscious form the substrate of this assimilative system. They are repositories of ancestral experience, of all the experience which man, as a species, has had of the world. Their "field" is Nature, the external world of objects, including the human collective and man himself as an assimilative-reactive, psychophysical unit. That is to say, there is in the collective psyche of man, as in all animals, but modified according to species, a layer built up of man's specifically human, instinctive reactions to his *natural* environment. A further layer contains group instincts, namely experiences of the specifically *human* environment, of the collective, race, tribe, group, etc. This layer covers herd instincts, specific group reactions which distinguish a particular race or people from others, and all differentiated relationships to the nonego. A final layer is formed by instinctive reactions to the psychophysical organism and its modifications. For example hunger, hormone constellations, etc., are answered by instinctive reactions. All these layers intercommunicate. Their common factor is that the reactions are purely instinctive, the psychophysical unit reacting as a whole by means of meaningful acts which are not the outcome of individual experience, but of ancestral experience, and which are performed without the participation of consciousness.

This ancestral experience is rooted in the body and expresses itself organically, through the body's reactions. The lowest and by far the largest layer of "incorporated" experience is physiochemical, and has no psychic representation whatever. Instincts and impulses, as vectors of action, are psychic, though they need not be centrally represented. The body-psyche totality regulated by the nervous system responds to them by acting. To take an example, hunger is the psychic representation of a deficiency in the cells, and, with the help of instinctive reactions and their combination, it sets the organism in motion, impels it to act. But only when hunger is centrally represented and is perceived by an ego center do we get the beginning of consciousness, not when instinct merely sets the body-whole in motion by reflex action.

Centroversion, Ego, and Consciousness

We must now consider the significance of the ego and consciousness for the totality of the psychophysical organism, and their relation to centroversion. Needless to say, we are not concerned to frame a theory of consciousness, but are only attempting to outline certain points of view which have proved their importance for the psychological development of the individual and the collective.

The excitability of organic matter is one of those elementary properties which facilitate its orientation to the world. Owing to this excitability the nerve tissue becomes differentiated and the sense organs are developed. Co-ordinated with them is consciousness, the control system of centroversion. The registration and combination of stimuli from outside and inside, balanced reaction to them, the storing of stimuli and reaction-patterns are among the essential functions of an ego-centered system of consciousness. In the course of millions of years of differentiation, ever more complicated relationships are created within the structure of the organism, but also an increasing need for registration, control, and balance. The majority of these innumerable points of balance are unconscious and incorporated; that is to say, they are built into the structure of the body system. But

293

with increasing differentiation the zones under control come to be increasingly represented in the control organ of consciousness. This representation takes the form of images, which are psychic equivalents of the physical processes going on in the organs.

Ego consciousness is a sense organ which perceives the world and the unconscious by means of images, but this image-forming capacity is itself a psychic product, not a quality of the world. Image formation alone makes perception and assimilation possible. A world that cannot be imagined, a nonplastic world like that of the lower animals, is of course a living world; there are instincts in it and the organism as a whole responds to it by unconscious action. But such a world never gets represented in a psychic system that reflects and shapes it. The psyche is here built up through a series of reflexes; it responds to stimuli with unconscious reactions, but with no central organ in which stimulus and reaction are represented. Only as centroversion develops and gives rise to systems of ever higher scope and caliber do we get the world represented in images, and an organ —consciousness—which perceives this plastic world of representations. The psychic world of images is a synthesis of experiences of the inner and outer world, as any symbol will show.

Thus the psychic image-symbol "fire," as something "red," "hot," "burning," contains as many elements of inner experience as of outer experience. "Red" possesses not only the perceptible quality of redness, but also the emotional component of heat as an inner process of excitation. "Fiery," "hot," "burning," "glowing," etc., are more emotional than perceptual images. We contend, therefore, that the physical process of oxidation, fire, is experienced with the aid of images which derive from the interior world of the psyche and are projected upon the external world, rather than that experiences of the external world are superimposed on the inner. The subjective reaction to the object always takes precedence historically, while the objective qualities of the object remain in the background. In human development the object becomes disentangled only very gradually and with extreme slowness from the mass of projections in which it is wrapped and which originate in the interior world of the psyche.

Centroversion is already at work as the primary function of the psyche, causing unconscious contents to present themselves to consciousness in the form of images. It leads firstly to the formation of symbolic images, secondly to the ego's reaction to them. We call the formation of images and the reactions of consciousness an expression of centroversion, because the interests of the psychophysical unit as a whole are more effectively conserved with the help of these processes than without them. The central representation of the image in consciousness gives the individual a more comprehensive and more total experience of the inner and outer world, and at the same time a better orientation in every department of life. Inner reaction, that is, adjustment of ego consciousness to the world of instinct, seems to have originated quite as early as reaction to externals.

When instincts are centrally represented, i.e., when they appear as images, Jung calls them archetypes. Archetypes take the form of images only where consciousness is present; in other words, the plastic self-portrayal of instincts is a psychic process of a higher order. It presupposes an organ capable of perceiving these primordial images. This organ is consciousness, which on that account is associated with eye, light, and sun symbols, so that in mythological cosmogony the origin of consciousness and the coming of light are one and the same.

In the dawn period the perception of images resulted in an immediate reflex action, because consciousness only took passive precedence over the executive organ of the body, but was not superordinate to it. The fact that its organic substrate derives embryologically from the ectoderm shows that consciousness was a kind of sense organ; yet it was already differentiated in two directions and could perceive images coming from outside as well as from inside. Originally it was impossible for the ego to distinguish the source of these images, for at the stage of *participation mystique* an outside could not be perceived as

295

distinct from an inside; the two sets of images overlapped, so that experience of the world coincided with inner experience.

This original phase, when consciousness was a sense organ, is marked by the functions of sensation and intuition, i.e., the perceptive functions [34] which are the first to appear both in the development of primitives and in that of the child.

Thus, evolving consciousness is at least as much open to internal as to external stimuli. But it is significant that the registering organ which receives these stimuli from inside and outside feels, and necessarily feels, itself remote from them, different and, as it were, extrinsic. It stands like a registration system halfway between the external world and the body as the field of inner excitations. This position of detachment is a primary condition of consciousness, and it is the essence of its functioning to intensify and differentiate this attitude still further. In other words, it is an historical necessity for the organ of registration and control which we call consciousness to be differentiated in two directions at once.

The nervous system, particularly the cerebrospinal system whose final exponent is consciousness, is an organic product of the unconscious, designed to hold the balance between the outer world and the inner. The inner world ranges in extent from physical reactions and their modifications to the most intricate psychic reactions. It is not reactive only to external stimuli, not just a stimulus-machine as the materialists imagine, but the source of spontaneous movements of the most varied kinds, which man-

[34] This is not the place to enter more specifically into function-psychology; we need only note that feeling and thinking, being rational functions, are the products of a later development. (Cf. Jung, *Psychological Types*, def. 44.) The rational functions are correlated with the laws of reasoning, which have only become accessible to consciousness as the deposits of ancestral experience. Jung gives the following definition: "Human reason, therefore, is nothing other than the expression of man's adaptedness to the average run of events, which have gradually become deposited in solidly organized complexes of ideas that constitute our objective values. Thus the laws of reason are those laws which characterize and regulate the average 'correct' or adapted attitude." So it is understandable that the rational functions are historically late products. Adaptation to average events and the formation of solidly organized complexes of ideas are the "work of human history," and into their organization has gone the "labor of countless generations."

ifest themselves as drives and complexes, physical and psychic tendencies. All these inner tendencies must be recognized by the conscious system and the ego, balanced, and adjusted to the external world; that is to say, consciousness has to protect one's person against wild animals and outbreaks of fire, and at the same time control all instinctual constellations and bring them to fulfillment. Its responsibility and its competence lie as much in modifying the environment for the production of food as in inner modifications which adapt the egocentric tendencies of the individual to the collective. So long as the system of ego consciousness is functioning soundly, it remains an organ affiliated to the whole, combining in itself the executive and the directive functions.

Pain and discomfort are among the earliest factors that build consciousness. They are "alarm-signals" sent out by centroversion to indicate that the unconscious equilibrium is disturbed. These signals were originally defense measures developed by the organism, though the manner of their development is as mysterious as that of all other organs and systems. The function of ego consciousness, however, is not merely to perceive, but to assimilate these alarm signals, for which purpose the ego, even when it suffers, has to hold aloof from them if it is to react appropriately. The ego, keeping its detachment as the center of the registering consciousness, is a differentiated organ exercising its controlling function in the interests of the whole, but is not identical with it.

The ego was originally only an organ of the unconscious and, impelled and directed by it, pursued the latter's aims, whether these were personal and vital aims such as the satisfaction of hunger and thirst, or those of the species, such as dominate the ego in sexuality. The discoveries of depth psychology have adduced a wealth of evidence to show that the conscious system is a product of the unconscious. Indeed, the profound and far-reaching dependence of this system upon its interior unconscious foundations is one of the crucial discoveries of modern times. It corresponds in importance to the equally profound and far-reaching external dependence of the individual upon the collective.

Although consciousness is a product of the unconscious, it is a product of a very special sort. All unconscious contents have, as complexes, a specific tendency, a striving to assert themselves. Like living organisms, they devour other complexes and enrich themselves with their libido. We can see in pathological cases, in fixed or compulsive ideas, manias, and states of possession, and again in every creative process where "the work" absorbs and drains dry all extraneous contents, how an unconscious content attracts all others to itself, consumes them, subordinates and co-ordinates them, and forms with them a system of relationships dominated by itself. We find the same process in normal life, too, when an idea—love, work, patriotism, or whatever else—comes to the top and asserts itself at the cost of others. One-sidedness, fixation, exclusiveness, etc., are the consequences of this tendency of all complexes to make themselves the center.

The peculiarity of the ego complex, however, is twofold; unlike all other complexes it tends to aggregate as the center of consciousness and to group the other conscious contents about itself; and secondly, it is oriented towards wholeness far more than any other complex.

Centroversion persistently strives to ensure that the ego shall not remain an organ of the unconscious, but shall become more and more the representative of wholeness. That is to say, the ego fights against the unconscious tendency that seeks to master it, and instead of allowing itself to be possessed, learns to keep its independence in relation to both inside and outside.

Although in the realm of nature, individuals are sacrificed in their myriads in order to subserve the will of the species for propagation and variation, this will of the Great Mother comes increasingly into conflict with ego consciousness, which does not see itself merely as the executor of the collective will, but more and more as a unique individuality opposed to the collective will of the Great Mother.

All instincts and impulses, all atavisms, and all collective tend-

298

encies can ally themselves with the image of the Great Mother and oppose the ego. Since there is such a variety of contents, and the number of symbols associated with the Great Mother is extraordinarily large, the Great Mother image acquires such a bewildering assortment of features that it coincides with the unconscious as symbolized by "The Mothers" in *Faust*.

Ego consciousness has, as the last-born, to fight for its position and secure it against the assaults of the Great Mother within and the World Mother without. Finally it has to extend its own territory in a long and bitter struggle.

With the emancipation of consciousness and the increasing tension between it and the unconscious, ego development leads to a stage in which the Great Mother no longer appears as friendly and good, but becomes the ego's enemy, the Terrible Mother. The devouring side of the uroboros is experienced as the tendency of the unconscious to destroy consciousness. This is identical with the basic fact that ego consciousness has to wrest libido from the unconscious for its own existence, for, unless it does so, its specific achievement falls back into the unconscious, in other words is "devoured."

Thus, the unconscious is not in itself destructive and is not experienced as such by the whole, but only by the ego. That is very important so far as the ego's further development is concerned. Only during the early stages does it feel threatened and fugitive, protesting that the unconscious is destructive. Later, when the personality feels itself allied not only to the ego but to the whole, consciousness no longer sees itself threatened to the degree that the adolescent ego was, and the unconscious now presents other aspects than those of danger and destruction.

What the ego experiences as destructiveness is firstly the overwhelming energy-charge of the unconscious itself, and secondly the feebleness, liability to fatigue, and inertia of its own conscious structure. The two elements appear projected in the archetype of the Antagonist.

The emergence of this image induces fear as a defensive reaction on the part of the conscious system. But the very fact

299

that it can become visible as an image shows that consciousness is growing stronger and more alert. The nebulous power of attraction hitherto exerted by the unconscious crystallizes into a negative quality, recognized as being inimical to consciousness and the ego, and a defensive mechanism is thereby set in motion. Fear of the unconscious leads to resistance and thus to a strengthening of the ego; indeed we shall always find that fear of the unconscious, and fear in general, is a symptom of centroversion, seeking to protect the ego.

The ego's resistance to the unconscious then passes from fear and flight to the defiant attitude of the "strugglers"—who are the mythological exponents of this intermediate phase—and finally to the aggressive attitude of the hero, who actively champions the position of consciousness against the dragon of the unconscious.

In the myths of the strugglers we have a clear instance of the aggressive intentions of the unconscious, of the Great Mother who constitutes the prime threat to the ego position of adolescent consciousness. The ego, as the center of a consciousness systematizing itself in the service of centroversion, is exposed to the disintegrative forces of the unconscious. It is to be noted that sexuality is only one of these forces, and by no means the most important. The tendency of unconscious contents to swamp consciousness corresponds to the danger of being "possessed"; it is one of the greatest "perils of the soul" even today. A man whose consciousness is possessed by a particular content has an enormous dynamism in him, namely that of the unconscious content; but this counteracts the centroversion tendency of the ego to work for the whole rather than for the individual content. Consequently the danger of disintegration and collapse becomes all the greater. Possession by an unconscious content entails loss of consciousness and has an intoxicating effect, so that one smitten by it is always under the sway of the Great Mother and is threatened with the fate of all her youthful lovers: either with effeminacy and castration, by being transformed into her, or with madness and death, by being dismembered.

The growing tension between the conscious ego system and the unconscious body system is the source of a psychic energy which distinguishes human beings from animals. The centroversion that makes possible this differentiation and individualization is an expression of the creative principle, and in the human species this principle performs its experiments upon the individual, who is the carrier of the ego.

Ego and consciousness are the organ of the unconscious force of centroversion which creates unity and balance within this unity. Not that its task is regulative only; it is also productive. It is in the nature of the organism not only to maintain the status of the whole with fine adjustments, but to develop in itself larger and more complicated unities by extending the empirical field with which it comes into contact.

What we called the alimentary uroboros has to be brought to fruition by the creative principle at work in it from the very beginning. Not only does this principle direct the metabolism of the life forces, not only does it balance and compensate; it also leads to the development of new unities, giving rise to new organs and systems of organs, and trying its hand at creative experiments. Just how these innovations are tested as to their performance and capacity for adaptation is a second problem, to the solution of which Darwinism has made a vital contribution. But it is another thing to explain the creative experiments themselves. Never yet have we succeeded in making it appear even remotely probable that an organ arises from an accumulation of infinitesimal chance variations. It is easy enough to explain the differentiation of organs in this manner, but not how they arise through gradual association.

Mythology represents the creative principle as the self-generative nature of the uroboros, which is associated with the symbol of creative masturbation. This symbolic masturbation has nothing to do with the later, markedly genital phase, but merely expresses the autonomy and autarchy of the creative uroboros, which begets in itself, impregnates itself, and gives birth to itself. The "closed circuit" stage changes into one of creative balance, and, in place of the former static passivity, a dynamic constellation now assumes autarchic control. The appropriate symbol here is not the quiescent sphere, but the "self-rolling wheel."

Man's historical and psychological development shows that the role of the individual is just as important for humanity as is that of the ego and consciousness for the unconscious. In both cases, what originally came into being as the organ and instrument of the whole is seen to possess a specific activity which, in spite of the conflicts it produces, has proved extremely fruitful over the wide field of evolution.

Centroversion is an irreducible, unitive function innate in the psychophysical structure. Aiming at unity, it is at the same time the expression of unity and assists ego formation; i.e., it produces the ego as center of a conscious system built up of contents and functions grouped round this ego nucleus.

Side by side, then, with the integrating process that welds a mass of individual cells and cell systems into the body-psyche unit, the process of differentiation produces an autonomous conscious system separate from the unconscious. Both processes are the expression and effect of centroversion. The conscious system is not just a central switchboard for establishing relations between inside and outside; it is at the same time an expression of the organism's creative urge for innovation. But whereas in the biological and animal realm this urge has to operate with infinities of time, in human consciousness it has evolved a time-saving organ by means of which innovations can be tested in far shorter periods. Human culture is a product of this creative urge for experimentation. In view of the shortness of human culture nothing final can yet be said about its success. But the fact remains that in the course of this—compared with biological evolution—tiny span of time during which human consciousness has shaped human culture, the most extraordinary changes have taken place. Technology and science, the tools of consciousness, have created a wealth of artificial organs, and the rapid growth and variety of creative inventions are proof of their superiority when compared with the slow formation and development of organs in biology. Life's experiment in enlisting the aid of consciousness for its creative work would seem to have been a lucky fluke.

In making these remarks we are fully aware of our anthropomorphic and teleological manner of speaking. But the very fact that consciousness necessarily experiences itself as the exponent of the creative experiments of the whole as soon as it begins to examine itself and its history gives new weight and new justification to our anthropocentric outlook. It is after all scientifically justifiable to regard consciousness as one of life's experimental organs, more justifiable at any rate than to gloss over the fundamental fact of man's spiritual existence and explain it away with reflexes or behaviorism. By postulating a creative principle at the beginning of his creation myths and placing these at the beginning of the world, man experienced his own—and by projection, God's—creativeness long before the idea of creative evolution was discovered.

As the vehicle of tradition, human consciousness collectively takes over the role formerly played by the biological factor. Organs are now no longer inherited but are transmitted. Thus there arises a spiritual world of consciousness which, as human culture, asserts its independence of life and nature. In this spiritual world, the individual, as carrier of the ego and of the conscious principle associated with it, is all-important. The prototype of the mature ego struggling to free itself from the grip of unconscious forces is the hero. He is the exemplar, the Great Individual, and all individual developments are modeled on him.

Before we examine the factors that make it possible to undermine the authority of the unconscious, we must briefly outline the stages leading from the germinal ego's containment in the uroboros to the ego of the hero fight. In tracing this mythological and symbolic sequence we can only tentatively suggest an interpretation in terms of psychic energy.

The transition from uroboros to Great Mother is characterized by a further development of the ego and a strengthening of the conscious system, as well as by the transition from the nonplastic to the plastic epoch.

The plastic epoch is the mythological age of cosmic ritual, re-enacting the sequence of cosmic and mythical events. The archetypes, as cosmic forces, appear above all in the astral, solar, and lunar mythologies and in the rites over which they preside. This is the age of the great mythologies, when the cosmic figures of the primordial deities—Great Mother and Great Father—crystallize out from the fluid mass of indeterminate powers, from the "vast, brooding God of prehistory," [35] and begin to take shape as creator-gods. The uroboric total divinity, envisaged in formless perfection as the "supreme God," is succeeded by the archetypal gods. They, too, are pure projections of the collective unconscious upon the remotest possible object —the heavens. Since there is as yet no developed ego consciousness, nor any effective individuality, there can be no relation between man and the cosmic events proceeding in "some heavenly place." It is as though in the beginning the figures were still autonomous, reflecting themselves as gods in the mirror of the heavens, without having passed through the medium of man and his personality, or without being altered in the passage.

The mythologies dealing with the creation of the world, and the first great sequences of gods and their battles, have often come down to us from later periods when they had already been worked over by speculative philosophy. But there is always an early mythological foundation. Local myths and rituals then spring up in countless places, all helping to shape the great gods. The unification of many separate cults into the more celebrated god-figures is of secondary importance. The salient feature is that the Mother and Father deities, the gods and goddesses of heaven and earth, are worshiped as figures, as operative factors with an ego center, to whom definite qualities are ascribed, and no longer as vague, magical daemonisms lurking in the background with manalike attributes.

[35] Rohde, *Psyche.*

A glance at the historical development shows over and over again how visible form springs from the formless, the definite from the indefinite, and how from the daemonic-animal level there arise centers of force, beings endowed with specifically human features. The clearest instance of this is the development of Greek religion. The gods of Olympus are the best example of this progressive configuration which goes beyond the archaic stage of vague numinosity,[36] though the same development can be seen everywhere, if not with the same degree of clarity.

The myths of the plastic epoch indicate a growing humanization in the life of the gods and in man's experience of them. Whereas the primitive numina were cosmic, charged with a symbolism whose power-content obscured their form, there is now a gradual approximation of the divine to the human. The battles and events that were formerly conceived as cosmic phenomena or as conflicts between the gods themselves now come down to the human level.

The first phases in the relation between ego consciousness and the unconscious were marked by dependence and resistance. In the uroboros the stage of nondifferentiation from the unconscious could still be experienced positively, but at the stage symbolized by the Great Mother, the son's dependence, though positive at first, soon takes on a negative form.

The uroboric unconscious symbolized by the Great Mother is a system which has to relax its hold upon the ego and consciousness—or rather, would have to relax its hold if the development were to proceed without friction.

But one of the facts we are always coming up against in our psychic experience is that growth takes place by fits and starts. There are retentions and blockages of libido which have to be breached by a new phase of development. Always the "old system" hangs on until the opposing forces are strong enough to overcome it. Here, too, "war is the father of all things." Psychic systems possess an inner stability which Jung has designated as the inertia of libido. Every system—and every archetype

[36] Murray, *Five Stages of Greek Religion,* pp. 39 f.

corresponds to a definite group of contents organized into a system—has an urge for self-preservation which shows itself in the possessive and retentive hold this system has over the ego. Liberation and free activity only become possible when the ego system has more libido at its disposal than the retentive system, i.e., when the ego's will is strong enough to break away from the corresponding archetype.

Further Phases of Ego Development

The increasing independence of consciousness only reaches a turning point in the hero myth; until then it is overshadowed by its unconscious origins. In its progress from uroboric self-destruction to adolescent resistance, we can discern a steady increase of ego activity and its polarization in respect of the unconscious, which it originally experienced as paradise, then as dangerous and fascinating, and finally as its enemy. And as the ego's activity and the intensity of its libido increase, so the symbolism varies. At first, plant symbols are the most prominent, with their passivity and earthiness. The youth is a vegetation deity—flower, corn, tree. His harvesting, death, and resurrection in the coming up of the seed belong to the natural rhythm of the matriarchate. Here sexuality is the instrument of the earth's fertility, follows the periodicity of the rutting seasons, and is unrelated to the world of ego consciousness.[37]

[37] Briffault (*The Mothers*, Vol. I, p. 141) discriminates between the primary, aggressive sex instinct and the social mating instinct. In the animal world the sex instinct is frequently accompanied by biting, and sometimes the partner is actually devoured. We discern in this situation the predominance of the alimentary uroboros in the presexual stage, i.e., of the alimentary over the sexual instinct.

We cannot, however, go all the way with Briffault in his interpretation of the material. Only in isolated and exceptional cases is the sexual instinct carried so far towards absurdity that the male eats the female he has fertilized. But the reverse situation, where the fertilized female eats the male, is by no means *contra naturam:* it corresponds to the archetype of the Terrible Mother. Moreover it is prefigured in the "eating" of the male spermatazoon by the fertilized ovum. Once the access of sexual instinct has subsided and fertilization is accomplished, the dominance of the alimentary uroboros reasserts itself in the mother. For her, the supreme principle is to develop the mother-child totality through the intake of food, i.e., to promote growth; and the male who is eaten is just an unattached object of alimentation like anything else. The short-lived onrush of sexual instinct evoked by the male produces and can produce no emotional attachment whatever.

The predominance of vegetation symbolism means not only the physiological predominance of the vegetative (sympathetic) nervous system; it also denotes, psychologically, the predominance of those processes of growth which go forward without the assistance of the ego. But for all their seeming independence, ego and consciousness are nevertheless characterized at this stage by their reliance upon the determining substrate of the unconscious in which they are rooted, and also upon the sustenance provided by this substrate.

As the activity of ego consciousness increases, the vegetation symbolism is followed by the animal phase, when the male experiences himself as a living, active, and savage animal, though still subordinate to the "mistress of wild beasts." This sounds paradoxical at first, for the animal phase would seem to correspond more to a strengthening of unconscious forces than to a strengthening of the ego.

In the animal phase the ego is indeed largely identical with its instinctive components, the vectors of the unconscious. The "mistress" is the directing force "behind" this activity, but the masculine ego is now no longer vegetative and passive: it is active and desirous. The ego's intentionality has gained in momentum, so that it is no longer a case of my "being driven" or of my "having the urge," but of "I want." The ego, hitherto quiescent, becomes actuated by animal instinct—in other words, the instinctive impetus communicates itself to the ego and to consciousness, is taken over by them, and extends their radius of activity.

Centroversion, during its first conscious phase, manifests itself as narcissism, a generalized body feeling in which the unity of the body is the first expression of individuality. This magical relation to the body is an essential characteristic of centroversion, and love of one's own body, its adornment and sacralization, constitute the most primitive stage of self-formation. This is evident from the widespread practice of tattooing among primitives and the fact that individual tattooing which does not conform to the stereotyped collective pattern is one of the earliest ways of expressing one's individuality. The individual is known and distinguished by the specific form he gives himself in his tattooing. The individual mode of tattooing shows his name, also the name of the more intimate circle with which he is identified—the clan, caste, sect, or professional guild. The magical correspondence between world and body scheme also belongs to this early narcissistic phase. In this connection the tendency to "embody" individual qualities and to display them on one's person is still alive today; it ranges from the world of costume and fashion to the military decoration, from the crown to the regimental button.

Leaving the narcissistic body stage, the ego then advances to the phallic stage, where consciousness of one's body and of oneself coincides with an aroused and actively desiring masculinity. The transition is marked by numerous phenomena in which the "intermediate stages" are accentuated.[38] Androgynous and hermaphroditic figures of gods and priests, and cults emphasizing the original bisexuality of the uroboric Great Mother, characterize the transition from the feminine to the masculine.[39]

Sexual perversion is only a morbid expression of dominance by this archetypal phase, but is not identical with it, for besides this morbid expression there are other, positive, and productive ones which operate over the wider field of culture.[40]

Phallicism [41] is symbolic of a primitive stage in man's con-

[38] Carpenter, *Intermediate Types among Primitive Folk.*

[39] No doubt biological intermediate types also play a part here, but the archetypal—i.e., psychological—situation is more important than the biological.

[40] Many contents which, in "perversion," come to be dominants of sexual life have their prototypes in this mythological intermediate stage of dominance by the Great Mother. As mythological facts they are transpersonal, i.e., beyond and outside personality, and are therefore events *sub specie aeternitatis* because they are symbolical and as such magically effective. Only when they intrude into the narrow personalistic sphere do they become "perverted," i.e., pathogenic factors, because these "erratic blocks" of mythology and transpersonality then act as foreign bodies which hamper individual development.

[41] We disregard here the special conditions that apply to the female.

sciousness of his masculinity. Only gradually does he come to realize his own value and his own world. The male begins by being the copulator, not the begetter; even when the phallus is worshiped by the female as the instrument of fertility, it is far more the opener of the womb—as in the case of certain primitives [42]—than the giver of seed, the bringer of joy rather than of fruitfulness.

Phallus worship may originally appear side by side with worship of the fertilizing god. Sexual pleasure and the phallus are experienced orgiastically without a direct connection necessarily being felt with propagation. The virgin-mother who conceives the god, and the phallus-worshiping maenads, correspond to two different forms of possession, where phallus and procreative god are not yet identical.

Mythologically, the phallic-chthonic deities are companions of the Great Mother, not representatives of the specifically masculine. Psychologically this means that phallic masculinity is still conditioned by the body and thus is under the rule of the Great Mother, whose instrument it remains.

Although in the phallic phase the masculine ego consciously and actively pursues its special goal, namely the satisfaction of instinct, it is still so much the organ of the unconscious that it cannot grasp that sexual satisfaction in mating has anything to do with propagation; in fact the dependence of instinct upon the will of the species for self-propagation remains quite unconscious.

As the male-chthonic element in phallicism becomes more conscious, masculinity gains in strength and self-realization, and the active, aggressive power components in it develop. At the same time, the males—even when they have the social leadership—may still submit to the great chthonic fertility goddess and worship her in a feminine representative, because of the Great Mother's dominance in the masculine unconscious.

The growing ascendency of phallicism then unites the family under its rule, and finally we come to the psychological struggle

[42] Malinowski, *The Father in Primitive Psychology*, p. 331.

between matriarchate and patriarchate, and a modification of masculinity itself.

Ego-accentuation leads from the uroboric to the hermaphroditic, and so to the narcissistic stage, which is autoerotic at first and represents a primitive form of centroversion. The next stage is that of phallic-chthonic masculinity, dominated by the body sphere, and this in turn is succeeded by a masculinity in which the activity of consciousness has become the specific activity of an autonomous ego. In other words, consciousness, as the "higher masculinity of the head," attains knowledge of its own reality as self-consciousness. This higher masculinity is the masculinity of the "higher phallus," with the head as the seat of creative realization.

The development of ego consciousness is paralleled by a tendency to make itself independent of the body. This tendency finds its most obvious expression in masculine asceticism, world negation, mortification of the body, and hatred of women, and is ritually practiced in the initiation ceremonies of adolescents. The point of all such endurance tests is to strengthen the ego's stability, the will, and the higher masculinity, and to establish a conscious sense of superiority over the body. In rising above it and triumphing over its pains, fears, and lusts the ego gains an elementary experience of its own manly spirituality. To these tribulations is added an illumination by the higher spiritual principle, whether this be vouchsafed by spiritual beings in individual or collective visions, or by the communication of secret doctrines.

The goal of all initiation, however, from the rites of puberty to the religious mysteries, is transformation. In all of them the higher spiritual man is begotten. But this higher man is the man possessed of consciousness or, as liturgical language expresses it, of the higher consciousness. In him, man experiences his fellowship with a spiritual and heavenly world. Whether this fellowship takes the form of an apotheosis, or the initiate becomes one of God's children, or a *sol invictus*, or the hero becomes a star or an angel among the heavenly host, or whether he identifies himself with the totem ancestors, is all one. Always he enters into an alliance with heaven, with light and wind, cosmic symbols of the spirit that is not of this earth, bodiless and the enemy of the body.

Heaven is the dwelling place of gods and genii, symbolizing the world of light and consciousness as contrasted with the earthy, body-bound world of the unconscious. Seeing and knowing are the distinctive functions of consciousness, light and sun the transpersonal heavenly factors that are its higher condition, and eye and head the physical organs that are correlated with conscious discrimination. Hence in the psychology of symbols the spiritual soul descends from heaven and in the psychic body scheme is apportioned to the head, just as the loss of this soul is mythologically represented as a blinding, as the death of the sun-horse, or as a plunge into the sea—in other words, the overthrow of masculinity always follows the path of regression. It entails dissolution of the higher masculinity in its lower phallic form and therefore loss of consciousness, of the light of knowledge, of the eye, and a relapse into the body-bound chthonic world of animality.

The fact that fear is a symptom of centroversion, an alarm signal sent out to warn the ego, can be seen most clearly from the fear of regressing to an older ego form which would destroy the new, and with it the new system of ego consciousness. The "self-preservative tendency" of a system determines its pleasure-pain reaction.[43]

The pleasurable qualities associated with the previous ego phase, once that system is outgrown, become painful for the ego of the next phase. Thus uroboric incest is pleasurable only for the feeble ego nucleus still embedded in the uroboros. But as the ego grows stronger, uroboric pleasure becomes uroboric fear of the Great Mother, since this pleasure harbors the danger

[43] Dissolution threatens from two sides: from regression to a lower level as well as from progression to a higher one. Hence the typical oscillation from pleasure to fear and fear to pleasure is most marked during the transitional phases of ego development, e.g., in childhood and puberty.

of regression and matriarchal castration which would mean its extinction.

The conquest of fear is therefore the essential characteristic of the ego-hero who dares the evolutionary leap to the next stage and does not, like the average man who clings to the conservatism of the existing system, remain the inveterate enemy of the new. Herein lies the real revolutionary quality of the hero. He alone, by overcoming the old phase, succeeds in casting out fear and changing it into joy.

B. The Separation of the Systems

(MYTHOLOGICAL STAGES:
SEPARATION OF THE WORLD PARENTS
AND DRAGON FIGHT)

Centroversion and Differentiation

THE FURTHER DEVELOPMENT of personality is determined by the splitting into two systems of the conscious and the unconscious, or rather by their separation, for it is only in the later development of Western consciousness that the separation takes the more dangerous form of a split. This development is mythologically depicted in the stages of the separation of the World Parents and the Hero Myth, the latter stage being partially contained in the former.

Through the separation of the World Parents heaven and earth are distinguished from one another, polarity is created, and the light set free. It is a mythological representation of the ego, poised between the lower, feminine world of earth and body, and the higher, masculine world of heaven and spirit. But since consciousness and the ego always experience themselves as masculine, this lower earth-world is taken to be the world of the Great Mother, and consequently hostile to the ego, while heaven is sensed as the ego-friendly world of the spirit, later personified as the All-Father.

The separation of the World Parents is the cosmic form of the hero fight, portraying the emancipation of the individual in mythological terms. Its first stage consists in overcoming the Great Mother dragon, in liberating the individual and the system of ego consciousness from her dominance.

The formation of the personality can now proceed further along the course of centroversion, which, by combining, systematizing, and organizing, accentuates ego formation and at the same time knits the originally diffuse contents of consciousness into a single system.

The prime task of consciousness with respect to the overmastering tendencies of the unconscious consists mainly in keeping its distance, in consolidating and defending its position, i.e., in strengthening the stability of the ego. All this time the ego is

315

becoming conscious of its differences and peculiarities; the libido available to the conscious system is increased—by processes still to be described—and from passive self-defense the ego launches forth into activity and a campaign of conquest. In the myths this stage comes under the motif of the Twin Brothers.

We showed in the section dealing with the Terrible Male how the destructive masculine power aspect of the uroboros and Great Mother is assimilated by the ego and co-ordinated with personality and consciousness. Part of the archetype of the antagonist—a figure of the collective unconscious—is incorporated into the personal system.

This antagonist represents the power of darkness as a transpersonal quantity, symbolized for instance by the ancient Egyptian Set, the Apopis serpent, or the man-killing boar. At first, the passive or only feebly resistant ego consciousness of the adolescent falls victim to him: the energy-charge of the archetype is stronger and ego consciousness is snuffed out. During the stage of the twins, however, the adolescent experiences part of this destructive force as belonging to him personally. He is no longer merely the victim of the Great Mother, but, through his own self-mutilation and suicide, he negatively assimilates the destructive tendency which has turned against him. The ego center gains control over this aggressive tendency of the unconscious and makes it an ego tendency and a content of consciousness; but although the Great Mother's destructive intentions toward the ego have now become conscious, she still continues to keep her old object in sight. The ego's resistance to the Great Mother and the conscious realization of her destructive policy go together. At first the ego is overpowered by the content newly emerging into consciousness—namely, the archetype of the antagonist—and goes under. Only gradually, and to the degree that the ego recognizes this destructive tendency as being not just a hostile content of the unconscious, but as part of itself, does consciousness begin to incorporate it, to digest and assimilate it, in other words, to make it conscious. The destruction is now separable from its old object, the ego,

316

and has become an ego function. The ego can now use at least a portion of this tendency in its own interests. In fact, what has happened is that the ego, as we have said, "turns the tables" upon the unconscious.

The assimilation of the destructive tendencies of the unconscious is closely connected with the "negative" qualities of consciousness. This is expressed not only in its capacity to distinguish itself from the unconscious and keep its distance but also in utilizing this capacity in its ever-renewed attempts to break down the world continuum into objects, thus making it assimilable for the ego. The assimilative powers of consciousness which enable it to grasp objects first as images and symbols, then as contents, and finally as concepts, and to absorb and arrange them in a new order, presuppose this analytical function. By its means the destructive tendency of the unconscious becomes a positive function of consciousness.

In the analytical-reductive function of consciousness there is always an active element of defense against the unconscious and against the danger of being overpowered by it. This negative activity is apparent wherever we meet with the symbolism of knives, swords, weapons, etc. In numerous world creation myths, the cutting up of the dragon precedes the building of a new world from its dismembered parts. Just as food must be cut up small before it can be digested and built into the structure of the organism, so the vast world continuum of the uroboros must be broken up and divided into objects for assimilation by consciousness.

The uroboric tendency of the unconscious to reabsorb all its products by destroying them so as to give them back in new, changed form is repeated on the higher plane of ego consciousness. Here, too, the analytical process precedes the synthesis, and differentiation is the prime requisite for a later integration.[1]

In this sense all knowledge rests on an aggressive act of incorporation. The psychic system, and to an even greater extent consciousness itself, is an organ for breaking up, digesting, and

[1] S. Spielrein, "Die Destruktion als Ursache des Werdens."

317

then rebuilding the objects of the world and the unconscious, in exactly the same way as our bodily digestive system decomposes matter physiochemically and uses it for the creation of new structures.

The activity of the hero in his fight with the dragon is that of the acting, willing, and discriminating ego which, no longer fascinated and overpowered, and abandoning its youthful attitude of passive defense, seeks out the danger, performs new and extraordinary deeds, and battles its way to victory. The supremacy of the Great Mother, the control she exercised through the instinctual power of the body, is superseded by the relative autonomy of the ego, of the higher spiritual man who has a will of his own and obeys his reason. Faust's wresting of the land from the sea symbolizes the primal deed of heroic consciousness, which snatches new territory from the unconscious and places it under the rule of the ego. Just as on the adolescent level the dominant features were passivity, fear, and defense against the unconscious, so on the heroic level the ego plucks up courage and goes over to the offensive. It is immaterial whether the direction of this offensive be introverted or extraverted, since both flanks are occupied by the Great Mother dragon, whether we call her nature, the world, or the unconscious psyche.

We now come to the active incest of the hero, the fight with the Great Mother and her defeat. The awe-inspiring character of this dragon consists essentially in her power to seduce the ego and then to castrate and destroy it in matriarchal incest. Fear of dissolution held the ego back from regressing to the Great Mother and to the uroboros; it was the protective reaction of the ego system against regression. But when the ego is no longer prepared to remain at the stage of the "strugglers," who are dominated by their fear of the Great Mother, it must conquer the fear that once protected it and do the very thing of which it was most afraid. It must expose itself to the annihilating force of the uroboric Mother Dragon without letting itself be destroyed.

318

By overcoming its fear, and by actually entering into the uro-boric Great Mother, the ego experiences its higher masculinity as a lasting quality, deathless and indestructible, and its fear is changed into joy. This connection between fear and pleasure plays a decisive part in normal psychology, but is particularly important in the psychology of neurosis. At this stage of devel-opment, and only at this stage, sexuality becomes the symbol for a struggle to "get on top," and here the Adlerian terminology of the power drive is altogether appropriate.[2] But perseveration in such symbolism, as found—consciously or unconsciously—in many neurotics, means that the archetypal stage of the dragon fight has still not been surmounted, and that the ego is arrested in it. In most cases the failure is not expressed by the symbol of castration and dismemberment, as at the stage of the Great Mother, but by the symbolism of defeat and captivity, and occa-sionally by blinding.

Like the blinding of Samson and of Oedipus, captivity, which in many myths and fairy tales takes the form of being eaten, is a higher form of failure than dismemberment or phallic castra-tion. Higher, because defeat at this stage affects a more highly developed and more stable ego consciousness. Hence this de-feat need not be final, as castration and death are bound to be, and in a certain sense blinding too. The vanquished may, for instance, subsequently be rescued by a hero, and defeat may yet end in victory. Consciousness, though sorely tried, may be able to hang on in captivity until rescue arrives. The different forms which the rescue takes correspond to different forms of progression. For instance, Oedipus remains a hero even though he regresses tragically to the mother, Samson transcends his de-feat and dies victorious, Theseus and Prometheus are freed from bondage by Herakles, and so on.

Equally, the ego-hero who falls in battle is not destroyed as an individual personality, in the sense that the ego is blotted out in uroboric or matriarchal incest. By passing through the archetypal stages of mythology, the ego advances toward the

[2] Alfred Adler, *The Neurotic Constitution.*

319

goal of the dragon fight, which, as we have seen, means immortality and everlastingness. The gaining of something suprapersonal and indestructible through this fight is the ultimate and deepest meaning of the treasure, so far as the development of personality is concerned.

It is not our intention to repeat here what has been said in Part I about the separation of the World Parents, the creation of light, and the hero myth in relation to the development and differentiation of consciousness. Our psychological task is rather to indicate some of the methods by which the ego detaches itself from the unconscious and forms itself into a relatively independent system; in other words, how the individual's personality is built up. We have to examine how the personal and individual emancipates itself from the transpersonal and collective.

The Fragmentation of Archetypes

The separation of the conscious from the unconscious may be effected by any of the following means: (1) the fragmentation—splitting up or splitting off—of archetypes and complexes; (2) the devaluation or deflation of the unconscious; (3) the secondary personalization of contents which were originally transpersonal; (4) the exhaustion of emotional components liable to overwhelm the ego; (5) abstractive processes whereby the unconscious is represented first as an image, then as an idea, and is finally rationalized as a concept. All these differentiations assist the formation, from a diffuse transpersonal unconscious which has no knowledge of individuals and is purely collective, of a system of personality whose highest representative is to be found in ego consciousness.

In order to trace the development of consciousness we have to make a necessary distinction between two components of the unconscious. This involves dividing the material content of the collective unconscious from its emotional or dynamic content.

320

Not only does the archetype represent, as an image, some content more or less accessible to consciousness, but it also has, independently of its contents or in association with them, an emotional and dynamic effect upon the personality. What we have called the "fragmentation of archetypes" is a process whereby consciousness seeks to wrest from the unconscious the material content of the archetypes in order to supply the needs of its own system.

Rudolf Otto, in his description of the numinous, names it the awe-inspiring mystery, fascinating and beatific, the "wholly Other," the Holy.[3] This *numinosum* is the central experience of the ego in respect of any and every archetype; it is the ego's basic experience of the collective unconscious and of the world upon which the archetypes are projected. It is as though the world of the unconscious were, in effect, an extension of the numinous, as though the inconceivable multiplicity of its aspects had been divided up into the separate figures of the collective unconscious, in order to become experienceable for the ego, either successively or in the aggregate. In the course of development, i.e., during the transition from the nonplastic to the plastic phase, the collective unconscious is split up into the pictorial world of archetypal images, and the same line of development leads to the fragmentation of the archetypes themselves.

Exhaustion of Emotional Components: Rationalization

Fragmentation occurs in the sense that, for consciousness, the primordial archetype breaks down into a sizable group of related archetypes and symbols. Or rather, this group may be thought of as the periphery enclosing an unknown and intangible center. The split-off archetypes and symbols are now easier to grasp and assimilate, so that they no longer overpower ego consciousness. This discursive experience of the archetypes,

[3] *The Idea of the Holy.*

one after another and from different sides, is the result of a development in the course of which consciousness learns to protect itself against the effect of the primordial archetype. The numinous grandeur of the archetype, as originally experienced by primitive man, is the unity of the archetypal group of symbols in which it now manifests itself, plus an unknown quantity which disappears in the fragmentation process.

Let us take as an example the archetype of the Great Mother. It combines a bewildering variety of contradictory aspects. If we regard these aspects as qualities of the Great Mother and list them as qualities of the archetype, that is itself the result of the process we are describing. A developed consciousness can recognize these qualities, but originally the archetype acted upon the ego en masse, in all the undifferentiated profusion of its paradoxical nature. This is the chief reason why the ego is overwhelmed, and consciousness disoriented, by the archetype, whose emergence from the depths is always new, different, unexpected, and terrifyingly vivid.

Thus the Great Mother is uroboric: terrible and devouring, beneficent and creative; a helper, but also alluring and destructive; a maddening enchantress, yet a bringer of wisdom; bestial and divine, voluptuous harlot and inviolable virgin, immemorially old and eternally young.[4]

This original bivalence of the archetype with its juxtaposed opposites is torn asunder when consciousness separates the World Parents. To the left, there is ranged a negative series of symbols—Deadly Mother, Great Whore of Babylon, Witch, Dragon, Moloch; to the right, a positive series in which we find the Good Mother who, as Sophia or Virgin, brings forth and nourishes, and leads the way to rebirth and salvation. Here Lilith, there Mary; here the toad, there the goddess; here a morass of blood, there the Eternal Feminine.

The fragmentation of the archetype is represented in myths as the deed of the hero; only when he has separated the World Parents can consciousness be born. We can follow the details

4 Jung, "Psychological Aspects of the Mother Archetype."

of this fragmentation process in the hero myth. At first the dragon fight is against the primordial archetype of the uroboros, but once it has been split up, the fight must be directed against the father and mother, and finally a constellation is reached where the dichotomy becomes absolute. Against the hero are ranged the Terrible Mother and Terrible Father; with him, the creative Father-God and Virgin Goddess. Thus the inchoate world of the uroboros becomes the human world, molded into shape by the life of the hero. Man, modeling himself on the hero, has now found his rightful place between the upper realm and the lower.

The power of the primordial Great Mother archetype rests on the original state where everything is intermingled and undifferentiated, not to be grasped because ever in flux. Only later do images emerge from this basal unity, forming a group of related archetypes and symbols revolving about this indescribable center. The wealth of images, qualities, and symbols is essentially a product of the fragmentation effected by a consciousness which perceives, discriminates, divides, and registers from a distance. *Determinatio est negatio.* The multiplicity of images corresponds to a multiplicity of possible attitudes and possible reactions of consciousness, contrasted with the original total-reaction that seizes upon primitive man.

The overpowering dynamism of the archetype is now held in check: it no longer releases paroxysms of dread, madness, ecstasy, delirium, and death. The unbearable white radiance of primordial light is broken up by the prism of consciousness into a multicolored rainbow of images and symbols. Thus from the image of the Great Mother the Good Mother is split off, recognized by consciousness, and established in the conscious world as a value. The other part, the Terrible Mother, is in our culture repressed and largely excluded from the conscious world. This repression has the result that, as the patriarchate develops, the Great Mother becomes simply the Good Mother, consort of the Father-Gods. Her dark animal side, her power as the uroboric Great Mother, is forgotten. Accordingly in all Western cultures, including those of antiquity, there are vestiges of female consorts side by side with the father deities who have supplanted them. Only in recent times were the ancient mother cults laboriously rediscovered, and it was reserved for an age versed in depth psychology to excavate the primeval world of the Terrible and Uroboric Mother. Her repression was understandable and necessary from the point of view of the patriarchate and of a conscious development with strong patriarchal tendencies. Ego consciousness had to consign these aspects to oblivion, because its fear of the abyss was still too uncomfortably close: although it had successfully fought the dragon the terrors of this fight were still very much alive. Hence consciousness, afraid lest "real knowledge" should call down the fate of regression that overtook Oedipus, represses the Sphinx and with euphemistic imprecations enthrones the Good Mother.

The fragmentation of archetypes should on no account be conceived as a conscious analytical process. The activity of consciousness has a differentiating effect only because of the variety of possible attitudes it can adopt. The emergence of a group of archetypes split off from the basic archetype, and of the corresponding group of symbols, is the expression of spontaneous processes in which the activity of the unconscious continues unimpaired. To the conscious ego these archetypes and symbols appear as products of the unconscious, even when they have been constellated by the conscious situation as a whole. So long as consciousness fails to constellate the unconscious, no differentiated symbols and archetypes will appear. The more acute the systemization of consciousness is, the more sharply it constellates the contents of the unconscious. That is to say, the manifestations of the unconscious vary with the intensity and scope of the conscious mind. The growth of consciousness and its mounting energy-charge assist the differentiation of the archetype, bringing it and the archetypal nexus of symbols more sharply into focus. Hence conscious activity is of crucial importance; but all visible manifestations remain, like the symbol itself, dependent on the spontaneity of the unconscious.

The breakdown of the amorphous unconscious into the picture world of archetypes enables them to be represented and perceived by the conscious mind. No longer do "dark" impulses and instincts exercise complete control of the totality; instead, the perception of an inner image produces a reaction on the part of the conscious ego. Originally this perception touched off a total reaction very like a reflex, as for instance the "panic terror" evoked by the Pan image.

Delayed reaction and de-emotionalization run parallel to this splitting of the archetype into groups of symbols. The ego ceases to be overwhelmed as consciousness becomes more capable of assimilating and understanding the individual symbols. The world grows clearer, orientation is more possible, and consciousness is enlarged. An anonymous and amorphous primal deity is inconceivably frightful; it is stupendous and unapproachable, incomprehensible and impossible to manipulate. The ego experiences its formlessness as something inhuman and hostile, if indeed it ever tackles the impossible task of experiencing it. So we often find an inhuman god at the beginning in the form of a beast, or some horrid anomaly and monster of miscegenation. These hideous creatures are expressions of the ego's inability to experience the featurelessness of the primal deity. The more anthropomorphic the world of gods becomes, the closer it is to the ego and the more it loses its overwhelming character. The Olympian gods are far more human and familiar than the primeval goddess of chaos.

During this process, the primal deity is split up into different gods with individualities of their own. God is now experienced and revealed under as many aspects as there are gods. This means that the ego's powers of expression and understanding have increased enormously. The growing differentiation of cults shows that man has learnt how to "deal with" the deity in the form of individual gods. He knows what they want and he understands how to manipulate them. Every god who can be seen

325

and ritually manipulated represents so much consciousness gained, so much unconsciousness made conscious.

It is a known fact that the "functional" gods of religion eventually become functions of consciousness. Originally, consciousness did not possess enough free libido to perform any activity—plowing, harvesting, hunting, waging war, etc.—of its own "free will," and was obliged to invoke the help of the god who "understood" these things. By means of ceremonial invocation, the ego activated the "help of the god" and thus conducted the flow of libido from the unconscious to the conscious system. The progressive development of consciousness assimilates the functional gods, who go on living as qualities and capacities of the conscious individual who plows, harvests, hunts, and wages war as and when he pleases. It is evident, however, that when the conscious manipulation is not successful, as in war, the war-god continues to act as a functional god even today.

Just as a symbolic multiplicity of gods surrounds the primordial God, so, as consciousness develops, every archetype surrounds itself with its appropriate group of symbols. The original unity breaks down into a solar system of archetypes and symbols grouped round a nuclear archetype, and the archetypal nexus of the collective unconscious comes forth from the darkness into the light.

Again, just as the digestive system decomposes food into its basic elements, so consciousness breaks up the great archetype into archetypal groups and symbols which can later be assimilated as split-off attributes and qualities by the perceptive and organizing powers of the conscious mind. With progressive abstraction the symbols turn into attributes of varying importance. Thus the animal nature of the archetypal deity appears alongside him as his "companion animal." With further rationalization the "human" element—i.e., his propinquity to the ego—comes so much to the fore that the god frequently fights against this animal, the animal side of himself.[5] If the abstraction, or exhaustion of the symbol's content by the assimilating conscious-

[5] Frazer, *Adonis, Attis, Osiris* (in *The Golden Bough*).

ness, is carried still further, then the symbol turns into a quality. For instance Mars, whose original meaning, like that of every god, was exceedingly complex, becomes the quality "martial." This fragmentation of the symbol group tends in the direction of rationalization. The more complex a content is, the less it can be grasped and measured by consciousness, whose structure is so one-sided that it can attain to clarity only over a limited area. In this respect consciousness is built analogously to the eye. There is *one* spot where vision is sharpest, and larger areas can be perceived clearly only by continuous eye-movements. In the same way, consciousness can only keep a small segment sharply in focus; consequently it has to break up a large content into partial aspects, experiencing them piecemeal, one after the other, and then learn to get a synoptic view of the whole terrain by comparison and abstraction.

The importance of this fragmentation is particularly clear in the case of a bivalent content such as we showed the Great Mother archetype to be. We say that the personality has a bivalent tendency when positive and negative trends are simultaneously present in it, e.g., love and hate towards the same object. The state of bivalence, which is innate in primitives and children, corresponds to a bivalent content composed of positive and negative elements. The antithetical structure of such a content makes conscious orientation impossible and eventually leads to fascination. Consciousness keeps on returning to this content, or to the person who embodies it or carries its projection, and is unable to get away from it. New reactions are constantly released, consciousness finds itself at a loss, and affective reactions begin to appear. All bivalent contents that simultaneously attract and repel act in like manner upon the organism as a whole and release powerfully affective reactions, because consciousness gives way, regresses, and primitive mechanisms take its place. Affective reactions resulting from fascination are dangerous; they amount to an invasion by the unconscious.

An advanced consciousness will therefore split the bivalent

327

content into a dialectic of contrary qualities. Before being so split, the content is not merely good and bad at once; it is beyond good and evil, attracting and repelling, and therefore irritating to consciousness. But if there is a division into good and evil, consciousness can then take up an attitude. It accepts and rejects, orientates itself, and thus gets outside the range of fascination. This conscious bias towards one-sidedness is reinforced by the rationalizing processes we have mentioned.

Rationalization, abstraction, and de-emotionalization are all expressions of the "devouring" tendency of ego consciousness to assimilate the symbols piecemeal. As the symbol is broken down into conscious contents, it loses its compulsive effect, its compelling significance, and becomes poorer in libido. Thus the "gods of Greece" are no longer for us, as they were for the Greeks, living forces and symbols of the unconscious requiring a ritualistic approach; they have been broken down into cultural contents, conscious principles, historical data, religious associations, and so on. They exist as contents of consciousness, and no longer —or only in special cases—as symbols of the unconscious.

However, it would be wrong to speak of the soul-destroying nature of consciousness, for we must not forget that consciousness constructs at the same time a new and spiritual world in which, transformed, the venerable but dangerous figures of the unconscious are allotted a new place.

This process of rationalization, which enables consciousness to form abstract concepts and to adopt a consistent view of the world, comes at the end of a development that is only just beginning to be realized in modern man.

The formation of symbols and groups of symbols played a large part in helping consciousness to understand and interpret the unconscious, and, for primitive man, the rational component of a symbol is particularly important. The symbol acts upon the whole of the psyche and not upon consciousness alone; but with the extension of consciousness there also ensues a modification and differentiation of the symbol's action. The complex content of the symbol still continues to "possess" consciousness, but in-

328

stead of being overwhelmed, consciousness becomes engrossed in it. Whereas its original archetypal effect led as it were to a "knockout" of consciousness and to the primary unconscious total reaction, the later effect of the symbol is stimulating and invigorating. Its intrinsic meaning addresses itself to the mind and conduces to reflection and understanding, precisely because it activates more than mere feeling and emotionality. Ernst Cassirer has demonstrated at great length how the intellectual, cognitive, conscious side of man develops out of "symbolic forms," [6] which from the point of view of analytical psychology are creative expressions of the unconscious.

Thus the emancipation of consciousness and the fragmentation of archetypes are far from being a negative process in the sense that primitive man experiences an "animated" world, while modern man knows only an "abstract" one. Pure existence in the unconscious, which primitive man shares with the animal, is indeed nonhuman and prehuman. The fact that the dawn of consciousness and the creation of the world are parallel processes which throw up the same symbolism indicates that the world actually "exists" only to the degree that it is cognized by an ego. A differentiated world is the reflection of a self-differentiating consciousness. The multiple archetypes and symbol groups split off from a primordial archetype are identical with the ego's greater range of experience, knowledge, and insight. Under the total impact of experience in the dawn period no particularized forms could be recognized, for the tremendous force of it extinguished the ego in a sort of numinous convulsion. But a more informed human consciousness can experience, in the multiplicity of religions and philosophies, theologies and psychologies, the innumerable facets and meanings of the numinous, now anatomized into image and symbol, attribute and revelation. That is to say, although the primal unity can only be experienced fragmentarily, it has at least come within range of conscious experience, whereas for the undeveloped ego it was utterly overwhelming.

[6] *The Philosophy of Symbolic Forms.*

A self-differentiating consciousness means that the ego complex can associate itself with any number of differentiated contents and thus gain experience. Primitive experience is total, but is not associated with an ego complex and consequently does not become personal experience which can be remembered. What makes the real psychology of childhood so extraordinarily difficult to describe is the fact that there is no developed ego complex capable of gaining experience, or at least of remembering its experience. For this reason child psychology, like that of the dawn man, is more transpersonal than personal.

The higher emotionality of primitives and children may easily bring about the extinction of the ego complex, whether because this emotionality is original, as in the child, or because it irrupts into consciousness in the form of an affect. If we imagine that the conscious function, in order to work at all, must carry a specific ballast of libido, but no more than that, then it is obvious that an overload of libido will unsettle the function and finally cause it to fail altogether, so that there is no possibility of ego experience and memory.

Concurrent with the fragmentation of archetypes and assisting, like it, the steady growth of ego consciousness, there is in man a tendency to exhaust his original reserves of emotionality in the interests of reason. This exhaustion of emotional components accompanies his evolutionary advance from the medullary man to the cortical man. Emotions and affects are bound up with the lowest reaches of the psyche, those closest to the instincts. The feeling tone basic to what we shall hereafter describe as the "emotional-dynamic" components has its organic roots in most primitive parts of the brain, namely the medullary region and the thalamus. Since these centers are linked up with the sympathetic nervous system, the emotional components are always intimately associated with unconscious contents. Hence the vicious circle we are constantly coming up against: unconscious contents release emotions, and emotions in their turn activate unconscious contents. The connection of both the emotions and the unconscious contents with the sympathetic nervous sys-

330

tem has its physiological basis at this point. Emotion manifests itself simultaneously with an alteration of the internal secretions, the circulation, blood pressure, respiration, etc., but equally, unconscious contents excite, and in neurotic cases disturb, the sympathetic nervous system either directly, or indirectly, via the emotions aroused.

The trend of evolution makes it clear that the medullary man is being superseded by the cortical man. This can be seen from the continuous deflation of the unconscious and the exhaustion of emotional components. It is only now, in the present crisis of modern man, whose overaccentuation of the conscious, cortical side of himself has led to excessive repression and dissociation of the unconscious, that it has become necessary for him to "link back" with the medullary region. (See Appendix II.)

The dawn man lives his affects and emotions to the full. We should not forget that "complexes," those contents of the unconscious which influence our lives to an extraordinary degree, have been explicitly characterized as feeling-toned. The tendency of any complex to lay hold on one's feelings forms the basis of Jung's association experiments. The disturbances in the rational structure of consciousness which manifest themselves during these experiments, and the physical excitation displayed in the psychogalvanic phenomenon, are due to the emotional component of the complex and to the feelings it arouses, which immediately lead to its detection.[7]

Human evolution runs from the primitive emotional man to the modern man, whose expanded consciousness protects—or endeavors to protect—him from this access of primitive emotionality. But so long as the dawn man continued to live in *participation mystique* with his unconscious contents, and his conscious system was unable to exist independently of the unconscious, the material and dynamic components were so closely linked together that we can speak of the identity and complete fusion of both. Or we can express it by saying that perception

[7] Jung, "On Psychophysical Relations of the Associative Experiment," "The Association Method," and *Studies in Word Association.*

and instinctive reaction were one. The emergence of an image—the material component—and the instinctive reaction which affected the whole psychophysical organism—the emotional-dynamic component—were coupled in the manner of a reflex arc. Originally, therefore, a perceptual image outside or inside resulted in an instantaneous reaction. In other words, the coupling of the image with the emotional-dynamic component instantly released flight or attack, an access of rage, paralysis, etc.

This primitive reaction and the coupling of the two components cease as consciousness grows stronger. With the steady development of the cerebrum, the instinctive reflex is delayed by conscious intervention in the form of reflection, deliberation, etc. Gradually instinctive reaction is suppressed in favor of consciousness.

There are, however, two sides to this replacement of the original, total reaction by the discontinuous, differentiated, "splinter" reaction of modern man. The loss of total reaction is regrettable, especially when it leads to the apathetic, dead-and-alive specimen of today who no longer responds to anything vital except when he is recollectivized, as part of a mass, or, debauched by special techniques, reverts to the primitive. Nevertheless, the total reactivity of primitive man is no subject for romanticism. We must realize that, like the child, he was forced into total reaction by any and every content that emerged, and, overpowered by his emotionality and the underlying images, acted as a totality, but without freedom.

For this reason the anti-emotional trend of consciousness, provided that it is not carried to extremes, is an unmixed blessing for humanity. The impulsiveness of primitive man and of people in the mass, who are likely to be stampeded into catastrophic action on the slightest provocation, is so dangerous, so unpredictable in its "brainless" suggestibility, that it is highly desirable for the community that it should be replaced by conscious directives.

Consciousness has to resist these instinctive reactions because the ego is liable to be overpowered by the blind force of instinct, against which the conscious system must protect itself if development is to proceed. Although instinctive reaction represents an "appropriate" pattern of behavior, there is nevertheless a conflict between the developing ego consciousness and the world of instinct. The former must always put its own specific mode of behavior, which pursues very different aims, in place of collective and instinctive reaction, for the latter is by no means always in accord with the individual aims of the ego, nor with its preservation.

Very often instinct is insufficiently adapted to the individual's situation, being appropriate only at a primitive level and to a primitive ego, but not at all appropriate to a developed one. For instance, an uprush of affective reaction for the deathblow may be extremely useful to savages in the jungle; but in the normal life of civilized man this kind of instinctive reaction—except in wartime—is not only inappropriate but positively dangerous. Bitter experience of mass psychology has taught us how senselessly and disastrously the instincts often work out from the standpoint of the individual, even though it may sometimes be for the good of the community.

Among primitives, and wherever the conditions are primitive, the conflict between individual consciousness and the collective tendencies of the unconscious is resolved in favor of the collective and at the cost of the individual. Often the instinctive reactions bear no relation to the ego, but only to the collective, the species, etc. Nature is always showing that she sets no store by the individual. As Goethe says:

The one thing she seems to aim at is Individuality; yet she cares nothing for individuals.[8]

In contrast with this, however, the development of consciousness also serves the interests of the individual. While the ego is coming to terms with the unconscious, more and more attempts are made to protect the personality, to consolidate the conscious

[8] "Nature," trans. by T. H. Huxley, from the *Metamorphosis of Plants*.

system, and to dam up the danger of inundation and invasion from the unconscious side.

Thus, as the ego develops, it is imperative to prevent a situation from arising in which the dynamic-emotional component of an unconscious image or archetype would drive the ego into an instinctive reaction and so overwhelm consciousness.

For this reason there is sound sense in the tendency to separate the reaction from the perceptual image which releases it and to break down the original reflex arc until the material and the dynamic components of the collective unconscious are finally segregated. If the emergence of an archetype is not immediately followed by an instinctive reflex action, so much the better for conscious development, because the effect of the emotional-dynamic components is to disturb, or even prevent, objective knowledge, whether this be of the external world or of the psychic world of the collective unconscious. Consciousness with all its four functions, introverted as well as extraverted, is the cognitive organ par excellence, and its differentiation and that of the functions is possible only when the emotional components of the unconscious are excluded. The sure aim of the differentiated function is continually being obscured by the intrusion of emotional components.

If the ego is to attain a condition of tranquillity in which to exercise discrimination, consciousness and the differentiated function must be as far removed as possible from the active field of emotional components. All differentiated functions are liable to be disturbed by them, but the disturbance is most evident in the case of thinking, which is by nature opposed to feeling and even more to emotionality. More than any other function, differentiated thinking requires a "cool head" and "cold blood."

Consciousness, ego, and will, which might be described as the *avant-garde* of conscious development, at least in the West, tend to loosen up the bonds between the material and the dynamic components of the unconscious, so as then, by repressing the latter—i.e., the feeling-toned instinctive actions and reactions—to control and assimilate the material components. This repres-

334

sion of the emotional-dynamic components is unavoidable, because conscious development demands that the ego be freed from the grip of emotion and instinct.[9]

The fragmentation of archetypes and exhaustion of emotional components, therefore, are as necessary for the development of consciousness and the real or imaginary depotentiation of the unconscious as are the processes of abstraction and the secondary personalization which we shall discuss later. These abstraction processes are not to be identified with the abstract trend of scientific thinking or with conscious rationalization; they set in very much earlier. The development from prelogical to logical thinking [10] represents a basic mutation which strives to establish the autonomy of the conscious system with the help of these same abstractive processes. In this way the archetype is replaced by the idea, of which it is the forerunner. The idea is the result of abstraction; it expresses "the meaning of a primordial image which has been 'abstracted' or detached from the concretism of the image." [11] It is a "product of thinking."

Thus the line runs from primitive man's total possession by the primordial images to a final situation in which deflation of the unconscious is so far advanced that the idea is regarded as a conscious content to which one can, though one need not, take up an attitude. Instead of being possessed by an archetype we now "have an idea" or, better still, "pursue an idea."

Secondary Personalization

The strengthening of the personal ego system and, simultaneously, the steady undermining of the unconscious tend in the

[9] The repressed component plays an important compensatory role in other departments of man's collective culture. It also forms a specific characteristic of the unconscious independently of the individual's attitude- or function-type. The peculiar atmosphere and coloring of the unconscious, its fascination, the nameless attraction and repulsion we feel for it, and the insidious influence it exerts upon the ego irrespective of content, are all manifestations of the dynamic components of the unconscious.

[10] Cassirer, op. cit.; Lévy-Bruhl, How Natives Think.

[11] Jung, Psychological Types, def. 23.

direction of secondary personalization. This principle holds that there is a persistent tendency in man to take primary and transpersonal contents as secondary and personal, and to reduce them to personal factors. Personalization is directly connected with the growth of the ego, of consciousness, and of individuality throughout human history, through which alone "personality" arises and the personal psychic sphere peculiar to the ego emerges from the torrent of transpersonal and collective events.

Secondary personalization is also connected with the processes of introjection and the interiorization of "outside" contents.

As we have seen, man begins by experiencing the transpersonal outside himself, i.e., projected upon the heavens or the world of gods, and ends by introjecting it and making it a personal psychic content. In the language of symbols, in ritual, myth, dreams, and childhood reality, these contents are "eaten," "incorporated," and so "digested." By such acts of introjection and the assimilation of previously projected contents the psyche builds itself up, the subject and the ego-centered conscious personality acquiring more and more "weight" as more and more contents are taken in. But, as we have already noted when discussing the fragmentation of archetypes, it is only through image formation—the giving of form to the formless—that conscious assimilation is made possible. The evolving consciousness gradually learns to distinguish shapes in the dimness, and, even more important, it elaborates them. Similarly, in secondary personalization the expanding system of personality draws the transpersonal figures into its own orbit. This involves not only introjection, but the anthropomorphic creation of images, which gives point to the old dictum of Xenophanes:

Why, if cattle and horses and lions had hands, and could use their hands to paint with and to produce works of art like men, then horses would paint the forms of gods like horses, and cattle like cattle, and each would make the bodies like their own.[12]

Secondary personalization brings a steady decrease in the effective power of the transpersonal and a steady increase in the

[12] Based on the citation in Burnet, *Early Greek Philosophy*, p. 119.

importance of the ego and personality. The sequence begins with the impersonal, all-powerful *numinosum,* cosmic mythology, and the ideas of the dynamistic or pre-animistic epoch, having as their corollary a more or less uncentered human being, unconscious, and existing psychologically as a group-unit. Next comes the plastic epoch, with vague forms looming behind the astral myths, then the gods with their earthly counterparts, the mana heroes, who possess an archetypal rather than an historical character.

Hence the dragon-slaying hero who represents the sun on its "night sea journey," or in other cultures the moon, is the archetypal exemplar and guiding figure of all historical heroes.[13]

Thus, the mythical age is followed by the early historical period with its god-kings, etc., when the mingling of the heavenly with the earthly, and the descent of the transpersonal to the human level, become more and more evident. Secondary personalization leads finally to the local deities becoming heroes and the totem animals domestic spirits.

As ego consciousness and individual personality gain in importance and thrust themselves increasingly to the fore in the historical period, there is a marked strengthening of the personal element. In consequence, the human and personal sphere is enriched at the expense of the extrahuman and transpersonal.

The weight that falls to ego consciousness and individuality makes a man conscious of himself as a human being, whereas in the stage of unconscious nondiscrimination he was for the most part a purely natural being. The fact that, in totemism, he can equally well "be" an animal, a plant, or even a thing is an expression of his incapacity for self-discrimination and of his undeveloped self-awareness as a person.

[13] For this reason the earliest historiographers always tried to bring the individual hero into line with the archetype of the primordial hero, and thus produced a kind of mythologized historiography. An example of this is the Christianization of the Jesus figure, where all the mythical traits peculiar to the hero and redeemer archetype were sketched in afterwards. The mythologizing process is the exact opposite of secondary personalization, but, here as there, the center of gravity of the hero-figure is displaced towards the human activity of the ego (cf. A. Jeremias, *Handbuch der altorientalischen Geisteskultur,* p. 205).

While the animal forms of the gods and ancestors originally symbolized and expressed man's oneness with nature, which was turned to practical account in sorcery, hunting magic, and the breeding of domestic animals, the theriomorphism of a later age is an expression of the transpersonal numen of prehistoric times. Thus the attendant animals of the gods everywhere betray the original form of the latter. In Egypt, for instance, we can trace the development of secondary personalization in the increasing humanization of the gods. In prehistoric times the ensigns of the various nomes were animals, plants, or objects of some kind, whether we choose to regard them as totemistic symbols or not. In the First Dynasty the falcons, fishes, etc., sprouted arms; at the end of the Second Dynasty hybrid shapes begin to appear, human bodies with the heads of the old animal figures that have become anthropomorphic gods; and from the Third Dynasty onwards the human form becomes the rule. The gods establish themselves in human form as lords of heaven, and the animals retire.[14] The advance of secondary personalization can be observed in literature too, where mythological motifs turn into fairy tales and finally into the earliest romances. A good example of this "descent" is the way in which the Set-Osiris or Set-Horus myth changes into the Story of the Two Brothers. What was originally the cosmic opposition of light and darkness becomes the conflict of divine twin brothers, and finally dwindles to a "family novel" in which the immemorial drama has taken on personalistic features.

This progressive assimilation of unconscious contents gradually builds up the personality, thus creating an enlarged psychic system which forms the basis of man's inner spiritual history as this makes itself increasingly independent of the collective history going on all round him. This process, initiated in the first instance by philosophy, has today reached what is chronologically its latest stage in psychology, still of course only in its infancy. Hand in hand with this there goes a "psychization" of the world. Gods, demons, heaven and hell are, as psychic forces,

[14] Moret, *The Nile*, p. 362.

withdrawn from the objective world and incorporated in the human sphere, which thereupon undergoes a very considerable expansion. When we give the name of "sexuality" to what was once experienced as a chthonic divinity, or speak of "hallucination" instead of revelation, and when the gods of heaven and the underworld are recognized as dominants of man's unconscious, it means that an immense tract of external world has dropped into the human psyche. Introjection and psychization are the other side of the process by which a world of physical objects becomes visible, and this world can no longer be modified by projections to the degree that it could before.

What now happens, however—and this is the most important result of secondary personalization so far as the individual is concerned—is that transpersonal contents are projected upon persons. Just as in the historical process god-images were projected upon human beings and were experienced in them, so now archetypal figures are projected into the personal environment, and this leads to a necessary but exceedingly dangerous confusion of the person with the archetype.

This process not only plays an important role in childhood, as the projection of parental archetypes upon the parents, but the fate of the collective is largely determined by such projections upon Great Individuals who influence human history, whether positively or negatively, as heroes, leaders, saints, and so forth. We shall see that a healthy collective culture is possible only when secondary personalization is not carried to the point of absurdity; if it is too radical, it leads to false projections of the transpersonal and to the phenomena of recollectivization, whereby vital elements of the cultural heritage are placed in jeopardy and may be lost altogether.

The deflation of the unconscious, resulting from all the processes we have described, brings about the systemization of consciousness and the separation of the two systems. The relative depotentiation of the unconscious is absolutely necessary if ego consciousness is to be reinforced and enriched with libido. At the same time, the great wall that marks the boundary between

339

conscious and unconscious is continually being strengthened by the revaluation—and devaluation—of unconscious contents. The patriarchal motto of the ego, "Away from the unconscious, away from the mother," sanctions all the devices of devaluation, suppression, and repression in order to exclude from its orbit contents potentially dangerous to consciousness. The activity of the latter as well as its further development depend on the resultant heightened tension with the unconscious.

The activity of masculine consciousness is heroic in so far as it voluntarily takes upon itself the archetypal struggle with the dragon of the unconscious and carries it to a successful conclusion. This dominance of masculinity, which is of crucial importance for the position of the female in patriarchal societies,[15] determines the spiritual development of Western man.

[15] The deflation of the unconscious, its "dethronement" by the patriarchal trend of conscious development, is closely connected with the depreciation of the female in the patriarchate. This fact will receive detailed treatment in my forthcoming work on the psychology of the feminine; here, it is only necessary to make the following observation: the psychological stage ruled by the unconscious is, as we saw, matriarchal, its emblem being the Great Mother who is overcome in the dragon fight. The association of the unconscious with feminine symbolism is archetypal, and the maternal character of the unconscious is further intensified by the anima figure which, in the masculine psyche, stands for the soul. Consequently the heroic-masculine trend of development is apt to confuse "away from the unconscious" with "away from the feminine" altogether. This trend towards patriarchal consciousness is reflected in the supersession of feminine moon myths by masculine sun myths and can be traced far back into primitive psychology. Whereas the moon myths, even when the moon is masculine, always indicate the dependence of consciousness and light upon the nocturnal side of life, i.e., the unconscious, this is no longer the case with the patriarchal solar mythologies. Here the sun is not the morning sun born of the night, but the sun in his zenith at high noon, symbolizing a masculine consciousness which knows itself to be free and independent even in its relations with the self, i.e., the creative world of heaven and spirit.

If Briffault's view is correct, that most mysteries were originally feminine mysteries and were adopted by the men only later, then the anti-feminine tendencies of the men's societies, whose archetypal basis we have already discussed (pp. 180 f.), also have an historical basis. The degradation of woman and her exclusion from many of the existing patriarchal systems of religion is evident even today. This depreciation of the feminine ranges from the intimidation of women by the ceremonial bull-roarers in primitive society (*The Mothers*, Vol. II, p. 544), to the "*taceat mulier in ecclesia*," the Jew's daily prayer of thanks at having been born a man, and the disenfranchisement of women in many European countries at the present time.

The correlation of consciousness with masculinity culminates in the development of science, as an attempt by the masculine spirit to emancipate itself from the power of the unconscious. Wherever science appears it breaks up the original character of the world, which was filled with unconscious projections. Thus, stripped of projection, the world becomes objective, a scientific construction of the mind. In contrast to the original unconsciousness and the illusory world corresponding to it, this objective world is now viewed as the only reality. In this way, under the continual tutelage of the discriminative, masculine spirit, ever searching for laws and principles, the "reality principle" comes to be represented by men.

In so far, then, as ego consciousness, with its discriminative functions, endeavors to break up the indeterminate character of the unconscious world, it is the organ of adaptation to reality. Hence, in primitive man and in children, its development is necessarily dependent upon their capacity to grasp reality, and to that extent the Freudian opposition between the pleasure principle and the reality principle is justified. But this adaptation to a purely external reality no longer meets the needs of later and more recent developments. Our modern consciousness is beginning to recognize the fact that constituents of reality are also to be found in the unconscious itself, as the dominants of our experience, as ideas or archetypes. Consciousness must therefore turn inwards. As the discriminative organ it has to function just as efficiently in respect of the objective psyche inside as of the objective physis outside. Introversion and extraversion are now governed by a broadened reality principle which, in the interests of centroversion, has to be applied to the world and the unconscious equally. The rise of depth psychology as a means for investigating the objective psyche is a symptom of this new orientation.[16]

[16] Cf. Gerhard Adler, "C. G. Jung's Contribution to Modern Consciousness," in *Studies in Analytical Psychology*.

The Transformation of Pleasure-Pain Components

The path of evolution, leading mankind from unconsciousness to consciousness, is the path traced by the transformations and ascent of the libido. On either side there stand the great images, the archetypes and their symbols. As man progresses along this path, ever greater units of libido are supplied to his ego consciousness, so that this system is continually being extended and strengthened. Thus the dawn man, with his momentary flashes of consciousness, is gradually replaced by the modern man, whose ego subsists more or less in a conscious continuum, within a cultural world produced by the collective consciousness of his group and of humanity at large.

We call this path an "ascent" because we experience consciousness and the world of light as being "above" us and unconsciousness and darkness "below," still under the spell of the primitive symbolism which associates the upright posture of the human figure with the development of the head as the seat of the "higher" centers and consciousness. The sequence of stages which begins with the Great Round and passes through the nexus of archetypes to the single archetype and the symbol group, and from the idea to the concept, is an ascending sequence, but it is also a limitation. What was originally experienced only as a vague something "in the depths," charged with energy and hence very real and fascinating, becomes, as a conceptual content, an item of thought, freely maneuverable by the mind and applicable at will. Such a content has certainly gained in utility value, but only at the cost of forfeiting an essential part of its initial libido charge to consciousness as a whole.

The fascination of an unconscious content lies in its power to attract the conscious libido, the first symptom of which is a riveting of attention upon that content. If the attraction grows stronger, the libido is sucked away from consciousness, and this may express itself in a lowering of consciousness, fatigue, de-

342

pression, etc. Whereas in an illness the activation of the unconscious content by an afflux of libido manifests itself in the form of disturbances, symptoms, and so forth, and in the creative individual this content spontaneously combines with consciousness and expresses itself in creativity, the act of conscious realization consists in the ego deliberately leading the mind and the free libido at its disposal towards the focus of fascination. The libido activating the unconscious system as its emotional component, and the libido of the recognizing and realizing ego system, flow together in the act of recognition into a single stream. This confluence is perceived by the ego as pleasurable, and this is so in any genuine realization, in any new recognition or discovery, and again whenever a complex is broken down or an unconscious content assimilated. It is immaterial whether the fascinating content is consciously realized as an image, a dream, a fantasy, an idea, a "hunch," or a projection. The assimilation of unconscious contents, in whatever form, leads not only to an enrichment of the conscious material but to an enrichment of libido, which makes itself felt, subjectively, as excitement, vivacity, and a joy that sometimes borders on intoxication; and, objectively, as a heightening of interest, a broadened and intensified capacity for work, mental alertness, etc.

In the process of realizing and assimilating an unconscious content, the ego makes a "descent," from the conscious standpoint, into the depths, in order to raise up the "treasure." In terms of psychic energy, the pleasure of the "conquering hero" arises from the combination of conscious libido with that of the newly acquired content which it incorporates.[17]

The grasping and assimilation of the content by consciousness are an expression of its enrichment with libido. But by no means

[17] The descent is from the conscious to the unconscious, and thus the reverse of the creative process which starts in the unconscious and works upwards. Manifestations of the unconscious in the form of images, ideas, thoughts, etc. are experienced by the ego as pleasurable. The joy of the creative process springs from the suffusion of consciousness with the libido of the hitherto unconsciously activated content. The pleasure and enrichment of libido resulting from conscious realization and creativity are symptomatic of a synthesis in which the polarity of the two systems, conscious and unconscious, is temporarily suspended.

343

the whole libido charge of the content can be absorbed. Simultaneously with the alteration and enrichment of consciousness, the splitting up of the content leads very frequently, if not always, to an activation of the unconscious as well. We may explain the mechanism as follows: a certain proportion of the liberated libido cannot be absorbed by consciousness and flows off into the unconscious, where it "libidinizes" associated groups of complexes or archetypal contents. These contents are then brought up by association and are produced as random ideas, etc.—in so far as they appear at all—or else a new unconscious constellation is effected. The combination of this new constellation with the original activity of realization is what constitutes the continuity of all creative work, the essential elements of which are always prepared in advance by the unconscious, and are there elaborated and enriched before being produced.

The continuity of these processes is manifest not only in creativity but in all dream series, visions, and fantasies, where we always find an inner consistency, a web of associations deposited around one or more nuclei, as though around a center.[18]

One of the most important attainments of consciousness is its ability to dispose at will of the libido supplied to its system, and to use it more or less independently of the source from which it came. Just as the animation occasioned in the reader by a "stimulating" book can be applied to a poem, a walk, a bridge party, or a flirtation, without there necessarily being any connection between the book and the ego's reaction, so the ego can apply as it pleases a portion of the libido accruing to it from the conscious realization of an unconscious content. This relative freedom of the ego, no matter how much it is abused, is one of its most precious accomplishments.

In the course of these developments, consciousness becomes capable of directing its attention upon any object it chooses, and at the same time the ego acquires a relative independence. The way leads from fascination, when the ego was passive and at the mercy of any activated unconscious content, to a state of

[18] Jung, *Psychology and Alchemy*, fig. 49.

344

consciousness having sufficient libido for the free and active application of interest to whatever the outside world or the collective demands, or to anything with which it chooses to occupy itself.

This is something that must constantly be borne in mind. Before the advent of depth psychology it seemed perfectly natural to identify psychology with the psychology of consciousness. The discoveries of depth psychology have now produced the reverse impression that all conscious contents are determined solely from the unconscious. But only through a better understanding of the dialectical play between conscious and unconscious is real psychological knowledge possible. The formation and consolidation of the conscious system and its struggle for autonomy and self-preservation are just as important a factor in the history of psychic development as the relativizing of this autonomy through the constant tension between conscious and unconscious.

One very important energy problem connected with the sequence of psychic stages is the modification of emotional components due to the change of pleasure-pain qualities. The pleasure-pain component depends on the libido-charge of a psychic system. Pleasure is the psychic equivalent of the proper functioning of a system, i.e., of its healthiness, and the symptom of this is balance and a capacity to expand with the help of surplus units of libido. The "inertia" of a system is proportionate to its specific gravity, i.e., to its powers of resistance. Every system resists dissolution and reacts to danger with pain, just as it reacts to stimulation and libido enrichment with pleasure.

Since the ego is the center of the conscious system, we identify ourselves primarily with the pleasure-pain reactions of this system as though they were our own. But in reality the source of the ego's pleasure-pain experience is by no means only the conscious system.

From the fact that the personality evolves into two systems, conscious and unconscious, it is evident that the conflict between them must also lead to psychic conflict between the

345

pleasure-pain positions, since every partial system strives to maintain itself and reacts to danger with pain, and to any reinforcement and extension of itself with pleasure, as we have said.

In consequence of this, however, the pleasure-conflict—as we can call this situation for short—depends as much upon the degree of integration reached by the personality as upon the stage of ego development which determines the relations between the ego and the unconscious. The more undeveloped consciousness is, the smaller the pleasure-conflict, which again diminishes with greater integration of the personality, since the pleasure-conflict expresses a dissociation between conscious and unconscious.

Not that these two lines of development always run parallel. In a small child a low ego level is combined with a high degree of integration; hence its relatively strong sense of pleasure in general, the mythological expression of which is the paradisal uroboric state. On the other hand, during the process of maturation in the first half of life, a decrease of integration is combined with an increase of ego and consciousness. Differentiation of personality leads to mounting tension within the psyche and hence to increasing conflict between the pleasurable experiences of the ego system and those of the autonomous unconscious system.

The idea of the unconscious having "pleasurable experiences" strikes one as paradoxical at first, indeed as quite meaningless, since every experience, including that of pleasure, appears to pass through consciousness and the ego. But such is not the case. The serenity of the infant is just as emphatic as its experience of pain, but in no sense is it associated with a strong ego consciousness. Indeed, primitive pain and pleasure are largely expressions of unconscious processes. This is corroboration of the fact that ego consciousnes is psychically only a partial system. In psychic illnesses it is patently clear that the impairment and disturbance of consciousness are far from being experienced as unrelievedly painful. Only to the degree that the

346

ego has become the center and carrier of the personality is its pain or pleasure identical with the latter's. In neurotic and particularly in hysterical reactions, the failure of the ego and its suffering are frequently accompanied by a "smile of pleasure" —the triumphant grin of the unconscious at having taken possession of the ego. The uncanniness of all such neurotic and psychotic manifestations—which correspond to a "dysfunction" of the pleasure positions—can be explained by a dissociation of the personality, i.e., its nonidentity with the ego.

In the psychology of primitives this phenomenon can be seen most strikingly in possession, where the pleasure or pain of the daemon—the unconscious complex causing the possession— manifests itself quite independently of the pleasure-pain experience of the ego.[19]

The uroboric stage is ruled by an undifferentiated pleasure-pain reaction; later this hybrid reaction sorts itself out with the differentiation of the two systems, and then, at the stage of the separation of the World Parents, divides into opposites. The original hybrid character of reaction is thereafter at an end: pleasure is pleasure and pain, pain, and there is in addition a clear co-ordination with the two psychic systems, so that the pleasure of the one becomes the pain of the other, and vice versa. A victorious ego consciousness experiences its victory as pleasurable, while the vanquished unconscious system experiences pain.

In spite of this co-ordination of pleasure and pain with the two systems, the pain of the "vanquished" unconscious system does not remain unconscious. The situation of consciousness is complicated by the fact that it has to take note of this pain and make it conscious, or at least not remain unaffected by it. This results in suffering for the ego, even when it triumphantly asserts itself against the unconscious.

Myths express this phenomenon in the feeling of primordial guilt which accompanies the separation of the World Parents. In reality the guilt experienced by the ego comes from the

19 Soeur Jeanne, *Memoiren einer Besessenen.*

sufferings of the unconscious. As we remarked earlier, it is in a sense the World Parents, the unconscious itself, which is the plaintiff, not the ego. Only by overcoming its guilt-feelings can ego consciousness realize its true values; only then does it stand its ground and approve its own deed. The pleasure-conflict is operative in these feelings too, and by conquering them the hero affirms life in the full light of consciousness, even in the midst of conflict.

Nevertheless, the assimilating ego can only conquer by dint of unremitting struggle, never at a single blow. The gods who have been overthrown still play a part in the religion of their conquerors. Thus the overthrow of the old matriarchal goddesses and their replacement by patriarchal gods in the *Oresteia* do not end simply with the expulsion of the Erinyes, but, quite the reverse, with the institution of a cult in their honor. We find this sort of thing happening everywhere.

So long as a content is totally unconscious, it regulates the whole and its power is then at its greatest. But if the ego succeeds in wresting it from the unconscious and making it a conscious content, it is—mythologically speaking—overcome. As, however, this content still goes on using up libido, the ego must continue to work at it until it is fully incorporated and assimilated. Ego consciousness cannot therefore avoid further dealings with the "conquered" content and is likely to suffer.

To take an example: the ascetic whose ego consciousness has triumphantly repulsed the instinctual components that threatened to master him experiences pleasure with his ego, but he "suffers" because the instinct he has denied is also a part of his total structure.

The pleasure-conflict between the two systems takes place mainly in consciousness and as such determines the life of the adult, just as the suffering it entails characterizes the life of the hero in mythology. Only with the onset of maturity is this suffering partially overcome in the individuation process. A high ego level then coincides once more with an integrated personality, and with the progressive balancing of the two systems the pleasure-conflict too is equalized.

The Formation of Authorities within the Personality

The archetypal phases of conscious development correspond to certain ego levels which are co-ordinated with definite periods in the individual's life, each with its wealth of experiences. They belong to the store of personal conscious or unconscious memories of the individual, who passes through the archetypal phases of conscious development in his own ontogenetic development.

Jung [20] has emphasized that the archetypes are not determined as to their content, but only as to their form:

A primordial image is evidently determined as to its contents only when it is conscious, and hence filled out with the material of conscious experience.

Conscious experience of the archetype consists accordingly in the uniquely personal manner in which the transpersonal becomes a reality for the individual.

How individually the archetypal phases are experienced therefore depends on the personality, one part of which is formed by the "personal" unconscious. Consequently, the ontogenetic "filling out" of the archetypal framework—its "padding," so to speak —can be made conscious through analysis of the personal unconscious, by actively rehearsing these contents in the memory and thus dissipating their hitherto unconscious effects. Once more we observe how archetypal structures preformed in the collective unconscious are bound up with uniquely personal contents, without the one being derivable from the other. The *kind* of experience we shall have is prescribed by the archetypes, but *what* we experience is always individual.

[20] "Psychological Aspects of the Mother Archetype."

This doubling of archetypal and individual features shows itself particularly clearly in a phenomenon of great importance for the formation and development of personality, namely the creation within it of various "authorities." Besides the ego, analytical psychology distinguishes as such authorities the self, i.e., the totality of the psyche, the persona, the anima (or animus in women), and the shadow.[21] The fact that these authorities appear as "persons" is consistent with the fundamental teaching of analytical theory that all unconscious contents manifest themselves "like partial personalities." [22] Each of these authorities can, as an autonomous complex, obsess the ego and lead to a state of possession, as the psychology of primitives and also of civilized man clearly shows. The psychology of the neuroses teems with such states of possession. The formation of psychic authorities as psychic organs has a very cogent meaning for the individual, since they facilitate the unity of the personality. Their growth in the course of human history—and the development of a personality in which these authorities are structurally united—is a process that continues still.

We are, unfortunately, not in a position to write a history of these formations, though we can follow their actualization onto-genetically in the development of the individual. We would only hint, very briefly, at what might be said about this process from the standpoint of stadial development.

In the course of its "heroic" encounter with the outside and inside world, the ego establishes objective relations with both by introjecting a variety of contents and building out of them its picture of reality. A complication arises here, because the ego system which seeks to master these external and internal realities is not fixed once and for all, but is itself an assimilatory mechanism with a history of its own, in the course of which it retraces, step by step, the archetypal phases of conscious development. Thus there are in the psychic system and in consciousness—so far as it represents that system—different phases

[21] Jung, "The Relations between the Ego and the Unconscious."
[22] "A Review of the Complex Theory."

of development as regards both the ego and the world, different modes of apprehension and different symbols, successful and unsuccessful attempts at assimilation, all co-existing side by side, so that orientation is made possible only through the hierarchical order imposed by stadial development. The introjection into consciousness of unconscious positions that have already been traversed, and of bygone levels of ego development, always complicates the situation of the ego by actualizing these positions and exposing consciousness to their influence.

The formation of personality, like that of the ego and consciousness, is regulated by centroversion, whose function it is to promote the creative unity of the living organism. The danger of dissolution through participation is extraordinarily great when the organism is unconscious, but less so for a conscious and integrated personality. The processes we have already described—namely, the fragmentation of archetypes, exhaustion of emotional components, secondary personalization, deflation of the unconscious, and rationalization, all of which enhance the stability of the ego and consciousness—prove, despite their tendency to become split off and differentiated, to be guided by centroversion, and the growth of personality and of the authorities constellated by them subserves its purposes likewise.

As the personality develops, it must take in wide areas of the unconscious. The task of the authorities is to protect the personality from the disintegrative forces of the collective unconscious without breaking the vital link with it, and to guarantee the continued existence of the individual without impairing his contacts with the group and the world.

The formation of the persona, as a defense mechanism against, and a means of adaptation to, the collective, has been fully described by Jung,[23] but it seems to be more difficult to account for the origins of the anima and the shadow.

A substantial part of the shadow, too, is the result of collective adaptation. It contains all those elements in the personality which the ego condemns as negative values. This selective

[23] "The Relations between the Ego and the Unconscious."

351

valuation is collectively determined by the class of values current in the individual's cultural canon. To the degree that his positive values are relative to a particular culture only, the shadow containing his negative values will be equally relative.

But the shadow only half belongs to the ego, since it is part of the personal unconscious and as such part of the collective. On the other hand, it is also constellated by the figure of the Antagonist in the collective unconscious, and the importance of the shadow as an authority rests precisely on its position midway between the personal conscious and the collective unconscious. Its effect on the personality as a whole lies in compensating the ego. It is as though centroversion had attached to the aspiring flights of ego consciousness, with its animosity to the body, the leaden weight of the shadow which takes good care that there shall be no "reaching for the moon" and that man's collective, historical, and biological conditions shall not pass unregarded by the generalizing and hypostatizing attitude of the conscious mind. The shadow thus prevents a dissociation of the personality such as always results from hypertrophy of consciousness and overaccentuation of the ego.[24]

The formation of the shadow goes together with the introjection of the antagonist, a figure we have already encountered when dealing with the psychology of myths. The assimilation of evil and the incorporation of aggressive tendencies always center on the shadow. The "dark brother" is as much a symbol of the shadow side as the bush-soul of primitives.[25] Only by incorporating this dark side does the personality put itself into a posture of defense. Evil, no matter by what cultural canon it be judged, is a necessary constituent of individuality as its egoism, its readiness to defend itself or to attack, and lastly, as its capacity to mark itself off from the collective and to maintain its

[24] An alchemical picture from the *Viridarium chymicum* of Daniel Stolcius de Stolcenberg (Frankfort, 1624; reprinted from Michael Maier, *Symbola aurea,* Frankfort, 1617), showing Avicenna with an eagle chained to a toad, illustrates the same problem symbolically. Cf. Read, *Prelude to Chemistry*, pl. 2, ii.

[25] Benedict, *Patterns of Culture;* Mead, *Sex and Temperament in Three Primitive Societies.*

"otherness" in face of the leveling demands of the community. The shadow roots the personality in the subsoil of the unconscious, and this shadowy link with the archetype of the antagonist, i.e., the devil, is in the deepest sense part of the creative abyss of every living personality. That is why in myths the shadow often appears as a twin, for he is not just the "hostile brother," but the companion and friend, and it is sometimes difficult to tell whether this twin is the shadow or the self, the deathless "other."

This paradox bears out the truth of the old law that upper and lower reflect one another. Indeed, in psychological development, the self lies hidden in the shadow; he is the "keeper of the gate," [26] the guardian of the threshold. The way to the self lies through him; behind the dark aspect he represents there stands the aspect of wholeness, and only by making friends with the shadow do we gain the friendship of the self.

We shall examine elsewhere [27] some of the cultural complications arising from the conflict between ego and shadow, and, in even greater degree, from that between the community and the shadow side of the individual.

These few hints at the psychology of the shadow must suffice, and in the same way we can only venture a few remarks about the formation of that other authority known as the soul-image or anima/animus.[28]

If we consider the sequence Uroboros, Great Mother, Princess, we note a steady progression away from monstrous confusion and paradoxicality to the clear human image of the freed captive. The further back we go, the more complex, intangible, and bafflingly mysterious the terms of the sequence become; but as we approach the ego they gain in definition and offer numerous points of relationship.

It is like one of those pictures which, so long as they are not

[26] Jung, "Archetypes of the Collective Unconscious." Cf. also the Moses-Chidher analysis in "Concerning Rebirth."

[27] Appendix II; also my *Depth Psychology and a New Ethic.*

[28] I am not concerned here with the "psychology of the feminine" and the extent to which it deviates from that of the masculine ego.

sharply focused, seem to be without contours and utterly confusing, but which fall into a pattern when the observer stands off at the right distance. Figures, masses, relations now become visible, whereas before they had remained blurred and indecipherable. The development of consciousness is more or less analogous to this alteration of vision; indeed it seems to be directly dependent upon how far consciousness succeeds in gaining the distance that will enable it to perceive distinct forms and meanings, where before was nothing but ambiguity and murk.

With the freeing of the anima from the power of the uroboric dragon, a feminine component is built into the structure of the hero's personality. He is assigned his own feminine counterpart, essentially like himself, whether it be a real woman or his own soul, and the ego's capacity to relate to this feminine element is the most valuable part of the capture. Herein, precisely, lies the difference between the princess and the Great Mother, with whom no relations on equal terms are possible. The union of male and female, inside and outside, bears fruit in the culture-hero and founder of kingdoms, in the family, or in creative work.

The link back to the Great Mother, to the ground and origin, passes through the anima princess, for she is the abyss of the feminine in altered, personal form. Only in her does the female become man's partner. His help consists essentially in delivering the princess from the power of the dragon, or in conjuring her forth from the dragon shape which distorts her and her humanity, as illustrated by the numerous myths and folk tales dealing with the theme of disenchantment.

A substantial part of the anima figure is formed through the fragmentation of the uroboric mother archetype and the introjection of its positive aspects. We have seen how this archetype gradually splits up into an archetypal group. For instance, qualities like good and bad, old and young, lie side by side in the uroboros and Great Mother, but in the course of development the "young" princess or anima splits off from the "old" mother, who continues undeterred to play her specific role of good and bad in the unconscious.

354

The anima is a symbolic and archetypal figure, being made up of magical, alluring, and dangerously fascinating elements which bring madness as well as wisdom. She has human, animal, and divine features, and can assume corresponding shapes when enchanted or disenchanted. As the soul, she can no more be defined than man can define woman; yet, although exceeding the heights and depths of a man, she has finally entered the human sphere, a "you" with whom "I" can commune, and not a mere idol to be worshiped.

With her mixed archetypal and personal characteristics, the anima stands on the frontiers of the personality, but as one of its "authorities" she is an assimilable part of its structure.

When, for instance, the anima figure is broken down in the individuation process and becomes a function of relationship between the ego and the unconscious,[29] we have an illustration of the fragmentation and assimilation of archetypes whose historic importance for the evolution of consciousness we have endeavored to describe.

Only by relating to the reality of the soul—the freed captive—can we make the link with the unconscious truly creative, for creativity in all its forms is always the product of a meeting between the masculine world of ego consciousness and the feminine world of the soul.

Just as the projection of the self upon the group, as the collective self, forms the libidinal basis of the group psyche and hence of all communal living,[30] so the anima or animus projection is the basis of life between the sexes. In the one case the all-embracing self-symbol is projected upon the all-embracing group; in the other the soul-image, which has closer ties with the ego and personality, is projected upon the more intimate figure of a woman. Whenever the anima (and, *mutatis mutandis*, the animus) is unconscious, she is projected and thereby forces the individual into a human relationship with the carrier of the projection, binds him to the collective through his partner, and

[29] Jung, "The Relations between the Ego and the Unconscious."
[30] Cf. Appendix I.

355

compels him to undergo the experience of a human "you," at the same time making him partially conscious of his own unconscious soul. Although both self and anima act as unconscious agencies at first, they gradually mark off, from the wide field of possible participations, smaller areas which are closer to the ego; while the powerful libido bond between the partners leads to progressive conscious realization and thus undermines the unconscious fascination.

The existence of the anima or animus figure means that the personality still possesses a system with strong unconscious motivations; but, judged by the situation of the dawn man, who was liable at any moment to uroboric dissolution through *participation mystique,* this component is a relatively stable structure capable of withstanding the onslaughts of the collective unconscious. Thus the divinatory powers of the psyche, giving guidance and warning of danger, serve the purposes of centroversion. When she appears in her highest form, as Sophia, the anima clearly reveals this basic function of hers as the sublime partner and helpmeet of the ego.

The Synthetic Function of the Ego

The militant or "heroic" functions of the ego, however, are not applied solely to the control of the unconscious; that the same functions are also used for dominating the external world need be pursued no further, since we can take it as known that this activity forms the basis of Western science. A no less important function of the ego is the synthetic function, which enables it to build a new whole out of the "decomposed" parts, through assimilation of the material previously broken down and modified by the analytical faculty. Our view of the world, in so far as we have a conscious conception of the whole, is the unity of a world transformed by ourselves, which once, as an unconscious unity, engulfed all consciousness.

We have described a number of processes illustrating the

356

polarity and collaboration of the two psychic systems, their separation and partial recombination, their tendency towards mutual insulation, and their mutual struggles to dominate one another. These processes would be disastrous for the individual in whom they take place, and would threaten his very existence, were they not all in large measure controlled and balanced by a striving for wholeness which regulates the psychophysical harmony and the interplay of the psychic systems themselves. This tendency we have introduced under the concept of centroversion. It sets to work whenever the whole is endangered through the ascendency of the unconscious and its autonomous contents, or, conversely, through the excessive insulation and overvaluation of the conscious system. With the help of compensation, a basic factor in all organic and psychic life, it binds psyche and physis into a unity, and its range of action extends from the balanced metabolism of unicellular organisms to the balance which obtains between conscious and unconscious.

The differentiation of conscious from unconscious and of the individual from the all-pervading collective is typical of the human species. Whereas the collective has its roots in ancestral experience and is represented by the collective unconscious, the individual is rooted in the ego, whose development proceeds largely with the help of consciousness. Both systems are amalgamated in a single psyche, but the one grows out of the other both phylogenetically and ontogenetically. The ego is the acting and willing center, but the consciousness of which it is the center also possesses, as the organ of representation and cognition, the power to perceive processes in the collective unconscious and the body.

All the objects of the outside and inside worlds are introjected as contents of consciousness and are there represented according to their value. The selection, arrangement, gradation, and delimitation of the contents so represented depend in large measure on the cultural canon within which consciousness develops and by which it is conditioned. But it is characteristic of every individual, under all circumstances, to create for himself a

357

consciously constellated and synthetically constructed view of the world, however great or small in scope.

The likeness between ego consciousness and the uroboros is the fundamental "family likeness" between ego and self, which corresponds mythologically to that between father and son. Because, psychologically, ego and consciousness are organs of centroversion, the ego rightly emphasizes its central position. This basic fact of the human situation has its mythological equivalent in the divine birth of the hero and his filiation to "heaven." What we are prone to call the "anthropocentric" belief of the primitive, that the existence of the world depends on his magical performances and that his rituals control the coursing of the sun, is in reality one of the deepest truths of mankind. The father-son likeness between self and ego is manifest not only in the martial exploits of the hero-son, but in the synthetic power of consciousness to create a new spiritual world of human culture in the likeness of the divine.

This synthetic function, taking its place alongside the analytical one, presupposes a faculty to which we have repeatedly drawn attention: the faculty for objectivation. Ego consciousness, poised between the outer and inner world of objects and driven to unceasing acts of introjection, is by virtue of its registering and balancing functions ever compelled to keep its distance, until it finally reaches a point where it becomes detached even from itself. This produces a kind of self-relativization which, as skepticism, humor, irony, and a sense of one's own relativity, promotes a higher form of psychic objectivity.

During this process ego consciousness proves its difference from all other partial psychic systems—of which it is one—by throwing off that fanatical obsession with itself which is symptomatic of every system's primary will to self-preservation. It is precisely this growing reflectiveness, self-criticism, and desire for truth and objectivity that enable consciousness to give better and more adequate representation even to the positions it opposes. This facilitates self-objectivation and finally, at the climax of its development, it learns to give up its ego-centeredness and allows itself to be integrated by the totality of the psyche, the self.

The synthetic activity, which is absolutely indispensable for the integration of a "self-centered" personality, is one of the elementary functions of consciousness. It is a direct offshoot of centroversion and of its synthesizing effects. The new and decisive factor here, however, is that the synthesis produced by the ego is a conscious one; in other words, the new unity does not remain at the biological level but is lifted onto the psychological level. Completeness is one of the desiderata of this synthesis.

As the integration process during the second half of life seems to indicate, the stability of the personality is determined by the scope of the synthesis it has reached. Only when the material has been synthesized to the requisite degree of completeness are the demands of centroversion satisfied; it then manifests itself by bringing the self into the center of the personality, with all the accompanying phenomena.

The integration of the personality is equivalent to an integration of the world. Just as an uncentered psyche which is dispersed in participations sees only a diffuse and chaotic world, so the world constellates itself in an hierarchical order about an integrated personality. The correspondence between one's view of the world and the formation of personality extends from the lowest level to the highest.

Only now, when the division of personality into two systems has been outgrown, is the unity of the psyche restored through the synthetic work of consciousness, but on the higher plane of integration. The visionary goal of the dragon fight—immortality and lastingness—is now attained. By the displacement of the center from the ego to the self, the inmost experience of the individuation process, the transitory character of the ego is relativized. The personality is no longer wholly identified with the ephemeral ego, but experiences its partial identity with the self, whether this experience take the form of "godlikeness" or of that

359

"cleaving to the godhead" (adherence)[31] of which the mystics speak. The salient feature is that the personality's sense of no longer being identical with the ego prevails over the mortality which clings to egohood. But that is the supreme goal of the hero myth. In his victorious struggle the hero proves his godlike descent and experiences the fulfillment of the primary condition on which he entered into battle, and which is expressed in the mythological formula "I and the Father are one."

[31] [Hebrew "dwᵉkut." The root "dwk" is the same as that of "dybbuk," the demon who "clings" to a person.—G. ADLER.]

C. The Balance and Crisis of Consciousness

Compensation of the Separated Systems:
Culture in Balance

IN APPENDIX I we trace some of the lines of development that lead from the original group situation to a collective formed of more or less strongly individualized persons, and try at the same time to show the role played by the Great Individual whom the myths represent as the hero. This development is paralleled by another, in which the differentiation of the conscious from the unconscious, their separation into two systems, and the emancipation of ego consciousness reach completion.

With this we have left the sphere of the dawn man and entered into the sphere of culture, and we now have to examine the cultural problems that emerge with the separation of the two systems.

The first part of the present section, dealing with "culture in balance," provides a tentative sketch of the situation that obtains when the psychic health of the collective is guaranteed by "nature," thanks to the operation of the same compensatory tendencies in mankind which can be shown to exist in the individual psyche.

The second part shows, equally tentatively, how far our cultural unease or dis-ease is due to the fact that the separation of the systems—in itself a necessary product of evolution—has degenerated into a schism and thus precipitated a psychic crisis whose catastrophic effects are reflected in contemporary history.[1]

*

We have emphasized that in the evolution of mankind the "sacred" and the "extraordinary" are precursors of processes

[1] In Appendix II an attempt is made to interpret this degeneration of the group into the mass and the various phenomena to which it gives rise, so that in a sense the present section, together with the two Appendices, form a self-contained whole.

which are later enacted in every individual. The wide discrepancy between ego consciousness on the one hand and the world and the unconscious on the other makes it imperative that the ego should be helped, if indeed the role of the individual and his ego consciousness is as important for the species as we take it to be. This help is granted to the individual, inwardly and outwardly, on condition that the maturing ego emulates the many heroic feats and dragon fights which mankind as a whole has accomplished before him. Or rather, it would be more correct to say that the individual must re-experience all the heroic deeds which mankind has accomplished in emulation of the Great Individuals, the original heroes and creators whose achievements have become part of the collective human heritage.

The collective transmits to the maturing individual, as cultural possessions in his world of values, such contents as have strengthened the growth of human consciousness, and it proscribes all developments and attitudes that run counter to this process. As the vehicle of spiritual tradition it supports from outside the a priori archetypal patterns laid down from the inside, and actualizes them through education.

The educative demands of the collective, and the need to adapt to these demands, together form one of the most important aids in the ego's struggle for independence. "Heaven" and the world of the fathers now constitute the superego or conscience which, as another "authority" within the personality, represents the collective conscious values, though these vary with the type of collective and its values, and also with the stage of consciousness which the collective has reached.

We have already indicated the significance of heaven and masculinity for the hero fight. Here we must emphasize yet again that in early childhood the personal father who represents the collective becomes the bearer of the authority complex which is bound up with collective values, and that later, in puberty, this representative role is taken over by the men's society. Both representatives are a great help in the dragon fight,

364

which in childhood and puberty determines the psychic situation of the normal ego.[2]

The collective places a conscious world of values at the ego's disposal in the cultural traditions of the group. A one-sided development of ego consciousness, however, would only heighten the danger of dissociation between the two systems and thus precipitate a psychic crisis. Hence there is an innate tendency in every collective and every culture to establish a balance between its own positions and those of the individual embedded within it.

These equilibrating tendencies in a culture generally operate through the spheres in which the collective unconscious impinges directly upon the life of the community, namely through religion, art, and the ceremonial group activities which may or may not be associated with these, such as the waging of war, feasts, processions, meetings, etc.

The importance of these spheres for cultural balance lies in the fact that they guarantee the unity of psychic functions by preventing a schism between conscious and unconscious.

In this connection we must elucidate the role of the symbol for consciousness. The world of symbols forms the bridge between a consciousness struggling to emancipate and systematize itself, and the collective unconscious with its transpersonal contents. So long as this world exists and continues to operate through the various rituals, cults, myths, religion, and art, it prevents the two realms from falling apart, because, owing to the effect of the symbol, one side of the psychic system continually influences the other and sets up a dialectical relationship between them.

As Jung has shown,[3] the symbol mediates the passage of psychic energy from the unconscious, in order that it may be applied consciously and turned to practical account. He describes

[2] Both of them become the dragon who must be conquered if the ego is to develop in any way out of the ordinary, as for instance in the case of the creative individual.

[3] *Symbols of Transformation [=Psychology of the Unconscious].*

365

the symbol as a "psychological machine" which "transforms energy." [4]

In early cultures, everyday habit is simply the unconscious existence of primitive man, the habitual clinging of his libido to the world in *participation mystique*, in which state his natural life is spent. Through the symbol, the energy is freed from this attachment and becomes available for conscious activity and work. The symbol is the transformer of energy, converting into other forms the libido which alone enables primitive man to achieve anything at all. That is why any activity of his has to be initiated and accompanied by a variety of religious and symbolic measures, whether it be farming, hunting, fishing, or any other "unaccustomed" work not done every day. Only with the help of the fascinating, libido-catching, and ego-absorbing effect of the symbol can the "unaccustomed activity" be undertaken.

The same conditions are still operative in modern man, only we are not so conscious of them. The "sanctification" of unaccustomed activity is still the best method of getting a man out of the rut of everyday habit and conditioning him for the required state of work. To take an example: the transformation of a petty office clerk into the responsible leader of a death-dealing bomber squadron is probably one of the most radical psychic transformations that can be demanded of modern man. This metamorphosis of the normal peace-loving citizen into a fighter is, even today, only possible with the help of symbols. Such a transformation of personality is achieved by invoking the symbols of God, King, Fatherland, Freedom, the "most sacred good of the nation," and by dedicatory acts steeped in symbolism, with the added assistance of all the elements in religion and art best calculated to stir the individual. Only in this way is it psychologically possible to divert psychic energy from the "natural channel" of peaceable private life into the "unaccustomed activity" of slaughter.

Like the individual symbol, the social symbol valid for the group is "never of exclusively conscious or exclusively uncon-

[4] "On Psychic Energy."

scious origin," but is produced by the "equal collaboration of both." The symbol therefore has a rational side "which accords with reason," and another side which is "inaccessible to reason, since it is composed not only of data of a rational nature, but of the irrational data of pure inward and outward perception." [5]

The sensuous, figurative component of the symbol—the component deriving from sensation or intuition, the irrational functions—cannot therefore be grasped by reason. While this is perfectly obvious with straightforward symbols like the flag, the cross, etc., it is also true of more abstract ideas in so far as these are concerned with symbolic realities. The symbolic significance of the idea "Fatherland," for instance, transcends the rational element it undoubtedly contains, and it is precisely the unconscious emotional factor activated whenever the Fatherland is invoked that shows the symbol to be an energy transformer which, by force of fascination, deflects the libido from its accustomed courses.

Generally speaking the symbol works in opposite ways for primitive and modern man.[6] Historically, the symbol led to the development of consciousness, to reality-adaptation and the discovery of the objective world. It is now known, for instance, that sacred animals came "before" stockbreeding, just as in general the sacred meaning of a thing is older than its profane meaning. Its objective significance is only perceived afterwards, behind its symbolic significance.

In the dawn period the rationalizable component of a symbol was of crucial importance, since it was at this point that man's view of the world passed from the symbolic to the rational. The advance from prelogical to logical thinking likewise proceeds via the symbol, and it can be shown that philosophical and scientific thinking gradually developed out of symbolic thinking

[5] Jung, *Psychological Types*, def. 51 [revised.—TRANS.].
[6] For modern man the emergence of symbols on the "way inward" has a different meaning and function. Here, the mediatory position of the symbol, which is due to its being a combination of conscious and unconscious elements, is proved by the fact that the link-back of conscious to unconscious proceeds via the symbol, just as with the dawn man the development went in the reverse direction from unconscious to conscious.

by progressively emancipating itself from the emotional-dynamic components of the unconscious.

Because primitive man projects his unconscious contents into the world and its objects, these appear to him as drenched in symbolism and charged with mana, and his interest is thereby focused upon the world. His consciousness and will are weak and hard to move; his libido is suspended in the unconscious and is available to the ego only in small amounts. But the symbol, as an object animated by projection, fascinates, and, to the extent that it "grips" and "stirs" him, sets his libido in motion and with it the whole man. This activating effect of the symbol is, as Jung has pointed out,[7] an important element in every cult. It was only through the symbolic animation of the earth that the drudgery of agriculture was overcome, just as symbolic possession in the *rites d'entrée* alone makes possible any activity requiring large amounts of libido.

The symbol, however, is also an expression of the spiritual side, of the formative principle dwelling in the unconscious, for "the spirit appears in the psyche as instinct," as a "principle *sui generis*." [8] So far as the development of human consciousness is concerned, this spiritual side of the symbol is *the* decisive factor. Over and above its "gripping" aspect the symbol also has a meaningful aspect: it is more than a sign; it assigns meaning, it signifies something and demands interpretation. It is this aspect that speaks to our understanding and rouses us to reflection, not just to feeling and emotionality. These two aspects working together in the symbol constitute its specific nature, unlike the sign or allegory which have fixed meanings. So long as the symbol is a living and effective force, it transcends the capacity of the experiencing consciousness and "formulates an essential unconscious component" [9]—the very reason why it is so attractive and disturbing. Consciousness keeps on returning to it and circles round it fascinated, meditating and cogitat-

[7] *Symbols of Transformation.*
[8] Jung, "On Psychic Energy."
[9] *Psychological Types*, def. 51.

ing, thus completing the *circumambulatio* which recurs in so many dramatically enacted rites and religious ceremonies.

In the "symbolic life," [10] the ego does not take up a content with the rational side of consciousness and then proceed to analyze it, breaking it down in order to digest it in disintegrated form; rather the whole of the psyche exposes itself to the action of the symbol and lets itself be permeated and "stirred" by it. This permeating quality affects the psychic whole and not just consciousness alone.

Images and symbols, being creative products of the unconscious, are so many formulations of the spiritual side of the human psyche. In them the meaning and "sense-giving" tendencies of the unconscious are expressing themselves, be it in a vision, a dream, or a fantasy, or again in an inner image which is seen outside, as the visible manifestation of a god. The inside "expresses" itself by way of the symbol.

Thanks to the symbol, man's consciousness becomes spiritualized and finally arrives at self-consciousness:

Man can apprehend and know his own being only insofar as he can make it visible in the image of his gods.[11]

Myth, art, religion, and language are all symbolic expressions of the creative spirit in man; in them this spirit takes on objective, perceptible form, becoming conscious of itself through man's consciousness of it.

But the "sense-giving" function of symbols and archetypes also has a powerful emotional side, and the emotionality they evoke is likewise directed; that is, it possesses a meaningful and ordering character. As Jung says:

Every relationship to the archetype, whether through experience or simply through the spoken word, is "stirring," that is to say, it works because it releases in us a mightier voice than our own. He who speaks in primordial images speaks with a thousand voices; he enthralls and overpowers, while at the same time he lifts the idea he is trying to express out of the occasional and the transitory into the realm of the ever-enduring. He trans-

[10] Jung, "The Symbolic Life," a lecture (1939) printed for private circulation.
[11] Cassirer, *The Philosophy of Symbolic Forms* (trans. Manheim), II, p. 218.

mutes our personal destiny into the destiny of mankind, thereby evoking in us all those beneficent forces that ever and anon have enabled mankind to find a refuge from every peril and to outlive the longest night.[12]

Consequently possession by the archetype brings meaning and deliverance at once, since it liberates part of the emotional forces that had been dammed up through the development of consciousness and the resultant exhaustion of emotional components. Moreover, in and through these experiences—which, as we saw, were originally group experiences—there ensues a reactivation of the group psyche which puts an end, at least temporarily, to the isolation of the individual ego.

Possession by the archetype links the individual to humanity again: he is dipped in the torrent of the collective unconscious and is regenerated through the activation of his own collective layers. Naturally enough this experience was originally a sacred event and was celebrated as a collective phenomenon by the group. Like religious celebrations, which were and for the most part still are group phenomena, art too was once a collective phenomenon. Apart from the fact that art, so far as it is concerned with the self-representation of archetypal symbols, was always associated with the sacral sphere in dancing, singing, sculpture, and the telling of myths, it preserved its collective sacramental character even in later times, as we can see from Greek tragedy, medieval mystery plays, church music, etc. Only gradually, with progressive individualization, did its collective character fall into abeyance and the individual worshiper, spectator, or listener emerge from the group.

The culture of a nation or group is determined by the operation within it of an archetypal canon which represents its highest and deepest values, and which organizes its religion, art, festivals, and everyday life. So long as culture is in a state of balance, the individual is secure in the network of the cultural canon, sustained by its vitality, but held fast.

That is to say, while he is contained in the culture of his group

[12] "On the Relation of Analytical Psychology to Poetry," p. 248 [revised.— TRANS.].

his psychic system is balanced, because his consciousness is protected, developed, and educated by the traditional "heavenly world" which lives on in the collective values, and his conscious system is compensated by the archetypes embodied in the projections of religion, art, custom, etc. Whenever a critical situation arises, be it individual or collective, an appeal is instantly made to the transmitters of the canon. Whether these are medicine men, prophets, and priests, or commissars, leaders, ministers, and officials, will depend upon the canon, and also upon whether its basic institutions are founded upon demons, spirits, gods, a single God, or the idea of a tree, stone, animal, hallowed place, and so on.

In every case the psychological effect of the appeal will be one of balance, bringing about a reorientation to the prevailing canon and a reunion with the collective, thus overcoming the crisis. So long as the network of values remains intact, the average individual is secure in his group and its culture. In other words, the existing values and the existing symbols of the collective unconscious are sufficient to guarantee psychic equilibrium.

All symbols and archetypes are projections of the formative side of human nature that creates order and assigns meaning. Hence, symbols and symbolic figures are the dominants of every civilization, early or late. They are the cocoon of meaning which humanity spins round itself, and all studies and interpretations of culture are the study and interpretation of archetypes and their symbols.

The collective re-enactment of the determining archetypes in religious festivities and the arts associated with them gives meaning to life and saturates it in the emotions set free by transpersonal psychic forces in the background. Besides the religious and sacramental experience of the archetypes, there is also their aesthetic and cathartic effect to be considered, if we disregard the primitive states of possession induced by intoxicating drinks, by sexual excesses or sadistic orgies. Here again we can trace a gradual change in the line of development.

371

At first everything is under the unconscious emotional compulsion of the symbols which appear in the ritual, whose aim it is to represent and "enact" them. In the old coronation rites, for example, symbol and ritual are still wholly identical with the exemplary life of the king. Later the ritual takes the form of a sacred action which is "played" by the collective for the collective, though it is still invested with all the force of magic and ritual efficacy.

Gradually the *meaning* of the symbol is crystallized out, detaches itself from the action, and becomes a cultural content capable of conscious realization and interpretation. Although the ritual is acted as before, it is something of a game with a meaning—like the initiation rites, for instance—and the interpretation of the symbols therein represented and enacted becomes an essential part of the initiation. The accent, then, has already fallen on conscious assimilation and the strengthening of the ego.[13]

The law of compensation continues to act as an expression of centroversion over the whole field of a culture so long as this culture is "in balance." Compensation of the collective through intervention of the transpersonal components of the cultural canon and their influence upon religion, art, and custom is by no means only "orientating" in its effects, i.e., productive of meaning and value; it also brings emotional freedom and a re-attunement. This emotional compensation becomes more and more important as the conscious system grows more differentiated and specialized.

A significant analogy may be found in dreams, which are compensations of consciousness directed by centroversion. The contents necessary to consciousness are supplied to it in the dream under the guidance of centroversion, which strives for balance

---

[13] We can trace the effect of secondary personalization all the way from the modification of the old symbolic ritual to the mysteries and classical tragedy, and finally to the modern theater. Once more we find the same line of development with its falling series of transpersonal factors and rising series of personal ones, beginning with the "play" of superhuman forces and gods and ending with the "boudoir" piece.

and tries to correct the aberrations, the one-sidednesses and oversights, which threaten the whole.

The dream, if it is understood, alters the conscious orientation and, in addition, brings about a reattunement of consciousness and personality. This reattunement shows itself in a complete change of attitude—for instance, after being asleep we wake up refreshed, alert, full of vigor, or again we may wake up feeling listless and out of sorts, depressed or on edge. It seems, also, that the contents of consciousness can be altered by a difference of emotional charge. Disagreeable contents suddenly appear delightful and therefore materially different; the things that attracted us before seem colorless, our desires disgust us, the unattainable becomes a pressing necessity, and so forth and so on.[14]

The emotional reattunement of consciousness thus produces an unconscious reorientation of its activity. In sick people it is effected by unconscious constellations which, because not built into the whole structure, may disrupt or possibly even destroy life, but in the healthy person the reattunement is directed by centroversion, and in his case emotionality is anything that stimulates him positively and sets him in motion, attracts, or repels. Where this is lacking, there is only deadness: dead knowledge, dead facts, meaningless data, disconnected, lifeless details, and dead relationships. But when the emotional component comes in, it arouses a libido-current of interest, and new constellations and new psychic contents start moving again. This interest may work for the most part unconsciously, as a kind of direction-giving affectivity; for the interest we ourselves can consciously direct is only a small tributary of the unconscious mainstream which flows through and regulates the life of the psyche.

This emotional current of vitality in a culture is canalized by the archetypes incorporated in the group's cultural canon. The

[14] This reattunement or re-emotionalization has so far been grossly neglected by depth psychology because investigators have been so fascinated by the study of the material components. But the material interpretation of a dream does nothing to explain how it causes the reattunement. Here we would only draw attention to the importance of emotional components for dream interpretation and therapy.

373

emotionality remains a living force and regenerates the individual, even though it is more or less bound to the conventional paths laid down by communal custom and habit.

However, the collective ceremonies of the group are not the only theaters for the play of transpersonal forces. The normal life of the individual, too, is embedded in a network of symbols. All the naturally important periods of life—birth, puberty, marriage, etc.—are singled out and commemorated. As they are felt to be collective and transpersonal, i.e., something beyond the purely individual, they are sacralized by being brought into contact with the cultural canon of the archetypes.

This contact with the great processes of nature regulates and sustains the life of the group and of the individual. The cosmic festivals held in honor of the sun and moon, the anniversaries that provide life with a sacred setting and give it direction, link up with the historical events in which the collective celebrates its history as human history. Everywhere life is studded with holy times, holy places, holy days. The landscape is thick-sown with shrines, temples, churches, monuments, and memorials, marking the spot where religion and art deposit their archetypal contents in our temporal space, and everywhere the transpersonal canon of values stamps itself upon the community it has gripped. In the same way, time too is caught up in a nexus of feast days with their solemn celebrations—dramas, contests, spring and autumn festivals, sacraments, and rites, in which cosmic life intermingles with the earthly.

Yet the sacred, emotive power of the transpersonal touches the life of the individual still more closely, and in a profounder sense. Birth and death, maturity, marriage, and childbirth are everywhere "sacred" for man, just as sickness and recovery, happiness and unhappiness, give him occasion to link his personal fate with that which transcends him. Everywhere contact with the archetypes modifies the purely personal world.

We have no wish to cite a mass of particulars showing how the continual influx of transpersonal life guarantees the vitality

374

of the personal.[15] Our sole concern is the basic situation; namely, that so long as culture is "in balance," the individuals contained in it normally stand in an adequate relationship to the collective unconscious, even if this is only a relationship to the archetypal projections of the cultural canon and to its highest values.

The organization of life inside this framework precludes—in the normal person—any dangerous invasions from the unconscious and guarantees him a relatively high degree of inner security, enabling him to lead an ordered existence in a world-system where the human and the cosmic, the personal and the transpersonal, are all articulated with one another.

The exceptions to this rule—exceptions, however, upon which the community depends—are the "outsiders," those who fall within an enlarged category of the type known in myth as the hero, the Great Individual.

The dialectical play between the Great Individual and the collective still continues today. For him the only thing that counts is the extraordinary. He must conquer the ordinary because it represents the power of the old order that constricts him. But conquering normal life—which is the life of the unheroic—always means sacrificing normal values and so coming into conflict with the collective. If later the hero is honored as a culture-bringer and savior, etc., this is generally only after he has been liquidated by the collective. The hero's mythological accession to power is only transpersonally true. He and his world of values may conquer and come to power, but often enough he never lives to experience this power personally.

The hero or Great Individual is always and pre-eminently the man with immediate inner experience who, as seer, artist, prophet, or revolutionary, sees, formulates, sets forth, and realizes the new values, the "new images." His orientation comes from the "voice," from the unique, inner utterance of the self, which has all the immediacy of a "dictate." Herein lies the extraordinary orientation of this type of individual. Not only is the canon always "founded," so far as we can judge, in accordance

[15] Van der Leeuw, *Religion in Essence and Manifestation:* "Sacred Life."

with the revelations enunciated by the voice, but to have experience of the voice often becomes an integral part of the canon, as is the case with the guardian spirits of the American Indians, or when the individual has to acquire his own particular totem. Even when he is pathologically overwhelmed by the spontaneous activity of the collective unconscious and, with mind deranged, proclaims the will of the Transpersonal, he is still regarded as holy precisely because he is crazed. Humanity, with profound psychological insight, sees in him a victim of the powers that be, sanctified through having been "touched" by the transpersonal.

We cannot enter here into the question of whether, in the case of the creative individual, possession results from the activity of the collective psyche or of his own consciousness, or of whether it is due to an excess or a deficit in his personal psychic system. All these possibilities exist, but they can only be examined in a separate study of the problem of creativity.

The important thing, however, is that the archetypal canon is always created and brought to birth by "eccentric" individuals. These are the founders of religions, sects, philosophies, political sciences, ideologies, and spiritual movements, in the security of which the collective man lives without needing to come into contact with the primordial fire of direct revelation, or to experience the throes of creation.

Speaking of the compensatory function of creative art, Jung writes:

In this lies the social significance of art: it labors without cease to educate the spirit of the age, bringing to birth those forms in which the age is most lacking. Recoiling from the discontents of the present, the yearning of the artist reaches back to that primordial image in the unconscious which is best fitted to compensate the insufficiency and one-sidedness of the spirit of the age. The artist seizes this image, and in the work of raising it from deepest unconsciousness and bringing it nearer to consciousness, he transforms its shape, until it can be accepted by his contemporaries according to their capacities.[16]

[16] "On the Relation of Analytical Psychology to Poetry," p. 248 [revised.— TRANS.].

376

The hero is not creative in the sense that he decorates and embellishes the existing canon, although his creativeness may also manifest itself in shaping and transforming the archetypal contents of his age. The true hero is one who brings the new and shatters the fabric of old values, namely the father-dragon which, backed by the whole weight of tradition and the power of the collective, ever strives to obstruct the birth of the new.

The creators form the progressive element in a community, but at the same time they are the conservatives who link back to the origins. In ever-renewed fights with the dragon they conquer new territory, establish new provinces of consciousness, and overthrow antiquated systems of knowledge and morality at the behest of the voice whose summons they follow, no matter whether they formulate their task as a religious vocation or as practical ethics. The depth of the unconscious layer from which the new springs, and the intensity with which this layer seizes upon the individual, are the real criteria of this summons by the voice, and not the ideology of the conscious mind.

By means of the symbol, the archetypes break through the creative person into the conscious world of culture. It is this deeper-lying reality that fertilizes, transforms, and broadens the life of the collective, giving it and the individual the background which alone endows life with a meaning. The meaning of religion and art is positive and synthetic, not only in primitive cultures, but also in our own overconscious culture, precisely because they provide an outlet for contents and emotional components that have been too rigorously suppressed. In the collective as in the individual the patriarchal world of culture, with its primacy of consciousness, forms only a segment of the whole. The positive forces of the collective unconscious which have been excluded struggle for expression in the creative person and flow through him into the community. Partly they are "old" forces, shut out through the overdifferentiation of culture, partly new and untried forces which are destined to shape the face of the future.

Both functions help to keep culture "in balance" by ensuring

377

that it does not stray too far from its roots or, on the other hand, ossify through conservatism.

But the hero, as the vehicle of this effort at compensation, becomes alienated from the normal human situation and from the collective. This decollectivization entails suffering, and he suffers at the same time because, in his struggle for freedom, he is also the victim and representative of the obsolete, old order and is forced to bear the burden of it in his own soul.

The significance of this fact has already been pointed out by Jung,[17] who speaks of the fatal compulsion that draws the hero towards sacrifice and suffering.

Whether his deeds are looked upon as services, as with Herakles, whose life, like the life of many if not all heroes, is a series of strenuous labors and difficult tasks, or whether this symbolism takes the form of a bull-sacrifice as with Mithras, or crucifixion as with Jesus, or being chained to the Caucasus as with Prometheus, always and everywhere we meet with the motif of sacrifice and suffering.

The sacrifice to be made may mean sacrificing the old matriarchal world of childhood or the real world of the adult; sometimes the future has to be sacrificed for the sake of the present, sometimes the present so that the hero may fulfill the future. The nature of the hero is as manifold as the agonizing situations of real life. But always he is compelled to sacrifice normal living in whatever form it may touch him, whether it be mother, father, child, homeland, sweetheart, brother, or friend.

Jung puts it that the danger to which the hero is exposed is "isolation in himself." [18] The suffering entailed by the very fact of being an ego and an individual is implicit in the hero's situation of having to distinguish himself psychologically from his fellows. He sees things they do not see, does not fall for the things they fall for—but that means that he is a different type of human being and therefore necessarily alone. The loneliness of Prometheus on the rock or of Christ on the cross is the sacrifice

[17] *Symbols of Transformation.*
[18] Ibid.

378

they have to endure for having brought fire and redemption to mankind.

Whereas the average individual has no soul of his own, because the group and its canon of values tell him what he may or may not be psychically, the hero is one who can call his soul his own because he has fought for it and won it. Hence there can be no heroic and creative activity without winning the anima, and the individual life of the hero is in the deepest sense bound up with the psychic reality of the anima.

Creation is always an individual achievement, for every creative work or deed is something new that was not there before, unique and not to be repeated. Thus the anima component of the personality is connected with the "voice" which expresses the creative element in the individual, contrasted with the conventionality of the father, of the collective, of conscience. The anima as prophetess and priestess is the archetype of the soul who conceives the Logos, the "spermatic word" of God. She is the inspirer and the inspired, the Virgin Sophia who conceives by the Holy Ghost, and the Virgin Mother who brings forth the Logos-spirit-son.

In the early uroboric and matriarchal phase there is only the type of the seer who, by sacrificing his ego, and so having become effeminate by identification with the Great Mother, delivers himself of his utterances under the overwhelming impact of the unconscious. This type of seer is widely distributed. The best known is the mantic form, in which a woman plays the prophetic role of seer and priestess, sibyl and Pythia. Her function is later taken over by the masculine seer-priest who is identified with her. This can still be seen in Wotan's relation to Erda. He receives the age-old wisdom of the Great Mother, the gift of prophecy, but in return has to sacrifice his right eye. Thus, with its ecstatic abandon and berserker frenzies of emotion, Wotanism, in its orgiastic as well as its mantic form, lacks the clear eye of the higher knowledge, which was lost through the "upper castration" performed by Erda.

The dark Wotan type of savage huntsman and of Flying

379

Dutchman belong to the retinue of the Great Mother. Behind their spiritual unrest there is the old longing for uroboric incest, the death wish that seems so deeply engrained in the Germanic soul.[19]

It is no accident that we find a powerful contrast to this mother-obsessed seer type in the kind of prophet who arose among the ancient Hebrews. His essential characteristic is his affinity with the father-figure, and the preservation and intensification of consciousness by means of this affinity. For him, mantic and oneiromantic prophecy is much inferior to prophecy with consciousness unimpaired. The prophetic intensity depends upon the intensity of consciousness, and Moses is rated the greatest prophet because he beheld God by day and face to face. In other words, the profound insight of the activated transpersonal layer, and the sharp vision of a highly developed consciousness, have to be brought into relationship, and not one developed at the expense of the other.

Thus the hero, like the ego, stands between two worlds: the inner world that threatens to overwhelm him, and the outer world that wants to liquidate him for breaking the old laws. Only the hero can stand his ground against these collective forces, because he is the exemplar of individuality and possesses the light of consciousness.

Notwithstanding its original hostility the collective later accepts the hero into its pantheon, and his creative quality lives on—at least in the Western canon—as a value. The paradox that the breaker of the old canon is incorporated in the canon itself is typical of the creative character of Western consciousness whose special position we have repeatedly stressed. The tradition in which the ego is brought up demands emulation of the hero in so far as he has created the canon of current values. That is to say, consciousness, moral responsibility, freedom, etc., count as the supreme good. The individual is educated up to them, but woe to any who dares to flout the cultural values, for

[19] Jung, "Wotan"; Ninck, *Wodan und germanischer Schicksalsglaube*.

he will instantly be outlawed by the collective as the breaker of the old tablets.

Only the hero can destroy the old and extricate himself from the toils of his culture by a creative assault upon it, but normally its compensatory structure must be preserved at all costs by the collective. Its resistance to the hero and its expulsion of him are justifiable as a defense against imminent collapse. For a collapse such as the innovations of the Great Individual bring with them is a portentous event for millions of people. When an old cultural canon is demolished, there follows a period of chaos and destruction which may last for centuries, and in which hecatombs of victims are sacrificed until a new, stable canon is established, with a compensatory structure strong enough to guarantee a modicum of security to the collective and the individual.

The Schism of the Systems: Culture in Crisis

It now remains for us to describe how, in the course of development, the emancipation of consciousness has precipitated a crisis, and how the separation of the conscious from the unconscious has led to the danger of a schism. At this point we enter into the cultural crisis of our time and of Western development as a whole. We can only attempt to follow out the psychological trends already described and thus make whatever contribution is possible, within the limits of our theme, towards an understanding of the cultural problems. The temptation to go beyond that is great, since the questions touched upon are of a burning topicality; but here, as in so many places, we must content ourselves with hints and can only point to the phenomena without embarking upon a discussion of causal connections.[20]

Western culture, whose crisis we are experiencing today, differs from all others known to us in that, although a continuum, it finds itself in continual process of change, even if the degree of change is not always equally apparent. The conventional

[20] In Appendix II we enlarge upon certain of the problems broached here.

division into classical, medieval, and modern is wholly fallacious. Any deeper analysis will show a picture of Western man in continuous movement and countermovement, but moving steadily in a direction fixed from the very beginning: toward the emancipation of man from nature and consciousness from unconscious. The cultural canon of the medieval man is likewise embedded in this continuum, not only because of the emphasis which that canon laid upon the individual soul and its salvation, but also because of its spiritual heritage from classical antiquity, which was far from being a mere matter of outward form, as all church history shows.

Despite the tendency to conservatism innate in every canon, the Western canon also has in it a revolutionary ingredient deriving from its acceptance of the hero archetype. It goes without saying that this hero figure is not the central point of the canon, nor is its revolutionary influence very easy to recognize; but when one sees in how short a space of time the most revolutionary figures of ecclesiastical history became assimilated and produced a new variation of the canon, one realizes the full significance of the acceptance into it of the hero archetype. The sanctity of the individual soul, which asserted itself throughout the Middle Ages in spite of all orthodoxy and all burnings of heretics, has become secularized since the Renaissance, though it was in existence long before that.

It is the same with the accentuation of individual consciousness. The recollectivization that was so conspicuous a feature of the Middle Ages as compared with antiquity is more a sociological than a theological problem. In recent times—that is, during the last one hundred and fifty years—we have witnessed an analogous process taking place in quite untheological form, and so are in a better position to understand the connection between them. We refer to the problem of the masses, which, owing to the Christianization of the backward peoples of Europe, led to a recollectivization that contrasted very strongly with the high standard of individual consciousness attained by the cultured man of antiquity. And today also, when the downtrodden masses

382

and the Asiatic masses are entering into history, there must inevitably be a temporary leveling down of consciousness and of individual culture in comparison with the single individual as the end product of Western civilization since the Renaissance.

The four phenomena—aggregation of masses, decay of the old canon, the schism between conscious and unconscious, and the divorce between individual and collective—run parallel to one another. How far they are causally connected is difficult to determine. At all events it is patently clear today that in the mass collective a new canon is being formed. Psychologically a primitive collective situation predominates, and in this new collective the old laws of *participation mystique* are more prevalent than at any time during the last few centuries of Western development.

This psychologically reactionary massing together of modern man coincides with another sociological phenomenon, namely the entry into history of new primary racial groups. That is to say, one must not confuse the primitive collective situation of the Asian masses now entering history with the phenomena of recollectivization, where untold millions of highly individualized and overspecialized city dwellers regress to a mass collective (see Appendix II). The intermingling of progressive and regressive lines of development is one of the complications of modern collective and cultural psychology.

Although standing from the very beginning under the motto "Away from the unconscious," the ego, as the organ of centroversion, must never lose touch with it, for it is an essential part of its natural balancing function to give the transpersonal world its due place.

The development that has brought about the division of the two systems is in accord with a necessary process of psychic differentiation, but, like all differentiation, it runs the risk of becoming overdifferentiated and perverse. Just as the differentiation of conscious functions in the individual harbors in itself the danger of overdifferentiation and one-sidedness, so the development of Western consciousness as a whole has not escaped

383

this danger. The question now arises of how far conscious differentiation can proceed and where it begins to turn into its opposite; that is, at what point in the hero's development there arises the danger of a mutation which, as so many of the myths tell us, will lead to his downfall.

Too much stability can cramp the ego, a too independent ego consciousness can become insulated from the unconscious, and self-esteem and self-responsibility can degenerate into presumption and megalomania. In other words, consciousness, standing at the opposite pole to the unconscious, and originally having to represent the personality's striving for wholeness, may lose its link with the whole and deteriorate.[21]

The danger of alienation from the unconscious presents itself in two forms: sclerosis of consciousness, and possession. In a sclerotic consciousness—a late product of development which on that account is unknown to mythology—the autonomy of the conscious system has been carried so far that the living link with the unconscious becomes dangerously atrophied. This atrophy expresses itself in the loss to ego consciousness of the function which strives for wholeness, and in a growing neuroticism of the personality.

Possession, the second form of loss of relationship to the unconscious, presents a different picture. Here the conscious system is overpowered by the spirit, with the help of which it had struggled to free itself from the tyranny of the unconscious. We have termed this phenomenon "patriarchal castration," because the creative activity of the ego is here impeded by the father, as previously by the mother.

In contrast to the swamping of the ego by the unconscious, which ends with the dismemberment of consciousness, the main feature here is an illimitable expansion of the ego.

Matriarchal castration involves loss of masculine consciousness, deflation, and degradation of the ego. Its symptoms are depression, a flowing off of libido into the unconscious, anemia of

[21] This phenomenon, which is central to all psychic illnesses, forms part of the general theory of neurosis.

384

the conscious system, and an *"abaissement du niveau mental"* (Janet).

In the inflation of patriarchal castration brought on by the ego's identification with the spirit, the process is the other way around. It leads to megalomania and overexpansion of the conscious system. The latter becomes surcharged with spiritual contents which it cannot assimilate and with libido units belonging to the unconscious. The ruling symbol of this condition is "ascension," and its symptoms are "losing the ground from under one's feet," loss of the body rather than dismemberment, mania rather than depression.

The mania is connected with all the signs of overaccentuation of the conscious system, such as intensified associations, sometimes amounting to an associative "fugue," paroxysms of will and action, senseless optimism, and so forth, all of which contrast with the slowing down of association, the enfeeblement of will and action, and the pessimism so evident in the depressive phase. Just as identification with the Great Mother causes enfeeblement of the masculine side of consciousness and impoverishes the activity of the will and the ego's directive powers, so identification with the spiritual father enfeebles the feminine side. Consciousness lacks the unconscious counterweights that would deepen and slow down the conscious processes. In both forms there is a disturbance of compensation, but in each case it is different.

Compensation is the first requisite for a productive relationship between the ego and the unconscious. This means that the princess, the soul, is lost to the ego just as much in the patriarchal as in the matriarchal form of castration.

But, as we have made clear in Part I of this book, behind both forms there looms the original uroboric castration, where the tendencies to differentiation cancel out. To put it in psychological language: just as mania and melancholia are merely two forms of madness, of the devouring uroboric state which destroys all ego consciousness, so regression to the unconscious, i.e., being devoured by the Great Mother, and the flight to "nothing but" consciousness, i.e., being devoured by the spiritual father, are two forms in which any truly compensated consciousness, and the striving for wholeness, are lost. Deflation as well as inflation destroys the efficacy of consciousness, and both of them are defeats for the ego.

Spiritual inflation, a perfect example of which is the frenziedness of Nietzsche's *Zarathustra,* is a typical Western development carried to extremes. Behind the overaccentuation of consciousness, ego, and reason—sensible enough in themselves as the guiding aims of psychic development—there stands the overwhelming might of "heaven" as the danger which goes beyond the heroic struggle with the earthly side of the dragon and culminates in a spirituality that has lost touch with reality and the instincts.

The form which this kind of degeneration usually takes in the West is not spiritual inflation, but sclerosis of consciousness, where the ego identifies with consciousness as a form of spirit. In most cases this means identifying spirit with intellect, and consciousness with thinking. Such a limitation is utterly unjustified, but the patriarchal trend of development "away from the unconscious" and towards consciousness and thinking makes the identification understandable.

Owing to this extremism the conscious system loses its true significance as the compensatory organ of centroversion whose function is to represent and realize the wholeness of the psyche. The ego degenerates into a psychic complex like any other, and exhibits in its egocentricity the self-obsession which is characteristic of every complex.

In this situation all the developments that have contributed in a meaningful way to the formation of consciousness go to extremes and become perverted. For instance, the splitting of an unconscious content into its material and emotional components was originally in the interests of conscious development, but now it is one of the critical features of a hypertrophied consciousness split off from the unconscious. The exhaustion of emotional components and the ego's alienation from the world of archetypal images result in its inability to react to sense-images at all, a fact which is particularly noticeable in modern man. Confrontation with an unconscious image, or even with an unexpected situation, finds him immune to reaction. Contrasted with the instantaneous reflex action of the primitive, the interval between situation and reaction is extraordinarily prolonged, if it is not abrogated altogether.

Loss of affectivity and emotionality, still further increased by the specialized differentiation of consciousness into separate functions, is certainly an essential condition of conscious activity and has undoubtedly helped modern man in his scientific pursuits, but it has a formidable shadow side. To the extent that conscious knowledge necessitates the suppression of emotional components, it is typical of and only advantageous to noncreative work. Creative processes, on the other hand, cannot and must not exclude powerfully emotional, and even excitatory, components; indeed they seem to be a necessary ingredient here. Every new conception and every creative idea comprise elements which up to that point were unconscious, and the inclusion of the emotional components associated with unconscious contents produces an excitation. The connection of the conscious system with the emotionally toned substrata of the unconscious alone makes creativity possible. Therefore, if carried to extremes, the differentiating and emotion-repressing trend of Western development has a sterilizing effect and hampers the widening of consciousness. This is confirmed by the fact that creative people always have something childlike and not fully differentiated about them; they are plasmatic centers of creativity, and it is quite beside the point to call such features "infantile" and try to reduce them to the level of the family romance.

This tendency to reduce all transpersonal contents to personalistic terms is the most extreme form of secondary personalization. The exhaustion of emotional components and secondary personalization have an important historical function to fulfill, in so far as they help to extricate ego consciousness and the individual from the clutches of the unconscious. That explains why they always appear during the transition from the prepersonal and suprapersonal to the personal. But when secondary personalization seeks to assert itself by devaluing the transpersonal forces, it produces a dangerous overvaluation of the ego. It is a typical false constellation of the modern mind, which is no longer capable of seeing anything that transcends the personal sphere of ego consciousness.

Secondary personalization is now being exploited by Western man in order to devalue the unconscious forces of which he is afraid. The supremacy of the transpersonal, and hence of the unconscious which, psychically speaking, is the seat of transpersonality, is denigrated and defamed. This form of apotropaic defense-magic invariably attempts to explain away and exorcize anything dangerous with a glib "nothing but" or "it's not half so bad as you think." Much as the wild and treacherous Black Sea was euphemistically called the "Euxine," the "hospitable sea," or the Erinyes were renamed the Eumenides, and the abysmal unknowableness of Godhead became the "All-loving and Merciful Father" and the "eiapopeia of children," so now we mistake the transpersonal for the merely personal. The primordial divinity of the Creator and the fierce, infinitely strange, ancestral totem-animal that dwells in the human soul have been so garbled that they now purport to derive from a prehistoric gorilla father or from a deposit of many such fathers, who have not conducted themselves well towards their "children."

Even the exaggerations of secondary personalization are expressions of man's efforts to regain possession of exteriorized psychic contents by introjecting them. But the necessary consequence of this process, whereby contents that before seemed to be outside are diagnosed as inside, is that transpersonal forces now appear in the human psyche and are recognized as "psychic factors." When this happens, partially in the psychology of instinct, and quite consciously in Jung's theory of archetypes, it means that an adequate assimilation has been achieved. But when secondary personalization is perverted, it leads to an over-

388

expansion of the ego, which thereupon tries to demolish the transpersonal by calling it mere illusion and reducing it to personalistic ego data.

As a result, the whole meaning of secondary personalization as a prerequisite for conscious assimilation is done away with, because the transpersonal is now in fact repressed. It can no longer be consciously assimilated, and proceeds to work negatively as a vague and powerful "unconscious" factor inside the psyche, just as it did outside at the beginning of man's development. The problematical thing about this turn of events is that in itself it is legitimate and necessary, and only leads to absurdity and danger if exaggerated.

We find a corresponding process in rationalization, where the archetype is elaborated into a concept. The line runs, as we saw, from the archetype as an effective transpersonal figure to the idea, and then to the "concept" which one "forms." A good example of this is the concept of God, which now derives wholly from the sphere of consciousness—or purports to derive from it, as the ego is deluded enough to pretend. There is no longer anything transpersonal, but only personal; there are no more archetypes, but only concepts; no more symbols, only signs.

This splitting off of the unconscious leads on the one hand to an ego life emptied of meaning, and on the other hand to an activation of the deeper-lying layers which, now grown destructive, devastate the autocratic world of the ego with transpersonal invasions, collective epidemics, and mass psychoses. For an upsetting of the compensatory relationship between conscious and unconscious is not a phenomenon to be taken lightly. Even when it is not so acute as to bring on a psychic sickness, the loss of instinct and the overaccentuation of the ego have consequences which, multiplied a millionfold, constellate the crisis of civilization.

While we cannot follow out here the psychological and ethical consequences of this situation as they affect the individual in his relation to the group,[22] we must still dwell for a moment

[22] See my *Depth Psychology and a New Ethic.*

upon what has been called the modern decay of values, and which we prefer to describe as the collapse of the archetypal canon.

The cultural canon originates in the projection of archetypal images from the unconscious. Its effectiveness may vary, either because the consciousness of the group undergoes a progressive or a regressive mutation, or because modifications occur in the collective unconscious, spontaneously, or in reaction to social and political changes. We shall have to leave unexamined the question of when, and in what circumstances, changes in the real world lead to reactions in the collective unconscious, and when and in what circumstances modifications in the collective unconscious express themselves in sociological upheavals. That the canon of values has steadily been disintegrating over the last few hundred years of Western development is a truism, which does not, however, prevent us from experiencing with horror and amazement the grim consequences of this process in the past, in the present, and in the future.

The disintegration of the old system of values is in full swing. God, King, Fatherland, have become problematical quantities, and so have Liberty, Equality, Fraternity, love and fair play, human progress, and the meaning of existence. This is not to say that they will not continue to influence our lives as transpersonal quantities of an archetypal nature; but their validity, or at least their position, has become precarious, their relation to one another questionable, and their old hierarchical order has been destroyed.

In this way the individual who lacks the support of a compensatory movement inside himself drops out of the ordered fabric of civilization. For him this means the breakdown of transpersonal experience, a shrinking of world horizons, and the loss of all certainty and meaning in life.

Two general reactions are to be observed in this situation. The first is regression to the Great Mother, into unconsciousness, a readiness to herd together in masses, and so, as a collective atom with new transpersonal experiences, to gain a new certainty and

390

a new point of vantage; the second is flight to the Great Father, into the isolation of individualism.

When the individual falls away from the cultural fabric like this, he finds himself completely isolated in an egotistically inflated private world. The restlessness, the discontents, the excesses, the formlessness and meaninglessness of a purely egocentric life—as compared with the symbolic life—are the unhappy results of this psychological apostasy.

Following the collapse of the archetypal canon, single archetypes then take possession of men and consume them like malevolent demons. Typical and symptomatic of this transitional phenomenon is the state of affairs in America, though the same holds good for practically the whole Western hemisphere. Every conceivable sort of dominant rules the personality, which is a personality only in name. The grotesque fact that murderers, brigands, gangsters, thieves, forgers, tyrants, and swindlers, in a guise that deceives nobody, have seized control of collective life is characteristic of our time. Their unscrupulousness and double-dealing are recognized—and admired. Their ruthless energy they obtain at best from some stray archetypal content that has got them in its power. The dynamism of a possessed personality is accordingly very great, because, in its one-track primitivity, it suffers from none of the differentiations that make men human. Worship of the "beast" is by no means confined to Germany; it prevails wherever one-sidedness, push, and moral blindness are applauded, i.e., wherever the aggravating complexities of civilized behavior are swept away in favor of bestial rapacity. One has only to look at the educative ideals now current in the West.

The possessed character of our financial and industrial magnates, for instance, is psychologically evident from the very fact that they are at the mercy of a suprapersonal factor—"work," "power," "money," or whatever they like to call it—which, in the telling phrase, "consumes" them and leaves them little or no room as private persons. Coupled with a nihilistic attitude towards civilization and humanity there goes a puffing up of the ego-sphere which expresses itself with brutish egotism in a total disregard for the common good and in the attempt to lead an egocentric existence, where personal power, money, and "experiences"—unbelievably trivial, but plentiful—occupy every hour of the day.

Formerly the stability of the cultural canon guaranteed the individual a set of ordered values in which everything had its proper place. This is now lost, and the atomized individual is possessed and eaten up by arbitrary dominants of a suprapersonal nature.

Not only power, money, and lust, but religion, art, and politics as exclusive determinants in the form of parties, nations, sects, movements, and "isms" of every description take possession of the masses and destroy the individual. Far be it from us to compare the predatory industrial man and power politician with the man who is dedicated to an idea; for the latter is possessed by the archetypes that shape the future of mankind, and to this driving daemon he sacrifices his life. Nevertheless, it is the task of a cultural psychology based on depth psychology to set forth a new ethos which shall take the collective effect of these daemonic possessions into account, and this means also accepting responsibility for them.

The disintegration of personality caused by an idea is no less dangerous than the disintegration caused by empty, personalistic power-strivings. The results of both can be seen in the disastrous massing together and recollectivization of modern man (see Appendix II). Elsewhere [23] we have attempted to show the connection between depth psychology and the new ethos. One of the most important consequences of the new ethos is that integration of the personality, its wholeness, becomes the supreme ethical goal upon which the fate of humanity depends. And even though depth psychology has taught us to understand how necessary it is, especially for the "highest men," to be possessed

[23] *Depth Psychology and a New Ethic.*

by the archetypes, this does not blind us to the possible fatal consequences of such possession.

The picture we have drawn of our age is not intended as an indictment, much less as a glorification of the "good old days"; for the phenomena we see around us are symptoms of an upheaval which, taken by and large, is necessary. The collapse of the old civilization, and its reconstruction on a lower level to begin with, will justify themselves because the new basis will have been immensely broadened. The civilization that is about to be born will be a human civilization in a far higher sense than any has ever been before, as it will have overcome important social, national, and racial limitations. These are not fantastic pipe dreams, but hard facts, and their birth pangs will bring infinite suffering upon infinite numbers of men. Spiritually, politically, and economically our world is an indivisible whole. By this standard the Napoleonic wars were minor *coups d'état*, and the world view of that age, in which anything outside Europe had hardly begun to appear, is almost inconceivable to us in its narrowness.

The collapse of the archetypal canon in our culture, which has produced such an extraordinary activation of the collective unconscious—or is perhaps its symptom, manifesting itself in mass movements that have a profound effect upon our personal destinies—is, however, only a passing phenomenon. Already, at a time when the internecine wars of the old canon are still being waged, we can discern, in single individuals, where the synthetic possibilities of the future lie, and almost how it will look. The turning of the mind from the conscious to the unconscious, the responsible *rapprochement* of human consciousness with the powers of the collective psyche, that is the task of the future. No outward tinkerings with the world and no social ameliorations can give the quietus to the daemon, to the gods and devils of the human soul, or prevent them from tearing down again and again what consciousness has built. Unless they are assigned their place in consciousness and culture they will never leave mankind in peace. But the preparation for this *rapprochement*

393

lies, as always, with the hero, the individual; he and his transformation are the great human prototypes; he is the testing ground of the collective, just as consciousness is the testing ground of the unconscious.

D. Centroversion and the Stages
of Life

Pilgrim, Pilgrimage, and Way
are but Myself toward Myself.
FARID UD-DIN ATTAR

Prolongation of Childhood and Differentiation of Consciousness

IN PART I we discussed the archetypal phases of conscious development as manifested in the mythological projections of humanity's collective unconscious. In Part II an attempt is made to show how and why the personality comes to be built up in the course of human history, and in what relation it stands to the archetypal phases.

Now, in this concluding chapter, we must show how the basic laws whose operation we have been tracing in the psychic history of mankind are recapitulated, in modified form, in the ontogenetic life history of the individual in our culture.

Only a tentative sketch is possible, because we cannot here present the reader with a detailed psychology of childhood and puberty. Nevertheless, it seems important to give a brief outline of this development, because in this way the connection between man's evolutionary history and modern life, and the life of every individual, will become apparent. Indeed, this link between ontogenesis and human history alone gives us the justification for having ranged so far afield in our exposition of the latter subject, and for claiming at the same time that the real concern of this book is the treatment of modern man and his urgent problems.

A psychotherapy of the individual, and a culture therapy of society as a whole, seem to us to be possible only when we have achieved a synoptic view of the origin and significance of consciousness and its history, such as will enable us to diagnose the conscious situation of the individual and of the collective.

The recognition of the crucial importance, for psychology and psychotherapy, of the stages of life, and the discovery of the individuation process as a development which takes place during the second half of life, we owe to the researches of C. G. Jung.[1]

[1] "The Stages of Life"; also cf. G. Adler, "The Ego and the Cycle of Life," in *Studies in Analytical Psychology*.

397

The most important factors for the understanding of individual development are the different direction and different effect of centroversion in the two life phases. The first phase, which is one of differentiation, has its historical prototype in the formation of the ego and its development, that is, when the activity of centroversion passes from the psychic totality of the unconscious self and moves towards the ego.

During the first half of life, a period of egocentering which is finalized in puberty, centroversion expresses itself as a compensatory relation between the conscious and unconscious systems, but remains unconscious; in other words, the central organ of centroversion, the ego, has no knowledge of its dependence upon the whole. During the second half of life, however, which is generally ushered in by a psychological change of personality in middle age, there is in the ego a growing awareness of centroversion. The individuation process may then be initiated, resulting in the constellation of the self as the psychic center of wholeness, which no longer acts only unconsciously but is consciously experienced.

The retardation of maturity and the dependence of the individual upon the social group for a period of almost sixteen years are, as we know, pre-eminently characteristic of the human species. This prolonged youth, contrasted with the early development of the rest of the animal world, is the most important prerequisite for human culture and its transmission. The inclusion of a lengthy period of learning and training until full maturity is reached has its counterpart in the unfolding of consciousness throughout human history. During this period the brain is developed up to the level to which man as a species has brought it. The learning period that ends with puberty is devoted to cultural education, consisting in the adoption of collective values and the differentiation of consciousness which facilitates the individual's adaptation to the world and the collective.[2]

[2] In his *Biologische Fragmente zur Lehre vom Menschen*, which became available to me only after the completion of my manuscript, A. Portmann expresses views that coincide to a surprising degree with my own. The fact that we have

Lastly, there also occurs in this period a further differentiation of personality, whose final stage we then find in the adult, and whose development, so far as it follows the patriarchal trend of conscious evolution, we shall briefly outline.

Education and increasing experience of life strengthen the adaptation to reality, which is more or less identical with adaptation to the collective and its demands. Meanwhile the collective compels the individual, however different his orientation may be at the different periods, to develop a one-sidedness which is at all times acceptable to itself.

Various factors collaborate in this adaptation. Their common denominator is the strengthening of consciousness and of its capacity for action, and the simultaneous exclusion of the disruptive forces of the unconscious.

One of these factors is the differentiation of the psychological type. That is to say, every individual will adopt a definite attitude to the world, either extraverted or introverted. Side by side with the habitual attitude there is a further differentiation of one of the main functions of consciousness, which function differs in every individual.[3] This differentiation of type, whether conditioned constitutionally or otherwise, guarantees him the maximum opportunities for adaptation, because the most efficient and congenitally the best function is developed as the main function. Simultaneously with this differentiation there is a suppression of the least efficient function, which, as the "inferior function," remains largely unconscious.

An important goal of childhood development and education is the utilization of the individual in the sense of making him a useful member of the community. This usefulness, achieved through differentiation of the separate components and functions of the personality, is necessarily bought at the cost of wholeness. The need to renounce the unconscious wholeness of the

---

arrived at the same conclusions, although approaching from two such different points of departure as biology and depth psychology, speaks not a little for the objectivity of these conclusions.

[3] Jung, *Psychological Types,* defs. 14, 22, 55.

399

personality is one of the most formidable developmental difficulties for the child, and particularly for the introverted child.

The transition from the "totality orientation" of the small child, from direction by the unconscious activity of the self to an ego-centered consciousness and the necessary division of the whole into two separate systems, forms a special difficulty. In this critical phase the heritage bequeathed to mankind by the hero—the systematic development of consciousness and its protection—must be re-experienced by the childhood ego and made fast in its possession if it is to gain access to the culture of the collective and command a place for itself in the community.

Development in the first half of life is marked by two decisive crises, each of which corresponds to a fight with the dragon. The first crisis is characterized by the encounter with the problem of the First Parents and by the formation of the ego. It is enacted between the ages of three and five, and psychoanalysis has made us familiar with certain aspects and forms of this parental encounter, under the guise of the Oedipus complex. The second crisis is puberty, when the dragon fight has to be fought out again on a new level. Here the form of the ego is finally fixed with the support of what we have called "heaven." That is to say, new archetypal constellations emerge, and with them a new relation of the ego to the self.

Characteristic of the process of differentiation in childhood is the loss and renunciation of all the elements of perfection and wholeness, which are inherent in the psychology of the child so far as this is determined by the pleroma, the uroboros. The very things which the child has in common with the man of genius, the creative artist, and the primitive, and which constitute the magic and charm of his existence, must be sacrificed. The aim of all education, and not in our culture alone, is to expel the child from the paradise of his native genius and, through differentiation and the renunciation of wholeness, to constrain the Old Adam into the paths of collective usefulness.

From the pleasure principle to the reality principle as we have defined it, from the mother's darling to the schoolboy, from uroboros to hero, such is the normal course of childhood development. The drying up of imagination and of creative ability, which the child naturally possesses in high degree, is one of the typical symptoms of impoverishment that growing up entails. A steady loss of the vitality of feeling and of spontaneous reactions in the interests of "sensibleness" and "good behavior" is the operative factor in the conduct now demanded of the child in relation to the collective. Increase in efficiency at the cost of depth and intensity is the hallmark of this process.

On the ontogenetic plane there now ensue all the developments which we have described as indispensable for ego formation and the separation of the conscious and unconscious systems. The child's primarily transpersonal and mythological apperception of the world [4] becomes limited owing to secondary personalization, and is finally abolished altogether. This personalization is necessary for the growth of personality now beginning and is effected with the help of ties to the personal environment upon which the archetypes are at first projected. As the personal ties grow stronger, the archetype is gradually replaced by the imago, in which personal and transpersonal characteristics are visibly blended and active. In this way the transpersonal archetypes are "blocked" by the personal figures of the environment to whom the ego relates. Or, as Rilke says:

... not quite can you call him away from that sinister company.
Truly, he tries, he escapes, and nestles disburdened
into your secret heart, where he takes and is newly begun.
But, did he ever begin himself?
Mother, you made him small, it was you who began him;
to you he was new, and over the young
eyes you bent down a world that was friendly and staved off the strange.
Where, O where are the years when you simply, by stepping in front of it,
screened with your slender figure the seething abyss?
Much you did hide from him thus; the room that was creepy at night
you made harmless, and out of your heart full of refuge
you mingled a humaner space with his night-space.[5]

[4] Jung, Seminar on children's dreams (unpublished); Wickes, *The Inner World of Childhood;* Fordham, *The Life of Childhood.*
[5] R. M. Rilke, Third Elegy.

Then follows the fragmentation of archetypes and the separation of the personal "good" side of the Mother figure from her transpersonal, negative side, or vice versa. The child's fear and feeling of being threatened does not derive from the traumatic character of the world, for no trauma exists under normal human conditions or even under primitive ones; it comes rather from the "night space," or, to be more precise, it arises when the ego steps forth from this night space. The germinal ego consciousness then experiences the overwhelming impact of the world-and-body stimulus, either directly or in projection. The importance of family relationships lies precisely in the fact that the personal figures of the environment who are the first form of society must be able, as soon as the ego emerges from the primary security of the uroboric state, to offer it the secondary security of the human world.

This development is paralleled by the exhaustion of emotional components and the outgrowing of the early accentuation of the body, and this in turn leads to the gradual building up of a superego through the demands and prohibitions of the environment.

Another general feature of conscious development, namely the deflation of the unconscious, can be traced in the normal growth of the child, when the primordial, unconscious world of childhood, the world of dream and fairy tale, and also of children's drawings and children's games, fades in increasing measure before the reality of the external world. The libido accruing from the activated unconscious is now employed to build up and extend the conscious system. The implementation of this process marks the transition from playing to learning. School in our culture is the architect whom the collective has commissioned to erect, systematically, a bastion between the deflated unconscious and a consciousness orientated towards collective adaptation.

The patriarchal line of conscious development with its watchword "Away from the Mother-world! Forward to the Father-world!" is enjoined upon male and female alike, although they

402

may follow it in different ways. To be a mother's darling is a sign of not having accomplished the initial dragon fight which brings infancy to a close. This failure makes entry into school and the world of other children impossible, just as failure in the rites of initiation at puberty precludes entry into the adult world of men and women.

We come now to the formation of those components of personality whose discovery we owe to the analytical psychology of Jung: the persona, the anima and animus figures, and the shadow. They are produced by the differentiation processes we have already described, which occur during the first half of life. In all of them, personalistic and individual features are combined with archetypal and transpersonal ones, and the personality components which ordinarily exist in the structure of the psyche as potential psychic organs now become amalgamated with the fateful, individual variants realized by the individual in the course of his development.

The development of the persona is the outcome of a process of adaptation that suppresses all individually significant features and potentialities, disguising and repressing them in favor of collective factors, or those deemed desirable by the collective. Here again, wholeness is exchanged for a workable and successful sham personality. The "inner voice" is stifled by the growth of a superego, of conscience, the representative of collective values. The voice, the individual experience of the transpersonal, which is particularly strong in childhood, is renounced in favor of conscience. When paradise is abandoned, the voice of God that spoke in the Garden is abandoned too, and the values of the collective, of the fathers, of law and conscience, of the current morality, etc., must be accepted as the supreme values in order to make social adaptation possible.

Whereas the natural disposition of every individual inclines him to be physically and psychically bisexual, the differential development of our culture forces him to thrust the contrasexual element into the unconscious. As a result, only those elements which accord with the outward characteristics of sex and which

403

conform to the collective valuation are recognized by the conscious mind. Thus "feminine" or "soulful" characteristics are considered undesirable in a boy, at least in our culture. Such a one-sided accentuation of one's specific sexuality ends by constellating the contrasexual element in the unconscious, in the form of the anima in men and the animus in women, which, as part souls, remain unconscious and dominate the conscious-unconscious relationship. This process has the support of the collective, and sexual differentiation, precisely because the repression of the contrasexual element is often difficult, is at first accompanied by typical forms of animosity towards the opposite sex. This development, too, follows the general principle of differentiation which presupposes the sacrifice of wholeness, here represented by the figure of the hermaphrodite.

Similarly, as we saw, the formation of the shadow, the dark side of the personality, is partly determined by adaptation to the collective conscience.

The training of the will and the pursuance of directed and disciplined action at the cost of unconscious, instinctive reactivity is equally necessary for the adaptation to reality demanded of the growing child. Once more there is a repression of emotional components. The passion and affectivity of the small child give way to the control of affects and the repression of feeling observable in well-brought-up children.

The formation of all these "authorities" strengthens the ego, consciousness, and the will, and, by more or less insulating the instinctual side, leads to an increased tension within the personality. The identification of the ego with consciousness robs it of contact with the unconscious and thus of psychic wholeness. Consciousness can now claim to represent unity, but this unity is only the relative unity of the conscious mind and not that of the personality. Psychic wholeness is lost and is replaced by the dualistic principle of opposites which governs all conscious and unconscious constellations.

In a sense, therefore, the development and cultivation of consciousness required by the collective constitute at the same time a process of uprooting. The inner collective tie to the instincts must in large measure be given up, and, as a secondary security for the ego, new roots must be sunk in the subsoil of the collective and in its ruling canon of cultural values. This process of transplantation means moving from instinct-centeredness to ego-centeredness, and any failure here brings a crop of developmental disorders and illnesses.

Progression through the archetypal phases, the patriarchal orientation of consciousness, the formation of the superego as the representative of collective values within the personality, the existence of a collective value-canon, all these things are necessary conditions of normal, ethical development. If any one of these factors is inhibited, developmental disturbances result. A disturbance of the first two factors, which are specifically psychic, leads to neuroticism; a disturbance of the other two, which are cultural, expresses itself more in social maladjustment, delinquency, or criminality.

The average child not only survives this process of uprooting, but derives from it an enhanced inner tension. Relative loss of unity, polarization into two psychic systems, insulation of the inner world and the building up of authorities within the personality may be productive of conflict, but they cannot be said to lay the foundations of any neurotic development. They are on the contrary normative, and it is their absence, or rather their incompleteness, that leads to illness.

A certain one-sidedness of development favorable to consciousness is largely characteristic of our specifically Western psychic structure, which therefore includes conflict and sacrifice from the start. At the same time, however, such a structure has the innate capacity to make the conflict fruitful and to endow the sacrifice with a meaning. Centroversion expresses itself in the psyche as a striving for wholeness which, as life goes on, balances the one-sidedness of the first half by a compensatory development during the second half. The tensional conflict between conscious and unconscious, provided that the natural compensatory tendencies of the unconscious are at work, leads

405

to a steady growth of personality; and, with an intensification of the conscious-unconscious relationship in such a maturing personality, the original conflict is replaced by an ever richer and more complete synthesis.

But, to begin with, the differentiation and division which we found to be necessary in the development of mankind are also necessary for the individual, who in his own development retraces the old paths that mankind has trod. The tension arising from his inner psychic polarization forms the personality's energy potential and relates him to the world in two ways.

As ego consciousness increases there is a progressive transference of libido to the world, a cumulative "investment" of it in external objects. This transference of libido derives from two sources: on the one hand from the application of conscious interest by the ego, and on the other hand from the projection of unconscious contents. Whenever the energy-charge of unconscious contents becomes excessive, they discharge themselves from the unconscious and are projected. They now approach the conscious mind as world-animating images, and the ego experiences them as contents of that world. In this way projection results in an intensified fixation to the world and to the carriers of the projection.

This process is particularly noticeable in puberty. Activation of the unconscious, which at this period occurs as a parallel symptom to psychophysical change, manifests itself in the increased activity of the collective unconscious and of the archetypes; it far exceeds the activation of the sexual sphere, and its manifestations consist not only in the danger of invasion, as evidenced by the frequency of psychoses at this period, but more particularly in a newly fledged and passionate interest in everything suprapersonal, in ideas and ideals of universal import, which many people evince only at this period of heightened activity in the collective unconscious. Puberty is further characterized by a change of emotional tone, a feeling for life and the world more akin to the universal oneness of the dawn man than to the mood of the modern adult. This lyrical animation and the relatively frequent emergence of mythological motifs in the dreams and poetic compositions of this period are typical symptoms of the activation of the collective unconscious layer.

But since the compensatory working of consciousness is also heightened in puberty, it is only with markedly introverted or creative natures that there is any direct perception of the movement in the unconscious. Generally it passes off behind the dividing wall between the ego and the unconscious, and only faint radiations reach the conscious mind. Besides radiating out into interest and feeling, the activated unconscious also makes itself felt through "fascinating" projections which initiate and guarantee the next stage of normal development.

The most important projections at this period are of the anima or animus, the contrasexual imagos lying dormant in the unconscious, which now become activated. These glamorous images are projected into the world and sought there, thus constellating the problem of a partner, the main theme during the first half of life.

Activation of Collective Unconscious and Ego Changes in Puberty

The detachment from the parental imagos, i.e., from the real parents, which has to be effected in puberty, is caused, as the primitive rites of initiation show, by the activation of the archetype of the transpersonal or First Parents. This activation is utilized institutionally by and for the collective, in the sense that the latter requires and assists the projection of parental archetypes upon transpersonal contents which are also recognized as transpersonal realities. That is to say, the relation to the figure of the master, teacher, and leader—in a word, the mana personality [6] —is, as a projection of the father archetype, no less important than the projection of the mother archetype upon one's country, or upon the community, the Church, or a political

[6] Jung, "The Relations between the Ego and the Unconscious."

movement. Henceforward the life of the adolescent who has emerged from the family circle into the collective will largely be claimed and used by these contents.

The criterion of being "grown up" is that the individual is led out of the family circle and initiated into the world of the Great Life-Givers. Accordingly, puberty is a time of rebirth, and its symbolism is that of the hero who regenerates himself through fighting the dragon. All the rites characteristic of this period have the purpose of renewing the personality through a night sea journey, when the spiritual or conscious principle conquers the mother dragon, and the tie to the mother and to childhood, and also to the unconscious, is severed. The final stabilization of the ego, toilsomely achieved stage by stage, has its counterpart in the final dispatch of the mother dragon in puberty. Just as the detachment of the anima from the mother is effected in real life at this point in ontogenetic development, and the mother's importance is eclipsed by that of the soul-partner, so this time normally sees the conclusion of the fight with the mother dragon. The reborn is reborn through the father principle with which he identified himself in the initiation. He becomes the father's son without a mother, and, inasmuch as he is identical with the father, he is also the father of himself.[7]

Through the prepubertal period the ego has gradually been taking up a central position; now, in puberty, it finally becomes the carrier of individuality. The detachment from the unconscious—so far as this is necessary for the production of tension between the two systems—is complete. The puberty initiations are an expression of the activated collective unconscious, which is now linked to the community, since, in these rites, the archetypal canon is handed down as the spiritual world of the collective by the elders who represent "heaven." In this way the neophyte, even when not vouchsafed a personal revelation, as he is in the "guardian spirit" initiations among the North Ameri-

[7] The partial relegation of these puberty rites to early childhood is a typical sign of patriarchally toned cultures. Here the mother is replaced by the father at the very beginning of life, in the rites of circumcision and baptism, so that the maternal sphere is consciously and decisively narrowed.

408

can Indians, is led to a new experience of his central position within the collective. Being initiated and being grown up mean being a responsible member of the collective, for from now on the suprapersonal significance of the ego and the individual is built into the culture of the collective and its canon.

Self-Realization of Centroversion in the Second Half of Life

The first condition of this development is the successful termination of the hero fight, when the victor unites himself with the suprapersonal forces which appear to him in the spiritual world of initiation. The neophyte feels himself to be the heir to this world, for whose sake he takes up the earthly struggle. Whether he effects his separation from the world of the unconscious by giving recognition to the world of religion and ethics, or by his acceptance of taboos and religious laws, is a matter of secondary importance.

Victory means the self-generation of masculinity, and, like the dragon slayer, the victor is rewarded with the princess. Now that he has reached adulthood, and sexuality has become admissible, the beloved takes the place of the mother. He now has a sexual role to play, and he has at the same time to pursue an individual as well as a collective aim.

The first half of life is largely taken up with adapting to the powers of the outside world and their suprapersonal demands. The projection of the archetypes of the First Parents, and of the anima and animus, alone makes it possible for consciousness to develop in a worldly direction. It is the fascination of the archetypal images operative "behind" the lure of external reality that gives the psyche its outward gradient, a characteristic feature of all normal development in this phase.

This phase of development is marked by the gradual unfolding of consciousness and the multiplication of relationships to reality. The underlying trend is given by nature herself, and it corresponds to those inborn instincts and psychic mechanisms which promote the growth and stabilization of consciousness. The very fact that the unconscious, as it becomes activated in puberty, is literally turned "inside out" through the natural processes of assimilation and projection is an instance of this same trend.[8]

After puberty, the normal adult has a firm but resilient ego consciousness with a relatively large amount of free libido at its disposal, well insulated against the inroads of the unconscious without being incapsulated, and, in proportion to its capacity and libido-charge, positively orientated to a greater or lesser portion of the objective world. Consciousness and personality are formed, in extraverts and introverts alike, by their progressive mastery of the world and adaptation to it. An exception is the creative individual, in whom there is a surcharge of unconscious activity but whose conscious capacity is able to withstand this surcharge, and the neurotic in whom, for whatever reason, conscious development is disturbed.

The absence in our culture of rites and institutions designed, like the rites of puberty, to smooth the adolescent's passage into the world is one reason for the incidence of neuroses in youth, common to all of which is the difficulty of facing up to the demands of life and of adapting to the collective and to one's partner. The absence of rites at the climacteric works in the same way. Common to the climacteric neuroses of the second half of life is the difficulty of freeing oneself from worldly attachments, as is necessary for a mellow old age and its tasks. The causes of these neuroses are therefore quite different from, indeed the opposite of, those occurring in the first half of life.

Whereas in the first half of life the central position of the ego does not allow the workings of centroversion to come to consciousness, the middle period is characterized by a decisive change of personality. Centroversion becomes conscious. The ego is exposed to a somewhat painful process which, starting

[8] The naturalness of this development is also proved by the analysis of developmental difficulties and neurotic disturbances in adult life.

in the unconscious, permeates the entire personality. This psychological mutation with its symptomatology and symbolism Jung has described as the individuation process, and he has amplified it with a wealth of material in his works on alchemy.

We can say, then, that with the phenomenon of the second half of life the personal development of centroversion enters upon a second phase. Whereas its initial phase led to the development of the ego and to the differentiation of the psychic system, its second phase brings development of the self and the integration of that system. But, although the transformation process runs in the opposite direction to the development which took place during the first half of life, the ego and consciousness are not disintegrated; on the contrary, there is an expansion of consciousness brought about by the ego reflecting upon itself. It is as though the ego were restored to its original position: it emerges from its monomaniac self-obsession and becomes once more the vehicle of the totality function.

The unconscious activity of the self dominates the whole of life, but it is only in the second half that this activity becomes conscious. While the ego is being built up in early childhood there is a gradual centering of consciousness, with the ego as the representative organ of wholeness. In puberty the individual, as an ego, feels himself to be the representative of collective wholeness. He becomes a responsible member of the collective, and between them there exists the same creative relationship as between the ego and the unconscious. From puberty up to the time of the climacteric, a period of active expansion which goes into reverse at the onset of the second half of life, the outward dialectic is conducted between individual and collective. Then, with individuation, comes the mastering of the inner dialectic between the ego and the collective unconscious.

In the integration process the personality goes back along the path it took during the phase of differentiation. It is now a question of reaching a synthesis between the conscious mind and the psyche as a whole, that is, between the ego and the self, so that a new wholeness may be constellated between the hitherto

411

diametrically opposed systems of conscious and unconscious. All the differentiations and personality components that were built up during the first half of life, when consciousness was developing, are now unbuilt. However, this does not take the form of a regression such as occurs in the phenomenon of mass recollectivization (see Appendix I), but is an integration in which the expansion and development of consciousness are simply continued in a new direction.

In this transformation process—which not only occurs in the conscious form of the individuation process, but, through the self-regulation of the psyche, also governs the maturation of all personality—the ego reaches consciousness of the self. With the growing self-awareness of the ego, the self evolves out of its unconscious activity and arrives at the stage of conscious activity. The path of transformation followed by the individuant resembles the hermetic process in alchemy; it is a new form of dragon fight culminating in a qualitative change of consciousness. The mythological stage which we called "Transformation, or Osiris," becomes a psychological reality when the conscious mind experiences the unity of the psyche.

In contrast to the previous deflation of the unconscious, differentiation, and the formation of an outward gradient to the collective, we now have deflation of the world, integration, and the formation of an inward gradient to the self. During the first half of life the impersonal and unconscious life of childhood had to mold itself into the personal life of the adult, who, while maintaining his position in the collective, must give a central place to the ego sphere, whether this be the sphere of personal achievement, human relationships, power, or creative work. This phase of personality development, dominated by the ego, is followed by another in which the assimilation of transpersonal and suprapersonal contents leads to a shifting of the center from the personal ego, the center of consciousness, to the self, the center of the total psyche.

The integration of all the authorities of the personality within this total psychic unity joins to the conscious mind those parts which were split off or had never been attached to it at all; and this process activates the emotional components as well as putting an end to secondary personalization. Although this development normally proceeds without impairing the integrity of consciousness, the crises and dangers involved are similar to those which threaten the primitive ego and may, in unlucky cases, even destroy the personality. Here, too, emotional and archetypal invasions threaten the ego as, on its heroic journey to the underworld, it voluntarily discards the limitations and defenses of conscious development. For instance, behind the parental imagos there now loom the primary archetypes, and the figures encountered become more various, more complex, more enigmatic and equivocal as the journey progresses. Just as the personality gives up the primacy of its specific sexuality and, by assimilating the anima or animus, regains its original hermaphroditism, so the archetypes lose their unambiguous character in a multiplicity of contradictory meanings. In contrast, however, to the primitive situation there is now a consciousness capable of experiencing them in all their polyvalency and paradoxicality, whereas formerly they would have led to its extinction. In the evolution of mankind the spontaneous expression of the unconscious through the natural symbol took precedence; but now, concurrently, we meet the phenomenon which Jung designates with the name of the "uniting symbol" and the "transcendent function." [9]

The uniting symbol is a product of a special situation in which, instead of the creativity of the unconscious predominating, as it does wherever natural symbols appear, the crucial factor is rather the attitude of the conscious ego, its stability in face of the unconscious. As a product of the transcendent function, the uniting symbol resolves the tension—of energy and content—existing between the ego stability of consciousness and the contrary tendency of the unconscious to overwhelm it.

The uniting symbol is therefore a direct manifestation of centroversion, of the individual's wholeness. Under the creative

[9] *Psychological Types,* def. 51.

influence of new and hitherto inactive elements the conscious and unconscious positions are overcome, i.e., "transcended." The uniting symbol is the highest form of synthesis, the most perfect product of the psyche's innate striving for wholeness and self-healing, which not only "makes whole" all conflict—provided that it is taken seriously and suffered to the end—by turning it into a creative process, but also makes it the point of departure for a new expansion of the total personality.

Jung observes: "The stability and positiveness of individuality, and the superior power of unconscious expression, are merely tokens of one and the same fact." [10] Stability and positiveness of individuality: that means the strength and integrity, also the moral integrity, of the conscious mind, its refusal to let itself be cast down by the demands of the unconscious and of the world. But the "superior power of unconscious expression" is the transcendent function, the creative elements in the psyche which can overcome a conflict situation not soluble by the conscious mind, by discovering a new way, a new value or image. Both together are an expression of the fact that a total constellation of the personality has been reached, in which the creativeness of the psyche and the positiveness of the conscious mind no longer function like two opposed systems split off from one another, but have achieved a synthesis.

This synthesis of the psyche is frequently accompanied by symbols representing the new unity of opposites, such as the symbol of the hermaphrodite. The hermaphroditic nature of the uroboros reappears here on a new level.

As in alchemy the initial hermaphroditic state of the *prima materia* is sublimated through successive transformations until it reaches the final, and once more hermaphroditic, state of the philosophers' stone, so the path of individuation leads through successive transformations to a higher synthesis of ego, consciousness and the unconscious. While in the beginning the ego germ lay in the embrace of the hermaphroditic uroboros, at the end the self proves to be the golden core of a sublimated uro-

[10] Ibid.

414

boros, combining in itself masculine and feminine, conscious and unconscious elements, a unity in which the ego does not perish but experiences itself, in the self, as the uniting symbol.

In this process there is a "sublimation" of the ego as it realizes its connection with the self, a connection which appears more than once in the paradoxical identity of Horus and Osiris. In the self the ego knows itself immortal, and in itself mortal; the connection between the two comes out in the Talmudic saying "Man and God are twins," [11] and also in the symbolism of the father-son and mother-daughter identity. By ceding its pretensions to uniqueness and its central position to the self, the ego, as its indirect representative, becomes "king of this world," just as the self is "king of the spirit-world."

The first phase of this process of "Osirification" and transformation, which is equivalent to the individuation process, still lies within the domain of the hero archetype; it is the phase of the dragon fight and of the *hieros gamos* with the anima. These two together constitute the preliminary stage of transformation which ends with the production of the self, of unity, as an inward act of self-generation and glorification. The introjection of the hero archetype, the union with the soul, the founding of the kingdom that "is not of this world," and the birth of the king are as much the mysteries of alchemy as of the individuation process.[12]

The act of self-generation which takes place right at the beginning of life, when ego consciousness frees itself from the devouring embrace of the dragon of the unconscious, has its counterpart in this rebirth of the ego as the self, when, in the second half of life, it breaks free from the embrace of the world dragon. The dragon fight of the first period begins with the encounter with the unconscious and ends with the heroic birth of the ego. The night sea journey of the second period begins with the encounter with the world and ends with the heroic birth of the self.

This last phase of conscious development is no longer

[11] Talmud, Sanhedrin 46 b.
[12] Jung, *Psychology and Alchemy,* index, s.v.

archetypal, i.e., collectively conditioned, but is individual. Archetypal materials may have to be assimilated as well, but they are assimilated consciously and by an individual who attains self-experience through his unique and idiosyncratic union with the transpersonal worlds within and without. It is no longer the unconscious, purely collective world of the uroboros that now dominates the ego, nor the conscious, purely collective world of the community, but both are combined and assimilated in a unique way. Whereas the fragmentary ego finds itself a mere atom tossed between the vast collective worlds of objective psyche and objective physis, the ego united with the self experiences itself anthropomorphically as the center of the universe.

After passing through all the phases of world-experience and self-experience, the individual reaches consciousness of his true meaning. He knows himself the beginning, middle, and end of the self-development of the psyche, which manifests itself first as the ego and is then experienced by this ego as the self.

This self-experience of the ego, however, is bound up with "everlastingness," with immortality, as in the Osiris myth. The wholeness that comes into being as a result of the individuation process corresponds to a profound structural change, a new configuration of the personality. Whereas in the first half of life there was a tendency to differentiation and ever-increasing tension at the expense of wholeness, the integration process tends towards increased stability and a lowering of tension. This trend of development is in accord with the natural maturation of all living structures. It has biological as well as physical equivalents. The genesis, stabilization, configuration, and consolidation of the personality are therefore associated with a symbolism whose ingredients are perfect form, balance, harmony, solidity. The mandala, whether appearing as the circle, sphere, pearl, or symmetrical flower, contains all these elements; while diamond, stone, or rock, as symbols of the self, represent the indestructibility and permanence of something that can no longer be split apart by the opposites.

But where the accent does not lie so much on indestructibility, eternity, and immortality, the stability of the psyche appears to be that of a living organism which grows, develops, and renews itself. Hence the decrease of tension between the opposites points rather to the agreement and harmony of the forces at work, to a qualitative change rather than to a quantitative diminution of their power. Here as everywhere, maturity denotes a transformation of quantitatively stronger tensions into qualitatively higher and more stable structures.

Structural wholeness, with the self as center of the psyche, is symbolized by the mandala, by the circle with a center, and by the hermaphroditic uroboros. But this uroboric circle now has the luminous core of the self for a center. Whereas in the beginning the uroboros existed at the animal level only, so that the ego germ contained in its midst was almost hidden, in the unfolding flower of the mandala the animal tension of opposites is overcome, transcended by a self which blossoms forth into a corolla of opposites. At the beginning of the development, consciousness was all but extinguished by the crushing superiority of the unconscious; at the end, it is broadened and strengthened by its connection with the self. This combination of the self with the stability of the ego serves to subdue and bind in a magic circle all contents, whether of the world or the unconscious, outside or inside.

The self-differentiating structure of the psyche is reflected in a world cleft asunder by the principle of opposites into outside and inside, conscious and unconscious, life and spirit, male and female, individual and collective. But to the maturing psyche, slowly integrating itself under the sign of the hermaphrodite, the world, too, assumes the appearance of the hermaphroditic ring of existence, within which a human center takes shape, be it the individual who comes to self-realization between the inner and outer worlds, or humanity itself. For humanity as a whole and the single individual have the same task, namely, to realize themselves as a unity. Both are cast forth into a reality, one half of which confronts them as nature and external world, while the other half approaches them as psyche and the unconscious,

417

spirit and daemonic power. Both must experience themselves as the center of this total reality.

We began with the ego in the womb of the parental uroboros dragon, curled up like an embryo in the sheltering fusion of inside and outside, world and unconscious. We end, as in an alchemical picture, with the hermaphrodite standing upon this dragon: by virtue of its own synthetic being it has overcome the primal situation, above it hangs the crown of the self, and in its heart glows the diamond.

But only when the conscious development of mankind as a whole, and not merely of single individuals, has reached this stage of synthesis, will the supra-individual uroboros situation truly be overcome, and with it the collective danger of the dragon. The collective unconscious of mankind must be experienced and apprehended by the consciousness of mankind as the ground common to all men. Not until the differentiation into races, nations, tribes, and groups has, by a process of integration, been resolved in a new synthesis, will the danger of recurrent invasions from the unconscious be averted. A future humanity will then realize the center, which the individual personality today experiences as his own self-center, to be one with humanity's very self, whose coming to birth will finally vanquish and cast out that old serpent, the primordial uroboric dragon.

APPENDICES

APPENDICES

I

THE GROUP AND THE GREAT
INDIVIDUAL

WE HAVE ATTEMPTED to clarify the psychological significance
of the uroboric situation and to represent it as the original
situation of the ego. Our task now is to show how the ego and
the individual develop out of the group. We have in the first
place to demonstrate the positive significance of the group for
the individual and to distinguish between the group and the
mass. The group is a living unit in which all members are connected with one another, whether the connection be a natural
biological one as in the tribal group, the family, clan, and the
primitive folk group, or whether it be institutional as in the
totem, the sect, and the religious group. But even in the institutional group the members are emotionally bound to one another
through common experience, initiations, and so forth. The formation of a group is thus dependent upon the existence of *participation mystique* between its members, upon unconscious
projection processes whose emotional significance we have
already discussed. Symptomatic of this situation is, for instance,
the fact that the group members call themselves brothers and
sisters, and so reproduce by analogy the original family group
where these ties are taken for granted.

Moreover, it is the nature of the group to have a permanent
character which is guaranteed by the unconscious ties between
the members. Every genuine group is a permanent group, and
through that permanence it also acquires an historical character.
Even temporary groups such as school classes, regiments, etc.,
show a tendency to manufacture a history for themselves so as
to become a genuine group. They try to make the original

experience upon which the group was founded—the shared experiences of youth or war—historic, and to demonstrate its permanence by means of conventions, rallies, records, minute-books, and the like.

Mass associations, on the other hand, are only nominal associations to which we cannot give the character and name of a group. In them it is always a question of what the Gestalt theory calls additive parts, i.e., an aggregation of individuals who are not bound together emotionally and between whom no unconscious projection processes occur. The common use of a train or theater, the herding together in unions, societies, guilds, corporations, parties, etc., do not constitute a group community. Certainly it is possible for such a mass association to become secondarily grouped, so that there is a partial resemblance to genuine group phenomena. But then the partial nature of the grouping comes to the fore. In an emergency it turns out that the pull of the primary group, e.g., the nation, is stronger than party membership. The fate of social democracy, for instance, has repeatedly shown that the political party is a mass association which collapses as soon as the primary group becomes activated, and that group allegiance to the nation reasserts itself in an emotional crisis, as on the outbreak of war.

Similarly, the associations resulting from the phenomena of recollectivization, to be discussed later, are mass associations. The carrying away of the atomized individual in a mass movement is a psychological process that can never form a group and has no permanent character. As we shall see, the mass lacks all the positive marks of the group, even though the individual in the mass may mistake it for a group and think he is experiencing a unity—whose illusory character, however, is manifest in its very transience.

Hence the group in our sense of the word is a psychological unit with a permanent character, whether natural or institutional, both contrasting with the associations of masses. The group in which the individual is contained represents a natural whole whose parts are integrated, as is seen most clearly in the original uroboric situation. The superiority of this group totality over the individual part invests the former with all the marks of an archetype. It is possessed of superior power, has a spiritual character and displays the qualities of leadership, is numinous, and is always the "wholly other," as is apparent in all institutional groups in which the founder of the group plays a part. The clearest example of this phenomenon—the projection of group wholeness—is totemism.

The spiritual nature of the totem has a religious and, in even higher degree, a social and ethical significance. It is the formative principle of all primitive life, since all conduct, rites, and festivals are determined by it, as well as the social hierarchy established by the totem.

The acquisition of an individual totem, as in North America, is by no means the rule; on the contrary we have here a collective demand that the individual should individualize himself through experience of the "voice," of direct inner revelation, which is quite in contrast to the ordinary life of primitives, where the totem is inherited. But even then, the totem is usually transmitted through the rites of initiation; i.e., is made the spiritual inheritance of the individual. The phenomenon of the guardian spirit is particularly interesting because in it we can observe, in collective form, the act which was normally the experience of the Great Individuals only, and which led to the formation of totemism everywhere. Not only is the spirit alive and active in the group psyche, that is, in the group's unconscious, but these spiritual phenomena of the collective unconscious manifest themselves in revelations which are perceived by particularly gifted individuals who, precisely because they become revelatory bearers of the transpersonal, prove to be Great Individuals.

The collective unconscious of the group manifests itself by taking possession of the individual, whose function it is, as an organ of the group, to convey to it the contents of the unconscious. Such manifestations are determined by the situation of the group and by the way in which the collective unconscious is constellated.

We have, therefore, a whole hierarchy of phenomena revealing the deeper layers of the psyche, and a corresponding hierarchy of revelation bearers who appear as Great Individuals. In the main, two things distinguish the revelation bearers from one another: the first is the degree of conscious participation in the phenomena of revelation; the second is the scope of the emergent contents.

The lowest place in this hierarchy is occupied by the Great Individual who is only a passive carrier of projections, that is to say, one whose conscious mind and personality stand in no kind of relationship to what is projected upon him. An instance of this is the widespread institution of symbolic victims who have to represent the god to be sacrificed. They may be chosen on account of their beauty, as in the case of fertility goddesses, or because they have some symbolic—and for us quite accidental—sign on their bodies, for instance they may be albinos or possess special stigmata like the witch marks of the Middle Ages. Often the symbol bearers are purely institutional, as with the sacrifice of war prisoners in ancient Mexico. This form, which shows no direct relationship between the personality and the contents projected upon it, is based on religious institutions with their retinue of priests, prophets, sorcerers, etc., who decide on the victim with the help of divination and other practices, and who are, therefore, the operative factors in the situation. But even here there is an active projection of an unconscious group-content upon an individual who thereby becomes a Great Individual, as is evident from the numerous dispensations which show him to be one "exempt," to whom the customary taboos no longer apply.

On a rather higher level stands the individual whose personality is possessed directly by the unconscious content—spirit, demon, God—even when his conscious mind does not participate in its assimilation or interpretation. This passive hypnosis by the unconscious is a very common phenomenon which is well

424

known as shamanism and can be observed in the possession states of practically all medicine men, prophets, and so forth. To this category also belongs the madman, in whom the transpersonal forces of the collective unconscious and of the spiritual world manifest themselves without the participation of the conscious mind and the ego. As we know, among primitive peoples, unless correspondingly gifted "psychopathic" personages are present, this state may be artificially induced by driving a member of the tribe mad and thus making him a medicine man. In this way he becomes the mouthpiece of the transpersonal and conveys to the group the contents it needs, which have been activated in the collective unconscious.

This stage has many forms and variants, for passive possession by a content of the collective unconscious may lead to identification with it, to inflation, but also to a "symbolic life" in which the content is actually "represented" in reality, as is partially the case among the Hebrew prophets and manifestly so wherever the life of a divine figure is "imitated."

Again, the temporary leader of a group, who is not related to it as the permanent leader but has only accomplished something outstanding in a unique situation and is therefore a Great Individual for the moment only,[1] is a typical example of this connection between unconscious possession and the importance of personality for the group.

The mediumistic Führer figure, the hypnotized hypnotist, likewise falls into the lower category of medicine men, for whom the daemonism of the Great Individual is simply a means for the self-daemonization of the mass, and whose significance as an individual personality is submerged, like that of the madman, in his function as a mere mouthpiece of the unconscious.

We come now to an important criterion. Many genuinely "great" men are distinguished from these lower stages by the fact that their conscious mind actively participates in the process and adopts a responsible attitude toward it. What characterizes

---

[1] This naturally does not apply to the "specialists," such as the professionals who wage a war, organize a fishing expedition, etc.

the hypnotist who is hypnotized by the unconscious is the banality of his mind, its lack of problems. For, if completely swamped by the invading content, consciousness becomes incapable of taking up any counterposition whatsoever, but is carried away and possessed by it to the point of identification.

The Great Individual, on the other hand, who really is a great man in the sense of being a great personality, is characterized not only by the fact that the unconscious content has him in its grip, but by the fact that his conscious mind also has an active grip on the content. It is immaterial whether his assimilation of the content takes the form of creation, or of interpretation, or of action; for common to all these is the responsible participation of the ego in coming to terms with the invading content, and not only its participation, but its ability to take up an attitude.

Only then does the Great Individual become a creative human being. The action no longer rests with the invading transpersonal alone, but with the centroversion operating through ego consciousness; in other words, there is now a creative total reaction in which the specifically human qualities of ego formation and conscious elaboration are preserved.

This category of Great Individuals serves as a model for the development of individuality in humankind generally. The individual fate of the hero—and the creative Great Individual is indeed a hero—may be the exception, but he is also the exemplar of a process which subsequently affects all individuals in varying degree.

The average ego, the average individual, remains fixed in the group, although in the course of development he is compelled to give up the original security of the unconscious, to evolve a conscious system, and to take upon himself all the complications and sufferings which such development entails. For the primary security of the unconscious he exchanges the secondary security of the group. He becomes a group member, and the average man spends at least half his life—the essential part of his development—adapting to the group and allowing himself to be molded by collective trends.

426

The role played by the collective in the human culture is decisive. Society, with its conscious postulates, sets up an authority, a spiritual tradition which, spoken or unspoken, forms the background of education. The individual is molded by the collective through its ethos, its customs, laws, morality, its ritual and religion, its institutions and collective undertakings. When one considers the original submergence of the individual in the collective, one sees why all collective orientations are so binding and are accepted without question.

Besides this tendency of the collective to form average members and to educate the ego up to the cultural norm represented by the elders, there is another tendency which is in the direction of the Great Individual.

For the group member, the Great Individual is primarily the carrier of projections. The unconscious psychic wholeness of the collective is experienced in the person of the Great Individual, who is at once the group self and the unconscious self of each member. What is present in every part of the group as the unconscious creative totality of the psyche, namely the self, becomes visible in the Great Individual or, at a higher level, is actualized in his life. The collective parts are still childishly dependent, with no ego center, no responsibility or will of their own to mark them off from the collective, so that the Great Individual is regarded as the directive force, as the very center of life, and is institutionally honored as such.

It is therefore completely inadmissible to reduce him to, or derive him from, the personal father figure. We find that, just as in the early history of man the Great Individual becomes the carrier for the projection of archetypal images such as the self, the mana figure, the hero, and the father archetype, so also in the course of ontogenetic development the figure representing authority, who in our civilization is the father, frequently becomes the carrier for these projections. But it is by no means only the father archetype that is projected upon him; very often it is quite another image, for instance that of the magician, the

427

wise old man, the hero or, conversely, of the devil, death, and so on.

The Great Individual who breaks away from the anonymity of the primordial collective is, on the heavenly plane, the god-figure, while on the earthly plane he is the medicine man, chief, and god-king. Sociological and religious developments are here closely bound together; they correspond to psychic changes, and the psychic differentiation by which the ego detaches itself from the undifferentiated unconscious is expressed in sociological changes as well as in a theological differentiation of man's view of the world.

Historically, the Great Individual is most accessible to us in the role of the god-king and, later, the king. The earliest cuneiform pictogram for "king" signifies "great man," and this was the way he was always pictured in the art of the ancient East. The Great King or the Great House, Pharaoh, is the embodiment and representative of the people. If the hieroglyph for the king of Lower Egypt is the bee, and the same image also occurs in the cultural sphere of the Euphrates, that only tells us the same thing. The "great" bee which rules the hive, and which today we call the queen bee, was regarded in antiquity as the king bee. But in Egypt the designation of the king as the "First Man" or "Great Man" is already a later development. It follows the stage of his god-identity, when even ritually he was as far removed from his people as a god. Speaking of this stage, the Pyramid Texts say the king was already in existence before the creation of the world,[2] an ideology which reappears later in connection with the Messiah.[3]

We have shown how, in the process of self-deification, the Egyptian king becomes the human bearer of an immortal soul. He is the only man who, by being ritually transformed into a

[2] Erman and Ranke, *Aegypten und aegyptisches Leben in Alterthum*, p. 62.

[3] We have explained earlier that a substantial part of the Egyptian worship of the dead served the purpose of making the king immortal after his death by the embalming of the body and the building of pyramids as symbols of immortality. Whereas at first only the king, who symbolized the collective self, gained immortality, and armies of men toiled for decades at his pyramids in order to assist his self-immortalization, this process was later not confined to him alone.

428

god in his own lifetime, unifies all parts of the soul and becomes the "perfect being"; [4] that is to say, he is the first and at this period the only man who is the simulacrum of God, a conception which in Judaism and in somewhat modified form in Christianity was to become a basic factor in man's psychic life.

The history of Egypt enables us to trace in a unique way how the ego grows out of its original collective identity and how the Great Individual, as carrier for the projection of the collective self, paves the way for the formation of each individual ego, and initiates and assists the process. Whereas in a collective composed of incomplete individuals the god-king is the archetypal representative of the group's totality, this figure gradually develops a mediatory function, that is, it gives up more and more of its mana to the group members and is thus disintegrated and "dismembered." The same process of incorporating and assimilating the greater, which was originally enacted between the king and God, now takes place between the individual and the king, who is "eaten." His divine kingship is continually reduced, but at the same time the incomplete members of the collective, who formerly existed only as instruments of his apotheosis, become complete individuals. The king now turns into a worldly ruler, and his despotism is a merely human and political one; but his demotion is accompanied by a process in which every individual acquires an immortal soul, that is, becomes Osiris, and introjects the self, the god-king, as the sacral center of his own being. We find the same secularization of a sacred content in the growing consciousness of a personal ancestry and a personal name. Originally both were the property of the king; later they became proper to each individual.[5]

The development of ego consciousness and individuality, via the Great Individual, is effected by the transmission of the contents he has revealed, and by making them part of the cultural canon, i.e., part of the suprapersonal values and agencies which regulate culture and life. For this the men's groups are mainly

[4] Moret, *The Nile and Egyptian Civilization*, pp. 181 f.
[5] Erman and Ranke, op. cit., pp. 185–90.

responsible, a fact of especial importance for the patriarchal line of conscious development and for the psychological understanding of the hero myth.

At the outset of culture, spiritual development is fostered by the men's societies in the form of secret societies, which later take the form of sects, mysteries, and religions. These secret societies seem from the very beginning to have arisen in opposition to the matriarchate. Koppers says:

The secret societies constitute a very ancient phenomenon in the history of mankind. They seem to have been founded by self-assertive men not very long after women had introduced the earliest agriculture. This may well have occurred in the Mesolithic Age.

Further:

The ethnological findings argue for the belief that it was woman who developed the plant gathering of the aboriginal period into agriculture. She made the soil valuable and consequently became its owner. First economically and then socially she achieved a dominant position: the complex of matriarchy developed.

The none too pleasant situation, into which men had thus been thrust, provoked a reaction. This is manifested in the male secret societies, whose secrecy and terror were directed primarily against the female part of the population. The males attempted by intellectual and religious-magical means to retrieve what they had lost in economic and social life.[6]

Apart from the fact that it is incorrect to reduce an historical and spiritual phenomenon like the rise of secret societies to personalistic feelings of resentment, the main point has been overlooked. Even if we accepted this "compensation theory," the fact remains—and it is precisely this fact that needs explaining—that for the men's groups religio-magical and spiritual contents were no less important than the social and economic supremacy of the matriarchate. This spiritual accent of masculinity, which is central to all secret societies and mysteries, is the point of significance. And if we invariably find, at the center

[6] "On the Origin of the Mysteries in the Light of Ethnology and Indology."

of the initiation ceremonies, that the neophytes are shown—on pain of death should they ever reveal the secret—that the ghosts and masks which have so terrified them are merely "play-acted" by men of their personal acquaintance, this does in fact amount to the passing on of a secret. We have no right to explain this in the modern scientific manner by saying that the neophyte is given much the same sort of enlightenment as one gives to a child today when he is told that Santa Claus is really Daddy or Uncle So-and-So.

Here, as later in the mysteries, we are dealing with a genuine transformation process which merits serious attention. In the same way that the primitive's identity with his totem is not just "represented," but is actually reproduced, in the dancing and the masks, the connection of the secret society with its tutelary spirit is a sacramental one. No more than the host is the wafer, is the ghost who appears in the initiation merely the man who plays him.

Thus Koppers says of the Kina festival of the Yamana Indians, of Tierra del Fuego:

Here the term "secret" is quite applicable; for the Kina is observed only by men. Women may not take part in it, and, indeed, the whole institution is directed *against* the women. The men are painted and masked to represent spirits, and the women are supposed to take them for real spirits. Thus the men consciously deceive the women, and, in principle at least, the death penalty attaches to betrayal of the secret of the Kina to women or the noninitiate.

The corresponding myth tells us that

It is a clear and distinct astral myth, according to which the women, led by the moon woman, Kina, formerly enacted the very same rite now enacted by the men. This servitude of the men was forcibly broken by the sun man. Led by the sun man, the men (of that time) killed all the women but spared the little girls in order to provide for the survival of the tribe.[7]

That the women are "consciously duped and deceived" is, if not entirely a false European interpretation, a late misunder-

[7] Ibid. This is a mother-murder myth as opposed to the father-murder myth concocted by Freud.

431

standing of their own mysteries by the natives themselves, such as we find all too frequently. Originally the mystery consisted precisely in the fact that the painted and masked men were "real ghosts." Besides experiencing his genuine transpersonality as an initiate, the individual also experiences a piece of ritualistic "secondary personalization." The detachment from the unconscious which is effected in the puberty initiation is enormously strengthened by his experiencing the mask-wearers as persons. It dispels fear and fortifies the ego and consciousness. But this knowledge in no way contradicts the initiate's other experience that he and the spiritual world belong together. On the contrary, the double relationship which enables the individualized, initiated ego to be apprehended both as a private person and as a mask, personal and transpersonal at once, is an elementary form of what the myths call the divine parentage of the hero.

The opposition of the men's society to all matriarchal tendencies is undeniable, but it is not to be explained by social factors, as we also find it under sociological conditions which rule out a suppression of the males—not proved even under matriarchal conditions—namely, in the patriarchate. On the other hand the psychological explanation which maintains that the matriarchate is not so much a sociological factor as a psychological stage will help to clear up the situation. Already in the Kina myth we find the archetypal opposition between Moon Woman and Sun Man, regarding which Koppers remarks: "In the light of universal ethnology totemic religion reveals a preference for solar conceptions." That is to say, the collective world of initiations, secret societies, sects, mysteries, and religions is a spiritual and masculine world, and, despite its communal character, the accent still falls on the individual, in that each man is initiated individually and undergoes an individual experience which stamps his individuality. This individual emphasis with its elective character stands in marked contrast to the matriarchal group, where the archetype of the Great Mother and the corresponding stage of consciousness predominate, bringing with them all the features we have described—*partici-*

432

pation mystique, emotionality, etc. In the opposed group of men's societies and secret organizations the dominant is the hero archetype and the dragon-fight mythology, i.e., the next stage of conscious development. It is true that the men's society also leads to a community life among the members, but this is braced by its individual character, the masculinity and accentuation of the ego. Consequently it favors the formation of the leader and hero type. Individualization, ego formation, and heroism belong to the very life of the male group and are in fact its expressions. Conditions in the female group seem to be markedly different in this respect, and it is this contrast which explains the antifeminine tendencies of the men's society. Woman and sex, the principal representatives of those unconscious instinctual constellations which are stirred up by anything feminine, are the danger zone: they are "the dragons to be overcome." That is why no women are ever admitted to the men's societies. On this level, where men are not yet sure of themselves, women are execrated as dangerous and seductive, and this is still largely true of cultures with patriarchal religions.[8]

Collective masculinity is a value-creating and educative force. Every ego and every consciousness is gripped and formed by it. In this way the masculine side helps the developing ego to live through the archetypal stages individually and to establish contact with the hero myth.

Even these bare indications will have sufficed to make it clear why we speak of a patriarchal line of conscious development. The development proceeds from the mother to the father. It is assisted by a series of collective authorities—heaven, the fathers, the superego—which are as emphatically masculine as the

[8] Patriarchal development brings a revaluation of the feminine, the best-known instance of which is the creation myth in Genesis. Here the Word is the creative principle: world and matter come from the abstract, from the spirit; the female is derived from the male and comes later. At the same time she is negative and seductive, the source of all evil, and must be subjugated by the male. The world of the Old Testament is very much colored by this revaluation in which all the maternal-chthonic characteristics of the primitive world of the Canaanites were devalued, reinterpreted, and replaced by the patriarchal Jehovah-valuation. This Jehovah-earth polarity is a basic factor in Jewish psychology, and unless it is understood it is not possible to understand the Jews.

433

conscious system itself. Further investigation might show that our terms "matriarchal" and "patriarchal" are characteristic only of the early Mediterranean cultures along the coast of Asia Minor and Africa. That fact would merely modify our terminology; it would not alter the content and substance of stadial development. Just as the father complex must be broken down and the authority complex delimited from him, so it is with the opposition between matriarchal and patriarchal. The archetypal symbolism of male and female is not biological and sociological, but psychological; in other words, it is possible for feminine people to be bearers of masculinity and vice versa. Always it is a question of relations, never of hard and fast definitions.

The figures of the Leader and Great Individual as projections of the collective unconscious are not confined to the male group, though the latter is more concerned with the spirituality of these figures than the female group, whose self-projection finds in the figure of the Great Mother a representative that is closer to nature than to the spirit. However that may be, the figure of the Great Individual is of crucial importance for the development of every single individual. His crystallization from the collective is obviously an evolutionary advance, since the progressive differentiation of the individual and the infinite variety of ego systems it produces lead to an infinite variety of experiments within the life of mankind. Whereas formerly, as we saw, only the "great man" possessed a consciousness and stood for the collective in the role of leader, the further course of evolution is characterized by a progressive democratization, in which a vast number of individual consciousnesses work productively at the common human task. In this sense the leader who is saddled with collective responsibility is an atavism, and democracy the future form of humanity, regardless of the political expedients that may be chosen.

This conscious democratization of humanity is compensated by the genius, the Great Individual who is leader and hero in an "inner" sense, that is, the true representative of the forces and contents which such a democratized consciousness lacks and

434

which reach consciousness for the first time in him. He is pre-eminently the theater for mankind's novel experiments, in whom are constellated those contents which will later extend the whole range of human consciousness.

Between the democratized consciousness of humanity which lives, functions, perceives, thinks, formulates, interprets, and understands in millions of representatives, and the creative centers, the men of genius, there is a continuous interchange. Together, as the spiritual and cultural side of humanity, they form a united front against the unconscious, even if, at first, the genius is hounded down, starved to death, and silenced by the democracy of consciousness. The fact that millions of human beings work together consciously and are simultaneously concerned with the vital problems of the collective—political, scientific, artistic, or religious—makes the probability of his acceptance ever greater. The time lag between the appearance of a genius and his assimilation by the democracy of consciousness is relatively small. For the genius himself it may be tragic, but so far as humanity is concerned it is irrelevant.

MASS MAN AND THE PHENOMENA
OF RECOLLECTIVIZATION

In the course of Western development, the essentially positive process of emancipating the ego and consciousness from the tyranny of the unconscious has become negative. It has gone far beyond the division of conscious and unconscious into two systems and has brought about a schism between them; and, just as differentiation and specialization have degenerated into overspecialization, so this development has gone beyond the formation of individual personality and given rise to an atomized individualism. Whereas on the one hand we see ever larger groups of overindividualized persons, there are on the other hand ever larger masses of humanity who have detached themselves from the original situation of the primary group and entered into the historical process. Both these developments tend to lower the significance of the group as a unit composed of persons consciously or uncoϡciously bound together, and to exalt the mass as a conglomeration of unrelated individuals.

Now, while the clan, tribe, or village is as a rule a homogeneous group descended from a common origin, the city, office, or factory is a mass unit. The growth of these mass units at the cost of the group unit only intensifies the process of alienation from the unconscious. All emotional participations are broken down and personalized; that is, they exist only in a narrowly restricted personal sphere. As has long been observed, in the place of a group or a people there now appears a mass unit like the State, a purely nominal structure which, in the manner of a concept, comprises a variety of different things, but does not represent an idea that springs as a central image from a homogeneous

436

group. Romantic attempts to revalue or to reverse this development necessarily result in regressions, because they take no account of its forward tendency and misunderstand its connection with the historically positive evolution of the ego and consciousness.

Owing to the process of mass aggregation, the original group continues to exist only in the form of the family; but here too we can already discern a disintegrative tendency which increasingly restricts the effectiveness of the family group and assigns it a place only in childhood, or rather, only in infancy. The existence of the family, however, is of paramount importance for the preconscious and transpersonal psychology of the child.

In our culture there has been a steady disintegration of small groups and small nations, and hence an undermining of the psychological foundations of the group which expresses itself in mass-mindedness, in the atomization and conscious internationalization of the individual. One result of this expansion of consciousness is that, regardless of conflicting national ideologies, every modern consciousness is confronted with that of other nations and races and with other cultures, other economic patterns, religions, and systems of value. In this way the original group psychology and the cultural canon determining it, once taken for granted, become relativized and profoundly disturbed. Modern man's view of the world has changed to a degree that is still very far from having been digested psychologically. The long perspective of human history stretching back beyond prehistoric times into the animal kingdom, the rise of ethnology and comparative religion, social revolutions advancing all over the world towards the same goal, the recognition of primitive psychology and its connection with modern psychology [1]— behind all this we perceive the same fundamental driving force. The common human background and substratum whose scientific discovery as the collective unconscious we owe to Jung is beginning to manifest its universal workings in humanity itself. The picture that now emerges of a starry heaven of archetypal

[1] Aldrich, *The Primitive Mind and Modern Civilization*, pp. 48 f.

437

forces arching over humanity is, however, accompanied by the disappearance of those fragmentary constellations which in the canon of individual groups were regarded as the whole of heaven. Knowledge of other religions may lead to the experience of a common religious tendency at work in humanity, but it also relativizes every individual form of religion, for at root this is always conditioned by the psychological, historical, social, and racial soil of the group from which it sprang.

The global revolution which has seized upon modern man and in whose storm center we find ourselves today has, with its transvaluation of all values, led to a loss of orientation in the part and in the whole, and daily we have new and painful experience of its repercussions in the political life of the collective, as well as in the psychological life of the individual.

The cultural process leads to a schism between conscious and unconscious in a form which we described above as characteristic of development during the first half of life. The building up of the persona, and the adaptation to reality under the guidance of the superego as the court of conscience representing collective values, together with the help of suppression and repression, constellate the shadow and the anima and animus components in the unconscious.

This shadow side of the personality, however, owing to its contamination with the inferior, undeveloped archaic side, bears all the marks of the primitive psyche and thus stands in significant contrast to the original group man.

On this account we prefer to call the sub-man who dwells in us moderns the "mass man" rather than the "group man," because his psychology differs in essential respects from that of the latter. Although the genuine group man is for the most part unconscious, he nevertheless lives under the rule of centroversion; he is a psychic whole in which powerful tendencies are at work, making for consciousness, individualization, and spiritual growth. We have followed these tendencies, and it will therefore be understandable if we now say that in spite of his unconsciousness, in spite of projections, emotionality, and so forth,

438

the group man possesses enormously constructive, synthetic, and creative powers which manifest themselves in his culture, his society, his religion, art, customs, and even in what we call his superstitions.

The mass man lurking in the unconscious of the modern, on the other hand, is psychically a fragment, a part-personality which, when integrated, brings with it a considerable expansion of the personality, but is bound to have disastrous consequences if it acts autonomously.

This unconscious mass component is opposed to consciousness and the world of culture. It resists conscious development, is irrational and emotional, anti-individual and destructive. It corresponds mythologically to the negative aspect of the Great Mother—it is her murderous accomplice, the adversary and man-slaying boar. This negative, unconscious part of the personality is archaic in the most negative sense, for it is the beast-man at bay. He becomes the shadow and dark brother of the ego only if, through a process of integration, the ego consciously descends into the depths of the unconscious, there to seek him out and bind him to the conscious mind. But when the reverse happens, when, that is to say, consciousness is overpowered and wholly possessed by him, we get the frightful phenomenon of regression to the mass man as manifested in the mass epidemics of recollectivization.

In these circumstances the disoriented, rationalistic consciousness of modern man, having become atomized and split off from the unconscious, gives up the fight because, understandably enough, his isolation in a mass which no longer offers him any psychic support becomes unendurable. For him the hero's task is too difficult, the task he ought to perform by following in the footsteps of humanity before him. The fabric of the archetypal canon which used to support the average man has given way, and real heroes capable of taking up the struggle for new values are naturally few and far between.

The renegade ego of modern man therefore succumbs to a reactionary mass-mindedness and falls victim to the collective shadow, to the mass man within. Whereas in a homogeneous psyche the negative element has a meaningful place as decomposition and death, as chaos and *prima materia,* or as the leaden counterweight which roots growing things to the earth, in a fragmented psyche with a defeatist, regressing ego it becomes a cancer and a nihilistic danger. With the disintegration of ego consciousness all the positions built up in the course of human development are regressively destroyed, as in psychosis.

As a result, the ego-sphere of the human and personal is lost. Personality values no longer count, and the supreme achievement of the individual—his behavior as an individual human being—is broken down and replaced by collective modes of behavior. The daemons and archetypes become autonomous again, the individual soul is swallowed back by the Terrible Mother, and along with it the experience of the voice and the individual's responsibility before man and God is invalidated.

That the mass phenomenon is statistically a regression to the lowest level is self-evident, since the position of consciousness itself then begins to decay. Simultaneously with this, however, there is a reactivation of the medullary man and of his overwhelming emotionality. With the collapse of a consciousness oriented by the cultural canon the effective power of conscience, of the superego, is also destroyed, and consciousness loses its virility. "Effeminacy" then makes its appearance as an invasion from the unconscious side, manifesting itself in the breakthrough of complexes, of the inferior function and the shadow, and finally in a semipsychotic eruption of archetypes. The whole defense position of the conscious mind crumples up and the spiritual world of values with it. The personal ego-sphere as well as the autarchy of the personality drop away, and all the essential marks of centroversion.

Every single one of these phenomena is discoverable today in the mass situation and in the phenomena of recollectivization.[2]

[2] Alfred Kubin's visionary book, *Die andere Seite,* written in 1908, not only anticipates the events that were to burst upon Germany many years later, but with remarkable intuition realizes their connection with the collective unconscious.

The unique and frightful thing about this recollectivization is that it does not and cannot possibly mean a genuine regeneration. Regression does not reproduce the original group situation, but only a mass such as has never existed before and is, psychologically, a novel phenomenon.

When masses of city-dwellers regress to the unconscious state, it does not create a psychological unit that is in any way comparable to the original group and its psychology. In the original group, as we must emphasize yet again, consciousness, individuality, and spirit existed in the germ and strove to express themselves through the collective unconscious of the group, whereas the unconsciousness to which people are resignedly regressing today is, as it were, an unconscious with no tendencies in this direction. The autonomy of the unconscious reigns supreme in the mass psyche with the collusion of the mass shadow-man who lurks in the unconscious personality, and for the time being at least there is no sign of the regulating intervention of centroversion or of the regulation of the group by the cultural canon. The mass, therefore, is the decay of a more complex unit not into a more primitive unit but into a centerless agglomeration. Regression to the mass-man is only possible given the extreme process of cleavage between ego consciousness and the unconscious, and the consequent loss of centroversion. This absence of regulation by the whole leads to chaos.

Using the analogy of psychic illness one might, even in these circumstances, speak of the action of centroversion. In the individual, too, a rigid exclusion of the unconscious and a systematic disregard of its efforts at compensation cause it to turn destructive. We then find that compensation ceases and that, as Jung says, the unconscious directs its destructive tendency against consciousness and the ego. This "if you won't, then I'll force you" attitude can sometimes bring about a conversion, just as punishment may bring the sinner to repentance. The destructive decay of the individual in the mass harbors this possibility in itself, but only if it is made conscious, understood, assimilated, and in this way integrated.

441

The great danger that evidently prevents a conscious realization of this situation lies in the illusory phenomena which appear with recollectivization and blind the ego. The toxic effect of the mass situation lies precisely in its intoxicating character, which is always a concomitant of the dissolution of consciousness and its powers of discrimination. As we saw earlier, the libido-link between the ego system and the unconscious is "pleasurable." So it is when the link snaps and the ego system sinks into regression. The old bait with which that wily ratcatcher, the "hypnotized hypnotist" of mass epidemics, seduces us is uroboric incest.

In recollectivization the image of the original group and its wholeness is projected by the renegade ego upon the mass. The ego surrenders and, re-emotionalized, pouring itself out in an orgy of mass participations, experiences with pleasure a mass self akin to the uroboros, which sucks it in, embraces, and engulfs it. But a nihilistic, regressive perversion of the motto "Be embraced, ye millions!" is truly of the devil. The mass shadow-man, the herd of atomized individuals, and the mass self combine to form a pseudo-unity which is sheer illusion. That it is purely a matter of mass unification and a travesty of unity is evident from the swift disillusionment which ensues, and from the fact that mass illusion is incapable of producing any genuine and durable participation, much less anything constructive. The illusion of unity at a mass meeting does not even lead to genuine *participation mystique* with the spirit of the mass, let alone to a relationship of the participants with one another. In the real group, the group phenomenon of participation brings a synthetic development, taking the form of mutual responsibility, increased readiness for self-sacrifice, etc., which appears not merely as a momentary intoxication but embodies itself in institutions and communal undertakings. For instance the orgiastic feasts among primitives and in the older cultures promote the growth of groups and communities, and establish religious forms and other phenomena whose importance for the development of consciousness we have already stressed.

But in mass phenomena the illusory elation is as transient as that induced by hypnosis; it does not impress itself upon the conscious mind by bringing it to a creative synthesis, but leaks away like any other momentary intoxication. Yet even this delusive frenzy of mass possession is zealously desired by an ego emptied of all meaning, and is one of the chief allurements with which the mass hypnotist successfully operates.

Modern mass propaganda seeks—in part quite consciously—to restore the old group unity and the mutual projections of the participants, together with all the symptoms of emotional possession that pertain thereto. This it does—as was particularly to be observed in National Socialism—by enlisting the aid of symbols and archetypes. We have already pointed out the basic error and also the dangers of these recollectivizing tendencies. The intended victims of this possession are—above all in the big cities—atomized individuals split off from the unconscious, and although they may be able to regress to this unconscious state for a little while by surrendering their egos, the subjective delirium which accompanies it harbors in itself the most dangerous and destructive consequences.

The modern worker and citizen, with his scientific education and proneness to "reduce" everything transpersonal, himself becomes a reduced individual when recollectivized by the mass. The primitive or archaic man, on the other hand, with his relatively undeveloped consciousness and ego system, experiences in a collective group event, such as an initiation ceremony or mystery cult, a progression and expansion of himself through his own experience of the symbols and archetypes. He is illuminated and not reduced by them. These group phenomena tend to constellate the higher man and a "higher brotherhood," and not, on the contrary, to weld the mass particles into a mere conglomeration of which Jung could say, "The masses are blind brutes." [3] Note that the accent lies on the blind, not on the brute. Group possession, therefore, is never destructive in the same sense that mass action is destructive, where the mass consists of psychologically unrelated, or only momentarily related,

[3] *Psychology and Alchemy*, p. 461.

atomized individuals. The group contains its own regulator not only in the form of the ruling canon, but in the mutual knowledge all members have of one another. The very anonymity of the individual in the mass intensifies the action of the shadow side. It is a significant fact that, in order to carry out their sadistic executions, the Nazis were obliged to remove the assassin from his own group. It is very much harder, if not actually impossible, for a village community to liquidate its own Jews. Not so much because of the group's greater humanity—we have learnt not to regard this as one of the fundamental decencies—but because the individual must do his deeds under the eyes of the group. Removed from his group and subjected to terrorism, however, he becomes capable of anything.

But even in the mass situation the quality of the individual is important, for the composition of the mass determines its deeds. Sighele [4] could still believe that the violence or peaceableness of a mass is determined by its criminals or by those of its members whose profession it is to "see blood"; but depth psychology takes a different view. The "mass man within," the shadow, is the determining factor, not just consciousness and its orientation. The quality of the individual is indeed decisive, yet this is formed not so much by the quality of consciousness as by the quality of the whole personality, which for that very reason must be the psycholoical basis of the new ethos.

The growth of conscience, the formation of the superego by adaptation to the values of the collective, of the old men, stops at the point where the collapse of the cultural canon deprives this collective tribunal of its transpersonal bases. Conscience then becomes a Jewish, capitalist, or Socialist "invention." But the "voice," that inward orientation which makes known the utterances of the self, will never speak in a disintegrated personality, in a bankrupt consciousness, and in a fragmented psychic system.

[4] Reiwald, *Vom Geist der Massen*, p. 123.

BIBLIOGRAPHY

BIBLIOGRAPHY

ABRAHAM, KARL. "A Short Study in the Development of the Libido, Viewed in the Light of Mental Disorders." In: *Selected Papers on Psycho-Analysis.* Translated by Douglas Bryan and Alix Strachey. (International Psycho-Analytical Library, ed. Ernest Jones 13.) London, 1927.

ABRAHAMSEN, DAVID. *The Mind and Death of a Genius.* New York, 1946.

ADLER, ALFRED. *The Neurotic Constitution.* Translated by B. Glueck and J. E. Lind. New York, 1917.

ADLER, GERHARD. *Studies in Analytical Psychology.* London and New York, 1948.

ALBRIGHT, WILLIAM FOXWELL. *Archaeology and the Religion of Israel.* (Ayer Lectures of the Colgate-Rochester Divinity School, 1941.) Baltimore, 1942.

———. *From the Stone Age to Christianity.* Baltimore, 1940.

ALDRICH, CHARLES ROBERTS. *The Primitive Mind and Modern Civilization.* With an introduction by Bronislaw Malinowski and a foreword by C. G. Jung. London and New York, 1931.

ANDERSON, JOHANNES C. *Myths and Legends of the Polynesians.* London, 1928.

BACHOFEN, JOHANN JAKOB. *Das Mutterrecht.* (Gesammelte Werke, Vols. II and III.) Basel, 1948. 2 vols.

———. *Urreligion und antike Symbole.* A selection from his works, systematically arranged; edited by Carl Albrecht Bernoulli. (Reclam edition.) Leipzig, 1926. 3 vols.

BARLACH, ERNST. *Der Tote Tag.* Berlin, 1912.

BENEDICT, RUTH. *Patterns of Culture.* Boston and New York, 1934.

BIN GORION, MICHA JOSEF, pseud. (Micha Joseph Berdyczewski). *Die Sagen der Juden.* Translated from Hebrew into German by Rahel Bin Gorion, pseud. (Rahel Ramberg Berdyczewski). Frankfort, 1913–27. 5 vols.

BISCHOFF, ERICH (ed. and trans.). *Die Elemente der Kabbalah.* Berlin, 1913. 2 vols.

BLACKMAN, AYLWARD. *See* HOOKE.

BREYSIG, KURT. *Die Völker ewiger Urzeit.* (Die Geschichte der Menschheit, Vol. I.) Berlin, 1907.

BRIFFAULT, ROBERT. *The Mothers.* London and New York, 1927. 3 vols.

BUDGE, E. A. WALLIS (ed.). *The Book of the Dead.* An English translation of the Theban Recension. London, 1938.

———. *Guide to the First, Second, and Third Egyptian Rooms.* (British Museum.) 3rd edition, London, 1924.

———. *Guide to the Fourth, Fifth, and Sixth Egyptian Rooms, and the Coptic Room.* (British Museum.) London, 1922.

——— and HALL, HARRY REGINALD HOLLAND. *Introductory Guide to the Egyptian Collections in the British Museum.* London, 1950.

BURNET, JOHN. *Early Greek Philosophy.* 4th edition, London, 1930.

Cambridge Ancient History, The. Cambridge and New York, 1923–39. 12 vols. and 5 vols. of plates.

CARPENTER, EDWARD. *Intermediate Types among Primitive Folk.* London, 1919.

CASSIRER, ERNST. *The Philosophy of Symbolic Forms.* Translated by Ralph Manheim. New Haven, 1953–57. 3 vols.

———. *An Essay on Man.* New Haven, 1944.

CHANTEPIE DE LA SAUSSAYE, PIERRE DANIEL. *Lehrbuch der Religionsgeschichte.* 4th edition, edited by Alfred Bertholet and Eduard Lehmann. Tübingen, 1925. 2 vols. (Contains "Die Griechen" by M. P. Nilsson and "Semitische Völker in Vorderasien" by F. Jeremias.)

CHILDE, V. GORDON. *New Light on the Most Ancient East*. London, 1934.

Ciba-Zeitschrift. Basel and Leipzig.

COOK, ARTHUR BERNARD. *Zeus: A Study in Ancient Religion*. Cambridge, 1914–1940. 3 vols.

COOMARASWAMY, ANANDA K. *Am I My Brother's Keeper?* New York, 1947.

———. "A Note on the Stickfast Motif," *Journal of American Folklore*, LVII (1944), 128–31.

———. *The Bugbear of Literacy*. London, 1949.

CORNFORD, W. F. *See* PLATO.

COVARRUBIAS, MIGUEL. *Island of Bali*. New York, 1937.

DANZEL, THEODOR-WILHELM. *Magie und Geheimwissenschaft*. Stuttgart, 1924.

DEUSSEN, PAUL (trans.). *Sechzig Upanishad's des Veda*. Leipzig, 1897.

DREWS, ARTHUR. *Die Marienmythe*. Jena, 1928.

ERMAN, ADOLF. *Die Religion der Ägypter*. Berlin and Leipzig, 1934.

———. *The Literature of the Ancient Egyptians*. Translated by Aylward M. Blackman. London, 1927.

——— and RANKE, HERMANN. *Aegypten und ägyptisches Leben im Altertum*. Tübingen, 1923.

EVANS-WENTZ, W. Y. (ed.). *The Tibetan Book of the Dead*. Lama Kazi Dawa-Samdup's English rendering. 3rd edition, London, 1957, with Commentary by C. G. Jung.

FARNELL, LEWIS RICHARD. *Cults of the Greek States*. Oxford, 1896–1909. 5 vols.

FORDHAM, MICHAEL. *The Life of Childhood*. London, 1944.

449

FRAZER, J. G. *Adonis, Attis, Osiris: Studies in the History of Oriental Religion.* (Part IV of *The Golden Bough.*) 3rd edition, New York and London, 1919. 2 vols.

——. *The Golden Bough.* Abridged edition. New York, 1951.

——. *The Worship of Nature.* (The Gifford Lectures, University of Edinburgh, 1924–25.) New York, 1926.

FREUD, SIGMUND. "From the History of an Infantile Neurosis." In: *Standard Edition of the Complete Psychological Works of Sigmund Freud,* Vol. XVII. (Translated by Alix and James Strachey.) London, 1955.

——. *Moses and Monotheism.* In: *Standard Edition,* Vol. XXIII. (Translated by James Strachey.) London, 1964.

——. "Civilization and Its Discontents." In: *Standard Edition of the Complete Psychological Works of Sigmund Freud,* Vol. XXI. (Translated by Joan Riviere.) London, 1961.

FROBENIUS, LEO. *Monumenta Africana.* Weimar, 1939. 6 vols.

——. *Kulturgeschichte Afrikas.* Zurich, 1933.

——. *Vom Kulturreich des Festlandes.* Berlin, 1923.

GADD, C. J. *See* HOOKE.

GELDNER, KARL F. *Vedismus und Brahmanismus.* (*Religionsgeschichtliches Lesebuch,* edited by Alfred Bertholet, No. 9.) Tübingen, 1928.

GLOTZ, GUSTAVE. *The Aegean Civilization.* Translated by M. R. Dobie and E. M. Riley. London and New York, 1925.

GOETHE, J. W. VON. "Nature," from *The Metamorphosis of Plants.* Translated by T. H. Huxley. *Nature* (London), I (1869).

GOLDENWEISER, ALEXANDER A. *Anthropology in North America.* London, 1937.

GOLDSCHMIDT, G. "Alchemie der Aegypter." *Ciba-Zeitschrift* (Basel and Leipzig), 1938. No. 57: "Der Ursprung der Alchemie."

GRESSMANN, HUGO. *Tod und Auferstehung des Osiris nach Fest-bräuchen und Umzügen.* (Der Alte Orient, Vol. XXIII, No. 3.) Leipzig, 1923.

GUÉNON, RENÉ. *Man and His Becoming According to the Vêdanta.* Translated by Richard C. Nicholson. London, 1945.

GUNKEL, HERMAN. *Schöpfung und Chaos in Urzeit und Endzeit.* Göttingen, 1895.

HARDING, M. ESTHER. *Woman's Mysteries, Ancient and Modern.* London and New York, 1935; rev. edn., 1955.

HASTINGS, JAMES (ed.). *Encyclopedia of Religion and Ethics.* Edinburgh and New York, 1908–27. 13 vols.

HAUSENSTEIN, WILHELM. *Die Bildnerei der Etrusker.* Munich, 1922.

HEYER, LUCY. "Erinnyen und Eumeniden." In: *Das Reich der Seele.* Edited by G. R. Heyer and F. Seifert. Vol. I. Munich, 1937.

HOERNES, MORITZ. *Urgeschichte der bildenden Kunst in Europa.* Completed by Oswald Menghin. Vienna, 1925.

HOOKE, SAMUEL HENRY (ed.). *Myth and Ritual.* London, 1933. (Contains essays by Aylward M. Blackman, C. J. Gadd, and others.)

HORNER, GEORGE WILLIAM (trans.). *Pistis Sophia.* London, 1924.

HORODEZKY, S. A. *Rabbi Nachman von Brazlaw.* Berlin, 1910.

HUME, ROBERT ERNEST (trans.). *The Thirteen Principal Upanishads.* Oxford, 1921.

JEANNE, SOEUR. *Memoiren einer Besessenen.* Edited by H. H. Ewers. Stuttgart, 1919.

JEREMIAS, ALFRED. *Das Alte Testament im Lichte des Alten Orients.* Leipzig, 1904.

451

———. *Handbuch der altorientalischen Geisteskultur.* Leipzig, 1913.

JEREMIAS, FRIEDRICH. *See* CHANTEPIE DE LA SAUSSAYE.

JONAS, HANS. *Gnosis und spätantiker Geist.* Göttingen, 1934.

JONES, ERNEST. "Psychoanalysis of Christianity." In: *Essays in Applied Psychoanalysis.* Vol. II. London, 1951.

JUNG, C. G. "Analytical Psychology and Education." In: *The Development of Personality. (Coll. Works,* Vol. 17.) New York and London, 1954.

———. "Analytical Psychology and *Weltanschauung.*" In: *The Structure and Dynamics of the Psyche. (Coll. Works,* Vol. 8.) New York and London, 1960; 2nd edn., 1969.

———. "Archetypes of the Collective Unconscious." In: *The Archetypes and the Collective Unconscious. (Coll. Works,* Vol. 9, i.) New York and London, 1959; 2nd edn., 1968.

———. "The Association Method." In: *Collected Papers on Analytical Psychology.* Edited by Constance Long. 2nd edition, London, 1917; New York, 1920. [In *Coll. Works,* Vol. 2.*]

* References are given in this way to still unpublished volumes of the edition of the *Collected Works of C. G. Jung,* translated by R. F. C. Hull, now in course of publication in London and New York. Published volumes are cited in the usual way. Titles of all volumes are as follows:

1. Psychiatric Studies.
2. Experimental Researches.
3. The Psychogenesis of Mental Disease.
4. Freud and Psychoanalysis.
5. Symbols of Transformation.
6. Psychological Types.
7. Two Essays on Analytical Psychology.
8. The Structure and Dynamics of the Psyche.

9, i. The Archetypes and the Collective Unconscious. 9, ii. Aion.
10. Civilization in Transition.
11. Psychology and Religion: West and East.
12. Psychology and Alchemy.
13. Alchemical Studies.
14. Mysterium Coniunctionis.
15. The Spirit in Man, Art, and Literature.
16. The Practice of Psychotherapy.
17. The Development of Personality.

Final Volumes: Miscellaneous Works, Bibliography, and General Index.

———. "Concerning Rebirth." In: *The Archetypes and the Collective Unconscious.* (*Coll. Works,* Vol. 9, part i.) New York and London, 1959; 2nd edn., 1968.

———. *Contributions to Analytical Psychology.* Translated by H. G. and Cary F. Baynes. New York and London, 1928.

———. "Freud and Jung: Contrasts." In *Freud and Psychoanalysis.* (*Coll. Works,* Vol. 4.) New York and London, 1961.

———. Kindertraumseminare [Seminars on children's dreams]. Multigraphed for private circulation only. 1936–39.

———. *Modern Man in Search of a Soul.* Translated by W. S. Dell and Cary F. Baynes. New York and London, 1933.

———. "On Psychic Energy." In: *The Structure and Dynamics of the Psyche.* (*Coll. Works,* Vol. 8.) New York and London, 1960; 2nd edn., 1969.

———. "On Psychophysical Relations of the Associative Experiment," *Journal of Abnormal Psychology* (Boston), I (1906). [In *Coll. Works,* Vol. 2.*]

———. "On the Relation of Analytical Psychology to Poetry." In: *The Spirit in Man, Art, and Literature.* (*Coll. Works,* Vol. 15.) New York and London, 1966.

———. "Paracelsus as a Spiritual Phenomenon." In: *Alchemical Studies.* (*Coll. Works,* Vol. 13.) New York and London, 1967.

———. "The Psychological Aspects of the Kore." In: *The Archetypes and the Collective Unconscious.* (*Coll. Works,* Vol. 9, part i.) New York and London, 1959; 2nd edn., 1968.

———. "Psychological Aspects of the Mother Archetype." In: *The Archetypes and the Collective Unconscious.* (*Coll. Works,* Vol. 9, part i.) New York and London, 1959; 2nd edn., 1968.

———. "The Psychological Foundations of Belief in Spirits." In: *The Structure and Dynamics of the Psyche.* (*Coll. Works,* Vol. 8.) New York and London, 1960; 2nd edn., 1969.

———. *Psychological Types.* Translated by H. G. Baynes. London and New York, 1923. [*Coll. Works,* Vol. 6.*]

——. *Psychology and Alchemy.* (*Coll. Works,* Vol. 12.) New York and London, 1953; 2nd ed., 1967.

——. "The Psychology of the Child Archetype." In: *The Archetypes and the Collective Unconscious.* (*Coll. Works,* Vol. 9, i.) New York and London, 1959; 2nd edn., 1968.

——. "Psychology of the Transference." In: *The Practice of Psychotherapy.* (*Coll. Works,* Vol. 16.) New York and London, 1953; 2nd edn., 1966.

——. *Psychology of the Unconscious.* Translated by Beatrice M. Hinkle. New York and London, 1921. [Revised as *Symbols of Transformation,* q. v.]

——. "The Relations between the Ego and the Unconscious." In: *Two Essays on Analytical Psychology.* (*Coll. Works,* Vol. 7.) New York and London, 1953; 2nd edn., 1966.

——. "A Review of the Complex Theory." In: *The Structure and Dynamics of the Psyche.* (*Coll. Works,* Vol. 8.) New York and London, 1960; 2nd edn., 1969.

——. "The Stages of Life." In: *The Structure and Dynamics of the Psyche.* (*Coll. Works,* Vol. 8.) New York and London, 1960; 2nd edn., 1969.

——. "The Structure of the Psyche." In: *The Structure and Dynamics of the Psyche.* (*Coll. Works,* Vol. 8.) New York and London, 1960; 2nd edn., 1969.

——. *Studies in Word Association.* Translated by M. D. Eder. London, 1918; New York, 1919. [In *Coll. Works,* Vol. 2.*]

——. *The Symbolic Life.* (Guild of Pastoral Psychology, Lecture No. 80; given April 5, 1939.) London, 1954. [In *Coll. Works,* Vol. 18. *]

——. *Symbols of Transformation.* (*Coll. Works,* Vol. 5.) New York and London, 1956; 2nd edn., 1967.

——. "The Visions of Zosimos." In: *Alchemical Studies.* (*Coll. Works,* Vol. 13.) New York and London, 1967.

* See footnote on p. 452.

———. *Wirklichkeit der Seele*. Zurich, 1934.

———. "Wotan." In: *Civilization in Transition*. (*Coll. Works*, Vol. 10.) New York and London, 1964.

——— and KERÉNYI, C. *Essays on a Science of Mythology*. Translated by R. F. C. Hull. New York, 1950, 2nd edn., 1969; London (entitled *Introduction to a . . .*), 1951. Princeton/ Bollingen Paperback edn., 1969.

JUNG, C. G., and WILHELM, RICHARD. *The Secret of the Golden Flower*. Translated by Cary F. Baynes. New York and London, 1931; rev. edn., 1962. [Jung's commentary in *Coll. Works*, Vol. 13.]

KEES, HERMANN. *Aegypten*. (*Religionsgeschichtliches Lesebuch*, edited by Alfred Bertholet, No. 10.) Tübingen, 1928.

———. "Die Befriedigung des Raubtiers," *Zeitschrift für Ägyptische Sprache und Altertumskunde* (Leipzig), LXVII (1931), 56–59.

———. *Der Götterglaube im alten Aegypten*. (Mitteilungen der Vorderasiatisch-Aegyptischen Gesellschaft, Vol. XLV.) Leipzig, 1941.

KERÉNYI, KARL (or CARL). "Die Göttin Natur," *Eranos-Jahrbuch 1946* (Zurich, 1947), 39–86.

———. "Kore." See JUNG and KERÉNYI.

KOPPERS, WILHELM. "On the Origin of the Mysteries in the Light of Ethnology and Indology," *The Mystic Vision* (Papers from the Eranos Yearbooks, 6; New York and London, 1969), 32–69.

KUBIN, ALFRED. *Die andere Seite*. Munich, 1923.

LAO-TZU. *Das Buch des Alten vom Sinn und Leben*. Translated by Richard Wilhelm. Jena, 1911.

———. *The Way and Its Power*. Translated by Arthur Waley. London, 1934.

LAWRENCE, D. H. *Last Poems*. Edited by Giuseppe Orioli and Richard Aldington. New York, 1933.

LEEUW, GERARDUS VAN DER. *Religion in Essence and Manifestation*. Translated by J. E. Turner. London, 1938.

LEISEGANG, HANS. *Die Gnosis*. Leipzig, 1924.

———. "The Mystery of the Serpent," *The Mysteries* (Papers from the Eranos Yearbooks, 2; New York and London, 1955), 194–260.

LEONARDO DA VINCI. *See* RICHTER.

LÉVY-BRUHL, LUCIEN. *How Natives Think*. Translated by Lilian A. Clare [from *Les Fonctions mentales dans les sociétés inférieures*]. New York and London, 1926.

———. *The "Soul" of the Primitive*. Translated by Lilian A. Clare. New York, 1928.

MALINOWSKI, BRONISLAW. *Crime and Custom in Savage Society*. New York and London, 1926.

———. *The Father in Primitive Psychology*. London, 1927.

———. *Mutterrechtliche Familie und Ödipus-Komplex*. Leipzig, 1924.

MEAD, MARGARET. *Sex and Temperament in Three Primitive Societies*. New York, 1935.

MEREZHKOVSKI, D. S. *The Secret of the West*. Translated by John Cournos. New York, 1931.

MORET, ALEXANDRE. *Mystères Égyptiens*. Revised and enlarged edition, Paris, 1922.

———. *The Nile and Egyptian Civilization*. Translated by M. R. Dobie. London, 1927.

MURRAY, GILBERT. *Five Stages of Greek Religion*. 3rd edition, Boston, 1952.

NEUMANN, ERICH. "Mystical Man," *The Mystic Vision* (Papers from the Eranos Yearbooks, 6; New York and London, 1969), 375–415.

————. *Depth Psychology and a New Ethic.* Translated by Eugene Rolfe. New York, 1969.

NEWCOMB, FRANC J., and REICHARD, GLADYS A. *Sandpaintings of the Navajo Shooting Chant.* New York, 1937.

NILSSON, MARTIN P. *Die Religion der Griechen.* (*Religionsgeschichtliches Lesebuch,* edited by Alfred Bertholet, No. 4.) Tübingen, 1927.

————. *See also* CHANTEPIE DE LA SAUSSAYE.

NINCK, MARTIN. *Wodan und germanischer Schicksalsglaube.* Jena, 1935.

OTTO, RUDOLF. *The Idea of the Holy.* Translated by John W. Harvey. London, 1923.

PETRIE, FLINDERS. *The Making of Egypt.* London and New York, 1939.

PHILIPPSON, PAULA. *Thessalische Mythologie.* Zurich, 1944.

————. *Untersuchungen über den Griechischen Mythos.* Zurich, 1944.

PICARD, CHARLES. "Die Ephesia von Anatolien" and "Die Grosse Mutter von Kreta bis Eleusis," *Eranos-Jahrbuch 1938* (Zurich, 1939), 59–120.

PIETSCHMANN, RICHARD. *Geschichte der Phönizier.* (Allgemeine Geschichte in Einzeldarstellungen, I, 4.) Berlin, 1889.

[PLATO.] *Plato's Cosmology; the Timaeus of Plato.* Translated by W. F. Cornford. New York and London, 1937.

PORTMANN, ADOLF. *Biologische Fragmente zu einer Lehre vom Menschen.* Basel, 1944.

PREUSS, KONRAD THEODOR. *Die geistige Kultur der Naturvölker.* Leipzig, 1923.

PRITCHARD, JAMES B. (ed.). *Ancient Near Eastern Texts.* Princeton, 1950; 3rd edn., 1969. (Contains E. A. Speiser's translation of the Gilgamesh Epic.)

457

PRZYLUSKI, JEAN. "Ursprünge und Entwicklung des Kultes der Mutter-Göttin," *Eranos-Jahrbuch 1938* (Zurich, 1939), 11–34.

Pyramid Texts. *See* SETHE; ERMAN, *Die Literatur der Aegypter.*

RAGLAN, LORD [Fitzroy Richard Somerset, 4th Baron Raglan]. *Jocasta's Crime.* (Thinker's Library, 80.) London, 1940.

RANK, OTTO. *The Myth of the Birth of the Hero.* Translated by F. Robins and Smith Ely Jelliffe. (Nervous and Mental Disease Monograph Series, No. 18.) New York, 1941.

———. *Psychoanalytische Beiträge zur Mythenforschung.* (Internationale Psychoanalytische Bibliothek, No. 4.) Leipzig and Vienna, 1919.

READ, JOHN. *Prelude to Chemistry.* London, 1936.

REICHARD, GLADYS A. *See* NEWCOMB.

REITZENSTEIN, I. R. *Die hellenistischen Mysterienreligionen.* Leipzig, 1910.

REIWALD, PAUL. *Vom Geist der Massen.* (Internationale Bibliothek für Psychologie und Soziologie, Vol. I.) Zurich, 1946.

RENAN, ERNEST. *Mission de Phénicie.* Paris, 1864–74. 2 vols.

RICHTER, J. P. (ed.). *The Literary Works of Leonardo da Vinci.* 2nd edition, enlarged and revised. Oxford, 1939. 2 vols.

ROEDER, GÜNTHER (ed. and trans.). *Urkunden zur Religion des alten Aegypten.* (Religiöse Stimmen der Völker.) Jena, 1915.

ROHDE, ERWIN. *Psyche.* Translated by W. B. Hillis [from the 8th German edition]. New York, 1925.

SCHEFTELOWITZ, ISIDOR. *Alt-palästinensischer Bauernglaube in religionsvergleichender Beleuchtung.* Hanover, 1925.

SCHOCH-BODMER, HELEN. "Die Spirale als Symbol und als Strukturelement des Lebendigen," *Schweizerische Zeitschrift für Psychologie und ihre Anwendungen* (Bern), IV (1945), 324 ff.

SCHOLEM, G. *Die Geheimnisse der Schöpfung: Ein Kapitel aus dem Sohar.* Berlin, 1935.

———. *Major Trends in Jewish Mysticism.* New York, 1946.

SEIDEL, ALFRED. *Bewusstsein als Verhängnis.* Edited from his remains by Hans Prinzhorn. Bonn, 1927.

SELIGMAN, C. G. *Egypt and Negro Africa: A Study in Divine Kingship.* London, 1934.

SETHE, KURT HEINRICH (ed.). *Die alt-aegyptischen Pyramidentexte, nach den Papierabdrücken und Photographien des Berliner Museums.* Leipzig, 1908–22. 4 vols.

SILBERER, HERBERT. *Problems of Mysticism and Its Symbolism.* Translated by Smith Ely Jelliffe. New York, 1917.

SMITH, G. ELLIOT. *The Evolution of the Dragon.* Manchester, 1919.

SPEISER, E. A. *See* PRITCHARD.

SPIELREIN, SABINA. "Die Destruktion als Ursache des Werdens," *Jahrbuch für psychoanalytische und psychopathologische Forschungen* (Leipzig and Vienna), IV (1912), 465 ff.

STEINEN, CARL VON DEN. *Unter den Naturvölkern Zentral-Brasiliens.* Berlin, 1894.

STREHLOW, CARL. *Die Aranda- und Loritja-Stämme in Zentral-Australien.* (Veröffentlichungen aus dem Städtischen Völker-Museum, Vol. I.) Frankfort on the Main, 1907–20. 5 vols.

THURNWALD, RICHARD. *Die Eingeborenen Australiens und der Südseeinseln.* (*Religionsgeschichtliches Lesebuch,* edited by Alfred Bertholet, No. 8.) Tübingen, 1927.

TISHBY, ISAIAH. [The Doctrine of Evil and the "Klipah" in the Lurian Cabala (in Hebrew).] Tel Aviv, 1942.

TROTTER, WILFRED. *Instincts of the Herd in Peace and War.* London, 1916.

459

VIROLLEAUD, CHARLES. "Ischtar, Isis, Astarte" and "Anat–Astarte," *Eranos-Jahrbuch 1938* (Zurich, 1939), 121–60.

WALEY, ARTHUR. *See* LAO-TZU.

WEININGER, OTTO. *Sex and Character*. Translated from the 6th German edition. London and New York, 1906.

WICKES, FRANCES G. *The Inner World of Childhood*. With an introduction by C. G. Jung. New York and London, 1927.

WILHELM II [Ex-Kaiser of Germany]. *Studien zur Gorgo*. Berlin, 1936.

WILHELM, RICHARD. *See* LAO-TZU; JUNG and WILHELM.

WINCKLER, HUGO. "Himmels- und Weltenbild der Babylonier als Grundlage der Weltanschauung und Mythologie aller Völker," *Der alte Orient* (Vorderasiatische Gesellschaft, Berlin), III (1901): 2–3.

WINLOCK, HERBERT EUSTIS. *Basreliefs from the Temple of Rameses I at Abydos*. (Metropolitan Museum of Art, Papers, Vol. I.) New York, 1921.

WOODWARD, JOCELYN M. *Perseus: A Study in Greek Art and Legend*. Cambridge, 1937.

WUNDT, WILHELM. *Elements of Folk Psychology*. Translated by E. L. Schaub. London and New York, 1916.

WÜNSCHE, AUGUST. *Aus Israels Lehrhallen: Kleine Midraschim zur späteren legendarischen Literatur des Alten Testaments*. 4 vols. in 2. Leipzig, 1907–9.

YEATS, W. B., and SHREE PUROHIT SWAMI (trans.). *The Ten Principal Upanishads*. New York and London, 1937.

ZIMMER, HEINRICH. *Maya, der Indische Mythos*. Stuttgart, 1936.

INDEX

INDEX

A

ab, 237

abaissement du niveau mental, 385

abortion, 189

Abraham, 174, 189

Abraham, Karl, 32*n*

Abrahamsen, David, 96*n*

abstinence, 59

abstraction, 328, 335

Abydos, Egypt, 71*n,* 85, 230, 232*f;*
  illus. 18 (*f*64), 28, 30 (*f*240)

acacia, 69

Acrisius, King, 213

Actaeon, 81, 83, 93

Adam, 71, 120, 178

Adamas, 188

adaptation: collective, 351–52; to
  reality, 341, 398–99

additive parts, 422

adherence, 360

aditi, 30

Adler, Alfred, 319

Adler, Gerhard, 341*n,* 360*n,* 397*n*

adolescence: and aggression, 316;
  effeminate nature of, 157–58; self-
  division, 95–101, 121; son-lover
  phase, 44–52, 53*n,* 114, 178–79,
  300; transition to adulthood, 409–
  10; *see also* puberty

Adonis: and boar, 78, 97, 224*n;* and
  castration, 59*f,* 188, 253; and
  Dionysus, 90; Gardens of, 227;
  and pig sacrifice, 86; son-lover
  stage, 46*f,* 57; as vegetation deity,
  73

adulthood, *see* individuation

Aegeus, 136

affectivity, loss of, 387

affects, 330, 333

Africa, 9, 434; *illus.* 6 (*f*32); and
  Great Mother, 54, 57, 79, 265

Agave, 81

"agenbite of inwit," 26

Agenor, 79–80

aggression: conversion of, 316–18;
  and ego development, 123–25

agriculture, 43, 368, 430

Aion, 10

Aitareya Upanishad, 28

Aithon, 93

akeru, 235

akhet, akhu, 243

Albright, W. F., 37*n,* 75*n,* 160*n,*
  189*n;* quoted, 73–74, 97–98

alchemy: and centroversion, 411;
  and hermaphrodite, 414, 418;
  homunculus, 34; and mutilation,
  121; and Osiris myth, 253, 255;
  retort, 34, 206; and shadow, 352*n;*
  and transformation, 239*n;* and
  uroboros, xiv, 8, *illus.* 9 (*f*32)

Aldrich, C. R., 183*n,* 269*n,* 437*n*

alimentary uroboros, 27–34, 290–93

All-Father, 315

All One, 10

Alpha and Omega, 10

Alphaic Artemis, 84

Amam/Am-mit, 69

Amasis, *illus.* 25 (*f*144)

INDEX

see also Osiris myth; symbols; transformation
Ares, 80
Argos, 81, 86, 213
Ariadne, 91, 201, 203
Aristotle, 264
Arsinoë Philadelphos, 223
art, 104, 370; creative, 376
Artemis, 59, 71*n*, 81, 215; cognomens of, 84; and Hippolytus, 91–92
Asar, 229*n*
ascension, 254, 255*n*, 385
ascetism, 189, 310, 348
Asherah, 74
Ashtaroth, 74–75, 134
Asia, 79, 383
Asia Minor, 54, 60, 75, 77, 79, 83, 85, 90, 434
asses, 224*n*
assimilation, 30–32, 372; of unconscious contents, 336–41, 343, 356, 410
association, 331*f*, 344
associative fugue, 385
Assyria, 75
Astar/Attar, 75
Astarte, 59, 66, 71, 73*ff*, 229; and higher castration, 159–60
astrology, 94–95
Astronoë, 77
atavism, 298
Athene: and Eternal Feminine, 21*ff*; and Great Mother, 80, 82, 92; and Orestes, 16, 248; and Perseus, 214*ff*, 248
atman, 9, 105, 290*n*
atomization, 392, 422, 436*f*; and regressive mass formation, 439–40, 443–44
Attar/Astar, 75
Attar, Farid ud-din, quoted, 395

Attis: and boar, 78, 95, 224*n*; and pig, 86; and self-castration, 88, 91, 93, 188, 253; as son-lover, 46, 48; as vegetation deity, 58*ff*, 73
Atum, 19, 20, 33, 238
Australian aborigines, symbolism of, 288–90
autarchy, uroboric, 33–35
authorities, 191, 204, 364, 404, 433–34; archetypal phases as ego phases, 349–51; shadow and anima, 351–56
autoeroticism, 34
Autonoë, 81
autosuggestion, 268
Avicenna, 352
ax (labrys), 76
Aztecs, *illus.* 7 (*f*32)

B

ba, 235, 237, 240, 243
Baal, 74, 97, 160, 179
Babylonia, 23, 49, 75, 118, 165; *illus.* 3 (*f*32), 16 (*f*64); Etana myth, 187–88; Gilgamesh Epic, 62–63, 93, 180–81
Bachofen, J. J., 27, 39, 65, 79, 83, 265–66; on Dionysus, 90–91; on masculine principle, 47–48, 92, 159; on matriarchate, 41–42, 45, 82, 94, 163, 168, 178; on Oedipus, 164
backbone, 100*n*, 230–32
Bali, 87*n*; *illus.* 19 (*f*64)
baptism, 408*n*
barbel-bynni fish, 71*n*
barbers, 59
Bardo Thödol, *see* Book of the Dead: Tibetan
Barlach, Ernst: *Der Tote Tag*, 165–68, 186; on hero, 174
barley, 223

C

science and "inner voice," 173–74; father image, 170–72; "fathers," and the collective, 172–73; matriarchate to patriarchate, 180–84; patriarchal castration, 186–90; Terrible Male, 178–80; transformation of kingship, 184–86; transpersonal and personal elements, 174–78

—: slaying of mother, 152–69; higher castration, 159–68; Jung's interpretation, 153–54; *Oresteia*, 168–69; rebirth through heroic incest, 154–58, 162–63

Herod, 43

Herodotus, 80*f*, 84*n*, 252*n*

heron, *illus*. 31 (*f*240)

Hesamut, 56–57

Heyer, Lucy, 168*n*

Hierapolis, 85

hieroglyphs, 20, 237, 428

hieros gamos, 17, 150, 198, 254, 415

higher castration, 159–68

higher ego, 123

higher femininity, 202–3

higher masculinity, 92, 141–43, 158–59, 203, 253–54, 310–11, 319

Hildegarde of Bingen, St., *illus*. 11 (*f*32)

Hinduism, 55, 149; *see also* India; Upanishads

Hippolytus, 89, 91–93, 178, 180

Hipponoüs, 219

hippopotamus, 56, 68*f*; *illus*. 17 (*f*64)

historiography, 337*n*

Hittites, 75

Hoernes, Moritz, 50*n*

Holy Ghost, 22, 76,* 134

homosexuality, 141*n*

homunculus, 34

Hooke, S. H., 135*n*, 165*n*, 211*n*, 212*n*, 213*n*

Horner, G. W., 10*n*

Horodezky, S. A., 24*n*

horse, 217–19

Horus, 55, 216*n*, 230*n*, 233*f*, 236; *illus*. 27, 30 (*f*240); and ascension, 233*f*; Edfu Feast, 135–36, 244; and fertility, 222*f*, 226*f*, 244*ff*; and Isis, 43, 64–68, 73, 156; and Pharaohs, 149; and Set, 182*f*, 338; as son of Osiris, 177, 246–52, 265, 415

hostile twins, 95–101

humanity, and individual, 444

humanization, 131

Hume, R. E., 9*n*, 28–30*n*, 105*n*, 107*n*

hunger, 293; symbolism of, 26–28

hunting, 55, 147

Huxley, T. H., 333*n*

Hyacinthus, 43

Hybristica, 86–87

Hypermnestra, 82

hypnosis by unconscious, 424–26, 442

hypostatization of group soul, 274–75

hysteria, 86, 347

I

Icarus, 188

Iliad, 84*n*

illness, 373

images, 294–95, 332, 336, 369; outside and inside, 295–96

imagos, 400, 407, 413

immortality, 195, 208, 221, 359, 416–17, 428*n*

impotence, 94*n*

impulses, 293

incarnation, 247

metabolic symbolism, 28–32, 290–93

metempsychosis, 238

Metternich stele, 85n, 222n, 237n

Mexico, 11, 25, 239n, 424; *illus.* 6 (ƒ32)

Meyer, Eduard, *illus.* 31 (ƒ240)

Michael (archangel), 162

Michelangelo Buonarroti, *illus.* 20 (ƒ106)

Middle Ages, 382, 424

midriff, 26

mill, treading of, 159–60

Min, 222, 248, 253n

Minos, 79f, 85

Minotaur, 79ff

miscegenation, 325

Mithraism, 98

Mithras, 378

Moloch, 178

monotheism, 19, 177, 282

monsters, 161–62, 176, 198, 214

moon, 149, 233, 337, 340n, 374

moon-cow, 80

moon-goddesses, 83

Moret, Alexandre, 64, 234n, 338n, 429n; quoted, 20, 237, 240–43, 245

Moscow, *illus.* 22 (ƒ144)

Moses, 146, 175, 353n, 380

Mot, 97, 179

Mot-Set, 74

Mother: cults, 324; Great, *see* Great Mother; slaying of, *see* hero myth; Terrible, *see* Terrible Mother

Mother Goddess, 49

mother-murder myth, 431n

Mother of All Living, 15

"Mothers, The," 14, 202–3, 299

mouse, 84n

Mueller, Nikolaus, *illus.* 8 (ƒ32)

mummification, 224–28, 230, 232, 234, 240, 249f

Mundaka Upanishad, 29

murder, parental, 121

Mut, 55, 228

Mutilation, 121f

Mycenae, 80

mystery religions, *see* religion

mysticism, 26, 253f, 360n

mythology, xiv; and collective unconscious, xvff *passim;* creation, *see* Great Mother, separation of World Parents, uroboros; and differentiation, 304–5; dual nature of, 195–97; hero, *see* hero myth; transformation, *see* transformation; *see also individual myths and places of origin*

N

Napoleonic wars, 393

narcissism, 25, 34, 158; *illus.* 14 (ƒ64); defined, 122–23; and Great Mother, 50–52; as phase of ego development, 307–8

Narcissus myth, 89–91, 93, 96

Nathan of Gaza, 120

nation, 275, 366

National Socialism, 443–44; *see also* Germany

nature, 15, 39, 40, 110, 139, 162, 191, 409–10; *illus.* 12, 13, 18 (ƒ64); and individual, 333; symbols, 76, 215, 374

Navajo Indians, 10

Nazi party, *see* National Socialism

Near Eastern cultures, 46, 75, 211

neck, 230

Nectanebo II, King, *illus.* 27 (ƒ240)

Neith, 55

Nekhbet of Nekhen, 246

481

T

493

ERICH NEUMANN

Born in Berlin in 1905, Erich Neumann earned his Ph.D. at the University of Berlin in 1927. He then began medical studies in Berlin and completed the examinations for the degree in 1933, after which he left Germany. He studied with C. G. Jung in 1934 and 1936, and from 1934 his permanent home was Tel Aviv, where he practiced as an analytical psychologist. For many years he returned regularly to Zurich to lecture at the C. G. Jung Institute. From 1948 until 1960 he was a regular contributor at the Eranos meetings in Ascona, Switzerland, and he also lectured frequently in England, France, and the Netherlands. He was a member of the International Association for Analytical Psychology and president of the Israel Association of Analytical Psychologists. He died in Tel Aviv on November 5, 1960.

Dr. Neumann had a theoretical and philosophical approach to analysis contrasting with the more clinical concern in England and the United States. His most valuable contribution to psychological theory is the empirical concept of "centroversion," a synthesis of extra- and introversion. His philosophical considerations of psychology are contained in *Tiefenpsychologie und neue Ethik* (1949), but he is best known for his statements of a coherent theory of feminine development. In *The Origins and History of Consciousness* (1949; tr. 1954), which illustrates by interpretations of basic mythologems the archetypal stages in the development of human consciousness, the emphasis on matriarchal symbolism foreshadowed his monumental work *The Great Mother* (first published in English, 1955), a study of the Magna Mater in the art of all times and in ethnological and mythological documents. Other works dealing with the idea of the feminine are *Amor and Psyche: The Psychic*

Development of the Feminine—A Commentary on the Tale by Apuleius (1952; tr. 1956) and *The Archetypal World of Henry Moore* (first published in English, 1959). The extent of his interests and his penetrating comprehension of the fine arts are demonstrated by essays on Leonardo da Vinci, Marc Chagall, Mozart, Kafka, Georg Trakl, Jewish symbolism, and many other topics. Some of these are contained in his collected essays *Umkreisung der Mitte* (3 vols., 1953–54), four of which are translated in his *Art and the Creative Unconscious* (1959).